PUBLIC POLICY
Scope and Logic

PUBLIC POLICY
Scope and Logic

FRED M. FROHOCK
Syracuse University

PRENTICE-HALL, INC., *Englewood Cliffs, New Jersey 07632*

Library of Congress Cataloging in Publication Data
Frohock, Fred M
   Public policy.

   Bibliography: p.
   Includes index.

    1. Policy sciences.   2. United States—Politics and
government—1945-   3. United States—Social policy.
I. Title.
H61.F68   300'.1'8   78-8382
ISBN 0-13-737932-3

© 1979 by PRENTICE-HALL, INC., *Englewood Cliffs, N.J. 07632*

PRINTED IN THE UNITED STATES OF AMERICA
10 9 8 7 6 5 4 3 2 1

PRENTICE-HALL INTERNATIONAL, INC., *London*
PRENTICE-HALL OF AUSTRALIA PTY. LIMITED, *Sydney*
PRENTICE-HALL OF CANADA, LTD., *Toronto*
PRENTICE-HALL OF INDIA, PRIVATE, LIMITED, *New Delhi*
PRENTICE-HALL OF JAPAN, INC., *Tokyo*
PRENTICE-HALL OF SOUTHEAST ASIA PTE. LTD., *Singapore*
WHITEHALL BOOKS LIMITED, *Wellington, New Zealand*

contents

3

GROUPS AND ELITES   *64*

4

THE PEOPLE IN POLICY:
POSITIVE AND NEGATIVE PARTICIPATION   *103*

5

ORGANIZATIONAL DECISIONS
AND PUBLIC PLANNING   145

6

PUBLIC POLICY
EVALUATION   *183*

7

ETHICS, JUSTICE, AND
PUBLIC POLICY   *221*

8

PUBLIC POLICY AND
DEMOCRACY   263

APPENDIX A: The
Fourteenth Ammendment

APPENDIX B: An Overview OF
Prominent Black
Organizations

preface

One of my colleagues is programmed to sneer whenever the study of public policy is discussed. "Public policy," he invariably announces, "is nothing more than the dependent variable in the study of politics." Delivered in the right way, this remark never fails to impress—until, in the short silence that usually follows, one reflects on public policy as also the independent variable, the intervening variable, the focal point for discussions of law and justice, and who knows what else.

I suppose what my colleague is trying to say, and would say if he could just get away from simplistic causal schemes, is that all of us in the social sciences study public policy in one way or another. Agreed—and to this self-evident truth I would add, those in law and philosophy also serve who only stand and wait, and even attend to the muse of public policy on more occasions than social scientists might admit. The study of public policy, to turn the truism in the direction of a cliché, is currently fair game for almost any discipline that is concerned with social things (and that, dear friends, covers a lot).

If the natural eclecticism of public policy studies can be appreciated, it might not seem so odd that someone devoted to political philosophy could have written a book on public policy. The truth is, political philosophy is more concerned than ever with social things, a turn of affairs due as much to a revival of interest in social justice as to anything else. To the skeptics, let me point out that political theory and political philosophy are still—*political* theory and *political* philosophy. And that even Plato and Aristotle had more than passing interest in the social issues of their day. The truth also is that the more standard treatments of public policy are beginning to edge toward topics like equity, the public interest, justice, as the recent events of politics push them in that direction. It seems like a happy moment to turn push into shove with a book like this one.

My personal motives in writing this book are less complicated. One motive, or hope, really, was that a return to politics and its practical literature would free my work in political philosophy from some self-created impediments. One item has already been produced by this exercise in psychic release: "The Structure of 'Politics'" in the September 1978 issue of *The American Political Science Review*. More will follow. The second motive was pecuniary. Much has been written about money, from Samuel Johnson's observation that there are few ways in which a man can be more innocently employed than in making (getting) money, to the more sombre identifications of money as "filthy lucre" (Norman O. Brown) or (as identified with success) the last repression of modern literature (Norman Podhoretz). My approach, by comparison, is straightforward Johnson: I freely and guiltlessly admit that this book is a commercial enterprise intended to make money for its author and publisher. Abbie Hoffman wrote a book in the heady years of the 1960's entitled "Steal This Book"—an Austinian performative as both title and imperative. My slogan is the reverse: "*Buy* This Book." At least one political philosopher in the world will be pleased.

I am quite aware that a book of any scope intersects the fields of specialists in a number of areas. I am ready to concede that any part of this book (with the possible exception of Chapter Seven) could have been written better by someone specializing on the topics discussed. But, as Bertram Russell pointed out in his survey of the history of philosophy, if such concessions are allowed to deter publication, then general books would never get written (and I think general overviews of a field of study are helpful).

Several people have attempted to correct my errors by reading all or parts of the book. Special thanks are due to the three anonymous readers Prentice-Hall used. They gave good advice in abundance, much of which I accepted and some of which I ignored (at my peril, I'm sure). Edwin Bock read the entire manuscript and made many helpful suggestions. Linda Fowler read and commented on parts of the book, and was especially helpful in weaning me away from the conflict-management model of politics to see the importance of the rational-incentive model (though since she has yet to read Appendix C, I still don't know whether I'm right or wrong in my understanding of Arrow's theorem). I have learned much about rational choice theory from Robert Wolfson. Several ideas about Rawls and Harsanyi have come to me from conversations with Eric von Magnus. Also, as usual, my colleague in theory here at Syracuse, James Reynolds, has given me more good thoughts than I like to admit, including the example of the ideological vote-shift I use in discussing the voting paradoxes in Appendix C. My graduate seminars over the years have been excellent testing grounds for these, and other, ideas. Dean Larson, Chris Quinn, William O'Brian, and Roger King were especially helpful critics as I worked out the thoughts presented in this book. Charles Smith assisted me throughout on the research, and Howard Birnbach was helpful with some late checking of references. At Prentice-Hall, Cathie Mahar was an excellent production editor; and Pat Cahalan did a competent, amazingly detailed job of copyediting. Thanks are also due Ms. J. F. Hausfeld, who unknowingly gave me the idea of opening the book with the Shakespeare quote. I am also pleased to acknowledge that I have learned much about public policy over the years from my brother Patrick's enlightening and very funny stories about Washington politics. None of these stories, unfortunately, has ever been printable exactly in the way he told it. Finally, my thanks to my typist, Mary Kay Orcutt, who always receives my totally unreasonable deadlines with good cheer and unfailing efficiency.

I am also grateful to the Free Press for permission to reprint pages of Chapter One, which originally appeared in slightly different form in my "Systems Theory and Structural-Functional Analysis," in Donald Freeman, Ed., *Foundations of Political Science: Scope, Research, Method* (Glencoe, Illinois: The Free Press, 1978, pp. 3–9). Acknowledgement of material from George Orwell's, *1984* p. 142 goes to Mrs. Sonia Brownell Orwell and Martin Secher and Warburg Ltd.

And, for those who believe in the usual solemn litany of a Preface, I do accept responsibility for all errors and failed ambitions that remain in this book. The critics, after all, have done their best to warn me, again and again, that the *hubris* of comprehensiveness goes before a fall.

FRED M. FROHOCK
Syracuse University

PUBLIC POLICY
Scope and Logic

politics and policy

1

THE NATURE OF POLITICS

> .... *Get thee glass eyes;*
> *And, like a scurvy politician, seem*
> *To see the things thou dost not."*
>
> (King Lear IV:6)

Shakespeare is not on historical record as endorsing this view of politicians expressed by one of his characters. With good reason, probably: "scurvy" is quite a mouthful even for an Elizabethan. What Shakespeare would do with the record of the last several years is anyone's guess. One certainty is that he, like us, would be inclined to pass some form of judgment on "politicians," as people have done in every age.

Good students all, we and Shakespeare would be better off suspending such judgments until we understand more about "politics." Which brings us to the purpose of this book: We will try here to lay out in general and concrete ways the fullest possible dimensions of political life through the study of public policy. The hubris fueling such a goal would do justice to King Lear himself. But ambitious effort is required for ambitious judgment. The actors cannot be evaluated without understanding the play. No guarantees can be given, no satisfaction-or-your-money-back pledges are offered. But throughout this book will be found various standards to judge "politics" and "politicians," all keyed to an understanding of public policy.

1

The immediate inquiry, however, is the basic one: What is "politics"? To answer, let's turn from drama on the stage to drama in the real world.

(1) In late September of 1957, President Dwight Eisenhower issued an executive order authorizing federalization of the Arkansas National Guard and the use of federal troops to enforce court orders to integrate Central High School in Little Rock, Arkansas. (2) On October 13, 1968, New York City and the Uniformed Sanitationmen's Association reached an agreement in a contract dispute that had precipitated a nine-day strike, ended only by New York State Governor Nelson Rockefeller's intervention. (3) On April 9, 1970, the New York State Senate voted thirty-one to twenty-six to repeal an 1830 law prohibiting abortion, making abortion now a matter between a woman and her doctor up to the twenty-fourth week of pregnancy. (4) In early 1964, the U.S. Congress passed the Civil Rights Act of 1964, which insured equal standards in voting registration procedures and outlawed discrimination based on race, color, religion, sex, or national origin in public facilities and employment. (5) In February 1976 candidates of both national parties entered the New Hampshire primary; Jimmy Carter won a Democratic plurality and President Gerald Ford edged Ronald Reagan in the Republican voting, 51 percent to 49 percent.

All five events above are normally seen as part of the operations of the political system. But they differ in important ways. Some are actions that govern imperatively, through the threat or use of physical force (presidential use of federal troops). Other actions, those we tend to call "political," are transactions that settle conflict through bargaining among disputing parties (the New York City settlement of the wage dispute with sanitation workers). Other actions rearrange the social context by providing new alternatives or maintaining old alternatives (the New York State Abortion Law, which also has ethical dimensions not shared by the other examples). Then there are actions that change or maintain fundamental rules of the political system, including even those rules identifying who can play the game (the 1964 Civil Rights Act). Some political events are like games, involving actions by autonomous players opposing one another in conditions of uncertainty and risk (the New Hampshire primary). That even these examples do not exhaust the possibilities of political events gives a sense of how complex the scope of politics can be.

Any reasonable observer of political life who looks at the range and diversity of "political" actions may well conclude that no single definition can cover the entire scope of political events. Yet from the beginnings of political theory serious students of politics have attempted to construct such a definition. Theorists of the past often defined politics in evaluative terms, stating not only what politics *is* but what it *ought* to be. Recent political theorists, in contrast, have distinguished between facts and values, and have offered empirical (or factual) definitions of politics. Early twentieth century political scientists often concentrated on institutions of politics, such social units as Congress, the presidency, the judicial branches of government. More recent students of politics have focused on units of behavior, those events that are political whatever the institution in which they occur.

One conceptualization of politics prominently discussed today is: politics is the *authoritative allocation of values*. While this definition contains no words as lively as "scurvy," it can open our inquiry into politics and policy.

POLITICS AS "THE AUTHORITATIVE ALLOCATION OF VALUES"

When David Easton published *The Political System* in 1953, political science was viewed as a discipline in search of a definition. One problem with the field of inquiry, now generally acknowledged, was the tendency of many students of politics to single out some institution as the proper locus for political inquiry. It is easy now to see the deficiencies of such an approach; for whatever institution is chosen as the point of study, a case can always be made, on slightly different facts, for a rival institution. For example, if Congress (or its committees) are selected, someone can always lay claim for the presidency as the controlling factor in political life; if the presidency is chosen, then someone can argue that a "power elite" is the *eminence grise* behind the office of the chief executive.

The simplest way to resolve disputes over institutions is to ask a different question. What is it that institutions *do* that makes them candidates for political study? Instead of asking the older, institutional question, "What is the *structure* for the expression of politics," we ask, "What is the expressing *function* of politics?"

Specifying politics as the *authoritative allocation of values* is an attempt to identify the defining function of political life (Easton, 1953; 1957). It defines that which all political systems do, whatever the arrangements for carrying out the defining function. All forms of government, dictatorships as well as democracies, are said to allocate values authoritatively. Perhaps even more important, it is no longer necessary to argue over which institution defines political life. We can now look for the function of politics, the *authoritative allocation of values*, and study politics in whatever institution performs this function. If the function is performed by the presidency, fine. If, however, it is performed by General Motors, fine also. In such a case we will simply take General Motors as the effective political unit in the society. This functional emphasis not only avoids criticisms that the wrong social unit has been chosen, but also conceptualizes politics as a system of actions with the defining function occupying the center space. A typical system design for politics is as follows:

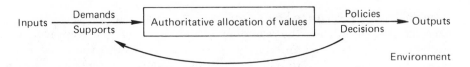

Whether politics can be successfully viewed as a system of actions will be discussed later in this chapter. For now it is important to see that shifting one's focus from institutions to functions also means adjusting the lens of one's viewing equipment; it means looking not at a static unit, but rather at the flow of a certain *type* of action that can occur in many social structures. Demands and supports become policies and decisions through actions that authoritatively allocate values, and this is a function that many institutions can carry out. If we set aside for the moment the issue of whether there is *any* single defining function, or characteristic, of political life, then the question we want to be sure of answering correctly is, "Does the *authoritative allocation of values* adequately define politics?"

One helpful way to inspect Easton's definition of politics is to look carefully at each word in the definition and try to determine if it covers all, or a substantial slice, of political life.

AUTHORITATIVE

Easton defines a policy as authoritative when "people feel they must or ought to obey it." One difficulty with this specification is that *feelings* may have little to do with some political events. In the strongest traditions of political life, social customs may govern behavior more effectively than any overt directive from political leaders. Preindustrial societies, indeed many small rural towns in America, are directed by the authority of "things have always been done this way." In such cases, policies may be carried out from habit, not from any feeling about what must or ought to be done.

We must also allow for the unintended consequences of action. It is commonly acknowledged today that many of the Head Start programs ambitiously developed for education in the 1960s had unforeseen and unplanned effects. Another example: the increased importance of early primaries, an unanticipated consequence of electoral reforms prior to the 1976 campaign, propelled Jimmy Carter into the White House by way of his stunning wins in New Hampshire and Florida. Policy may be the outcome of a decision process, but these outcomes can authoritatively affect behavior in a way quite unforeseen by those who initially form the policy.

A second difficulty with *authoritative* is its suggestion of *obedience*. Certainly many policies do elicit "obey" responses. Calling in federal troops, as in the example, disposes the average citizen to comply by obeying orders.

4

But other policies are not imperative and do not require obedience for compliance. Look at the language of the Civil Rights Act of 1964, for example. Two main provisions of the Act prohibit (1) unequal standards in voter registration procedures and (2) discrimination or segregation in public accommodations because of race, color, religion, or natural origin. Furthermore, the attorney general is required to act on behalf of any person denied equal access to public accommodations. Fines and imprisonment are cited as modes of enforcement.

Certainly this act contains strong rules that registrars, owners of public accommodations, members of school boards, and employers (among others) have to obey. But the act does not require those minority groups who are affected to do anything. The law is more accurately seen, from the perspective of minority groups, as providing access and opportunity, not as issuing commands they must obey. Similarly, extending the vote to women in 1920 did not require women to vote any more than the legalization of abortion today requires women to have abortions. Such actions can be called rule-establishing, or rule-permissive, policies. Either they change the framework of politics by establishing new rules and/or new players or they provide the conditions for doing certain things. In neither case can the appropriate responses of *all* citizens be accurately described by the word "obey."

ALLOCATION

Is politics always a form of allocation? When we allocate items, we distribute them. Distribution is a common enough theme in contemporary politics. It is even easy to see the political system as primarily concerned with distribution as it extracts resources (primarily through taxes) and spends moneys. Such policies as social security, welfare payments, poverty programs, aid to education, and urban reform are "strong" allocationist programs: they take resources from some segments of society and distribute them to others. But other policies are not so easily seen as allocationist formulas. Such regulatory policies as civil rights laws, law enforcement, and electoral reform are only marginally allocationist. Rather they seem directed at insuring conformity with certain rules, perhaps even as establishing access to the allocation process, not with allocating resources as such. Still other political actions do not seem to fit the idea of allocation at all: establishing roles and offices at all levels of government, organizing groups (like political parties or congressional committees) to maintain social practices, reinforcing symbolic values.

Two types of policy issues are not even logical candidates for allocation: (1) public goods, and (2) ethical issues that must be resolved within a public policy framework. A "pure" public good is generally defined as any good that is (a) *nonexcludable,* meaning that it is consumable by everybody if available at all, and (b) *supply-irreducible*, meaning that consumption does not diminish supply (Samuelson, 1954–55). Pure public goods are rare, but many goods either approximate this standard, or are characterized by one of the two defining attributes of pure public goods. Clean air, for example, is a good example of a public good. All can consume it whenever it is available and the supply, while not technically inexhaustible, has been only marginally diminished by consumption up to now. National security policies often represent *nonexcludability*, for insuring the defenses of an entire society will benefit all within the society, no matter who finances or arranges the defenses. Whatever we want to say about the efforts to make public goods available (with some expending more time and resources than others), such goods cannot be allocated in the sense of making things available to some while denying them to others. Certainly public goods are unlike, say, welfare payments, which *do* distribute society's resources. A public good, unlike a distributive good, is available to all once it has been made available at all.

The second kind of issue not adequately described by *allocation* is ethical. Frequently, ethical issues are not within the public domain. Whether one is obligated to attend church services every Sunday may be a proper topic for moral or religious regulation, but is in many societies a matter of indifference to public authorities. However, some moral issues do intertwine with legal rules. Killing is typically prohibited by both moral and legal rules, though for different reasons in each case (against God's law morally, say, and contrary to social stability legally).

Occasionally moral issues require public resolution to sanction certain practices. Abortion is a moral issue currently supported and condemned by those of opposite moral convictions. But because it involves the joint actions of doctors, hospital staffs, and patients, the law must stipulate what is permitted. Again, whatever the distributive effects for a society of abortion policy, disputes over the legalization of abortion are not primarily concerned with distribution, but rather with whether abortion is desirable as a public practice. Sometimes, as with the 1977–78 Congressional conflicts over whether to use Medicaid funds for abortions, allocation is an issue. But even in these disputes, the justice, or fairness, of cutting Medicaid funds for elective abortions was a focal issue. Successfully resolving social disputes over abortions is not simply a question of allocating values, or even of choosing one allocative arrangement of values over another, but of settling on what *ought* to be valued by the society.

It is also helpful to distinguish between maximization (or production) and allocation. Economists tend to use pie-slicing as an analogy for allocation. If one group gets a larger slice of the pie, then the others must get less. In politics, such activities are often called zero-sum, for gains to some require commensurate losses to others. But, although the idea of pie-slicing is excellent for understanding family dinners and even many forms of politics, the *size* of the social pie can also be an issue for political action. Government incentives to businesses to increase production, for example, may unavoidably favor some groups at the expense of others. But the primary goal of such policies may be only to increase the resources of a society, something not even indirectly intended by primarily allocationist policies like welfare programs. Increasing the productive capacity of a society may even affect purely distributive policies, for if the pie gets larger as it is being cut, then proportionate losses to a group may be compensated by the group's overall gains. Given that political societies can increase production of goods as well as distribute available goods, then the term *allocationist politics* seems to capture only the distributive dimension of political activity.

VALUES

One of the more difficult words to interpret in any language is *value*, and the difficulties are no less pronounced in political discourse. Political policy can allocate values in two prominent ways: (1) by rearranging the attitudes of citizens that express values, or (2) by distributing the things that are valued by citizens. In the first, policy aims at changing or maintaining the values of a population; this might happen when a government decides to "educate" its citizens about a policy it regards as necessary. For example, from 1947 onwards the Truman administration became convinced that an aggressive defense policy, including commitments to the security of Western Europe, would have to replace the demobilization policies in effect since the end of World War II. Public warnings in subsequent years about the Communist threat were designed, in part, to elicit popular support for the changed defense policies. In other words, for the policy to be fully successful, popular attitudes had to be changed.

Policy also distributes the goods and services that are held in favor by the public. Distributing "things" are among the more visible actions of a political system. That family of policies roughly grouped under urban affairs is an example of such allocation. On the assumption that houses, public and private, are items of value, the variety of programs sponsored by the Federal Housing Administration and the Urban Renewal Administration are attempts to allocate valued items. This type of allocation, of valued things, is different from the change or maintenance of attitudes that express values, even though they sometimes overlap in practice.

Still a third sense of *values*, however, is not covered by (1) or (2). This is the sense in which the term refers to disputes over what *ought* to be valued. An allocationist formula is most comfortably fitted to what *is* valued, either the expression of values in attitudes or the range of items held in favor. Authentic disputes over what ought to be held valuable are not equivalent to efforts aimed at changing or maintaining attitudes, or to distributions of valued things. They are actions aimed at clarifying, at settling on primary standards and rules, and at reaching basic conclusions about the "good life." Public debates over euthanasia, for example, are evaluative activities of singular importance for medical policies. But they are unlike the more familiar types of allocationist politics in not being action aimed at distributing anything.

DIMENSIONS OF POLITICAL LIFE

The failures of the phrase, *the authoritative allocation of values*, to cover all, or even most, phases of political life are easily explained: Politics is too diverse for a single-phrase definition. Though it is a distortion to view politics as analogous to any single game, the diversity of political life can be illustrated by comparing it to several quite different games. Sometimes politics is like *Monopoly*, commanding a player to "Go" to the next point, or "Stop," and inflicting penalties and rewards in conjunction with those commands. At other times politics is more like the trading of cards with pictures of star athletes: outcomes are effective only if each trader is satisfied that he is gaining in the give and take of the exchange (a Pareto-Optimal outcome, as will be explained later). Still other political actions are like games of poker, or chess, or even dice games, where tactical calculations must be made without knowing what an opponent will do next.

Sometimes—perhaps most often—politics is like prize fighting, a game between combative, self-interested players (egoists). At other times it can be selfless and other-directed, a successful basketball team with no superstars but many team players. Some political actions are like those conferences held in the off-season to change, or maintain, the rules for playing a game, much as the owners of professional football or baseball teams will covenant about the basic structure of their games. Some political action is like a game where the players change positions—someone wins the deal in blackjack or switches from cornerback to flanker in football. Other political action is like a game where the patterns can be altered without touching the defining, or constitutive, rules—the changes Bobby Fischer initiated in chess strategy, for example. None of these analogies taken singly captures the full scope of politics, but together they suggest the possible diversity of political life.

If we try to group all types of political events under a concept, the concept will not be statable in a single phrase. Rather, it will include a cluster of items. "Politics" includes regulation, bargaining, assigning roles and offices, extracting resources, maximizing, allocating, changing the rules or conditions of the game, and other actions that both overlap each other and extend to forms probably impossible to catalog exhaustively, and certainly impossible to describe with a single phrase.

This variety of political life also makes possible a variety of theoretical approaches to politics. Perhaps the most important distinction in approaches is between a power-oriented approach (control, authority) and an exchange-oriented approach (bargaining). Although supporters of each approach often try to reduce the opposition to their own terms, it seems more reasonable to adopt a nonreductive approach and investigate political events in all their apparent diversity rather than within some imposed uniformity.

In recognizing this variety, we should not assume that distinctions will always emerge in terms of separate events. A family of units can converge in a single political experience. Look, for example, at the number of items represented by just the defense lawyer in a criminal trial. He (a) represents his client, (b) is an egoist in earning his fee and maintaining his reputation, but (c) is operating to insure the interests of his client. He (d) opposes the prosecuting attorney in such game conditions as uncertain outcome, risk, imperfect knowledge, and payoffs, yet (e) is constrained in his actions by regulations on procedures and evidence. He can (f) bargain with the opposition, as in plea-bargaining, but (g) is subject to the imperatives issued by the judge and backed by coercion (for example, contempt citations), and so on. A law court is not a microcosm of the political arena, but as this example of a convergence of political dimensions suggests, any political experience may be a mixed and complicated combination of family items.

THREE MAIN TYPES OF POLITICAL ACTION

As students of politics, we are obligated to sort out the members of the "politics" family with as much precision as possible. If, as seems likely, a single-phrase definition such as the *authoritative allocation of values* will not work, perhaps a multiple-phrase approach will better cover all the cousins, brothers, sisters, aunts, and uncles of the "politics" family. As a matter of intellectual fact, three main approaches to the study of politics have reached prominence in recent years.

POWER, CONTROL

The oldest approach to politics is the *imperative* model. In this approach, political action is viewed as a *command* backed up, usually, with force. Max Weber, considered by many the originator of modern social science, defined the state as that institution in a territory which has a monopoly of force: The state has final or ultimate power; nothing can be more powerful than the state. This *sovereign* power of the state fits well with some recent views on the political system. Gabriel Almond (1960) defines the political system as that system of interactions which performs certain functions by means of "legitimate physical compulsion." The *power* or *control* model of politics helps us understand many forms of politics, especially the police function of the state. But, although politics is frequently an imperative transaction, it does not appear *always* to be a kind of command.

BARGAINING

Some recent studies of politics have emphasized the *exchange* nature of political transactions. One of the principle means of exchanging political goods is *bargaining*. A bargain is struck between people who cannot or will not control one another through commands. In bargaining, all parties give and take to reach a satisfactory outcome. A policy that expresses a bargained outcome, as did New York City's settlement with the sanitation workers, is the result of transactions. A command-type policy, like President Eisenhower's dispatch of troops to Little Rock, is formed prior to interactions or, sometimes, because bargaining transactions have broken down and consultation-with-adjustment is no longer possible. The interesting feature of exchange transactions is that they frequently occur among parties roughly equal (for whatever reason) in power. Bargaining represents the mutual adjustment of claims among competing individuals or groups.

GAMING

The theory of games, contrary to rumor, was not invented by Bobby Riggs, though much of his "gamesmanship" can be expressed in the theory. Game theory was created and introduced in a single, important book (*Theory of Games and Economic Behavior*, Von Neumann and Morgenstern, 1944). The theory explains with mathematical models the patterns of conflict and cooperation among two or more autonomous players. Unlike *power/control* theories and even theories of *bargaining*, the players in formal games need not act directly upon each other. Rather, as the candidates in the New Hampshire primary did, they may act on the conditions in which they find themselves (including other people) to secure an outcome. Game players usually do not command one another, at least not with the success found in authority relationships. Sometimes, in certain cooperative games, players bargain with each other and often exchange side payments to reach an outcome. But in other, more competitive games (especially zero-sum games), the players do not bargain with one another, although they may, in turns, command and bargain with spectators, like the electorate. The aim of an election, for example, is to win the most votes in competition with other players. A *gaming* approach to politics concentrates on the tactics or strategies of people in conditions of no authority. It helps illuminate the curiously competitive or cooperative actions of political actors who neither control one another, nor, sometimes, even directly exchange goods with one another.

These three approaches to politics—(a) power/control, (b) bargaining, and (c) gaming—do not exhaust the complicated family of political action. But they will serve as helpful guides as we explore public policy.

TYPES OF PUBLIC POLICY

We would expect public policies to correspond at least roughly to the dimensions and types of political action, since policy is, in its most general sense, the pattern of action that resolves conflicting claims or provides incentives for cooperation. Our expectations are not far off the mark, as we shall see, although defining policy in a neat phrase is probably as difficult and fruitless as looking for a single-phrase definition of politics.

Within the broad term "policy," two features stand out. First, policy is a social *practice*, not a singular or isolated event. An assassination, for example, is a political event, even if it happens once in the entire history of a country. But it is not a policy, or an issue for policy resolution, unless it is adopted as a recurring activity, a practice by some social unit—say, a revolutionary group. Second, policy is occasioned by the need either (1) to reconcile conflicting claims or (2) to establish incentives for collective action among those who do share goals but find it irrational to cooperate with one another. (This latter condition requires a solution to the "free rider" problem, explained in Chapter 2.) If we look back at the examples set out at the opening of this chapter, all are characterized by a nonutopian atmosphere of things-gone-wrong: people are making demands, or expressing goals, in ways that can be settled neither spontaneously nor through some happy operation of natural law.

Sometimes conflicting claims are actually expressed by claimants, a type of policy issue both visible and common enough in daily life. When, for example, blacks want access to public schools and whites want to keep them out, opposing claims are represented by opposing groups. At other times, claims stand only as opposed courses of action that seem to require a resolution. Creating new offices, organizing groups, even extending the franchise, may be actions that are taken not in response to group endorsement but as a result of, say, leadership perception of what is required for order, or even moral rightness. At still other times we might have goals shared by rational individuals who cannot rationally, on their own, find a successful way of cooperating to obtain these goals. What is not found in any examples of policy is the contemplative sense that nothing is to be resolved by way of action. The architect, for example, who has three plans on his desk, A, B, and C, is not acting in a way analogous to policy actions until he implements one plan in opposition to the others. Policy is action, not reflection on alternative claims.

Some of the most important types of public policy are made in conditions of *scarce resources*. If we all had enough material goods, many of the most important types of political quarrels would vanish. The amount of goods available also favors one type of policy or another. Many economic theorists maintain that increasing scarce resources (*maximizing*) are high priority problems in impoverished societies, and that *distributive* problems become prominent in conditions of abundance. But even if we had everything we needed materially, and if goods were distributed to the satisfaction of all, disputes could still occur over ethical practices. To claim that abortion either is or is not acceptable, for example, is to stake out a *moral* claim that cannot be resolved by more goods or better distribution. Public policy must occasionally be made even when scarce resources are not at issue.

Perhaps the most helpful way to see "public policy" is as a *patterned* attempt either to resolve or manage political disputes or to provide rational incentives to secure agreed-upon goals, with public policy issues capable of ranging far and wide over both material goods and ethical issues. Political events can occur outside the net of policy issues—one-time assassinations, for example. But if a political event becomes an issue for policy resolution—as would recurrent assassinations—then some patterned response will characterize the public policy that is made.

The *types* of public policy that have caught the attention of scholars lately can be drawn from our understanding of political life. Theodore Lowi (1964), for example, has suggested a threefold typology for policy actions.

REGULATORY

One of the more visible types of public policy is *regulatory*. The most dramatic form of regulation is through criminal law statutes. These statutes are, on the whole, state rather than federal laws and generally regulate how people can act toward one another. Federal regulatory policy occurs primarily through the actions of independent regulatory commissions. The Food and Drug Administration, Federal Communications Commission, and Interstate Commerce Commission, for example, are charged with the regulation of trade, rates, safety, communication, general practices of numerous businesses, and other areas of social life too numerous to list. We also have federal regulation of civil rights, which is buttressed by both civil and criminal law.

DISTRIBUTIVE

Distributive policies grant goods and services to specific segments of the population. One of the most prominent areas of distributive policies is welfare and health. All public assistance welfare programs are distributive. Both Medicare and Medicaid, as well as the Food Stamp Program, Aid to Families with Dependent Children, Veterans Administration programs, and a host of other programs, provide cash and transfers-in-kind (services; facilities; purchasing paper, such as food stamps) to people who meet certain criteria of need. Less direct, though still distributive, are "social insurance" policies. Programs such as social security distribute moneys to classes of people who meet criteria other than need.

REDISTRIBUTIVE

Redistributive policies aim at rearranging one or more of the basic schedules of social and economic rewards. Progressive tax policies are often cited as examples of redistributive policies, for they take proportionately more money from the rich than from the poor. Basic alterations in productive arrangements, as in government appropriation of industry, or changes in comprehensive services, as in socialized medicine, are also redistributive in their rearrangement of wealth. Some distributive policies transfer goods and services so strongly that they amount to redistributions. The growing cost of welfare programs, for example, may affect some basic structures for distributing wealth. In comparison to most European countries, redistributive programs have not been strong in American society. Because they involve a direct loss to the rich (and thus powerful) in society, they are the most difficult and controversial to implement.

To Lowi's three-fold division of public policy, we can add a fourth and fifth:

CAPITALIZATION

Businesses and governments (both local and state) also receive distributive largesse from the federal government. Such distribution, in theory if not in practice, is aimed at increasing the productive capacity of society's institutions. Although normally included in simple distributive policies, *capitalization* policies are not like the primarily *consumptive* distribution of welfare programs. Federal subsidies to economic institutions are vast and growing. They include (1) cash payments to farmers (for example, sugar beet and cane growers) to improve the farm industry; (2) tax subsidies, as in the oil depletion allowance, to encourage exploration and production in selected industries; and (3) credit subsidies, for example low-interest loans to municipalities (such as New York City), generous financing of public works projects, and loan guarantees (such as that given to the Lockheed Aircraft Corporation). Subsidies also reach private individuals, for example college students who are the beneficiaries of low-interest, deferred federal loans or work-study money.

Distributive policies are a substantial part of our public policy landscape. Some provide goods and services to consumers, as do programs for the needy or aged. Others aim at maximization or production goals, as do subsidies to certain industries. We have recognized a separate type of policy, *capitalization*, to describe this second form of distribution. With the additional form we must also recognize a hybrid type: funds allocated to city and state governments, who in turn allocate the moneys in distributive programs for consumption *or* capitalization. The growth of government subsidies has made it difficult, if not impossible, to locate any dividing line between private and public sectors of American society.

ETHICAL

Public policies can also establish the correct practice for some moral issue. The Supreme Court's decision in 1973 (*Roe* v. *Wade*) made abortion-on-demand a legally acceptable alternative in the first three months of term. The Court did not settle the moral issue of abortion: many people still view abortions as morally wrong, even though they are now legally permitted. But the public policies following the Court's decision set out what ought and ought not to be done in an area marked off by deep moral convictions. In effect, the Supreme Court decision established legally permissible practices on a moral matter. The aim of policies on abortion is to regulate actions. But the distinguishing feature of such policies is their intersection with moral issues. Some actions attempt to establish fundamental rules of an ethical nature, as did the U.S. Senate's 1977 passage of a moral code for itself. Again, such laws may be primarily regulatory in form. But the ethical nature of the acts warrants a category separate from other regulative policies of law and commerce.

In addition to these five policy types, we may describe public policy in terms of certain logical forms. Donna Kerr (1976) has suggested a basic division between two types of policies:

Rule Policies.   Some policies specify actions to be performed. The 1965 Elementary and Secondary Education Act outlined types of financial aid to be given to schools and pupils. This is an example of *rule* policy.

Goal Policies.   Other policies set goals to be achieved by any of a number of actions. When the U.S. Congress passed the Economic Opportunity Act in 1964, it called for "maximum feasible participation" by the poor in the administration of the program. How to achieve that goal was generally left open; the methods could (and did) vary greatly. This is an example of *goal* policy.

Still another division can be established between *substantive* and *procedural* policies. Both rule and goal policies are *substantive:* they set out *what* is to be accomplished. But sometimes a policy will simply state a procedure—in particular, *who* is to carry out some action. For example, "revenue sharing" is intended to shift many urban policies from the federal to the state and local levels of government. The State and Local Fiscal Assistance Act of 1972 provides for distribution of federal funds amounting to over $5 billion per year to states and communities. What is to be done with the money is only generally restricted; the important feature of the policy is a change in the *who* from federal to state and local authorities.

A neat separation between *substantive* and *procedural* policies is rarely possible. One of the favorite ploys of politicians is to turn a policy measure over to some agency in a procedural move designed to insure a certain substantive outcome. President Johnson, for example, conducted his "War on Poverty" with the newly created Office of Economic Opportunity, rather than through the more established Housing, Economics, and Welfare or Housing and Urban Development offices, in order to control and bring about the policy outcomes he judged desirable. Members of Congress frequently assign bills to committees to see that they die a quiet substantive death. The successful manipulation of procedure is one sure indication of a politician's mastery of substance.

THE POLICY PROCESS AS A SYSTEM OF ACTIONS

In addition to establishing types and logical forms for policies, students of policy have also attempted to conceptualize, to "see," the entire policy process. *Policy* lends itself easily to such a view. Even the most rudimentary study of how bills are passed through Congress suggests a beginning and a middle, if not an end, in a series of actions extending over time. The success of *process* perspectives makes for a predictable acceptance of *systems* approaches to the study of public policy.

Several definitions are important to an understanding of *systems theory* as applied to public policy.

1. A "system" is, technically, (a) any interaction of two or more mutually interdependent units that (b) persists over time. A lawn is a system, as is the solar system and a university classroom. Systems may be *closed* or *open*. A closed system is unresponsive to its environment. Example: the mind of an autistic child or a hermetically sealed laboratory. An open system responds to its environment. Example: a column of mercury or an airplane. Any

system is distinguishable from its environment by the characteristics of the units composing the system. Example: the solar system comprises nine planets and the sun. Anything else is "outside" the system and thus its environment.

2. Open systems are subject to both internal and external stress and respond to such stress in a variety of ways. Many of the responses contribute to the persistence of the system. Example: a herd of elephants must cope with internal population growth as well as external food shortages. The method of coping with stress may include thinning the herd by abandoning some young, foraging in new feeding areas, modifying mating habits, retaining leadership patterns. (While we don't want to make our elephant herd a society of intelligent planners, we can see that coping with stress to maintain the system might require the herd to change some internal and external factors and retain others. Moreover, as any one factor changes, the system itself changes, calling for further modifications.)

3. A *political* system is the subset of activities within a social system that we designate as "political." Example: defining *politics* as the *authoritative allocation of values* provides a system comprising all actions describable by the defining phrase. Unfortunately, if *politics* is a cluster of items rather than a class of actions all with one defining feature, then there can be as many different kinds of political systems as there are different kinds of political actions. Nevertheless, systems theorists in political thought frequently talk as if there is *a* political system; they assume a single definition of *politics*. This problem aside, however, any political system is *open*, continually coping with stress from its social and physical environment.

These three definitions above suggest the main outlines of a systems approach to politics. If we transplant the idea of a system to public policy *and* if we avoid the mistake of assuming a *single* policy system, then the basic model for the policy process will look like this: (Feedback refers to the effect that the outcome can have in modifying, influencing, or correcting any further input into the system.)

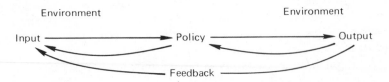

This can be interpreted as: Policy is an interaction of interdependent actions occurring over time and tending to persist in the face of stress from the environment of policy-making. A systems model allows you to see the total picture of policy. But to see the total picture accurately requires more details. We must fill in the policy features:

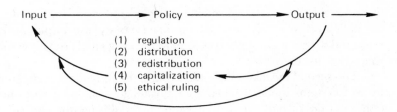

Now we can see how a systems model of policy locates—fixes in our sights really—the policy forms outlined earlier. In a systems model, *input* activities activate the conceptual "center" of policy—the five-fold policy forms—and these forms of policy provide *outputs* affecting the environment of the policy system. We now can sketch in some additional details on each side of the policy center (Jones, 1970).

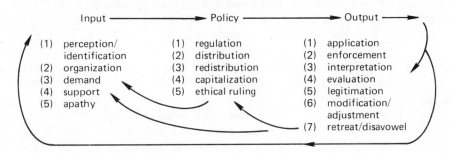

Here the picture is more complete. The general flow of policy indicated by the arrows suggests the interdependence of the activities, including the effect of feedback on both policy and input. Certain activities listed under *input*, for example the identification of a problem, lead to a *policy* made by the relevant authorities in the system, and this policy then flows to the right side of the model for application, enforcement, or other form of *output*. These activities in turn affect further inputs and policies. The advantages of a systems model are these: (a) the *process* character of policy is easily caught, thus avoiding the mistake of seeing policy as a static, random, or totally disjointed collection of activities; and (b) a high level of generality is maintained, persuading us to see a more total picture of policy than partial models or simple case studies permit.

In understanding and using a systems model of policy, however, we should be careful to avoid two mistakes. The first is supposing, with naivete uncharacteristic of students of politics, that the arrows depict a smooth continuum of *actual* policy activities, with no breaks or interruptions. The methods of implementing policies more often resemble the tactics of a streetfighter than a classic standup boxer: a whirl of disconnected motions, clumsily effective with only an occasional smooth line of pure form. The systems model of the policy process only sets out the diagrams we use to plot action in the mind and does not always correspond to the rough and uneven world of political action itself.

The second mistake we should avoid is thinking that the greater generality of a systems model is always an advantage in helping us to understand either politics or public policy. A general model is highly interesting in both its scope and, quite frequently, its elegance. But generalities can easily pass over the particular light and heat of real events. The study of public policy is the study of particulars, of real-life experiences. So to use systems models we must bring them down to earth, connect them to actual events. These connecting efforts are known as problems of interpretation in any general theory.

Sometimes interpretations of concepts are easy. Take *inflation*, for example: The indicators of inflation, while disputable, are still generally recognized (by economists) and provide a basis for measuring it. But many concepts of systems theory are not so easily attached even to disputable indicators. Take the idea of an "environment," for example. We know that a system's environment is anything outside the range of activities defined by its features. What is not so clear is what this can mean in real-life situations. Many groups in American society are at once in and out of the policy system: sometimes they make policy, and sometimes outputs of policy are aimed at them. With such complications we seem to need secondary theories of interpretation to tell us how to connect systems models to real-world politics. But we can avoid this additional theorizing by keeping in mind the limitations of general theory, and by remaining close to actual events even as we use systems models to see the overall policy process.

PLAN OF THE BOOK

In keeping with the strictures suggested for the use of systems models, the basic plan of the book is to combine theory with practice as closely as possible. Textbooks in public policy, like all textbooks, should consolidate the good literature in a field, allowing the student to grasp conventional wisdoms. This will be attempted here. But public policy texts must also communicate the excitement of actual politics, letting the student sense the keen struggle of making and implementing policy. This also will be attempted. If achieving these two goals sounds like a balancing act, it is. Theory will grace every chapter. But every chapter will also contain one or more extended case studies designed to clear the air of abstractions. Ideally, the case studies will illustrate the theory. But the rough-and-tumble world of politics does not always happily fit theoretical requirements, so sometimes the case studies will simply introduce actual events to the text, and nothing more.

This textbook is unlike many in the field in at least one important respect: Normative issues of public policy are treated as seriously as empirical issues. The introduction of an ethical form to Lowi's three-fold typology of policy gives a clue to what is ahead. We will look at such standard topics as decision models and interest groups, but we will also spend considerable time on such topics as abortion, reverse discrimination, genetic research, and distributive justice. This extended treatment of ethical issues and social justice serves two purposes. First, some excellent studies have made inquiry into such topics once more a respectable enterprise. Second, students of public policy can no longer ignore the ethical issues of the day. The policy issues of today and tomorrow are unavoidably intertwined with ethical matters, as we shall see as we proceed in this text.

THE EXAMPLES REVISITED

Shortly before President Eisenhower ordered federal troops to Little Rock, Arkansas, he met with Arkansas Governor Orville Faubus to reach an accord. Following the meeting Governor Faubus pledged to obey federal law, but asked for "patience." The Arkansas governor also announced that he would remove the state National Guard under "conditions of tranquility." But in the next few days violence erupted when blacks attempted to enter Central High School, prompting President Eisenhower to dispatch federal troops. After the deployment Eisenhower conferred with the Southern Governors Conference and agreed to withdraw the federal troops. Faubus promised there would be no disturbances. However, when the Arkansas governor weakened his pledge against disturbance by adding the phrase "by me," Eisenhower rapidly reversed his stand and maintained the presence of the troops. In late May of 1958, as the school term ended, federal troops were withdrawn. The following fall the state closed all four high schools and the civil rights struggles characterizing the painful and exhilarating events of the 1960s began.

On February 2, 1968, when New York City sanitation workers had been on strike nine days in defiance of the state's Taylor Law prohibiting such strikes, Governor Rockefeller ended the strike by temporarily assuming on behalf of the state the city's debt on sanitation funding. The following fall the city and the union reached an accord on the contract dispute. This accord was disrupted briefly when the incinerator workers struck a few weeks later for higher wages, a dispute ending after seven days when the city and the workers reached an agreement that included the payment of almost $3,000 in back pay to the workers. In February of the same year New York City had committed itself for the first time to submit a labor problem, the sanitation dispute, to binding arbitration, specifically to the chairman of the New York State Mediation Board.

Just over two months after the New York State Senate made abortion a matter between the woman and her doctor up to the twenty-fourth week of pregnancy, the American Medical Association, for the first time in its history, voted to allow all doctors to perform abortions for social and economic as well as medical reasons. In the first six months of the law, an estimated sixty-nine thousand abortions were performed in New York City alone, approximately one-half of these on women from outside the state. In May 1972, the New York State Senate repealed the two-year-old abortion law on a vote of thirty to twenty-seven. Governor Rockefeller quickly vetoed the repeal, reinstating the abortion law. On January 22, 1973, the United States Supreme Court overruled all state laws that prohibit or restrict any woman's right to obtain an abortion during the first three months of pregnancy.

Just these three examples indicate the heterogeneity of political life stressed in this chapter. Even so imperative an action as troop deployment can lead easily to bargaining over their maintenance or withdrawal. (Indeed, President Eisenhower had originally dispatched troops only after bargaining efforts with Governor Faubus had broken down.) The bargaining efforts for new distributions by the New York City sanitation workers dispute are overshadowed by the imperatives of binding arbitration. The New York State Abortion Law is a mixture of ethics, regulation, and gaming strategies. The opening conclusion we want to draw out is that, even if politicians are "scurvy," the study of politics and public policy is an investigation of events rich in distinctions and, above all else, provocative and always interesting. Politics must also be looked at with the thought that what we study has continuing implications for the world we live in, as these three examples demonstrate.

SUMMARY

1. A prominent definition of *politics* as the *authoritative allocation of values* fails to reflect the natural diversity of political life.

2. The word "politics" covers a family of items impossible to describe in a single phrase.

3. Three main approaches to the diversity of politics are (a) *power/control*; (b) *bargaining*; and (c) *gaming*.

4. Public policy can be organized along the lines of a five-fold typology: (a) *regulatory*; (b) *distributive*; (c) *redistributive*; (d) *capitalization*; and (e) *ethical*.

5. Some important logical forms of policy include (a) *rule* policies and (b)

goal policies, as well as a division of policy into (c) *substance* and (d) *procedure*.

6. A *systems* model can help in understanding the entire process of public policy, though it must be carefully balanced against the real-world events of political life.

7. All theoretical distinctions, types, forms, models, may fragment into tiny pieces when applied to the complications of actual policy events.

FOR FURTHER READING

THE CONCEPT OF POLITICS

ALMOND, GABRIEL, *The Politics of Developing Nations.* Princeton, N.J.: Princeton University Press, 1960.

ALMOND, GABRIEL, AND G. BINGHAM POWELL, *Comparative Politics: A Developmental Approach.* Boston: Little, Brown, 1966, pp. 195–201.

CONNOLLY, WILLIAM, *The Terms of Political Discourse.* Lexington, Mass.: D. C. Heath, 1974, pp. 1–44.

EASTON, DAVID, *The Political System.* New York: Knopf, 1953.

ECKSTEIN, HARRY, "Authority Patterns: A Structural Basis for Political Inquiry," *American Political Science Review,* December 1973.

ECKSTEIN, HARRY, AND TED ROBERT GURR, *Patterns of Authority: A Structural Basis for Political Inquiry.* New York: Wiley Interscience, 1975.

FROHOCK, FRED M., "Notes on the Concept of Politics," *The Journal of Politics,* May 1974.

————, "The Structure of 'Politics,'" *American Political Science Review* 71, September 1978.

MITCHELL, WILLIAM, "Politics as the Allocation of Values: A Critique," *Ethics* 71, January 1961.

SORZANO, J. S., "David Easton and the Invisible Hand," *American Political Science Review,* March 1975.

————, "Values in Political Science: The Concept of Allocation," *The Journal of Politics,* February 1977.

STRAUSS, LEO, *What Is Political Philosophy?* Glencoe, Ill.: Free Press, 1959, pp. 9–55.

WEBER, MAX, *Economy and Society,* I. New York: Bedminster Press, 1968.

GAMING AND BARGAINING

BRAMS, STEVE, *Game Theory and Politics.* New York: Free Press, 1975.

LUCE, R. DUNCAN, AND HOWARD RAIFFA, *Games and Decisions.* New York: John Wiley, 1957.

RAPOPORT, ANATOL, *Fights, Games, and Debates.* Ann Arbor, Mich.: University of Michigan Press, 1960.

RAPOPORT, ANATOL, AND ALBERT CHAMMAH, *Prisoner's Dilemma.* Ann Arbor, Mich.: University of Michigan Press, 1965.

RIKER, WILLIAM, *The Theory of Political Coalitions*. New Haven, Conn.: Yale University Press, 1963.
SCHELLING, THOMAS, *The Strategy of Conflict*. New York: Oxford University Press, 1963.
VON NEUMANN, JOHN, AND OSKAR MORGENSTERN, *Theory of Games and Economic Behavior*. New York: John Wiley, 1944, 1964.

PUBLIC POLICY: TYPES AND FORMS

KERR, DONNA, *Educational Policy: Analysis, Structure and Justification*. New York: David McKay, 1976.
————, *The End of Liberalism*. New York: Norton, 1969.
LOWI, THEODORE, "American Business, Public Policy, Case Studies, and Political Theory," *World Politics*, July 1964.
MITCHELL, JOYCE, AND WILLIAM MITCHELL, *Political Analysis and Public Policy*. Chicago: Rand McNally, 1969.
SALISBURY, ROBERT, "The Analysis of Public Policy: A Search for Theories and Roles," in *Political Science and Public Policy*, ed. Austin Ranney. Chicago: Markam, 1968.

SYSTEMS THEORY AND THE POLICY PROCESS

ALMOND, GABRIEL, "Comparative Political Systems," *Journal of Politics* 18, (1956), pp. 391–409.
BLALOCK, H., AND A. BLALOCK, "Toward a Clarification of Systems Analysis in the Social Sciences," *Philosophy of Science* 26, (1959), pp. 84–92.
BUCKLEY, WALTER, ED., *Modern Systems Research for the Behavioral Scientist*. Chicago: Aldine, 1968.
EASTON, DAVID, "An Approach to the Analysis of Political Systems," *World Politics*, April 1957.
————, *A Framework for Political Analysis*. Englewood Cliffs, N.J.: Prentice-Hall, 1965.
————, *A Systems Analysis of Political Life*. New York: John Wiley, 1965.
JONES, CHARLES O., *An Introduction to the Study of Public Policy*. Belmont, Calif.: Duxbury Press, 1970, especially pp. 1–16.
LINDBLOM, CHARLES, *The Policy-Making Process*. Englewood Cliffs, N.J.: Prentice-Hall, 1968.
MITCHELL, WILLIAM, *The American Polity*. New York: Free Press, 1962.
PARSONS, TALCOTT, "The Political Aspect of Social Structure and Process," in *Varieties of Political Theory*, ed. David Easton. Englewood Cliffs, N.J.: Prentice-Hall, 1966, pp. 71–112.

PUBLIC GOODS

SAMUELSON, PAUL, "The Pure Theory of Public Expenditure," *Review of Economics and Statistics*, 1954–55.
————, "A Diagrammatic Exposition of a Theory of Public Expenditure," *Review of Economics and Statistics*, 1954–55.
————, "Aspects of Public Expenditure Theories," *Review of Economics and Statistics*, 1958.

decision models of policy

2

SOCIAL POLICIES: CROSSING PATTERNS

If a society needs anything, we would think it needs a system for educating its young. Yet the primal status of education is no guarantee of either its success or its ability to generate consensus. Recent educational policy in the United States reads like a primer on social conflict and expert disagreement.

Shortly after World War II, many educators, and a good share of the general public, became convinced that federal aid to education was necessary. But, in spite of strong public support, two decades of political effort were required before the U.S. Congress passed the aid-to-education bill of 1965. Two issues figured prominently in the delay: race and religion. The first, southern opposition to the racial integration goals of aid-to-education bills, was set aside by the Civil Rights Act of 1964. The second, whether federal aid to education would include parochial schools, was effectively finessed by emphasizing aid to children rather than to schools. The Elementary and Secondary Education Act of 1965 provided compensatory aid for disadvantaged children as well as grants to public and private schools for general instructional resources.

Title I, the compensatory provision of the act, was challenged in an explosive report by James Coleman (1966). The Coleman Report argued that the effect of financial support for ghetto schools is insignificant, but that integration with advantaged children *is* important in student development. Though itself challenged, the Coleman Report furnished support for proponents of school integration, including those who advocated busing as a means to achieve racial balance in public schools. In 1975, after a decade of white

23

flight to the suburbs (in part to escape school integration), Coleman qualified the *busing* implications of his 1966 Report (Coleman, 1975). Today, forced busing is the most volatile political issue in the field of education, and school financing has re-emerged in different form as possibly the most intractable issue.

Educational policies, as this brief chronology suggests, often seem like a patchwork quilt: patterns of action crisscross in stunning ways, presenting to the student of public policy an uneven collection of issues and problems. Only extended bargaining and compromise by all groups made possible the Elementary and Secondary Education Act of 1965. But shortly after its passage a basic provision was challenged in a systematic policy study. Some of the act's programs have failed to have their intended effects (Head Start Programs), and unforeseen consequences (such as white exodus from the inner cities) have undermined some of the act's purposes. Currently, one attempt to rectify its apparent early miscalculations (forced busing) has enflamed partisan forces, and school financing is being rethought from the bottom up. If we assume that educational policies are, on the whole, the results of *decisions* by political actors, then the mosaic of actions since passage of the 1965 act provides the perfect laboratory for perceiving the two poles in social policy: not only what can be right and effective, but also how policies consciously decided can go terribly wrong.

RATIONAL DECISIONS AND SOCIOLOGICAL EXPLANATIONS

One direct way to explain social policies is to see them as the outcomes of decisions by individual policy planners. Such a concept is at the heart of democratic theory, for we cannot ascribe responsibility to elected officials unless we assume that events are, in some important way, the results of their decisions. The use of decision models in public policy explanations is closely aligned to the idea of *rationality*. In its simplest sense (one we will complicate very rapidly), a rational decision is one that maximizes the utility (or, roughly, works to the greatest advantage) of the person making the decision (Riker, 1973). The prime rival to a rational decision explanation is a *sociological* explanation. A "sociological" explanation attempts to show the events that led to a particular behavior, perhaps even subsuming these events under general laws.

Though "rational decision" and "sociological" approaches to explanation may complement each other in important ways, they differ in one crucial respect. A rational decision approach is normative; it sets rational requirements for measuring a person's actions. Indeed, if we call our friends irrational, they know we are finding fault—they do not "measure up" to some standard. A sociological explanation, on the other hand, while it must conform to the standards required for good explanations, requires nothing of the participant whose behavior is being explained. If behavior does not accord with our explanations, then we change our explanations—we do not judge the behavioral deviation as not "measuring up." (In such cases, it is our explanation that does not measure up.)

The importance of this difference between the two approaches can be illustrated with a famous dispute in the area of educational policy. In the late 1960s, the Ford Foundation and New York City Mayor John Lindsay's Advisory Panel on Decentralization of New York City Schools sponsored local control of the Ocean Hill-Brownsville school district. During the first year of the community project (1967/68), intense hostility occurred between the white teachers and administrators and the black local school board. Charges of racism and anti-Semitism were the common language of the dispute, a dispute that led to the sudden dismissal by the school board of nineteen white teachers in May 1968, and a subsequent citywide strike by the United Federation of Teachers in protest over the dismissals.

An explanation of the actions of parties to this dispute could reasonably begin with the introduction of rationality models. These models could assess the degree to which the behavior of the participants accorded with the requirements of rationality. Did they act to maximize their utilities (that is, did they choose those actions that would produce the greatest benefit to themselves)? But the rhetoric and counterproductive activities quickly call for a sociological explanation. A sociological explanation, in this case, would concentrate not on whether the participants in the dispute maximized utility, but on what caused them to behave irrationally.

It is tempting to view sociological explanations as the more powerful approach, since they cast the wider net and catch behaviors that rationality models cannot. But this would be a mistake. The power of a rationality model is precisely its normative form: it tells us not only *how* social policies come to be made (when they are rational), but also how to *judge* them. The most fruitful approach to explanation is in some combination of rationality and sociological explanations. We will develop such a combination here, beginning with the components of rational decision-making, and then discovering how the normal complications of social conditions finally force some fundamental modifications in the rationality requirements of policy decisions.

LOGICAL FEATURES OF RATIONALITY

We should expect to find certain background conditions in any rational policy decision. The most important background conditions are (1) the presence of policy alternatives, even if they are merely *go* or *stop;* (2) at least minimum information; and (3) policy actors capable of selecting from the alternatives. These background conditions are nothing more or less than those found in any rudimentary theory of choice. They exclude from rationality all actions without alternatives, actions taken in total ignorance, and actors who, for whatever reason, are incapable of choice (very small children, some of the mentally ill, and so on).

Once background conditions are established, rational decisions are expected to meet two minimum criteria: consistency and transitivity.

CONSISTENCY

A consistency requirement is most clearly stated in terms of the rule, "Treat like cases alike." Basically, it means that if two events are alike, then they must be treated in like fashion unless there is some reason for not doing so. For example, if two children appear for class, and both are alike in all relevant respects, then the teacher cannot teach one and turn away the other without explaining his actions. To do so is to act arbitrarily. An arbitrary public policy is irrational, unreasoned in the basic sense of following no intelligible rule.

A *consistent* public policy, however, may be undesirable on other grounds. Bad policies may be made worse by consistency. To those opposed to the Vietnam War, some measure of logical inconsistency in the search-and-kill policies would have been sweet relief. Moreover, a consistent policy can still be unjustified (as well as wrong). If the teacher in our example explains that the class is so crowded that only one more pupil can squeeze into the room, he explains his exclusatory actions. But we may still wish to see either both children admitted or both turned away. In fact, we may view the teacher's action as consistent but unfair.

The possibility of disputing the *reasons* for treating cases as alike or unalike is an important source of public policy issues. Through most of the history of social security, for example, widowers or husbands of retired women had to prove they were financially dependent on their wives as a condition for receiving social security benefits. Women have not had to offer similar proof, largely because women have traditionally been viewed as dependent partners in marriage. In 1977, the U.S. Supreme Court ruled (in *Califano* v. *Goldfarb*) that the government cannot demand such proof from men *because* it does not require it from women in similar circumstances. (One immediate result of the Court's decision was an increase in benefits to elderly and disabled widowers of approximately $210 million a year.) The rationality rule of "Treat like cases alike" was used by the Court, but only on the reversal of a long-standing tradition of viewing women as relevantly unlike men for the allocation of survival benefits.

No two events are ever the same in all respects. When two events are judged the same, we mean that they are alike in some relevant respects. The Court, like many other agencies, reversed what traditionally counted as a relevant respect—sex—in the ruling on social security benefits. American society, like all societies, operates with standard distinctions between what is and is not a relevant difference between individuals and groups. In recent history, race has been considered irrelevant for most public policy decisions. However, the reintroduction of race in compensatory policies, in what are called "reverse discrimination" decisions, is now an issue of some importance in several policy areas (see Chapter 7). Income level, on the other hand, has since the 1930s consistently been considered a relevant difference in administering various forms of public relief. That persons are below a certain minimum income qualifies them for welfare, for example, while those above the level are not eligible.

Consistency, then, must be maintained if policy is to be rational. But consistent policies can still be wrong or unjustified. And the rule of consistency, "Treat like cases alike," still permits policy disputes over what to count as relevant in judging cases as like or unlike one another.

TRANSITIVITY

A special case of consistency is "transitivity," which amounts to consistency in an order of items. Stated formally, three items, a, b, c, are in a transitive relationship (R = relationship) if aRb, bRc, then aRc. Let's loosen this statement up with some examples. Equality is a transitive concept. If a is equal to b, and b is equal to c, then a must be equal to c. Fatherhood is not transitive. If a is the father of b, and b is the father of c, then a is *not* the father of c. (He is the grandfather of c.)

"Transitivity" is an important requirement in the ordering of individual preferences. If a person prefers policy A to policy B, and policy B to policy C, then we would expect him to prefer policy A to C as well if he is rational. Whether this logical requirement of rationality—transitivity—can be maintained in all orderings of public policy alternatives will be explored shortly. (See especially Appendix C for the more technical development.) But, for now, we can consider transitivity a minimum criterion of rationality in the ordering of individual preferences—so long as we do not complicate the conditions in which the ordering is expressed.

CONDITIONS AND CALCULATIONS IN RATIONAL DECISIONS

Decisions in policy can also be arranged in terms of several types of conditions and calculations.

1. Policy decisions can be made under either conditions of *uncertainty*,

of *risk,* or of *certainty.* Uncertainty conditions are those that provide more than one possible outcome for a decision *and* the probability of outcome is not known. Conditions of risk also provide multiple outcomes, but the probability of outcomes *is* known. If the probability of outcomes is constant for the method that produces outcomes, then we have *objective* probability. Coin tossing, for example, is a method producing outcomes on objective probability: either heads or tails results, and the 0.5 probability of either a head or a tail does not vary with who is tossing the coin (if the toss is fair). If, on the other hand, the probability of outcomes is uncertain or unknown, but an individual still has clear and consistent preferences for some outcomes over others, we can say that the individual is acting on *subjective* probabilities. For example, horse racing is a sport with notoriously uncertain outcomes. But if an individual consistently bets the favorite to show, he is deciding on a probability index which can be unique to him; hence subjective.

Conditions of certainty provide one outcome, or set of outcomes, for a decision. Unlike decisions in uncertainty or risk, there is no doubt about what outcome will result from a given choice. A decision that is typically made under conditions of certainty is that of how to spend money for food—whether, say, to buy more meat or more eggs on a fixed budget. Once preferences are established, the problem can be solved for a single set of "best" outcomes. For example, some balance between meat and eggs can be set to reflect preferences (an economist would use indifference curves). The outcome can logically follow from the preferences. On the other hand, in uncertainty or risk, one can settle on what is preferred, but the outcome is still in doubt. The bettor on horse races may not get his payoff even after he ranks the horses in a preferential ordering.

2. Policy decisions also rely on types of evaluative calculations. One important calculation is *expected value.* A person who is deciding whether to change jobs or remain in his present employment can calculate the expected value of the change by weighing the benefits against the costs. An increase in salary might be compared to the trouble of moving to a new location, shorter hours may be weighted against the problems of adjusting to new colleagues, and so on. The expected value is, roughly, the anticipated benefits minus the costs of the effort. In conditions of uncertainty or risk, the prospect of cost versus benefit can appear in hazardous form. Suppose a person is faced with the prospect of winning a million dollars if heads turns up on the toss of a coin, but losing his house and job if tails turns up. The possible benefit, though high (one million dollars), may not be enough to override the possibility of prohibitive loss in the venture.

3. Another pair of calculations in policy decisions is *maximax* and *maximin.* A *maximax* decision occurs when one chooses to maximize the best

payoff among a set of outcomes. In the coin-toss example, a maximax decision-maker would go for the toss in an attempt to win the million dollars. A *maximin* decision occurs when one chooses to maximize the minimum outcome. Thus a maximin decision-maker would choose to avoid the loss of his house and job by not gambling on the coin toss. Maximax and maximin decisions can also be taken in conditions without probability calculations. One simply constructs, on the basis of existing knowledge, the set of best and worst outcomes in any situation and then either acts to secure the optimum of the best set (maximax) or the optimum of the worst set (maximin) that can happen.

Maximax and maximin strategies can be combined by assigning weights to best and worst outcomes, so that a trade-off between best and worst leads to a more moderate strategy somewhere between the two. Trade-offs are impossible in either–or situations like the coin-toss example (one either bets or not), but are helpful in many other types of decisions. If, say, selling I.B.M. stock would avoid losses if the stock goes down in value but buying more would result in profits if it goes up in value, then weighing the value of losses against profits in terms of one's own resources might lead to a partial decision: maintain the current holdings, or sell only a few, or buy only a few, and so on.

These three components of decisions, (1) uncertainty, risk, and certainty, (2) expected value, and (3) maximin versus maximax, suggest that rational action varies depending on situations and inclinations. What is rational in conditions of uncertainty may not be rational in conditions of certainty. Whether to choose maximums over minimums, to gamble when the stakes are high for either loss or gain, to some degree will be a matter of psychological inclinations. Certainly the person who gambles his life in a game of Russian roulette for a possible payoff of five dollars is a candidate for irrationality, so that we do normally operate with rough models of psychological rationality. But the roughness of these models can be seen quickly enough when the schedule of rewards and penalties is altered. What if a person risks twenty years of servitude against a gain of $500,000 on the legal and fair toss of a coin? Suppose a person decides against taking such a risk? Either decision seems defensible on rational grounds. Recognizing the various calculations of rationality also requires recognizing the difficulty of designating some calculations as rational and others as not.

Both the minimum criteria (consistency and transitivity) and the components of rational decisions (uncertainty, risk, certainty; expected value; maximin versus maximax) will be important to remember. They will reappear in likely and unlikely places throughout this text. Now, however, it is time to turn to our first case study to see how these and other features in decision-making theory operate in the real world of public policy.

A CASE STUDY: EDUCATION

Education is a peculiar social commodity: (1) It is a *primary* good. Everybody needs some education, both because being educated is desirable in itself and because rudimentary education is instrumental to getting other valued goods. Even knowing how to eat a balanced diet depends on some health education. (2) But education is also a competitive, or divisible, commodity. Unlike, say, national defense, educational goods are not public goods. They can be allocated to some people and denied to others. (3) People vary in their abilities to "consume" education. Even if education is made available uniformly to a population, the educational level of the population will vary.

These three features create some unusual problems in educational policy. First, because education is a primary good, many people feel that society ought to provide education before many other things are provided. Yet, second, because education can be distributed, many disagreements can occur over which of society's institutions ought to provide education. With such public goods as national defense, the fact of everyone equally consuming (*not* producing) defense arrangements leads naturally to government financing of defense policies through taxation. But education can be provided by the market system, packaged and sold on a private basis. Third, the natural divisibility of educational goods is made even more competitive by their uneven consumption even when uniformly available. If we give students identical schooling, it is a melancholy fact of life that some will come out better educated than others.

Education is, in sum, both primary and doubly competitive. We all need it. It is a priority item on life's scale of values. Yet it can be allocated to some, denied to others. And it is distributed unevenly even when uniformly available because of different capabilities among students. These features alone suggest the difficulty of issues in the area of education policy. Add one more feature to get a fuller picture: educational policies and formal institutions of education do not always go together. A variety of informal arrangements (for example, the family) can educate people, and formal educational institutions frequently—too frequently, critics say—deal in noneducative concerns like personnel policies, public and private finance, lobbying, and so on. So education is a primary good that is doubly competitive, while spread unevenly across society's institutions.

We will look at two areas of educational policy: (1) educational finance and (2) mandatory busing. The first is perhaps the most intellectually difficult area of education today. The second is the most volatile. Together they give a picture of the real world of education, which, while not exhaustive, can still illustrate the pleasures and perils of decision models in the study of public policy.

EDUCATIONAL FINANCE

Both primary and secondary schools in America are currently financed through local property taxes. This system of local financing has two important implications for education from kindergarten through twelfth grade. First, control is largely localized at the school district level. Though state and federal aid can be, and typically are, important additions to school budgets, once federal and state guidelines are followed, local officials generally set and implement budgets. School officials are not solely in control of local resources. Some states have imposed freezes on school tax increases, thus limiting local control. Of more importance, in most areas those who own property in a school district can vote on tax rates, a practice that amounts to having a veto power on school budgets (a veto voters are increasingly prone to exercise). Second, as might be expected, the resources available to school districts vary with the property values of the local districts. Generally, the greater the value of property in a district, the more money is available for the district schools on a constant tax rate. (A rate of five percent levied on a base of $1,000,000, for example, provides a lot more money than five percent on $100,000.)

Differences in financial resources from district to district have been challenged legally. This challenge has placed the system of financing public education in the United States under a scrutiny unique in the country's history: scientific, legal, and political senses of rationality have joined and occasionally collided as court cases on the issue have been decided. The basic issue at stake in the current system of educational financing is very simple. The fact that some children, by virtue of residence, go to better endowed schools than others has struck some people as unconstitutional. The geographical accident of physical residence, critics of the current system complain, ought not to count in the vital matter of education. Everyone ought to have access to equal educational facilities wherever they happen to live. On the other hand, supporters of the current system maintain that local residents have the right to set up their own educational institutions within the provisions of state and federal law, and that differences in allocation of funds is no violation of the constitutional rights of those in poorer districts.

Supporters of these two points of view argued before the Supreme Court in 1973 in a case warranting that slogan "landmark decision": *San Antonio* v. *Rodriguez*. In deciding cases of this nature, two standards for review are available to the courts. One is "strict judicial scrutiny." This standard requires that basic constitutional rights be maintained. The other standard of review is the "rational relationship test." Here the educational system must merely be in accord with the purposes of state educational policy and law. Which standard of review the court adopts turns on whether the court believes education is a constitutional right or not. If it is so regarded, then"strict judicial scrutiny" is required. If not, then the "rational relationship test" is appropriate.

The case of *San Antonio* v. *Rodriguez* was decided in favor of the plaintiffs against the San Antonio school board by the lower courts. The lower court accepted education as a constitutional right and, on the standard of "strict judicial scrutiny," found that the San Antonio system of financing had (1) infringed upon education as a fundamental interest, and (2) discriminated against poor people as a suspect class. Since the basis of financing education throughout the country was identical in all important respects to the San Antonio system, the lower court decision had, in effect, found the entire system of educational finance in the United States unconstitutional.

The Supreme Court, however, decided otherwise. Two important issues were addressed by the Court: (1) whether the Texas system operates to the disadvantage of children in "low wealth" school districts *as a suspect class*, and (2) whether education is a constitutional right. Justice Lewis Powell, writing for the Court majority, argued *no* on both issues. On the first, the Court maintained that the fact that the poor receive less expensive education than the affluent is not decisive. It must also be proved that a *class* of people is being deprived of education. On this point, the Court ruled that the class of deprived people is not well-defined: Such people are not necessarily concentrated in the poorest school districts, nor marked off in the usual ways, for example with disabilities, a history of unequal treatment, political powerlessness warranting legal remedy, and so on. Nor, Justice Powell argued, are people in low-wealth school districts absolutely deprived of education.

On the second issue, the Court maintained that no fundamental interest is involved in school finance, because education is not a constitutional right. The Court therefore need judge, on the "rational relationship test," only whether the San Antonio system of educational finance carried out state purposes, which amounted to a basic education for every child, and local control of school districts. The Court found that an "adequate" level of education was provided (although the Court did not define *adequate*) by the Texas educational system. Also, the Court, because of the absence of any satisfactory correlation between the assignment of financial resources and educational benefits, suggested that the judiciary ought to keep out of the field of education. By historical precedent and law, Justice Powell argued, education is a state responsibility.

The case of *San Antonio* v. *Rodriguez* did not, however, close the door on litigation over school financing. In *Serrano* v. *Priest* (1974), the California Supreme Court found differently from the U.S. Supreme Court decision in *Rodriguez*. The California case was under review when the *Rodriguez* decision was announced. Had the California judge in the case, Bernard S. Jefferson, decided that the lower court decision on *Serrano* was based on the

Table 2.1
LITIGATION OVER EDUCATIONAL FINANCE*

State (Chronological Order)	Operative Language of Educational Provision	Violation of Such Educational Provision	State Equal Protection Analysis	Violation of State Equal Protection Clause
New Jersey	"thorough and efficient"	Yes	—independent of federal —rational basis test —education ≠ fundamental right	No
Arizona	"general and uniform"	No (dicta)	—independent of federal —rational basis test —education = fundamental right	No
California	"system of common schools"	No (Calif. Sup. Court)	—independent but "substantially the equivalent" of federal —educational = fundamental right	Yes (Superior Ct.)
Washington	"ample provision" "general and uniform"	No	—federal and state are "construed alike" —rational basis test —education ≠ fundamental right	No
Connecticut	"appropriate"	Yes (Superior Ct.)	—federal and state have "same meaning" —strict scrutiny test —education = fundamental right	Yes (Superior Ct.)
Idaho	"general, uniform and thorough"	No	—independent, but "substantially equivalent" to federal —rational basis test —education ≠ fundamental right	No
New York	"system of free common schools"	?	—federal and state are "precisely the same" —rational basis test —education ≠ fundamental right (dicta)	?

*Reprinted from Thomas P. Dugan, "The Constitutionality of School Finance Systems under State Law: New York's Twin," *Syracuse Law Review* (Spring 1976), Vol. 27, No. 2, p. 595.

Fourteenth Amendment, then of course the *Rodriguez* decision would have been controlling. But he did not. He judged that the *Serrano* case was grounded in California's equal protection statutes, not on the equal protection of the Fourteenth Amendment. The California court, thus free to decide the case, judged that education is a fundamental interest and, on "strict judicial scrutiny," that the state does not provide the uniform and equal treatment this interest requires. The "adequate education" of *Rodriguez* was found not to be an adequate standard. The California court based much of its decision on its acceptance of an empirical relationship between expenditure of resources and educational quality.

Litigation over educational finance is currently in a mixed and complicated state of affairs (see Table 2.1). The *Serrano* decision apparently provided new possibilities for state court reviews of educational systems on the basis of state equal-protection provisions. How these reviews will turn out is not easy to say. But the fundamental issues these reviews raise for educational policy, and how they are resolved (if they ever are), will affect the field of education for decades. Two of the issues are central to court decisions: (1) whether education is a fundamental interest protected by the Constitution, and (2) what relationship, if any, exists between the expenditure of money and the quality of education. A third issue, more general than the first two and not considered in all of its dimensions by the courts, is the role of the judiciary in the field of educational policy.

FINANCE REFORM: PRO AND CON

Those favoring some reform of educational finance have developed several formulas over the years. One is full state funding of elementary and secondary schools, a measure proposed by a gubernatorial commission in New York State in 1972. Opposition to full state funding is strong, however. It would effectively eliminate local control of schools (even many proponents of finance reform favor local control). It would also lead, in all likelihood, to greater costs as state-level bureaucracies are established to administer the schools. Finally, it would tax already overburdened state budgets, especially if equity-with-quality is the state goal for school districts.

Another approach to reform is "district equalizing" through state intervention. In this method, the state would permit local taxing and control, but underwrite a certain sum for school expenditures in all districts. Thus, if a school district with a low property tax base is unable to generate revenues to meet the agreed-upon expenditures, the state would make up the difference. In this way, the inequities of district expenditures would be eliminated through state guarantees to low-wealth districts. States may also "recapture" excess funds from wealthy districts to finance these guarantees. The advantage that "district equalizing" has over full state funding is that it respects local revenue raising and control while insuring equal district expenditures with, proponents hope, a minimum bureaucratic involvement by the state.

Even the most glowing interpretations of "district equalizing," however, have been subject to several criticisms by opponents. One is that of "municipal overburden." Many officials in large cities maintain that merely equalizing district school expenditures is not enough. High and increasing inner-city costs—police, fire, maintenance, and other services—are also found in education. Thus, even an equalizing formula would discriminate against large cities, for urban areas must pay more for the "same" units of education than do suburban and rural areas.

Other opponents of "district equalizing" argue from the other direction: that any state leveling of financial expenditures for education is wrong. First is the argument for freedom: that taxpayers ought to be free to choose educational priorities and determine the amounts of money they want to spend on them. The "freedom" argument is especially opposed to "recapture" policies, where moneys are taken from wealthy districts and given to poorer areas. Second, there is the "misperception" argument: that high property values in a district do not necessarily reflect high wealth. Some districts, it is maintained, are composed of property-rich and money-poor people. Such districts cannot support poorer districts just because of high property values. Robert Young, superintendent of schools in Eastchester, New York, claims, "Property taxes and taxes are high because we are near New York City. The only way people could realize this supposed wealth is by selling their house" (N.Y. Times, 2/17/77). Thus, this argument might conclude, high expenditures in a school district might represent voluntary sacrifices for better schools rather than surplus moneys that could be redistributed.

Opponents of "district equalizing" also question the relationship between expenditures and quality. Suburban schools are admittedly better than their urban counterparts, but opponents of equalizing formulas attribute this quality to such factors as better students, attitudes in the home toward education, and other factors not improved by greater expenditures of moneys. Diverting funds to poorer districts, opponents argue, may only lower the quality of the better schools by impoverishment while not improving the quality of poorer school districts lacking those key factors in good education.

Thus, opponents of "district equalizing" attack, among other things, the resource–quality relationship, which is at the heart of arguments on the inequitability of present systems of school finance.

THE STATE OF EDUCATION: SOME EMPIRICAL RELATIONSHIPS

The two issues "internally" prominent in the area of educational finance—(1) education as a fundamental interest and (2) the resource–quality relationship—combine (not always happily) two types of reasoning. The first is a matter of legal and philosophical thought, decidable only by examination of the law and our definitions of key concepts. The second is what can be called a scientific issue: Whether and how the expenditure of money leads to quality education is an empirical question, decidable only by an investigation of actual states of affairs in school districts. Let us put off for now a description of how the reasoning in (1) works and instead concentrate on what we know about the data and theory in (2). What *is* the relationship between money and quality in education?

THE COLEMAN REPORT

The Civil Rights Act of 1964 directed the commissioner of education to conduct a study "concerning the lack of availability of equal educational opportunities for individuals by reason of race, color, religion, or national origin in public educational institutions at all levels in the United States. . . ." A group of sociologists, led by James Coleman, conducted such a study and in 1966 published their report, *Equality of Educational Opportunity* (generally known today as the Coleman Report). The report, 737 pages long, represents the first comprehensive study and evaluation of the American educational system. Its conclusions challenged the then popular wisdom on education, and occasioned a debate that has persisted to the present time on both the validity and even the motives of the report.

The most controversial parts of the report are in Sections 2 and 3. Here the Coleman team (1) concluded that, on the basis of objective characteristics (teachers' salary, books per student, age of buildings and textbooks, teacher and student attitudes toward their school, and so on), the differences between predominantly white and black schools is surprisingly small. Differences are greater between locales (especially northern versus southern regions of the country) than between schools within locales. The most striking difference between schools is race itself: students and teachers segregated on racial grounds. The allocation of resources to schools, including financial outlays, was discovered to be more nearly equal than had been thought up to that time.

The Coleman Report also (2) established a causal, or at least correlative, chain between certain factors and school output that startled educators in all professional areas. Educational results, measured by standard test scores, were found to be most strongly related to family background. Among factors within schools, student peers accounted for more variance in test scores than any other factor. The second strongest in-school factor was found to be teachers' characteristics. Other school characteristics, including the vital factor of expenditures of moneys, had little effect on academic performance. The conclusion the Coleman Report drew was that school integration across socioeconomic lines—in effect, an effort at utilizing the important peer-group variable—would increase black achievement. Increasing the resources at schools would generally not be effective.

The implications of the Coleman Report for busing students between predominantly white and black schools, indeed between high-quality and low-quality schools, regardless of race, are obvious. They will be discussed in a moment. But on the second issue of educational finance, the resource–quality relationship, the Coleman Report found few important connections between expenditures and educational quality.

THE JENCKS HARVARD STUDY

In late 1972, a team of eight scholars at the Harvard Center for Educational Policy Research, led by Christopher Jencks, published the *Jencks' Harvard Study*, later published as *A Reassessment of the Effect of Family and Schooling in America*. Jencks and his associates advanced and defended two major conclusions in the study: First, resource allocations like budgets, teachers, and so on, have no appreciable effect on raising the test scores of minority or disadvantaged children. (No link was found between expenditures and quality.) The character of a school's output, its academic quality, is a variable of the quality of children entering the school. Second, even *if* education is improved, neither the quality of education nor a student's background will significantly improve his or her future level of income. Jencks made the stunning claim that fully 78 percent of the variation in income is not accounted for by education or family background, leading him to speculate that such variation is due to "luck, personality, and competence." Jencks and his team recommended that the social order ought to stop relying on "marginal" institutions like schools to alleviate income inequalities and should pursue a more direct route to income leveling: progressive tax reforms, income floors and ceilings, guaranteed income maintenance, and so on.

Both the Coleman Report and the Jencks Harvard Study have been severely criticized, though not entirely discredited. Critics of the Coleman Report have alleged methodological shortcomings, including design flaws, inadequate responses, weak data analysis, and the usual difficulties of a cross-sectional (one point in time) rather than a longitudinal study. There is also at least one other study, *The Stockholm Report* (1973), which is both more comprehensive and contrary to the Coleman Report on (1) the importance of schooling in technical subjects like math, and (2) the power of education to make lower-class students upwardly mobile. On the relationship between monetary resources and quality, however, the *Stockholm Report* is silent.

The Jencks study has been subjected to a number of similar criticisms. These criticisms concentrate on the speciousness of using standard test scores, the unfortunate reliance on ambiguous "luck" language, some possible confusion in equating successful education with earning power, and—especially—the claim of the study that education and family background are unrelated to income. Both studies, however, have on the whole been able to maintain the empirical validity of one central assertion: the absence of important links between expenditures of money and school quality. In fact, there is even general agreement among critics of Jencks' study that the reform of schools does not raise the academic scores of students (Anosike, 1975).

If a connection between financial resources and educational quality is at least problematic, and perhaps specious, then a contradiction appears: scientific research suggests a conclusion at variance with the legal reasoning of some court decisions, for example in the *Serrano* case. The contradiction does not invalidate the legal decision in *Serrano*, but it shifts the entire weight of the argument to the first issue in educational finance, education as a fundamental interest, and even a right—a point to be elaborated in a moment.

MANDATORY BUSING

The apparent absence of a connection between the allocation of expenditures and the quality of schooling, and the additional finding that predominantly black schools are generally not as good as predominantly white schools, leads naturally to a policy of racial integration across specific schools. Integration policy is supported by sociological theory through the decades of the 1940s, 1950s, and even the 1960s. Beginning with Gunnar Myrdal's classic, *An American Dilemma*, through works by Kenneth Clark, Samuel Stouffer, and Gordon Allport, the dominant model in social theory held that integration (or "contact") between the races is good, segregation is bad. The Supreme Court decision of 1954 ending segregation in the nation's public schools relied on many of these sociological theories in arguing that school segregation irrevocably harms black children. The Coleman Report, among other things, supports again the assertion that separate *and* equal school facilities are in fact impossible.

The policy of school integration, accepted as an article of faith by the dominant political and intellectual leaders of American society for at least a decade (1954–64), is now being challenged both politically and intellectually. The challenge is a complicated one, not always warranted, and seems to be both historically based on and occasioned by a response to the most volatile educational policy in operation today: mandatory busing to achieve racial integration in public schools. It is important, in coming to understand what is happening to the integration model, to see two things. First, the political and intellectual consensus on the integration model has splintered and even collapsed in the years from 1964 to the present time. Second, and independent of this collapse, mandatory busing is a policy reasonably, though not necessarily, inferred from the basic components of the integration model and the pattern of residential life characteristic of American society today.

The collapse of political consensus on integration can be traced to major events of the late 1960s and early 1970s. (1) In 1964, the black movement was essentially united behind a policy of racial integration. By 1966, the movement was divided on the issue: both the Student Nonviolent Coordinating Committee and the Congress of Racial Equality had changed from a stance of prointegration to one of support for various forms of black separatism. (2) The Vietnam War, divisive in so many ways, both diverted attention from educational reform (thus diluting integration efforts) and, being fought disproportionately by black Americans, further divided the races. (3) But the sharpest opposition to school integration came about as integration efforts shifted from de jure to de facto segregation, affecting metropolitan areas in the North for the first time.

To any observer, the chronology of events in education from 1965 to the present offers a melancholy picture. Northern opposition to integration begins with Chicago, when the Department of Health, Education, and Welfare (HEW) in 1965 began pressuring local districts to integrate across residentially separate school systems. Resistance to the policies of HEW (then headed by John Gardiner) grew in Congress, forcing the Department to begin accepting limitations on its power to cut off federal aid to deficient districts. (The 1967 Education Act, for example, required HEW to give six months notice before cutting off aid, a compromise requirement accepted in the face of harsher Congressional limitations proposed on the floor.) The election of Richard Nixon in 1968 resulted in weakening enforcement (if any) of the 1964 Civil Rights Act by the U.S. attorney general.

The key court decision acting as a catalyst on the political changes was *Swann* v. *Charlotte-Mecklenburg* (1971), a case in which the Supreme Court supported the requirement of massive crosstown busing to achieve school integration. The *Swann* decision set in motion busing efforts in all parts of the country, and also motivated a number of proposed constitutional amendments in Congress. A typical proposal: "No public school student shall, because of his race, creed, or color, be assigned to or required to attend a particular school" (Representative Norman Lent). The sometimes strident clash of views on busing, and the resulting compromises, are reflected in several provisions of the 1974 Education Act. First, the bill states that school assignment practices do not violate student rights unless the practices are *intentionally* designed to segregate students. Second, the Ashbrook amendment, denying federal money for busing, was retained, although it was weakened with the allowance that local authorities can use the unrestricted impacted areas funds for busing (or any other purpose). Third, it was mandated that HEW cannot order busing beyond the next nearest school. Although the language of the 1974 Education Act is consistent with some mandatory busing, it is clear that the twentieth anniversary of the *Brown* decision witnessed an unprecedented hostility in Congress and the presidency to busing as a means to implement school integration.

Some recent court decisions have also come down against busing to achieve integrated schools. In early 1977, the Supreme Court vacated a federal appeals court decision that had earlier affirmed a broad desegregation order. Black children were to be bused from Indianapolis city schools to suburban schools under the desegregation plan. The aim of the plan was to achieve at least a 15 percent proportion of blacks in the surrounding school districts. The Court indicated that unless proof could be furnished that Indianapolis *intended* to discriminate, the mere *effects* of discrimination were not sufficient to justify the desegregation plan.

SOME EVIDENCE ON BUSING

The opposition to busing now has intellectual as well as political support. In a famous and provocative article, David Armour (1972, 1973) has challenged the basic integration model assumed until recently by both social scientists and jurists. Armour claimed to test the results of forced busing along five dimensions: academic achievement, aspirations, concepts of the self, race relations, and education opportunities. On all but educational opportunity, Armour found that forced busing led to poor or mixed results. Reading level of blacks in schools integrated through forced busing, for example, was only slightly ahead of the reading level of blacks in segregated schools, but was three years below their white colleagues. The low self-esteem of minority children seemed unaffected by integration. Even race relations, assumed to be improved by contact, actually deteriorated in the integrated schools studied. Only educational opportunities for blacks improved in integrated schools. Middle-class suburban or prep schools seemed to have a "channeling" effect for blacks not present in black schools: black students in integrated schools went to college in greater numbers, and to better colleges, than non-integrated black students.

How are such conclusions possible in the face of earlier sociological theory? Several answers are possible. One could simply maintain, of course, that Armour's conclusions are false or misleading, something some social scientists and educators have done (Pettigrew et al., 1973). On the assumption that they are at least prima facie valid, however, several explanations for the variance are possible, most made by Armour himself. First, the early integration model was generally based on (1) cross-sectional analysis (one point in time) rather than longitudinal analysis (extended over time), and (2) hypothetical conditions about *projected* racial contact. In contrast, Armour claims for his work both longitudinal dimensions and tests on *actual* integration (how it works, not how it might work). Second, mandatory busing is contrived (claims Armour), induced rather than natural. The fact of contrivance may create additional negative variables not foreseen in earlier studies. Third, the racial climate in America, as the brief historical sketch offered here suggests, has changed in important ways. Armour concludes with a recommendation for voluntary rather than forced busing.

Armour's case against mandatory busing has been strongly challenged (Pettigrew et al., 1973). It has been claimed, first, that Armour sets impossibly high standards for success: the longitudinal dimension is only one year and no distinction is made between desegregated schools (where the races are simply together physically) and integrated schools (where there is positive intergroup contact, cross-racial acceptance, equal dignity and access, and so on). The early integration model assumed both a longer time period and authentic integration in the second, more positive, sense. Second, it has been maintained that Armour's study commits methodological errors: the survey is incomplete and black students are compared with whites rather than with still segregated blacks. Third, the study ignores (a) the effects of integration on white children; (b) the racist climate in America negatively affecting the success of integration; and (c) the legal aspects of the problem, in particular the Fourteenth Amendment's equal protection requirements, valid regardless of hostile outcomes.

The responses to these objections are predictable. It may be said, first, that a demonstration of parallel gains by both blacks and whites is not enough, for the overriding fact is that integration by forced busing does not seem to reduce the disparities *between* the races (Armour, 1972, 1973). Here, however, the response is not completely adequate. Certainly something is lacking, for example, in an economic change that gives more money to both A and B, though not reducing the gap between them. What is missing is any progress on relative equality. On the other hand, the lower member of the set, let us say B, may still be better off than some other figure, C. This is roughly what occurs in integration through busing. Integrated blacks (B) are better off on reading achievement than segregated blacks (C), though not nearly equal to whites (A). To judge whether an improvement has occurred, however, we would want to know the difference between A and B, and between the lower member, B, and some non-integrated population, C. Here, unfortunately, the disparity is great: three years difference between A and B, and two months between B and C. Then, Armour suggests, we must weigh the relative harm to B in competing with A versus the slight advantage B has over C.

The methodological errors in any study are usually too technical to assess decisively. Armour's fundamental line of defense is a simple one: the conclusions he advances are at least as valid as, and in many ways better than, those of the early integration model. Therefore, one cannot endorse the early model in spite of its methodological limitations and reject his (Armour's) study because of methodological errors. It does seem, however, that the exclusion of effects on white children is a severe limitation. Supporters of forced-busing integration could well argue that whites, at least as much as blacks, are deprived of important experiences in a segregated society, and that white children are at least as appropriate a subject of study as black children. It is more difficult, however, to evaluate the effects of racist society on the integrated conditions, since forced busing is designed, in part, precisely to resolve the problems of racism; if the resolution is incomplete, this counts against the busing, not against the validity of the study revealing the incompleteness.

A report by the U.S. Civil Rights Commission in 1976, however, supports the general case for successful desegregation through busing where communities and community leaders want desegregation. The commission found that peaceful desegregation raises educational quality and minority achievement, though it also involves social costs such as lost jobs for minority teachers. Generally the response to mandatory school busing has been mixed. Although Boston met busing with social conflict, other cities—including Harrisburg, Pennsylvania—have peacefully accepted busing plans. The racial balance brought about in Harrisburg through busing has also been correlated with a general improvement in reading test scores in the city's schools. The Civil Rights Commission report suggests that the receptivity of an area to mandated busing weighs heavily in the overall success of busing measures to achieve desegregation.

It is on the legal aspects of the problem that the sharpest exchanges have occurred. Armour maintains that his critics unwittingly endorse a "double double" standard. First, his critics used research conducted prior to integration to demonstrate the benefits of integration. Now, when Armour draws some negative conclusions based on integration that is an actuality, his critics reject these conclusions, although actual integration should furnish more definitive results than projected integration. Second, the critics now maintain that the issue is really constitutional, not factual. Yet the definitive constitutional decisions were based on research which did purport to be factual. The critics are, according to Armour, trying to have it both ways.

The critics, in turn, can respond on the first double standard by questioning the scope, time period, and general validity of Armour's study (as we have seen). The second of the alleged double double standards, however, is of most interest here, because it revives the dual standards used in court decisions on educational finance. The critics can answer Armour by stressing the principle of constitutional rights used in these cases: while the law may be supported by empirical evidence, such evidence itself is never decisive; it must be intertwined with, and perhaps even subordinated to, the legal and moral reasoning of precedents and rights.

EDUCATIONAL POLICY:
TWO ISSUES IN SEARCH OF RESOLUTION

Throughout the discussion of educational policy we have seen two issues dominate the rational deliberations of policy-makers. The first is factual: how two variables, financial resources and mandatory busing, each affect a third, school quality—if in fact they do. The research seems to indicate at least an uncertain relationship and perhaps no real relationship between each independent variable, (a) financial resources and (b) mandatory busing, and the dependent variable, (c) school quality. School quality is not identical in each of the two causal relationships, for the Coleman and Jencks studies measure quality in ways different from Armour's. But in each case the research has tended to contradict the common wisdom about what is required to make quality schools equally accessible to all children.

The second issue is legal/moral, and is framed by the courts in terms of the equal-protection clause of the Fourteenth Amendment and a definition of what education means in contemporary democratic society. The judiciary has frequently allowed factual relationships established by social science to substantiate legal decisions. The classic example of this was *Brown* v. *Board of Education* (1954), the case in which the Supreme Court ruled openly, on the basis of social science data and conclusions, that segregation in public schools is unconstitutional. More recently, in *Rodriguez*, Justice Powell, in writing the majority opinion, seized on the absence of any proven correlation between expenditures of money and quality as partial justification for the Court's decision against the challenge to Texas' system of school finance. But the judiciary may also stress the legal or moral dimensions of its decisions.

The easiest way to see how legal and moral considerations properly enter judicial rationality is by inspecting what a judge considers in making his decision. He may consider, for example, (1) precedent, or what the law has said in the past; (2) what is fair under the legal system, for example, whether all people are being treated equally; (3) the status of an issue: for example, whether education is a fundamental interest. Now, none of these considerations can be settled by scientific inquiry. A social scientist is interested in determining what society is like, and what makes it the way it is.

But a judge may also be legitimately interested in deciding how society ought to be, and his decision, while frequently guided by facts, can also adjudicate facts on the basis of the legal or moral references he uses.

The adjudication of facts in judicial rationality can take several forms. In its strongest form, a court can simply subordinate facts to legal considerations. Whether a case is subjected to a "rational relationship test" or "strict judicial scrutiny" will call for different legal interpretations of the facts, and which of these evaluative standards is selected depends not on the state of society but on the conceptual status we give to education. Justice Thurgood Marshall, dissenting in the *Rodriguez* case, emphasized a close relationship between education and the capacity of citizens to exercise other rights and to participate successfully in the political process. He viewed education as a necessary condition for the more explicit constitutional guarantees. Granting education this conceptual status then led him to endorse the review standard of strict judicial scrutiny, and to come to conclusions at variance with the majority of the Court. A judiciary may also endorse a principle like fairness regardless of what the facts say. Although the *Brown* decision was based on social science findings, few today would want to deny equal opportunity even if the facts demonstrated that racial segregation caused no social and psychological harm (Rosen, 1972). We would likely say that *justice* requires enforcement of equal-protection clauses, the facts aside.

The judiciary may also use legal standards to decide which facts to utilize in its decisions. Whether any fact is legally relevant, for example, is something for a court to decide. Courts may even decide what the facts are. Sometimes the court will use the fact of contrary social theories or histories as a justification for ignoring both. Justice Earl Warren, in the *Brown* decision, summarily dismissed the question of historical intent on the Fourteenth Amendment because, in the face of various and conflicting constitutional histories, he judged it an inconclusive matter. But often the court will select one of several conflicting accounts of the facts. Justice Powell, in *Rodriguez,* accepted one set of facts (lack of correlation on cost–quality), and dismissed other contrary accounts. Given the tentative nature of most scientific theories (Karl Popper calls them hypotheses that have so far resisted falsification), the judiciary can be expected to have considerable freedom in subordinating or choosing facts to support its legal decisions.

At best the judiciary is engaged in an ongoing discourse with social science. Constitutional principles change with new perceptions of social reality, but not exactly as social reality changes. Those favoring a close relationship between law and fact can stress the ambivalent and perhaps negative relationships between cost and busing on the one hand and educational quality on the other. But since law is not merely fact, but also prescription for fact, a dissatisfaction with recent social theories on education can lead the judiciary to emphasize the legal/moral components in social decisions. A perfect balance between factual and legal/moral components is too much to expect, but it is important to know that both kinds of issues are prominent in educational policy today.

Cutting across the specific issues in educational policy are the theoretical issues found in decision theory. What *types* of decisions are found in educational policy? What are the models of decision-making generally used in public policy? Two models of decision-making are especially prominent today: classical and incremental. Let's turn to these two models before exploring educational decisions further.

CLASSICAL RATIONALITY: DECISIONS IN CERTAINTY CONDITIONS

At one extreme of decision theory is the oldest model of decision-making, the *classical* model of rationality. Classical rationality assumes that policy figures make decisions in the following way: First, they rank their goals in a hierarchy, from most to least preferable. Second, they rank the means to obtain these goals in a hierarchy from most to least effective. Third, they have perfect information (perfect, anyway, for the purposes of ranking) at their disposal. Finally, the decisions they make and implement are without strong consideration of important costs ("costs" here referring both to information-gathering, consultation, and so on, in *making* decisions, as well as to the costs of *implementing* decisions). These four features of classical rationality outline a form of decision-making almost rustic in its innocence and simplicity, yet with relevance, as we shall see, in conditions of certainty and with the use of overriding values.

Let's look at classical decisions in more visual terms. First, goals are ranked:

Goals: A_1 A_2 A_3

Then, means are ranked under each goal.

Goals:	A_1	A_2	A_3
Means:	X_1	Y_1	Z_1
	X_2	Y_2	Z_2
	X_3	Y_3	Z_3

Finally, choosing an optimal means leads unfailingly to an appropriate goal.

$X_1 \longrightarrow A_1$ $Y_1 \longrightarrow A_2$ $Z_1 \longrightarrow A_3$

Sometimes, both means and ends can be chosen. Let us call this the *double-choice* version of classical rationality. At other times, the ends are given, or fixed, and only means can be chosen. Let us call this the *single-choice* version.

Single-choice versions of classical rationality are found in Plato's works, where the goals or ends of rational deliberation are discovered, not chosen. A more modern example of single-choice rationality can be found in a mathematical system. The right answer in mathematics is not chosen, but discovered by applying the correct methods. (Imagine the chaos in a mathematics class if the right answers were determined by a vote, expressing the preference of the class.) A highly technical issue in policy may sometimes rule out the choice of goals. Whether, for example, to adopt a particular stance on disarmament is often mandated by technical considerations, not chosen by negotiators.

Double-choice versions of classical rationality, however, where both the means and ends are chosen, are more typical of current policy decisions. Any local school budget can illustrate some of the features of classical rationality, usually of the double-choice version. For example, a district budget in Syracuse, New York, in 1976, was set at $54 million. Of these $54 million, approximately $12 million were in fixed costs, those required to pay for power, retirement funding, and so on. To balance its budget, the district had to cut 12 percent from its elastic expenditures. Now, given that neither property assessments nor taxes would be scaled upward for the coming school year, nor state or federal aid increased, the choice of a strategy to reduce spending would with certainty lead to identifiable outcomes. One full-time teacher would be released, or two half-time teachers of art and music let go, and so on. In each case, the choice determines the outcome: If one full-time teacher is released, class size in the chosen area must increase. If two half-time art and music teachers are released, art and music classes must be cancelled altogether. The decision model of *classical rationality* roughly fits the situation (if we minimize some decision costs). The harried school principal might take issue with the thought that he chooses means *and* ends, for the goals of his budget might be dictated to him by the local taxpayers and the state legislature. But such goals, though mandated, are chosen by others and so are not fixed, as are the outcomes in Platonic political thought and mathematical systems.

CRITIQUES OF CLASSICAL RATIONALITY

Criticism of the classical model of rationality in studies of policy decisions is quite common today, so common that the best way to elaborate the model seems to be in terms of these critiques. The criticisms can be organized in terms of each characteristic of the model.

1. The possibility of arranging goals hierarchically has been questioned. Let us suppose that we are deciding which career to pursue, and, being alert students of rational decision-making, we order our preferences like this: first, full-time writing; second, teaching; third, law. So the hierarchy of goals is:

A_1 (Writing)
A_2 (Teaching)
A_3 (Law)

This arrangement of goals, however, is rational only if it is supported with certain facts, for example one's aptitudes, capabilities, financial resources, perhaps the current state of each profession (opportunities, restrictions, rewards, and so on). A change in the facts can alter the hierarchy. For example, the current overcrowded state of the teaching profession is a rational deterrent; therefore, the anticipated misfortunes of trying to enter the field of teaching may invert A_2 and A_3, placing law second. A reassessment of one's creative capabilities may bring about a reordering of writing, perhaps dropping it to last place. Now this dependence of hierarchical ordering on facts does not deny the possibility of a hierarchy, but it does qualify it. If an alteration of facts can rearrange any hierarchy, then no hierarchies are fixed; at least as important a consideration in decisions must then be the social (factual) context in which goals are ordered.

The outright denial of hierarchical ordering can be developed by pursuing the example. Suppose that our deliberating person decides that he can have a little of each goal, that he can write while teaching law and perhaps even practice some law on the side. If even partially successful, the person has engaged in a trade-off among his goals: instead of a strict hierarchy he has pursued a mixed strategy, partially acquiring all three goals. In trade-off strategies the goals are not ranked and pursued in serial fashion, but rather in a piecemeal manner that effectively levels the goals to a lateral relationship. If b, c, d represent the portions of each goal acquired, then $bA_1 \longleftrightarrow cA_2 \longleftrightarrow dA_3$.

Those denying the very possibility of hierarchical ordering in social planning argue that trade-offs are required by the very nature of the policy process: as goals are implemented and facts taken into account, the hierarchy is flattened out to provide a variety of partial goals.

2. If changing facts and conditions can upset our ranking of goals, they can also upset our ranking of the means we will choose to reach the goals. When we choose a means to accomplish a particular end, we may find we have produced not just the one desired outcome, nor even the intended outcome, but rather have set up a situation with several outcomes, some more probable than others.

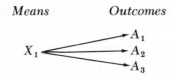

For example, if a person wants to become a writer, then he will (if he is rational) identify the means to develop writing skill. Let us suppose he chooses to study under an established author. One outcome of such study may well be the goal he seeks: he will become an established writer himself. But other outcomes are possible. The neophyte may turn out to be a writer of catalog copy for a department store. Or he might use the skills he acquires as an apprentice to become a speech writer for some prominent politician. Or he might end up as a newspaper reporter. Each of these goals can be seen as rational outcomes of the original means, which suggests that means are related to ends with uncertainty or risk.

3. Once we admit that a variety of outcomes is consistent with any means, it is but a small step to see the conditions of decisions as uncertain or probable rather than certain. This emphasis on uncertainty or risk is a key component of critiques aimed at the classical model: that, except on a small scale and within severely restricted conditions, we cannot *know* the results of our actions with anything approaching certitude. We can only know probable outcomes at best, a restriction of possible outcomes at worst. We can feel fairly certain that studying with an established author will not prepare a person to become a botanist (though it might make a marginal contribution), and we may be able to list all of the goals that can be reached by the apprentice-writer. Then, if we are lucky and have good data, we may be able to assign rough probabilities to various outcomes. Those who argue against the classical model maintain that what we cannot do is link the pursuit of any means with an assured outcome. This critique amounts to a denial of the possibility of perfect knowledge, a denial supported with the introduction of decisions in conditions of uncertainty or risk.

Perfect knowledge on a general scale *is* a staggering prospect. Taken literally, it presumes that we can become gods. Taken metaphorically and not literally, the prospect is still breathtaking. Even a partial realization requires the establishment of a necessary relationship between means and ends, a relationship seeming to violate common sense when the scope and complexity of political policy are appreciated. To think that we can know the outcomes of something as far-reaching as the Education Act of 1965 seems, to critics of the classical model, a gross underestimation of the practical range of policy consequences.

4. Finally, critics maintain that while the *costs* of decisions are among the most important rational considerations in public policy, the classical model

underestimates or ignores them. Costs, like friction in Newtonian physics, are unavoidable calculations in any real-world situation. Not only do decisions themselves require time and resources to make, but their implementation also involves expenditures of effort. If costs were strong considerations, a satisfactory model of social decision-making would be more sensitive to the modifications required by the conditions of decisions. The classical model, however, with its concentration on hierarchically arranged means and goals, largely ignores the conditions in which decisions are made. It makes insufficient allowance for cost, and as a result is insensitive to the changing conditions that the decision-making process itself imposes.

ALTERNATIVES TO CLASSICAL RATIONALITY: DISJOINTED INCREMENTALISM

Two strategies are available to critics of the classical model of rationality. First, they might introduce alternative models that avoid the difficulties of the classical model without incurring additional problems. Or, second, they could restrict the classical model to a more narrow range of policy situations. If they choose the second, they would then have to develop alternative models for the territory not covered by the classical model, but the classical model could still be maintained, though restricted in its range of validity. Students of policy have generally chosen the first, replacement option, dismissing all pretensions to classical rationality. The replacement model is drawn from a rejection of the classical features of policy-making.

Let's review the classical features once more: (1) a hierarchical arrangement of goals, (2) a hierarchical arrangement of means, (3) perfect information, and (4) a low estimate of decision costs.   Next, let's look at the models opposing classical rationality. They have been variously labeled "sufficing" (Simon, 1947) or incrementalism (Braybrooke and Lindblom, 1963). The general features are the opposite of the classical model: (1) *no* hierarchical arrangement of goals *or* means, (2) imperfect, limited information, and (3) the elevation of cost as an important considerations. If we think of decision models as calling our attention to one type of consideration versus another, then the incremental model (and, for convenience, *incrementalism* will be the term used from now on to describe the alternative tradition to classical rationality) shifts our attention *to* the policy process itself and away from the formation of goals and means.

To see this shift in attention, let's look again at the earlier example of a person deciding on a profession. In the classical model, the goals are ranked (A_1, A_2, A_3) and the means are scaled optimally (X_1, X_2, X_3). Rational action then consists of choosing and acting on the optimal means to a given goal $(X_1 \rightarrow A_1)$. In an incremental model, uncertain outcomes combined with cost and risk factors minimize the importance of goals formed prior to the implementation process. What happens as goals are being realized provides rational considerations that in turn affect the status of both means *and* ends.

This shift makes an important addition to rationality. Concentrating on the *process* of policy introduces a *time* dimension into policy decisions: instead of the static model of classical rationality, a longitudinal model is introduced. The means and ends of policy can continually be adjusted as policy is made and carried out. This concentration on the policy process follows naturally once uncertainty or risk, and decision costs, are added; for these are factors requiring calculations and recalculations of the outcomes of action. So the appropriate incremental models are $X_1 \longrightarrow A_1, A_2$ at time t_1; $X_2 \longrightarrow A_2, A_3$ at time t_2, where each later time in the policy process can bring new considerations, even new means and goals, for public policy. Policy, for the incrementalist, is a *serial* process of constant *adjustment* to the outcomes (proximate and long-range) of action.

What is it about the conditions of policy that favors the incrementalist model?

1. Information is typically inadequate because of (a) acquisition problems and (b) knowledge problems. In acquiring information, the policy authority is usually constrained both by time and by the simple fact that information costs money. We need not visualize a harried policy figure making decisions under the constant ticking of the second-hand on a clock (a sort of James Bond). The pressure of the calendar is enough, and the added pressure of the budget may be too much. The plain fact is that acquiring information, even imperfect information, has its costs in time and resources. Therefore, it must be calculated as a part of the decision process (perhaps even in terms of cost-benefit analysis); it cannot be assumed as a premise of decisions (as in the classical model of rationality). Even worse, some information is impossible to secure, either because it touches on sensitive matters (the sexual preferences of junior-high students, for example) or is unreachable with current research tools (the effect of television viewing on the dream patterns of small children, for example).

On the knowledge problem, an incrementalist assumes that the human mind is limited in its understanding of the world. The outcomes of action are not known with certainty. Even sound information varies in its reliability over time, so that (as we have seen) both means and ends must be adjusted in the policy process. In short, the world is complex, so rich in events that it surpasses any satisfactory comprehension. Complexity is roughly a matter of (1) the number of units, (2) the variation of units over time, and (3) the heterogeneity of units (how unlike one another the units are). Therefore, a policy decision covering a large number of issues and people, where the issues and people affected change quickly and are quite diverse, will be more complex than a policy decision involving only a few issues and people, where the issues and participants are stable over time, and the issues and participants form a homogeneous family of units.

Incrementalist proponents are convinced that complexity is the order of the day in policy decisions, that to view the world as simple is to commit an error of omission in failing to allow for an as yet unknown factor in policy analysis. So, even if the acquisition costs of information were somehow neutralized, the knowledge problem raised by incrementalists would rule out the possibility of perfect information: the world is just too complex for human intelligence to master.

2. Policy is made in divisive conditions, or in conditions lacking the proper reasons for collective action. Recall yet again the occasions for political action: conflicting claims, or cooperative goals lacking rational incentives for joint efforts. If claims conflict, then public policy is made and implemented against opposition of one sort or another. Sometimes the opposition is severe: individuals or groups are strongly opposed to one another on the basis of widely differing convictions. This was true in the Ocean Hill-Brownsville dispute on educational policy. At other times the divisiveness of politics is modest: opposition is neither intense nor based on widely separated convictions. Sometimes political action is required to provide reasons for the joint pursuit of common goals, as happened when the political system had to work through a labyrinth of negative incentives to produce a generally desired aid-to-education act in 1965. But whether opposition is severe or tepid, whether incentives for joint action are strong or puny, policy is not made in conditions of natural harmony, where coordinated actions occur without effort. It is made among people with differing interests, inclinations, points of view, and perhaps even ideologies, or in conditions where rational incentives for collective action are weak or altogether missing. Therefore, policy is always to some degree *complicated*, in that a number of different people and reasons must be taken into account in policy decisions.

To say that events are *complicated* is not the same as saying that events are *complex*. Complex events are those that are not easily understood. The conditions for policy may be simple to understand, yet be complicated in the time and effort required to successfully realize policy goals. The process of getting a bill through the U.S. Senate, for example, is understandable, but it is complicated in the number and delicacy of consultations required to get a bill through the chamber. The complicated nature of policy conditions, then, fractures policy into a series of events, each dealing with a piece of the policy context. Again: to get, say, an education bill through the U.S. Senate will not, as in the classical model, be an action captured in a single photograph. It will be a series of actions, analogous to motion pictures (critics would say those run in slow-motion), where each of the ideas and actors requires consideration.

This piecemeal, or disjointed, procedure that complicated conditions require is characteristic of the incrementalist model. So the second condition favoring incrementalism is the complicated nature of politics, a complication stemming from the natural opposition characterizing politics in the first place.

These two conditions favoring the incremental model, (1) inadequate information (due to complex conditions) and (2) the complicated nature of policy, suggest how goals and means are flattened out in policy decisions. A hierarchical arrangement is impossible to establish without adequate information, and negotiating a complicated network of actors and ideas will require a flexibility that hierarchical arrangements cannot easily tolerate. It should also be noticed that even the separation between means and ends is jeopardized under these conditions. Means can become ends, and ends become means in the tumble of policy conceived by incrementalists.

What is the type of policy administered in an incrementalist program?

It should be no surprise by now to announce that incrementalist policy takes the status quo very seriously. If we view policy decisions as affected sharply by facts, and we view these facts as complex and complicated, then any motion is almost frozen, and at least slowed. An incrementalist policy is one that departs from previous conditions and policies only in small steps. It is largely remedial, rarely therapeutic in any grand sense. General reform is out, unless it is modest in its demands. This restraint is required on rational grounds. If a decision-maker knows little with certainty, and if any action has the possibility of loss, then it behooves him to move carefully from established positions. He must, almost by default, trust to the rationality of the *system* of incrementalist actors and actions.

Thus, an incrementalist decision-maker expects other actors, in other sections of institutions, to correct the mistakes he may make as he operates even within his limitations, and even this remedial function of incrementalist systems depends upon the limited scope of decisions taken by everyone. So while the incrementalist model directly rejects the *form* of classical rationality, it indirectly denies something more: the *scope* of change that classical rationality provides. Synoptic policy (comprehensive policy) is ruled out with incrementalism.

CRITIQUES OF DISJOINTED INCREMENTALISM

Several types of criticisms can be leveled against incrementalist models. These criticisms may be viewed as external and internal. The external criticism is the easiest to state and the most difficult to refute on its own terms: that incrementalism is the planning model for ideological conservatism. On the face of it, such a charge seems true. Incrementalism does place the status quo in a preeminent position, so that change comes hard and in small doses. But the justification for incremental as opposed to sweeping change is rational, not ideological, in form. Proponents of incrementalism argue that real-world conditions make this model the only intelligent way to make policy decisions. If the policy model is conservative, it is not through any preference for the status quo.

This argument of rational necessity is not likely to impress a thoroughgoing radical, who may well counter that even irrational change is preferable to tolerating an unjust status quo (and he may be right). But at least the charge of ideological conservatism will have to wait for general validation on the internal inspection of incrementalism, for we cannot in general attach ideological labels to people if their method of operation is necessary on rational grounds. So the pressing question is, are the incremental models rational methods of making policy decisions?

The immediate answer to this question is yes. But the quick yes addresses the issue of rational requirements. Let us allow that a rational policy decision is one made by policy authorities who can make choices in conditions with alternatives, and on the basis of existing knowledge (assumptions of Section 3 of this chapter). The form of such a decision can vary. Some rational decisions are virtually required by conditions. The decision by the United States to intervene in World War II appears to be of this type. Other decisions are less conclusive: although the facts favor some courses of action, they do not decisively rule out alternatives. The recent jumble of court decisions on educational finance seem to be such decisions. But whatever the form of the decision, any decision that follows the weight of its considerations and is minimally fair in collecting and appraising facts is a rational decision. In conditions of uncertainty or risk, especially when the stakes are high, incremental decisions are rational decisions.

But the issue of rationality may be approached in a different way. Is the choice of incrementalism over other decision models itself always a rational choice? Do rational considerations invariably favor incrementalism over some modified, or restricted, version of classical rationality? The incrementalist proponent again answers yes, on the grounds that public policy is made in conditions of uncertainty. Thus an incrementalist model, in its more realistic appreciation of the way things are, will be justified in terms of better outcomes. Since it is rational to choose a decision-rule that, over the long run, has better outcomes than its rivals, incrementalism is said to be rational as an operating method as well.

Here, however, the evidence is mixed. One strong justification for incrementalism is that it avoids disasters, disasters that classical rationality is prone to produce in its insensitivity to social realities. But does it avoid disasters? Consider the following scenario, a script for a possible nightmare. Let's say that all available evidence suggests that the world will run out of fossil fuel in the year 2,000 and that alternative energy sources will not be adequately developed until 2,050. The only policy that will avoid the disaster of a world without fuel and the consequent breakdown in civilization itself turns out to be a severe and comprehensive rationing of all fuel for the next seventy years. Such rationing will require authoritarian policies in all major societies.

Regardless of how one feels about the alternatives in such a situation—breakdowns in civilized life versus authoritarian policies—an incrementalist planner could never choose the policy that would avoid the breakdown. He could never trust his information on future projections enough to *justify* the kind of absolutist policies the avoidance of breakdown requires in this situation. The information can be sound as information goes. But the incrementalist assumptions on what we can know are tentative enough to rule out decisive decisions of this scope. So if the avoidance of disaster requires, or seems to require, synoptic (or comprehensive) policy, the logic of incrementalist decision-making will not permit doing what is required.

An actual correlate of this hypothetical example is the energy program that President Carter introduced in April 1977. The program combined taxes, rebates, and price rises in an attempt to reduce domestic consumption of energy. President Carter justified the program with a picture of catastrophe: the United States without sufficient fuel and dependent on foreign sources of energy—conditions the President felt would "threaten our free institutions [and] endanger our freedom as a sovereign nation." No sooner had the program been communicated to Congress than dispute arose over whether, in fact, "we are now running out of gas and oil." A United Nations conference of experts maintained that enough fossil fuel exists in the world for another hundred years. This *uncertainty* in information naturally worked against the President's program, for, to the degree that we do not know what is needed, the status quo is favored against change (especially difficult changes like reductions in energy consumption). The incrementalist logic assumes that we can never know enough to warrant categoric, large-scale change.

Let's look at another policy close to current realities. Throughout the 1960s, the Vietnam War weighed heavily in debates on American public policy. In historical perspective, many scholars and policy actors (even those once favoring it) now view the United States' role in the war as a disaster of the first order. Over fifty thousand U.S. citizens were killed in the conflict; many more were severely wounded. Vietnam was devastated by the time that the war ended in 1975. American society was itself torn apart by divisions over the war, and even now many Americans who fled from the military draft live in other countries. The climate of suspicion and revolution brought about by the war strongly affected an administration later brought down by the Watergate scandal. Some might say that the aftereffects of the war are yet to be played out in American society.

One does not have to agree on a condemnation of the war to view it as a policy of considerable magnitude: resources and people were committed substantially, and strong convictions divided opponents and supporters of the war. Yet the Vietnam War is almost a perfect example of incremental policy. One small step after another, built on past and prevailing policies, gradually (incrementally) led American society into a vast policy commitment that subsequently could not be turned around incrementally. In short, a series of incremental decisions produced a policy that most now view as a disaster, for whatever reasons, and that at the very least rivaled any synoptic alternative to incrementalism in its scope and importance.

These three cases, one fanciful and two real, suggest that incrementalism is consistent with disasters of great magnitude, that modest policy moves can still lead to policies or circumstances immodest in scope. It is precisely because of such deficiencies that alternatives to incrementalism have been introduced, including a form of "mixed scanning" that includes incrementalism as a possibility among nonincremental policy strategies (Etzioni, 1968). A demonstration that incrementalism is *consistent* with disaster does not, of course, mean that this method of decision-making is worse than other forms. The outcomes of incrementalist decisions may still be better overall than those of alternative decision-rules. This is difficult to evaluate, however, because of the various interpretations we can make of exactly what an increment in policy is.

Let's try out four specifications of an increment: (1) An increment is a small departure from previous policy. (2) An increment represents a middle-range compromise of conflicting demands. (3) An increment is any policy that is modest in resources and scope. (4) An increment is any policy that accords with the more modest of claims made on any policy issue.

Each of these specifications is a plausible interpretation of an "incremental" policy. An example of the first would be the decision by the Kennedy Administration to send advisors to Vietnam. An example of the second, the Elementary and Secondary Education Act of 1965. An example of the third could be any decision to issue a new stamp. An example of the fourth would be a decision to support the National Association for the Advancement of Colored People in opposition to the Black Panthers in the 1960s.

Each of these four types of decisions can be counted as "a small or incremental move(s) on particular problems" (Braybrooke-Lindblom, 1963), or as the satisfaction of compromise standards short of maximization (Simon's "satisficing," 1955). Yet each can conflict with any of the others. A policy can be a small departure from previous policy, yet be comprehensive in its use of resources or be counter to the weight of policy demands. A policy with modest claims can be a significant departure from previous policies and can even be viewed as excessive by those whose extreme claims are being denied.

The possibility of internal contradictions on the term *incremental* increases as policy is more closely examined. Let us say that, roughly, there is a distinction among (1) decision-makers, (2) the content or substance of decisions, (3) the way decisions are implemented, (4) the consequences of decisions, (5) the social context in which decisions are made, and (6) the way decisions are justified. Now decision-makers can have synoptic *or* incremental goals and strategies; decisions can be comprehensive *or* restricted; implementation methods decisive *or* tentative; consequences large *or* small; the social context open *or* resistant to change; justifications dogmatic *or* provisional.

In each case, the first term in the pair is what we normally associate with synoptic policies; the second term, with incrementalist policies. But of course a mix can easily occur. Modest decisions can be harshly imposed, or have large, unforeseen consequences; they can fall into pliable social conditions that change drastically with little impetus, or they can be dogmatically defended. And the order may be reversed for synoptic policy: even the brightest of synoptic planners may find his policies contracted to infinitesimal levels by unlucky circumstances.

These observations do not rule out all possibility for identifying incremental policies. But they do suggest that the natural variety of political life (stressed in the opening chapter) can also wreak havoc with any simplistic attempt to separate into neat categories incremental policies from all other kinds of policies. As proponents of incrementalism remind us, the land of policy is a wild and unruly place. And its wild and unruly nature makes comparative judgments on rational decision-rules as difficult as separating them realistically in the first place. But the one conclusion we can draw from the variety of political life is that somewhere in this variety is surely a place for classical rationality. If we can identify the conditions favoring incrementalism, then the converse of these conditions will logically favor the classical model: a limited, simple, and uncomplicated policy setting where valid information can be acquired quickly and easily for little cost—in short, restricted conditions of certainty. Though such conditions are seldom found in contemporary industrial society, they do suggest a possible society that may have existed somewhere in the past. And perhaps local areas of modern society still harbor such places. Thus, one main claim of incrementalist champions of "the analyst's inevitable failure to construct a completely rational-deductive system" can be amicably denied (Braybrooke-Lindblom, 1963, p. 113).

Can the costs of decisions ever be rationally ignored? It depends. Certainly the incrementalist is on strong grounds when he points out that information is costly and that public policy typically succeeds only through costs in time and effort. And certainly it is rational to balance costs against benefits in evaluating the success of any policy. But, on the other hand, if the values to be implemented in public policy are important enough, almost any cost may be worth the benefits such, values represent. Think about constitutional rights. Even if the costs were quite high, it still might be rational to guarantee such rights. The model of classical rationality suggests that we might have values so preeminent that costs are not important considerations. No rational person could deny the logic of this suggestion.

THE JUDICIARY IN EDUCATION: CLASSICAL OR INCREMENTAL

If we look again at the two issues in educational policy, the factual and the legal/moral, we can see that each issue favors a different decision model, although the judiciary process as a whole is strongly incremental. It was once thought that legal reasoning was, by definition, based on fixed principles. The doctrine of *stare decisis* (that judicial decisions are based on precedent) assumed that the law contained immutable principles to be discovered by judges and applied to particular cases. In such a doctrine judicial decisions are types of classical rationality, single-choice version. More recently, it has been argued that the law requires neutral principles that, once decided upon, will be applicable to all like cases (Wechsler, 1959). This later doctrine also exhibits many features of classical rationality, this time of the double-choice version.

Each of these legal doctrines has been shattered by the facts of judiciary practice. No court case seems to have a single principle on which a decision can be made. Several principles are typically available for rational choice, and even the standards of review (the "rational relationship test" versus "strict judicial scrutiny") call for a decision. Students of the judiciary now generally concede that we cannot make sense of the judicial process as a series of decisions around a locus of principles. It seems more sensible to see it as a response to changing social realities.

In short, judicial decisions are incremental in form and logic: they (1) are strongly based on the status quo (the legal order), (2) consider concrete cases (restricted alternatives), (3) are remedial in addressing claims for redress of wrongs, (4) operate with established procedures (legal doctrines and rules), (5) reconstruct data in selecting facts and law, (6) build on multiple small decisions (especially in the case-by-case development of the common law), and (7) are made by one agency, the courts, and counterbalanced by other decision-making agencies in the political system (Shapiro, 1969; Dahl, 1957).

The incremental model of decision-making is clearly supported in the educational decisions based on the two causal relationships discussed earlier: cost–quality and mandatory busing–quality. In the cost–quality chain, the initial allocation of resources is not identical to the distribution of benefits for students in the outcomes of policy. In the busing–quality chain, expected results are frustrated; they are perhaps inversely related to initial expectations. In each case the clear and unbroken chain between efforts and results assumed in the classical model of rationality is missing. There is also uncertainty because of the tentative status of any explanatory theory. Therefore, the incremental model is favored: if we are not sure of what we know, we proceed cautiously.

On the other hand, the legal and moral issues of educational policy seem to present a peremptory, or absolute, value: the equal-protection clause of the Fourteenth Amendment can be maintained as right or just in the face of uncertainty and change. The classical model is favored by the equal-protection clause, at least those aspects of it that resist the pressure for change that new facts produce. The logic of peremptory values can also produce the indifference to costs characteristic of classical rationality. When constitutional rights are enforced, costs may not be decisive considerations.

Notice, however, that even the peremptory status of the equal-protection clause is subordinate to a variety of decisions. *Who* is to be counted in equality cases (the poor in *Serrano*, but not the poor in *Rodriguez*), and *what* is to count as equality, is a matter of decision. Like the concept of *sameness* mentioned earlier, equality can be used as a principle to resolve issues or it can be an issue itself to be resolved by other means. Both the *Swann* decision, requiring busing, and the proposed amendments against the decision, deal with equality but in different senses.

Unfortunately, if different senses of equality are all defensible on one ground or another, then "equality" cannot function successfully as a principle with absolute status. It is, though resistant to change from facts alone, an item that itself requires decisions. These decisions may be guided (not mandated) by our views of social reality and the status we grant to social practices. Even peremptory values, in short, seem to require the sensitivity to social conditions characteristic of the incremental model. Some may find uncertainty nourishing: in an unsettled world the most charitable values and hypotheses can be chosen (Connolly, 1973). But whatever the choice, even the judiciary seems to be incremental in its decisions.

SUMMARY AND PROSPECTS

We have looked at the prospect of rational decisions in public policy and concentrated on the differences between *classical* and *incremental* models of policy decisions. Our case study has been education policy. Obviously not all recent education policy can be summed up in terms of rational decisions. The heat and rhetoric of the Ocean Hill-Brownsville conflict is ill-suited for rational treatment. Even the passage of the Elementary and Secondary Education Act of 1965 is perhaps best characterized as a series of bargaining transactions among groups rather than as a set of rational decisions—classical *or* incremental—by those making and implementing policy. But rational models of decision-making, as we have seen, do illuminate great stretches of recent education policy, especially that vital side of it treated by the judiciary. We also should better understand our decision models as a result of our investigation of education policy. To think of policy in terms of *decisions* is to think in terms of *individuals* in the political system, not aggregate units of the policy process. It is not clear that individual decisions can always be transformed into policy, a problem of *linkage* (how the individual influences public policy) that we will look at more closely in later chapters (especially Chapter 4). But it is important to understand that a decision-oriented view of policy normally begins with individuals. Some enthusiasts have maintained an organic theory of the state, arguing that the society as a whole can "decide" questions of policy. Such arguments are very complicated and not at all common ways of approaching politics; for to say that groups or collections of people can make decisions without reference to the individuals composing the groups is an odd way to proceed. Still, organic theories of the state, which rest on such a claim, were at one time prominent in the history of political theory. And the relationships of the individual to his society, shortly to be discussed, may give credence to some variation of this theory. But for now, we can accept that an emphasis on decisions in policy is normally also an emphasis on individuals making these decisions.

What we must do now, to expand our perspective on public policy, is look at larger units in the policy process. The idea of *decisions* in policy will not be left entirely behind, but the move to units like groups, elites, and classes will tend to emphasize the types of transactions these units have with one another rather than the models of policy decisions we have been concerned with up to now.

The main points of this chapter can be summarized as follows:

1.   Social policy can be seen in terms of the *decisions* made by individual actors.

2.   *Rational* models are distinct from *sociological* explanations, though each may complement the other.

3.   Rational decisions can be organized into (a) *logical features:* consistency and transitivity; (b) *conditions:* certainty, uncertainty, and risk; and (c) types of *calculations:* expected value, maximin *vs.* maximax.

4.   Two prominent models of decision-making in public policy are the *classical* and *incremental* models. Each model requires, and is appropriate for, different conditions of social policy.

5.   Education policy can be seen in important ways as reasoned decisions on two issues: (a) empirical (cost–quality; busing–quality), and (b) legal/moral (equal protection).

THE CLASSICAL MODEL OF RATIONALITY SUMMARIZED

1. Outstanding features:
   (a) hierarchy of goals
   (b) hierarchy of means
   (c) perfect information
   (d) indifference to decision costs
2. Main criticisms:
   (a) goals are too often lateral, their rank altering as new facts are introduced; goals can be traded off with each other
   (b) means are not related to goals and outcomes with certainty
   (c) information is limited and often faulty
   (d) costs cannot be eliminated from policy decisions

A SUMMARY OF DISJOINTED INCREMENTALISM

1. Outstanding features:
   (a) relates means and ends laterally, even including means being transformed into ends and vice versa
   (b) can use imperfect, limited information
   (c) concentrates on costs
   (d) emphasizes serial, or sequential, policy that continually readjusts means and ends
   (e) uses goals short of maximums—those that "satisfy"
   (f) departs from existing policies or states of affairs in small steps
   (g) oriented to remedial action rather than reform
2. Main criticisms:
   (a) not inconsistent with disasters
   (b) ambiguous over what an "increment" means
   (c) mixed cases, both incremental *and* synoptic, are possible
   (d) classical rationality is valid in restricted circumstances (simple, uncomplicated, easy and quick information), and in the implementation of peremptory values (like constitutional rights)

FOR FURTHER READING

The literature in both decision-models and education policy is vast and uneven. I have tried to identify only those works that seem to me both intrinsically good and relevant to the discussion of this chapter.

DECISION MODELS AND RATIONAL CHOICE

ALLISON, GRAHAM, *Essence of Decision*. Boston: Little, Brown, 1971.
BRAYBROOKE, DAVID, AND CHARLES LINDBLOM, *A Strategy of Decision*. New York: Free Press, 1963.
BUCHANAN, JAMES, AND GORDON TULLOCK, *The Calculus of Consent*. Ann Arbor, Mich.: University of Michigan Press, 1965.
CONNOLLY, WILLIAM, "Theoretical Self-Consciousness," in *Social Structure and Political Theory*, ed. Connolly. Lexington, Mass.: D. C. Heath, 1974.
DAHL, ROBERT, AND CHARLES LINDBLOM, *Politics, Economics and Welfare*. New York: Harper & Row, 1953.
DOWNS, ANTHONY, *An Economic Theory of Democracy*. New York: Harper & Row, 1957.
ETZIONI, AMITAI, *The Active Society*. New York: Free Press, 1968.
HARE, R. M., *Freedom and Reason*. New York: Oxford University Press, 1965.
HICKS, J. R., *A Revision of Demand Theory*. Oxford: Oxford University Press, 1956. (For a defense of unbounded, or classical, rationality in economics.)
KASSOUF, SHEEN, *Normative Decision Making*. Englewood Cliffs, N.J.: Prentice-Hall, 1970.
LINDBLOM, CHARLES, *The Policy-Making Process*. Englewood Cliffs, N.J.: Prentice-Hall, 1968.
——, "The Science of Muddling Through," *Public Administration Review*, 19 (Spring 1959).
QUADE, E. S., *Analysis for Public Decisions*. New York: American Elsevier, 1975.
RIKER, WILLIAM, AND PETER ORDESHOOK, *An Introduction to Positive Political Theory*. Englewood Cliffs, N.J.: Prentice-Hall, 1973.
SIMON, HERBERT, *Administrative Behavior*. New York: MacMillan, 1947.
——, "A Behavioral Model of Rational Choice," *Quarterly Journal of Economics*, 1955.
——, "Theories of Bounded Rationality," in *Decision and Organization*, eds. C. B. McGuire and R. Rander. Amsterdam: Noth-Holland, 1972.
TISDELL, CLEM, "Concepts of Rationality in Economics," *Philosophy of Social Science*, September 1975. (A summary of some recent views.)
WILSON, BRYAN, ED., *Rationality*. New York: Harper & Row, 1970.

JUDICIAL REASONING

BICKEL, ALEXANDER, *The Least Dangerous Branch*. New York: Bobbs-Merrill, 1960.
DAHL, ROBERT, "Decision-Making in a Democracy: The Supreme Court as a National Policy-Maker," *Journal of Public Law*, 6, No. 2 (1957), pp. 279–295. Reprinted in *The Supreme Court and Public Policy*, ed. Martin Shapiro. Glenview, Ill.: Scott-Foresman, 1969, pp. 57–64.
MILLER, ARTHUR SELWYN, "On the Choice of Major Premises in Supreme Court Opinions," *Journal of Public Law*, 14, No. 2 (1965), pp. 251–275. Reprinted in *The Supreme Court and Public Policy*, ed. Martin Shapiro. Glenview, Ill.: Scott-Foresman, 1969, pp. 118–132.
PELTASON, JACK, *Federal Courts in the Political Process*. New York: Random House, 1955.
ROSEN, PAUL, *The Supreme Court and Social Science*. Chicago: Ill.: University of Illinois Press, 1972, especially pp. 182–196, "The Adequacy of Social Science Findings," and pp. 197–229, "Using Social Science: Reflections and Conclusions."

SHAPIRO, MARTIN, "Stability and Change in Judicial Decision-Making: Incrementalism or Stare Decisis?" in *The Supreme Court and Public Policy*, ed. Martin Shapiro. Glenview, Ill.: Scott-Foresman, 1969, pp. 22–32.

WECHSLER, HERBERT, "Toward Neutral Principles of Constitutional Law," 73 *Harvard Law Review* 1 (1959).

EDUCATION POLICY

ANOSIKE, BENJI O., "The Jencks' Harvard Study Revisited," *The Educational Forum* (May 1975), Vol. 3, No. 4, pp. 435–446.

ARMOUR, DAVID, "The Evidence on Busing," *The Public Interest*, No. 28 (Summer 1972), pp. 90–126. Reprinted in *The Great School Bus Controversy*, ed. Nicolaus Mills. New York: Teachers College Press, 1973, pp. 81–122.

———, "The Double Double Standard: A Reply," *The Public Interest*, No. 30 (Winter 1973), pp. 119–131. Reprinted in *The Great School Bus Controversy*, ed. Nicolaus Mills. New York: Teachers College Press, 1973, pp. 159–173.

BARATZ, JOAN C., "Court Decisions and Educational Change: A Case History of the D.C. Public Schools, 1954–1974," *Journal of Law and Education* (Jan. 1975), Vol. 4, No. 1, pp. 63–80.

BENSON, CHARLES S., *Education Finance in the Coming Decade*. Bloomington, Ind.: Phi Delta Kappa, 1975.

BILLINGS, C. DAVID, AND JOHN B. LEGLER, "Factors Affecting Educational Opportunity and Their Implication for School Reform: An Empirical Study," *Journal of Law and Education* (Oct. 1975), Vol. 4, No. 4, pp. 633–640.

COLEMAN, JAMES, *Equality of Educational Opportunity*. United States Department of Health, Education, and Welfare, Office of Education, 1966.

———, "Integration, Yes: Busing, No," Interview by W. Goodman, *New York Times Magazine*, Aug. 1975, pp. 10–11, ff.

DUGAN, THOMAS P., "The Constitutionality of School Finance Systems Under State Law: New York's Twin, " *Syracuse Law Review* (Spring 1976), Vol. 27, No. 2, pp. 573–610.

FISCHER, THOMAS C., "*Defunis* in the Supreme Court: Is That All There Is?", *Journal of Law and Education* (July 1975), Vol. 4, No. 3, pp. 487–509.

HARVARD EDUCATIONAL REVIEW, *Equal Educational Opportunity*. Cambridge, Mass.: Harvard University Press, 1969. (Contains excellent commentary on the Coleman Report.)

JENCKS, CHRISTOPHER, *Inequality: A Reassessment of the Effect of Family and Schooling in America*. New York: Basic Books, 1972.

JOHNS, ROE L., AND EDGAR MORPHET, *The Economics and Financing of Education: A Systems Approach*. Englewood Cliffs, N.J.: Prentice-Hall, 1975.

KELLY, GEORGE A., ED., *Government Aid to Nonpublic Schools: Yes or No?* New York: St. John's University Press, 1972.

LEVIN, BETSY, ED., "Future Direction for School Finance Reform," A Symposium in *Law and Contemporary Problems* (Winter-Spring, 1974), Vol. 38, pp. 293–581.

———, "Recent Developments in the Law of Equal Educational Opportunity," *Journal of Law and Education* (July 1975), Vol. 4, No. 3, pp. 411–447.

LINDQUIST, ROBERT E., AND ARTHUR E. WISE, "Developments in Education Litigation: Equal Protection," *Journal of Law and Education* (Jan. 1976), Vol. 5, No. 1.

MARSHALL, MARGARET H., "The Standard of Interest: Two Recent Michigan Cases," *Journal of Law and Education* (Jan. 1975), Vol. 4, No. 1, pp. 227–241.

MILLS, NICOLAUS, ED., *The Great School Bus Controversy*. New York: Teachers College Press, 1973. (See other articles in addition to the Armour-Pettigrew exchange cited separately.)

MUNGER, FRANK, AND RICHARD FENNO, *National Politics and Federal Aid to Education*. Syracuse, N.Y.: Syracuse University Press, 1962.

MYRDAL, GUNNAR, *An American Dilemma*. New York: Harper & Row, 1962.

ORFIELD, GARY, "Congress, the President, and Anti-Busing Legislation, 1966–1974," *Journal of Law and Education* (January 1975), Vol. 4, No. 1, pp. 81–140.

PETTIGREW, THOMAS F., ELIZABETH L. USEEM, CLARENCE NORMOND, AND MARSHALL S. SMITH, "Busing: A Review of 'The Evidence,'" *The Public Interest*, No. 30 (Winter 1973), pp. 88–118. Reprinted in *The Great School Bus Controversy*, ed. Nicolaus Mills. New York: Teachers College Press, 1973, pp. 123–158.

Stockholm Report (Stockholm: International Association for the Evaluation of International Achievement, 1973).

groups and elites

3

ACTORS IN THE POLICY PROCESS

If any of us were to try to bring about some political action, we would likely encounter a bewildering spectacle of organizations. Suppose, for example, we tried to change a zoning law so that we could open a pizza stand in a residential neighborhood. Although the idea of such a stand might appeal to pizza lovers in the area, many residents would object. Neighborhood associations might oppose the change. Rival business groups might also object, especially if they find current zoning arrangements an orderly way of insuring profits. A budding pizza entrepreneur would find himself facing not other individuals, but *spokesmen* for associations of individuals. He would quickly discover a fundamental truth of politics: that people tend to group together when they become politically active, that they generally do not go it alone.

The idea of "clusters" of people in politics is as old as political theory itself. Plato's *Republic* is an arrangement of intellectually based *classes*. In *The Federalist Papers* James Madison claimed that people will tend to form *factions* in the political process. Marx gave the notion of *class* an economic base. In this century, American political theorists like Arthur Bentley, Earl Latham, and David Truman stressed the importance of *groups* in politics. If our pizza entrepreneur had read these theorists, he would have discovered a second important truth about politics: that people can be associated with each other in a variety of ways, by class, strata, groups, elites, and even systems.

Sometimes these associations are actual organizations. People *do* in fact

64

organize in groups, and we can readily identify these groups and observe how they operate politically: the American Medical Association, the AFL-CIO, the Farm Bureau, the American Association of University Professors, the Congress of Racial Equality, to name a few. All of these associations have names and exist in what we might call the real world (meaning, roughly, that we can observe their existence). Other associations, while useful as research tools, are not so clearly defined in our everyday world. Recognizing latent, or potential, groups, for example—those consisting of people with common interests who have not yet recognized and acted on this interest—can help us understand political life. They do not, however, exist in the same sense that overtly organized groups exist. As a case in point, women in America before about 1960 had common though unrecognized interests. Viewing them as a latent group would have helped in predicting and understanding the feminist movements of the 1970s, even though *in fact* women were not organized as a recent movement until after 1960.

In this chapter we will be concerned primarily with some *groupings*, actual *and* hypothetical, important to political life and with the theories of politics that go with them. We will continue to advance the idea of *rationality* through our discussion. But, to borrow a distinction from the last chapter, our primary interest will be in *sociological* explanations—the behavior of associations of various kinds and the effects of associations on the rational decisions that individuals in politics are required to make.

INTEREST GROUPS IN POLITICS

A basic unit in the American political system is the *interest group*. Interest group theory begins with an irresistible thought: that any society can be divided up into an infinite number of categories. The sparkling variety of human features can be categorized according to hair color, sex, height, salary, voice tone, residence, education—endless divisions on infinitely various features. Such groups are called *categoric*, or tertiary, groups.

Categoric groups are not, however, authentic social groups. They lack the "glue" of interaction. All redheads in the country may represent a simple classification, with no activity among them *as* redheads. A social group would occur if redheads organized on the basis of shared hair color (perhaps to further the social standing of a neglected pigmentation). Interaction does often occur on the basis of a categoric property. The objective datum of having school-age children leads parents to interact in groups concerned with education. The subjective datum of having an interest in monitoring school budgets frequently follows.

The "glue" of interaction can bring about an organization of the group, or can be caused by organization. Obviously, groups frequently organize on the basis of interaction. Labor, as a class activity, was characterized by economic interactions long before labor unions effectively organized workers. Interaction by these with class interests finally, some would say inexorably, led to labor organizations. But the existence of an organization can also create the interactions. Many women had "consciousness-raising" experiences in the 1960s after attending feminist meetings. Without structured feminist organizations, the categoric distinction of sexual identification might never have produced the interactions that led many women into feminist movements. So it works both ways: interaction can bring about organizations and organizations can create interactions.

Interactions commonly take place on the basis of one or more overlapping interests. Doctors form medical associations because they share certain professional interests. Again, however, while interests can lead to interactions, the reverse is also true. People who, for whatever reason, interact with each other may come to discover, and perhaps even form, mutual interests. Frequency of contact may itself come to be an interest shared by those who interact. Interest can be either objective or subjective. Children, for example, may have interests as children which they do not perceive; hence these interests are objective. Social groups, however, typically have subjective interests, those that *are* perceived by group members. In group theory human interaction is not just a statistical correlation; it is frequent contact on the basis of shared attitudes. These common attitudes are formed because of the wants or needs of the group, and frequently express the subjective interests of the group.

An *interest group* in American politics is "any group that, on the basis of one or more shared attitudes, makes certain claims upon other groups in the society for the establishment, maintenance, or enhancement of forms of behavior that are implied by the shared attitudes" (Truman, 1971, p. 33).

If we go back to our budding pizza parlor magnate, his entrance into politics would be filled with group encounters. Interest groups would act to further their interests in opposition to his. It may even be necessary to introduce the machinery of government to resolve this opposition. But the pizza entrepreneur would also discover an interesting thing. Unless he stumbles on certain interests of the Mafia or other groups outside the law, the resolution of his conflicts with opposing interest groups will be peaceful and generally within a stable framework of rules. Trial by combat, for example, will not be a likely decision-rule adopted by any of the interest groups he encounters.

What are the sources of stability in interest-group politics? First, interactions constituting an interest group are themselves stable. Purely random, sporadic, or chance encounters do not make an interest group. Saying "Hello" to a stranger while walking the dog is an interaction remote from interest-group activity. Attending regular meetings of the PTA *is* a type of interest-group interaction. This stability of interaction tends toward some point of equilibrium precisely on the basis of shared interests. Like a family that has lost one of the parents through death, shared interests among interest group members press toward restabilizing the interactions of the group if disturbances occur. So interest groups themselves operate against chaotic solutions to conflicting claims.

Second, certain types of groups provide an additional "glue" that binds together people who would otherwise disagree. The term *association* has a specialized meaning for some interest group theorists. They define it as an interest group that extends across two or more other groups by virtue of common membership in the different groups (Truman, 1971). For example, the would-be pizza capitalist may form an interest group making claims on society on behalf of pizza-oriented interests. This pizza group may then find itself opposed to an interest group formed by certain other fast-food restaurants. But suppose that our pizza representative regularly attends meetings of a local group developing the public relations of businesses in the area. There he meets and interacts with the representatives of the fast-food interest group. This interaction is a *tangent* relationship, which, if continued, forms an *association* that binds the representatives of the two opposed interest groups, pizza versus fast food. Such an association is a bridge that helps stabilize the conflicting interactions of otherwise separate and opposed interest groups.

Third, the formation and development of interest groups keep the general distribution of interests in balance. Latent, or potential, unorganized interests more or less dwell all around us. For example, senior citizens are a categoric group with a long-standing set of shared interests as elders. Recent history has seen this latent interest group emerge as an actual interest group. Why? Because, according to standard interest-group theory, (1) the interests of the elderly have been threatened by a variety of social and economic pressures, and (2) there are more of the elderly than ever before in American society. Disturbances against numerically large groupings generally result in the formation of an organization to protect the interests of the group. The system of interest groups stays in balance by precisely this kind of response: rational individuals binding together to further their interests in response to *external* pressures on those interests.

In addition to the stablizing influences of interest groups themselves, the American political system is also said to contribute to the stability of interest-group politics. First, American politics is generally characterized by multiple points of access to power. The formal apparatus of the federal government is open to influence at numerous points—the presidency, Congress, various departments and bureaus. The American political system is decentralized and available. This accessibility is a stabilizing factor in at least one important respect: claims on behalf of interests may be pressed effectively at numerous points, thus minimizing the possibility of excluding groups who could powerfully affect society in other, not so peaceful, ways.

At one time traditional group theorists also had faith in the soothing effects of overlapping and general unorganized interests. Overlapping interests are those shared by people who might be opposed to one another on other grounds. The pizza group and the fast-food operators might find that they have a joint interest in promoting business in general. Thus their opposition is not categorical; they do not occupy mutually exclusive turfs. Rather, they have something important in common: furthering the interests of business in general. Overlapping interests can be explored to find points of agreement, and even grounds for tangent relationships. Such shared concerns smooth over the severity of differences in obvious ways.

The "rules of the game" are also important unorganized interests in American politics. Although groups can have sharply conflicting interests, theorists assumed for a long time that all groups also had a common interest in maintaining the institutional framework within which conflict is resolved. The appeal of such an assumption is intuitive as well as observational. If we disagree, only a decision-rule of some sort will resolve our disagreement. Turning the dispute on the decision-rule would seem to remove hope of resolving the disagreement. In fact, the older interest groups in American society have traditionally behaved *as if* such unorganized interests exist. Take, for example, farm, labor, business, or professional groups—generally, the claims advanced by standard interest groups have not challenged basic decision-rules so much as they have laid out stakes on the outcomes of these decision-rules.

The general model of politics represented by interest-group theories is straightforward and uncluttered by messy ideological issues. Group theories depict politics as a competitive arena within which groups interact on the basis of adversary interests. These interests are not peremptory, but pragmatic. Compromise is not only possible but typical. Both the nature of groups and the nature of the political system contribute to the stability of interest-oriented conflict.

Although the interest-group model is frankly interesting, some of its basic assumptions and key conclusions have been challenged recently. Let's turn to another way of organizing *groupings* in the social system to see some helpful contrasts between interest-group politics and other models of the political process.

ELITES

An "interest group" view of the political system is essentially lateral: the society is seen as broken up into a variety of unranked associations (the word is used generically here) making demands upon one another and upon the larger society. But associations can also be ranked in terms of effectiveness, prestige, wealth—or any other indicator that places one association of people "above" another. This vertical, or hierarchical view of society, introduces the concept of *elites*. An *elite*, according to the dictionary, is the choice or select part; when applied to groups, an elite is the socially superior segment of society. When applied to political matters, an elite would be the ruling parts of society. If, then, all parts of society ruled equally, as happens in direct democracy or a unanimity principle, we would have no ruling parts and thus no political elite.

One of the oldest, and still vital, issues in political thought is whether elites of some sort are needed for political societies to function successfully. Certainly some division of labor is required if societies are sufficiently large. In an assembly of even five-hundred members, to hear from everyone on even a single measure would exhaust both time and patience. The same point can be made about a complex society: the greater the diversity among citizens, the more difficult it is for the society to operate with full and effective participation on every policy issue. These limitations are almost mathematical in form, and have been recognized since the time of Pericles as constraints on democracy (Dahl, 1971). They are generally thought to re-quire the division of political labor into speciality units, like committees and representatives. Such units do the work of politics by concentrating both their time and efforts on political matters, and by focusing their attention on specialized areas. Thus we have both professional politicians, those who work at political matters and little else, and experts within the field of politics who know a lot about a few specific issues.

A division of labor does not necessarily lead to a political elite which rules on its own counsel. But it does lead to the traditional distinction between those who rule and those who are ruled (though perhaps on their consent and authority). The conditions that produce a political division of labor also need not extend to all political societies. Obviously, a simple and small society can be run on the unanimous and direct consent of every member. But it is a nostalgic fact that today's world is neither simple nor small. So modern society is characterized by a class of rulers, whatever the political form (despotism, democracy, etc.) of the society.

Two interesting questions arise when we concede that political rulers exist: (1) What is the *form* of political elites operating in modern de-mocracies? and (2) Is democracy compatible with elite rule?

To the first question we have two general answers: (a) pluralist (Dahl, 1971), and (b) uniform (Mills, 1957).

(a) The pluralist view of political rule maintains that minorities govern effectively at least in American society. These minorities are elites as they govern, but they exercise effective power only within separate issue areas. In effect, the pluralist model specifies *revolving* elites, a fluidity of political power instead of fixed authorities. In practice, the model asserts that democratic political arrangements work like this: issues *A*, *B*, *C*, and *D* are salient for the political society. Each issue activates groups with an interest in seeing certain things done. Say issue *A* occasions groups *a*, *b*, and *c* to become active, issue B moves groups *d*, *e*, and *f* to political action, and so on. Now as each of these issues moves into the political arena and becomes a *public* or *political* issue, each group with an interest in the issue gets busy. Essentially, the groups bargain with each other to arrive at a decision all can support. This bargained decision then becomes public policy through various political means (executive decree, legislative enactment, policy board announcement, or such).

Where is the public in all this? They're largely inactive, which is what makes the pluralist model an elitist theory in the descriptive sense. How then can the system be called democratic? Because supporters of the pluralist model make a distinction between those who are inactive because they are coerced or forced and those who are inactive because they are satisfied or disinterested. If the public were inactive in the first sense, then obviously we would not have a democratic system. However, inactivity in the second sense can be interpreted (not without some disagreement) as indicating at least an acquiescence in, and perhaps even consensus on, what is going on politically. Also, if the political system provides *access* to the means of power, then supporters of the pluralist model are prepared to grant democratic status to such systems even if people do not generally avail themselves of this access. Again, inactivity can be interpreted as an agreement with the decisions made on policy issues. Most pluralist supporters recognize that the public occasionally participates, and decisively, when bargaining among elite factions breaks down. But the system can also function happily without such breakdowns and in the face of public apathy. What furnishes the lubricant for the system are unorganized interests, or a general (though uneven) consensus on fundamental values (Dahl, 1961).

(b) The uniformity, or power elite, view of political rule maintains that there are *fixed*, not revolving, authorities. In this model of political power, the ruling elite remains constant even as policy issues change. Again, let us suppose that issues *A*, *B*, and *C* are prominent. Then, on the uniformity model, issue *A* will have groups *a*, *b*, and *c* as decisive figures for policy-making, issue *B* will also have *a*, *b*, and *c*, and issue *C* will have *a*, *b*, and *c*. In short, the same groups exercise power regardless of issue content. A single, rather than multiple, elite governs. Naturally the personnel can change (people do not live forever, or even necessarily hold power for long periods of time). But the elite as a governing body is maintained even with changes in personnel. Such an elite, by its nature and function, occupies strategic positions in society, both institutional and informal. Corporate boards combine with military staffs, congressional committees, and so on to exercise power in the common interests of the elite they constitute (Mills, 1957; Hunter, 1953).

In the uniformity model the public fares no better, and in fact is worse off, than in the pluralist model. By and large, people are inactive in both models. But the inactivity is more pernicious for democracy in the uniformity model. The power elite here determines the *framework* that operates to form and discuss policy alternatives. So consensus, when it occurs, is determined by institutional manipulation; the options open to the public are carefully guarded by the elite, and do not exceed the limits of elite interest. Supporters of the uniformity model, for example, would interpret the choices between presidential candidates as limited *because* an elite constrains the range of political alternatives presented to the public (Mills, 1957). Even the attitudes of the public are sometimes said to be determined by institutional manipulation, so that false needs are created in order to further the interests, usually economic, of the elite (Marcuse, 1964). The absence of decisions in such a model becomes more important than the making of decisions, for what is left out of the policy area is often more revealing for understanding the system than what is allowed in for public resolution (Bachrach, 1967; Bachrach and Baratz, 1962, 1963, 1975).

The question that begs to be asked after examining these two models of elite rule is this: How is it possible for social scientists looking at the "same" evidence (the state of American society) to develop two such different theories of political rule? The answers go far toward illuminating both the two models and the role of ideology in the conduct and study of public policy.

The immediate, but least satisfactory, reaction to two contrary models is that one is a correct reading of American society and the other mistaken. This reaction will probably be enthusiastically accepted by partisans for each model, but each will claim the other is wrong. The problem, then, is resolving the dispute by either settling on how one is wrong and the other right, or determining that both can stand as alternative interpretations because of fundamental differences in key concepts and rules of evidence. As we shall see, the latter strategy appears to be more rewarding in understanding elite theory.

CONCEPTS OF POWER

The key concept, which is given different emphasis in each of the two models, is *power*. Power is traditionally defined as a one-sided transaction between two or more actors, A and B: A has power over B if A can get B to take some action, X, that B would not otherwise take (Dahl, 1957). Any power transaction is notoriously difficult to confirm. The problem is that we must know what actually causes an action to determine if power has, in fact, been exercised. Were A's actions the only cause of B's behavior? Did some combination of circumstances produce B's actions? Did B in any way influence A's actions (was there feedback from B to A)? These are problems intrinsic to power. What is revealing is how each of the two models of elite rule emphasizes different interpretations of the concept of power.

Getting someone to do something, the central action of a power transaction, can be accomplished in many ways. Perhaps the most obvious is by command: A can command B to do X. This species of action is characteristic of military rule and traditional parent-child relationships, as well as older theories of the state (Weber). Although command transactions can fit both the pluralist and uniformity models, each model interprets *getting* differently.

In the pluralist model, bargaining seems to be the dominant transactional form, at least among the elite groups. When the public enters the policy dialogue, a form of persuasion seems to predominate. Spokesmen for elite factions (and they are factions in this theory, divided and at odds with each other, when they must appeal to the public) attempt to enlist the support of the voting population by standard campaign techniques. In the pluralist model all power transactions are face-to-face, or at least transactions between an A and a B.

In the uniformity model the distinctive characteristic of power is the absence of a direct $A \rightarrow B$ transaction. The uniformity model assumes that A gets B to do X primarily by manipulating the conditions in which B operates. So the power transaction is $A \rightarrow Z$, where Z is the social setting for B. In the uniformity model, for example, an elite might maintain the seniority system in Congress in order to insure its interests. These elite interests might require the maintenance of tax shelters for the rich, a maintenance perhaps impossible under a merit system in Congress. But the public in such an arrangement is not directly required to do anything. Institutions are manipulated, not the public, but the results are the same: interests of the elite (A) are fulfilled. The difference is that the public doesn't feel the "sting," or at least not immediately, in such indirect exercises of power. The public might never find out what is going on, for indirect power, unlike commands and bargaining, does not require that the one over whom power is exercised be aware of the power transaction.

The different emphasis on the concept, *power*, in each of the elite models not surprisingly leads to different interpretations of American society, for each emphasis will lead its supporters to "see" different aspects of the political system. Supporters of the pluralist model naturally concentrate on overt decisions, and on overt participation in decisions about important issues. They view the political system as a series of direct transactions among elite groups, and between elite groups and the general public. Supporters of the uniformity model, on the other hand, just as naturally focus on decisions *not* made and on the alternative possibilities that nondecisions leave unrealized. They also view the political system as a series of indirect transactions by those in power to manipulate the institutional arrangements that affect the way the public lives and chooses. So each model operates on different dimensions of the political system by virtue of their different concepts of power.

RULES OF EVIDENCE

Each model of politics also assumes different rules of evidence. In the pluralist model, propositions are supported with the evidence of events, things that actually occur. Events can be observed in any of the standard ways. For example, a meeting between elite figures, a board decision, an election—these are the kinds of events that figure heavily in the pluralist picture of politics. In the uniformity model propositions can be supported with the evidence of nonevents, things that don't actually happen.

How nonevents can be used as evidence sounds puzzling, for nothing happening might be thought to show nothing in the way of evidence. What makes nonevents plausible as evidence are pictures of possible realities. Imagine, for example, a society where public transportation has replaced private automobiles (not a hard feat, for in some European societies the two systems of transportation at least compete equally). Now *if* we can construct a cost-feasibility plan for such a society, and *if* we can show that the denial of the plan increased the profits of an economic elite, *then* the fact that such a society did *not* develop (a nonevent) can count in the uniformity model as evidence of elite manipulation.

Note that the concept of "interest" receives an additional twist with each of the two different rules of evidence. The reliance on actual, as opposed to possible, events predisposes the pluralist model toward a *consent* view of interest: something is in a person's interest if he agrees that it is in his interest, or at least if he is capable of agreeing that it is in his interest under different, though actual, circumstances. The reliance on possible, or nonoccurring, events in the uniformity model opens up additional variations on interest: something can be in a person's interest if he would have viewed it in his interest *in another* reality, one that could have but did not occur.

In our imaginary world of public transportation, for example, we can speculate that the public would not have wanted or needed automobiles and would have viewed it as in their interest *not* to own a car. This development of possible worlds gives the supporters of the uniformity model a powerful tool to use against the consent basis of pluralism: what people *think* they want or need is irrelevant, because the institutional arrangements of society do not take into account the wants or needs possible under different circumstances. Whether these different circumstances accurately reflect *real* human needs is, of course, more difficult to say.

Given these two theoretical differences, on (1) the concept of power and (2) rules of evidence, it no longer matters which model, the pluralist or uniformity, is "right." A more judicious view appeals: each of the two models operates with a different concept of the political system because each sees "power" differently and uses different rules of evidence. Those inclined to attach ideological labels to theoretical differences will not be satisfied with such bland judgment. Instead they prefer to explain theoretical distinctions as symptoms of ideological bias. Certainly the case can always be drawn for bias, though if it is applied to one model, it can be applied to the other. Perhaps a more modest observation is that supporters of each model are viewing *dimensions* of the political system, rather than the entire system. In a sense, both are right and both are wrong. From the point of view of a more general theory of politics, however, both are clearly inadequate.

On question (2) posed above—Is democracy compatible with elite rule?—the answers will have to wait for the discussion of democracy in Chapter 8. But it can be suggested here that how one answers this question will be determined both by what we mean by *democracy* and by which sort of elite rule we have in mind.

BLACK POLITICS: A BRIEF SKETCH

One of the most important events in American history has been the emergence in this century of black political awareness. The status of minorities in the United States has always been intertwined with the more fundamental values of democracy, and the mass demonstrations of the 1960s were closely involved with changes in the politics of black groups. One might say that black politics tests the deepest commitments of American society and also reflects the society's most fundamental changes. If these claims seem exaggerated, at the very least it must be conceded that black politics provides a provocative and complex testing ground for the theories of *groups* and *elites*.

Although any history is distorted when divided into periods of time and perhaps further distorted when events are seen as part of a movement, recognizing the changes in the black movement (read: concerted efforts) from one time period to another can help us understand the impact of black interest groups on conventional theories of politics. For convenience, and with deference to the limitations of historiography in a brief sketch, black politics in recent American society can be separated into four very rough time periods.

THE FIRST PERIOD

The first period of important black political activity took place from 1900 to about 1960. It was characterized by the dominance of the NAACP in the movement, with attendant action by the Urban League and CORE. Although some separatist activities occurred, the tactics employed were primarily integrationist and legalistic: the Legal Defense Fund and Educational Fund of the NAACP fought many successful legal battles against segregation, cases that concluded with favorable court decisions that struck at the legal basis of segregation. It is not an exaggeration to say that by the end of the 1950s, black organizations had, in effect, made segregation in public institutions illegal. But still racial barriers existed in various forms throughout the United States.

THE SECOND PERIOD

The second important period of black activity covers the years from about 1961 to 1965. During this time integrationist efforts frequently took the form of mass demonstrations. Intense rivalry among black organizations heightened, and the beginning of later schisms in the movement occurred. Representative of this period were the 1961 sit-ins by college students in Greensborough, North Carolina, the 1963 March on Washington, D.C., the successful attempt by the Mississippi Freedom Democratic Party to be seated as delegates to the Democratic National Convention of 1964, and the Selma-Montgomery March of 1965. In this period the Civil Rights Act of 1964 and the Voting Rights Act of 1965 were passed. The major provisions of each of these two important acts express the success of litigation efforts. The Civil Rights Act contained these major provisions: Title I barred unequal application of registration procedures, made a sixth-grade education proof of literacy, and required written literacy tests (as record of voter registration). Title II barred discrimination in public accommodations. Title III permitted the Justice Department to initiate desegregation suits. Title IV authorized the Attorney General to file school desegregation suits and called for a study of desegregation (later to emerge as the Coleman Report). Title VI barred discrimination in federally supported activities. Title VII barred discrimination by employers or unions with more than one-hundred employees or members. The Voting Rights Act, passed a year later, in effect amended Title I of the Civil Rights Bill by suspending the use of literacy tests or other voter qualification tests and authorizing the appointment of federal voting examiners for black registration in areas not meeting federal voter-participation requirements.

Two changes in tactics distinguished the second period of black activity. First, though legal challenges still played a role in the black movement—and in fact the legal arm of the NAACP defended those arrested in the mass movements—legislative action supplanted court decisions in efforts to bring about social change. Second, the pressures for change themselves shifted from "internal" initiatives on the legal and political components of the social system to "external" confrontations with the system.

In many ways, the two Selma marches represent this second period of black activity as well as any other events, and also seem in historical perspective to be harbingers of the violence to come. In early January of 1965, Martin Luther King announced in Selma the start of an Alabama-wide drive to register black voters. The mass demonstrations (and mass arrests) began in Selma at the start of February. Then, on March 7, 1965, the first of two marches began from Selma to the state capitol in Montgomery, Alabama. A vanguard of about five hundred marchers started slowly across a bridge leading away from Selma. Poised on the other side of the bridge was a phalanx of two hundred state troopers on foot and on horses. At a signal given by the head of the troopers, the armed force converged head-on with the marchers. The slow collision of the two groups on the dusty bridge and the swift chaos in the ranks of the marchers as troopers used nightsticks and whips to disperse the group were televised on all three networks. It was over in a matter of minutes, but the scene, like so many that were to follow in the media events of the late 1960s, seemed etched into American culture. Two days later King made another attempt to stage the march, this time a token effort arranged beforehand that traveled one mile. Though barely reaching the outskirts of Selma, King declared afterwards that "we had the greatest demonstration for freedom today that we've ever had in the South." Those who sensed the future naturally assumed he had been referring to the violent confrontation two days earlier.

THE THIRD PERIOD

The third period of black activism covered the years from 1965 to the early 1970s. Black separatism was seriously endorsed and the black movement was convulsed by inner divisions. The formation and proliferation of Afro-American Societies began. Black student unions were started on college campuses. The Black Panthers consciously conveyed a new image of the black man: armed and presumed dangerous. The mass demonstrations of the early sixties gave way to riots and increased hostility between the races. In 1965, the Los Angeles district of Watts erupted in a major riot of six days duration. An estimated 7,000 to 10,000 blacks looted, burned, and shot up the 150-block area of southwestern Los Angeles. Destruction of property was set at more than $40 million. Thirty-four persons were killed. Chicago,

Omaha, Cleveland, Baltimore, Dayton, Atlanta, San Francisco, Oakland, and other cities—including Watts again—were hit by riots in the "long hot summer" of 1966. The following year was worse. Riots occurred in Newark, Plainfield, New Jersey, Detroit, Harlem, and other areas. More violent disorders followed the assassination of Martin Luther King in 1968.

The riots, violent as they were, were not political rebellions. No organized attempts were made to overthrow the local authorities or secure physical control of the affected territories. The aim of the disorders seemed to be to inflict damage on hostile institutions, often prearranged targets but sometimes random selections (Oberschall, 1967). The riots quite frequently began in a combination of minor, unplanned events coupled with conditions ripe for civil disorders. A somewhat simplified though still helpful picture of these conditions includes (a) the presence of a black subculture, (b) limited opportunity for area residents in the larger social system, (c) a remote power structure, (d) low levels of political skill among residents, (e) high visibility of "privileged" groups and the police forces, (f) the apparent effectiveness of a disturbance on the social system (seen after the initial Watts riot), (g) the tacit legitimization of protest by the society, (h) a sanctioning of riots "by default" because of the reluctance of the society to supply effective counterforce, and (i) the presence of core groups whose agitation provided sanction to dissent (Lang and Lang, 1971). In the presence of all or some of these conditions, a minor incident like a traffic citation could be sufficient to set off a riot (it was, in fact, what occasioned the Watts riot).

Civil rights organizations carefully and prudently condemned the violence of the riots while pressuring for a change in the conditions precipitating racial violence. The Report of the National Advisory Commission on Civil Disorder (the Kerner Commission Report) in 1968 advocated as remedies (1) creating two million new jobs, (2) bringing six million housing units within the reach of low income families in the next five years, (3) expanding public housing, (4) providing greater federal funding of education, (5) establishing national (and higher) standards of welfare assistance, (6) developing "a basic floor of economic and social security for all Americans." It also recommended measures for security control of incidents.

The dialectic between civil rights groups and riots is complicated and controversial, but at least the recommendations of agencies like the Kerner Commission were beneficial to blacks. Civil rights groups are obviously stable, negotiating units; violent factions are not. But there is evidence that civil rights groups can, and did, use unplanned violence to try to negotiate favorable social outcomes. That these outcomes were not always implemented is due primarily to the inertia and outright resistance of the social system, not to the indifference of civil rights groups to the opportunities that civil disturbances provided.

Table 3.1
UNEMPLOYMENT BY RACE (PERCENT OF LABOR FORCE)

Year	1960	1965	1970	1975	1976
White	4.9	4.1	4.5	7.8	7.0
Black (and other)	10.2	8.1	8.2	13.9	13.1

Source: U.S. Bureau of the Census, *Statistical Abstract 1977*, p. 395.

THE FOURTH PERIOD

The final period of black activism covers the years from the early 1970s to the present. Although each of these four "historical" periods of time is too close to us to yield full understanding, the fourth one is literally the present and even more difficult to comprehend. Generally, both confrontation and rioting have subsided. Black activism seems to have renewed its pressure on the political system through traditional channels. Older black organizations like the NAACP have regained influence, though not dominance, in the black movement. Unlike the uniformity found during the early part of this century, today's black movement is heterogeneous, with a variety of factions and tactics. The experiences of the last two decades have changed even the older groups. The future, as with any movement, is open to speculation.

At present, however, the record of black economic success is mixed. Unemployment figures for blacks are chronically higher than for whites and, in fact, are usually more than double (in August, 1977, for example, 15.5 percent for blacks; less than half this figure for whites). An even more volatile

Table 3.2
MEDIAN INCOME IN CONSTANT (1975) DOLLARS OF FAMILIES AND INDIVIDUALS, BY RACE: 1947–1975

Year		1947	1960	1975
All Races	Family	$7,303	10,214	13,719
	Unrelated Individuals	$2,362	3,126	4,882
White	Family	$7,608	10,604	14,268
	Unrelated Individuals	$2,495	3,380	5,099
Black and other Races	Family	$3,888	5,871	9,321
	Unrelated Individuals	$1,798	1,940	3,392

Source: U.S. Bureau of the Census, *Statistical Abstract 1976*, p. 405.

Table 3.3
UNEMPLOYMENT BY RACE AND AGE (JULY 1977) (PERCENT OF LABOR FORCE)

Age	16–19	20–24	25–54	55–64	65 and Over
White	13.4	8.4	3.5	2.5	4.5
Black and other races	37.5	21.6	8.0	6.2	2.9

Source: U.S. Bureau of Labor Statistics, *Employment and Earnings* (Aug. 1977) Vol. 24, No. 8, p. 30.

situation is the high unemployment of black teenagers, a group that increased in numbers by 43 percent in the ten-year period from 1967 to 1977. In August of 1977, almost 40 percent of all black teenagers were unemployed. The pattern of "last hired, first fired" still seems to be a problem for black workers. To the degree that unemployment among urban black youths contributed to the riots of the late 1960s, the inner city is facing the prospect of continued social instability.

Median income for nonwhite *families* is more promising, rising from $3,888 in 1947 to $9,321 in 1975, an increase of 140 percent. White family income rose 88 percent in the same period. The income difference between white and nonwhite families narrowed in the twenty-eight year period. In 1947, nonwhite families earned 51 percent of white family income; in 1975, 65 percent. Black leaders pointed out, however, that such figures could be more pessimistically explained: more members of a black family were likely to be working (of economic necessity). The differences, in fact, between individual incomes of each race widened. Nonwhite individuals earned 72 percent of the income of white individuals in 1947; only 67 percent in 1977. The economic status of blacks (based on income figures) obviously does not satisfy the goals of the black movement.

BLACK ORGANIZATIONS AS INTEREST GROUPS

Standard theories of interest-group politics present a clear picture of how at least supporters of the theories think the American political system operates. The picture is drawn along the following lines: (1) American society is a pluralistic setting of conflicting, overlapping, and unorganized interests. (2) Groups express interests by making claims upon one another and upon the general society. (3) The system is more or less stable because of (a) the stabilizing origins and actions of interest groups, and (b) the responsiveness of the political system to interest claims. In general, interest-group politics is a series of balanced, pragmatic resolutions to interest-oriented demands. (See Bentley, 1949; Truman, 1971.)

Does the activity of black organizations generally correspond to this pluralistic model of interest groups?

Let us understand that many black organizations have a high percentage of whites as members. We will be using the label "black organization" to refer roughly to groups (a) primarily concerned with pursuing the interests and rights of black people, and (b) also composed of blacks to some substantial degree. Only in some cases, like the Muslims and, more recently, CORE, will such groups be limited to blacks only.

Black organizations, seen in this way, are similar to traditional interest groups in many ways. First, they are groups (obviously) and they act to maximize the interests of their members. Black groups also use many of the standard tactics of interest groups, including lobbying, publicizing the causes they endorse, supporting and opposing candidates in elections, legally challenging hostile bills and practices, and so on. On the other hand, there are significant differences between black organizations and traditional interest groups:

1. The degree of effective access to the political system, though not an easily measurable commodity, has *historically* been more limited for black organizations. The intractability of the race issue is well documented in the sociology of American society. In spite of the legal successes at the federal level in the 1940s and 1950s, racial segregation persisted informally in a wide range of American institutions (including, especially in the North, the educational system at the primary and secondary levels). The very exhaustion of legal remedies provides a rational explanation for the shift to mass demonstrations characterizing black activity in the 1960s.

Voting itself proved an inadequate way to change the system. Even with successful registration of blacks, the vote—long regarded as among the most effective of political resources (Dahl, 1971)—turned out to be moderately successful at securing black interest only where the white voters are evenly divided, where residential areas are heavily black, where party attachment is weak, and where blacks are mobile between the major political parties (Mathews and Prothro, 1966; Keech, 1968). The mixed effectiveness of both legal and voting resources is consistent with symbolic access to the political system (blacks talking with political leaders), but presents a restricted picture of effective access.

2. Interest groups make claims on the basis of shared attitudes, which express their interests. Black organizations do make interest-oriented demands, but they also, and perhaps most importantly, seek *rights*.

The differences between *interests* and *rights* can be shown with a simple example. Let us say that I have an interest in having my salary raised. I go to my employer with a request for a $5,000 raise. (Inflation, remember?) He balks, citing increased expenses in the business. I remind him of my value to the company. He counters with an offer of a $2,000 increment. We haggle for several minutes, finally settling on a $3,500 increase. Not bad by any standards. In contrast, suppose that I have a clause in my contract stating that this year I am to get a $5,000 raise. I still have an interest in raising my salary. Now, however, I also have *right* to a raise, and for a precise amount, at that. Now, when I go to my employer's office, I do not bargain; I point out what is mine by lawful agreement.

Put more formally, an interest is, roughly, anything that increases opportunities to get what one wants or needs (Barry, 1965). A right, on the other hand, is that which is due one by virtue of a just claim. *Interests*, as expected, easily cover such concrete gains as salary increases, shorter working hours, improved working conditions, and so on. *Rights* cover contractual agreements on any of these matters, and also such fundamental values as free speech, equality before the law, and so on. *Interests* are negotiable terms; *rights* are not. Whether, for example, the minimum wage is set at one figure or another can be settled by bargaining among the interested parties. But whether a group has equality before the law is not an issue open to adjustment or compromise. The concern of black organizations with rights as well as interests makes black interest groups, by the logic of rights, less able to adjust *all* of their demands to the demands of competing interest groups. On this token, some of the pragmatic restraint of interest-group politics did in fact give way in the 1960s to black slogans of "nonnegotiable" demands.

3. White interest groups typically represent segments of the white community, in a dual sense: (a) particular populations are represented by such organizations as labor unions or professional associations and (b) only some interests of each individual are represented by each organization—an individual is not, for example, totally represented by his economic interests alone. Black organizations, on the other hand, sometimes represent (a) the entire black population and (b) a more complete sense of the individuals that make up the black population. This two-fold sense of complete representation is in large part a function of black organizations' attempts to secure rights. The right, say, to equality before the law is not divided among those seeking it, nor is the right something that some need and others don't. Rather, it is uniformly required by all relevant individuals. Most rights are also central to the identity of each individual, not a separable part of him, like an economic interest, that competes with other parts. For example, an individual may trade off economic benefit with other interests (making money versus raising a family). But we do not usually view our constitutional rights as goods to be traded for other things.

Black organizations, in the dual sense of complete and inseparable representation, more totally represent their constituents. A more total representation operates against the moderating character of interest-group politics in one important respect: the issues sought are, once more, less amenable to compromise than partially representative issues, which can be traded off with each other.

The features of black politics outlined here—limited effective access to the political system, demands for rights, and a concern with more totally representative issues—quite reasonably lead to the distinctive political tactics employed by black groups. These include (1) an appeal to the *moral* (as opposed to self-interested) concerns of the larger community; (2) a concentration on the general public as well as on particular government agencies (including the reliance on mass demonstrations of the early 1960s); (3) a reformist, instead of a maintenance, orientation (progressive change rather than status quo); and (4) a parasitic dependence, at the beginning, on white support, with a later shift to independence.

These tactics do not differ in kind from those used by white groups, but they do differ significantly in emphasis. The moral, general, and reformist character of black groups is unlike the traditional activity of such groups as, say, the Teamsters or American Association of University Professors. Also, the rapid change from dependence to autonomy represents a polar shift not found in the history of most white interest groups.

These differences between black organizations and white interest groups do not imply that standard interest group theories are white theories and, therefore, inappropriate for understanding black political activity. The differences do suggest that recent black politics introduces factors that standard group theories do not emphasize. We know from recent experience that the American political system is not always "in balance." When access to the political system is ineffective, interests may be overriden by more total, peremptory values that seek violent outlets. We also know that the rules of the game are not always adequate restraints when stakes are high, nor even stable objects of consensus when fundamental values clash with each other.

ELITE CONCEPTS IN THE BLACK EXPERIENCE

The black movement has been replete with popular myths of elitism on both sides of the political struggles. Those outside the movement saw a few black leaders bringing about the entire sequence of events known as "the black revolution." (Remember the phrase "outside agitators"?) The "black power" slogan of recent history no doubt reinforced this view. Those inside the movement, on the other hand, saw a homogeneous elite extending from red-necked sheriffs to society's power structure as the source of all black troubles. (Remember the references to a uniform "Whitey"?)

But mythology aside, we have seen how different concepts of *power* and *interest* can lead to radically divergent views of the American political system. Though no single view of history can rule on the differences between the pluralist and uniformity models of elite rule, the uniformity model does seem more valuable in explaining the black movement, for several reasons.

First, the idea of "nondecisions" has great appeal in explaining obstructions to reformist movements. A reform effort in politics aims at changing some state of affairs and the degree of change is the measure of success: to what extent has the status quo changed into the desired end? To avoid reform only requires doing nothing. Therefore, the two key ingredients of a nondecision are present if reform fails: (1) the idea of what might have been, and (2) the explanation of the failure to reach it as the absence of needed decisions. Of course, it is easy to fall into paranoia with such analysis. But it is also easy to see how nondecisions appeal to failed reformists.

Second, the emphasis on rights in the black movement favors the hypothetical worlds central to the uniformity model. Recall that the uniformity model dismisses any strong reliance on what people may in fact *want* in the real world. Just because people want to drive private automobiles does not mean a system of private transportation is more desirable. People might have preferred public transportation if such a system had been allowed to develop. Hypothesizing a world of public transportation thus creates a source of "real" preferences in the uniformity model. A similar use of hypothetical worlds in part forms the logic of "rights" arguments. What black people would be capable of doing in a hypothetical world of completely granted rights fueled the thoughts and pronouncements of black leaders. Actual social conditions, deprived as they were, could not stand as conditions for the suppression of "real" preferences.

Third. the tactics of both white and black groups involved manipulating social conditions to achieve an indirect power transaction. Recall again that the uniformity model stresses the exercise of power through institutions, not in direct relationships. The black movement's reliance on economic boycotts and its general emphasis on structural change favors the uniformity model's view of power.

The explanation of the black movement made by the uniformity model is of course strongest when the movement is granted rationality from the point of view of its supporters. Its detractors may want to explain it in terms of purely random historical occurrences, giving it no sense in terms of either the pluralist or uniformity models. But if we accept that the movement is rational, then those ideas of nondecision, hypothetical worlds, and indirect power transactions—all part of the uniformity model—are what make most sense.

On the other hand, the dangers of such an assignment are only too real. Besides the obvious risk of glibness, the key ideas of the uniformity model only partially account for events in the black movement. The concepts of the uniformity model apply unevenly to different dimensions of black politics. (For example, *nondecisions* can explain the role of the white power structure; *indirect power* more appropriately explains black activity.) The key concepts of *power*, *interest*, and even *elites*, seem themselves to capture only a section of political life.

Like interest group theory, the use of *elite* concepts seems restricted when the complexities of the entire policy process are entertained seriously.

THE WOMEN'S MOVEMENT: EARLY HISTORY

The women's movement is like the black movement in one important respect: participants have joined together on the basis of shared attitudes *and* a common biological feature. As race is the physical denominator in black interest groups, so sex is in the women's movement. In both cases, because of the biological basis for unity, the groupings are unlike standard economic or social associations. While a machinist, for example, can become a teacher, it is almost impossible for a black to become a white or a woman to become a man. Physical identity is the foundation for each respective social movement.

The women's movement is both old and new, with early feminist activity beginning in the nineteenth century. One of the first goals of the women's movement was to secure equal educational opportunities for women, and in 1833 Oberlin became the first college to accept both men and women. These early feminist activities merged quickly with the abolitionist movement. But when women joined the general efforts to abolish slavery, they encountered a problem to be repeated in this century's civil rights movement: male abolitionist leaders did not permit them to function as equals. Women were expected to take on the biblical role of dependence and passivity.

Biblical roles, then and now, were not universally acclaimed by women. Feminist activities persisted through and after the Civil War in an attempt to gain women legal rights to their own property and wealth, guardianship of their children, and divorce rights. After the Civil War, the Thirteenth Amendment, abolishing slavery, was ratified. The Fourteenth Amendment, designed to insure the general rights under law of all persons regardless of race, was not interpreted as applying to women. The male proponents of "equal rights" were adamant in keeping feminist issues out of the drive for racial equality. Women were equally unsuccessful in extending to both sexes the Fifteenth Amendment's enfranchisement of all races.

Failure to gain the vote through the Fifteenth Amendment turned the feminist movement toward the goal of suffrage for women. From 1870 until 1920, it was the first priority of the women's movement. In 1869, however, the movement divided into two major factions on the issue of tactics. The National Women Suffrage Association developed a broad program of women's rights, with the vote seen as an instrument to secure these rights. The American Women Suffrage Association concentrated its attention on the vote itself, not other more controversial issues like divorce (espoused by the National groups). Both groups worked in their own ways toward enfranchising women.

Still another reform movement arose later in the nineteenth century: the temperance movement. Temperance reformers sought legal restrictions on the sale and consumption of alcohol. Many feminist leaders joined temperance efforts, and even formed their own temperance groups when denied membership in male-dominated associations. Restrictions on alcohol were in the interests of women in the nineteenth century, for the laws gave married women no protection against drunken husbands. Nevertheless, some feminist leaders sought a strategy separating temperance issues and women's suffrage, on the prudent grounds that linking the two would consolidate the liquor and brewing industries' opposition to *both* temperance and feminist movements.

By 1890, the two major factions of the women's movement, the National and American suffrage groups, had merged, and securing the vote for women became the sole feminist issue. More militant suffragists took over the movement in the early twentieth century, and a splinter group, the Congressional Union, was formed in 1913 to work on a constitutional amendment to enfranchise women. These efforts succeeded finally in 1920, when the Nineteenth Amendment was ratified. The achievement of the vote and the assumption that it would lead to equality led the women's movement into a dormant state from which it would not awaken for forty years.

THE NEW WOMEN'S MOVEMENT

Pat Haven, in "Why We Came Together," describes what it was like to sense the budding feminist movement of the 1960s:

But as much as we talked about men even then we had begun to talk about ourselves as women, as separate from men—about sex and about our bodies—the shame, pride, fear and pain and probably above all, of course, the lack of ownership. . . . finally we did decide to meet (as women). (Quoted in Hole and Levine, 1971, p. 121)

Meetings of the type described by Ms. Haven were inspired by several earlier events. Millions of women were called into industry in World War II, forever dispelling the myth that women were incapable of holding jobs traditionally reserved for men. Post-war expansion of the economy produced many service industries with appropriate openings for women. Rising costs often compelled many women to seek, and find, such jobs. Working wives made middle-class life possible for many families. Ideas changed in the 1950s with changes in birth control techniques, wider educational experiences, smaller families. The 1960s increased the sensitivity of the American people to deprived groups through the Vietnam War protests, the civil rights movement, the general rebellion of youth. Though even protest leaders were frequently male and chauvinistic, the recognition of minority exploitation by American society established the conditions for the growing self-awareness of women as a deprived group.

The recent women's movement is unlike earlier feminist activities in stressing two goals equally.

First, like earlier efforts in the nineteenth century, the women's movement today aims at changing the legal and social institutions that discriminate on the basis of sex. The movement, for example, has campaigned for "equal pay for equal work," and was successful in adding *sex* to the bans against discrimination on grounds of race, color, creed, and national origin contained in Title VII of the 1964 Civil Rights Act. Today's efforts to change formal or institutional sex bias are like the nineteenth and early twentieth century movements at institutional reform: they aim to alter the external social structures of sex discrimination.

Second, and unlike earlier efforts, the women's movement today also concentrates on changing the internal restrictions brought about by sexist attitudes. Stereotypes of women's roles, while less and less biblical in origin, still maintain a passive, secondary role for women while stressing the activist, primary role for men. For example, little girls too often see themselves as nurses, boys as doctors; women are housekeepers (or worse, "housewives," as if married to the house); men are breadwinners. These stereotypes are held by both men and women. The second, equally important, goal of the new women's movement is to change such sexist attitudes in both sexes.

Any recent chronology of institutional change suggests that the first goal of the women's movement has met with some success. In 1961, President John Kennedy established the first Presidential Commission on the Status of Women in the history of the country. In the following year the president issued a directive reversing a traditional ban on women in high-level civil service jobs. In 1965, a bill was passed in Congress requiring equal pay for women employed in the same capacity as men. The Civil Rights Act of 1964

Table 3.4
UNEMPLOYMENT BY SEX (PERCENT OF LABOR FORCE)

Year	1967	1970	1973	1976
Male	3.1	4.4	4.1	7.0
Female	5.2	5.9	6.0	8.6

Source: U.S. Bureau of Labor Statistics, *Employment and Earnings* (Aug. 1977) Vol. 24, No. 8, p. 29.

mandated equal opportunity in employment for both sexes. In 1967, President Lyndon Johnson signed an executive order prohibiting sex discrimination in federal employment and by federal contractors and subcontractors. Later that year Johnson also eliminated restrictions that prohibited a woman from attaining rank higher than a colonel in the armed forces. Although a considerable distance separates enactments from real equality between the sexes, the *laws* on sexual equality have undergone major changes.

The Ninety-second Congress was especially responsive to the needs of women. The 1972 Equal Employment Opportunity Act extended the coverage of equal opportunity requirements to public and private educational institutions, state and local governments, and employers and unions with fifteen (in contrast to the older threshold of twenty-five) or more members—all previously exempt. In addition, legislation barred sex discrimination in the administration of the Comprehensive Health Manpower Act of 1971 and the Nurses Training Act of 1971. Income tax deductions were provided for child care. Title IX of the Educational Amendments Act of 1972 prohibited sex discrimination in all federally aided education programs. *Legal* equality was becoming a reality by the early and mid seventies.

More recent efforts at institutional change have focused on a state-by-state campaign to gain ratification of the Equal Rights Amendment (ERA) to the U.S. Constitution. The Amendment states: "Equality of Rights under the law shall not be denied or abridged by the United States or by any State on account of sex." The ERA was in Congress, held in the House Judiciary Committee, for twenty-two years before reaching the floor of the House of Representatives. In 1970, Representative Martha Griffiths got the ERA to the House floor by means of a discharge petition, where it passed by a surprising majority of 352 to 15. The amendment had a rougher time in the Senate, but finally emerged from Congress in 1972 for ratification efforts in the separate states.

Where efforts at institutional reform seem *not* to be succeeding at the same pace is in *jobs*. In 1956, preliberation days, the median pay for women working full time was 63 percent of the midpoint in the men's scale. In 1976, the figure for women was down to 60 percent. Census figures show that, in 1960, women with full-time jobs had median earnings of $3,296, compared to a median figure of $5,435 for men. But while median earnings for men had climbed to $13,859 by 1976, women's earnings only increased to $8,312. Though the gap between men and women's earnings is not increasing dramatically, women's earnings are not keeping pace with men's. There are many explanations for these figures, including an optimistic one: the doubling of the number of women in the labor force in the last quarter-century, to 38.4 million, has unavoidably resulted in an increase of women in low-paying jobs. But whatever the interpretation (and there are far more pessimistic ones), the spectacle of women in the president's cabinet, in our highest

Table 3.5
MEDIAN INCOME BY SEX (IN DOLLARS)

Year	1960	1970	1976
Male	5,435	9,184	13,859
Female	3,296	5,440	8,312

Source: U.S. Bureau of the Census, *Statistical Abstract 1976*, and *1977*, p. 414 (1976) and p. 452 (1977).

courts, and in the corporate executive suites, obscures the economic plight of comparatively low-paid women in more ordinary work.

How successful the women's movement has been in achieving this second goal is more difficult to assess. One indicator of success may be the growing tendency of women in all walks of life to challenge what they regard as sexist rules and attitudes. In 1970, for example, damage suits against employers were filed by women in professions as disparate as airline stewardesses (against TWA) and military officers (a woman air force captain against the U.S. military). Another indicator might be the increasing willingness of traditional male bastions to open their doors to women (though often under the duress of court orders). The National Press Club of Washington, D.C., voted in 1970 to admit women to its membership. Both the Boy Scouts and U.S. Senate pages can now be girls. Though many such changes are trivial, they indicate a slow and painful change in sexist attitudes.

Resistance to the women's movement is still strong. In a memorable quote, Shirley Chisholm reflected on being the first black woman elected to the House of Representatives in 1968: "In the political world I have been far oftener discriminated against because I am a woman than because I am black. When I decided to run for Congress I knew I would encounter both antiblack and antifeminist sentiments. What surprised me was the much greater virulence of the sex discrimination." (Hole and Levine, 1971, p. 408) Sometimes opposition to feminist ideas can come from women. A Denver-based project of the Education Commission of the States released in 1977 the results of a survey of 4,600 seventeen-year-olds on the role of women in society. The results showed that almost one in four of the females in the survey felt that a woman's place is in the home "where she can cook, clean house and take care of the children" (in the words of one respondent).

Also, reservations have been expressed on the realistic possibilities for full equality between the sexes. Dr. Judith Bardwick, a psychologist, a feminist, and a dean at the University of Michigan, is beginning to believe that biology may yet place ceilings on feminine goals: "If you define dominance as who occupies formal roles of responsibility, then there is no society where males are not dominant," she has said. "When something is so universal, the probability is—as reluctant as I am to say it—that there is some quality of the organism that leads to this condition. So women may achieve greater parity, but will they achieve full parity? I don't know." (New York Times, November 30, 1977)

SOME BASIC FEMINIST CONCERNS

The central idea in the modern women's movement is perhaps the simplest: that sex should make no difference in how human beings are treated. In this respect, the black and women's movements are similar. Both deny the *social* or *psychological* importance of a biological distinction. The inequalities between men and women in society have occurred not because of innate differences, feminists maintain, but because of the reversible values societies have conventionally placed on these biological differences. These values have caused great harm to men and women, the argument continues, and should be discarded. By discarding them we can find the key to our general liberation as human beings.

One problem that the women's movement, old and new, has encountered is the tendency of men to ridicule feminist efforts. Some of the humor is well grounded. For example, feminist attempts to change words with male components sometimes have ludicrous outcomes. Transforming *gentlemen* to *gentlepeople* or something similar not only changes meaning but opens the door to satire. Similarly, changing *mankind* to *genuskind*, as one feminist urged, only results in the absurd term *kind-kind* (*genus* meaning *kind*). But the central goal of the new women's movement, that of liberating ourselves from historical cages of our own making, is so powerful in its implications that ridicule cannot do serious damage.

The view that sex is not a difference that makes a difference is new. Even as recently as 1970, a physician, Dr. Edgar Berman, argued before the Democratic Party's Committee on National Priorities that the menstrual cycle and menopause make a woman executive less reliable than a male counterpart of the same age. Unfortunately for the good doctor, he chose President John Kennedy as his exemplar, when it was well known that Kennedy had been under cortisone treatment for Addison's disease during his entire incumbency. The women's movement is more inclined to favor another doctor's response to sexual differences: Samuel Johnson, when asked whether man or woman is more intelligent, replied, "Which man and which woman?" Feminists maintain that no general superiority distinguishes the sexes and that the best *persons* should be selected for any job at any time.

Feminists do not, however, stop at the rejection of differences based on the biological distinction of sex. The women's movement also maintains that *beliefs* in the fallacy of biological differences have caused a sex-role system assigning an inferior status to women. Language reflects such a system. The absurdities of *gentlepeople* and *genuskind* aside, the subtle value distinctions between *bachelor* and *spinster*, the negative connotations of *bitch*, or the chronic use of *he* to denote any person—all, and more, represent subtle sexual bias. Feminists maintain that such institutions of society as the family, the educational system, and the business world both consciously and unwittingly reinforce a false male superiority. Because of this social bias, the women's movement has also actively criticized sex-role stereotyping and emphasized general education on how the sexes are in fact equal.

The two dominant concerns of the feminist movement seem to be (1) a rejection of the importance of sexual differences and (2) a radical critique of sex-role stereotyping in Western societies (Hole and Levine, 1971).

INTERESTS AND RIGHTS IN THE WOMEN'S MOVEMENT

Many women are currently organized in interest groups. The National Organization for Women (NOW), for example, was organized in 1968 with express demands to be made on other interest groups and on the social system in general. The list of demands in the 1968 NOW charter included (1) the Equal Rights Amendment, (2) laws banning sex discrimination in employment, (3) maternity leave rights in employment and in Social Security benefits, (4) tax deduction for home and child care expenses for working parents, (5) child care centers, (6) equal and unsegregated education, (6) equal job training opportunities and allowances for women in poverty, and (7) the right of women to control their reproductive lives.

Certainly these demands are in the interests of women, on the whole, to achieve. Many, such as tax deductions for child care, have become laws clearly in the interests of women to maintain. But of greater significance, the 1968 NOW charter, while elaborating the seven items as demands, outlined them in a preface as a bill of *rights*. The women's movement, like much of the black movement, is demanding what it perceives as due women on the basis of just claims, not simply interests.

The reappearance of rights in interest group activity gives us a chance to see some more general relationships between rights and interests in American politics. We have seen how demands based on rights are, by the logic of rights, less amenable to compromise than are demands based on interests. Let us add to the general idea of rights these further considerations (Okun, 1975): (1) There is no monetary charge for rights. The provisions of the ERA, for example, have no market value, while wages, retirement plans, and peanuts do. (2) One consequence of the nonmonetary status of rights (already noted) is that they are not suitable for trading, or buying and selling. We can trade away free tuition at colleges for better instructors, but "equality before the law" is not an appropriate barter for higher take-home pay. Constitutional rights have no price tags. King John in Magna Carta (A.D. 1215) declared a long-standing conviction: "To none will we sell. . . . justice."

(3) In addition, rights are universally distributed to all members of the class of people covered by the rights. They are not parceled out to some at the expense of others. The rights of women, for example, even though acquired through the efforts of a few, are available to all women once they are available at all. (They are, in this sense, "public goods.") (4) Also, by virtue of their universality, rights stress equality at the expense of other goods, especially market commodities. The ERA, for example, would likely be pushed by women's groups even if it meant a lower standard of living for men and women. (5) Finally, rights are not distributed as rewards, or withheld as penalties. Women, for example, demand "equal pay for equal work" not because it would be nice to have, but because they have a *right* to such pay.

The picture of "rights" outlined in one through five above is in part an idealized one. It represents the common view that inequalities in other social areas ought not to affect basic rights, a view developed recently by John Rawls on the right to liberty (which we will discuss in Chapter 7). But in the real world, economic inequalities chronically affect rights. "Equality before the law," for example, is a basic constitutional right in America. In reality, having the money to hire superior legal services gives the wealthy a decided advantage before the law. Campaign contributions, lobbying, and so on—studies of politics are replete with the influence money can have on even the most basic rights.

This reality, that social inequalities affect rights, injects politics into group efforts to secure rights. Women's groups, like black groups, demand basic rights. But to guarantee such rights frequently requires a general adjustment of economic interests. The women's movement, like all interest groups, has concentrated on political and economic reform as a *means* to acquire equal status in society. Feminist groups have gone further and attempted attitudinal reform, involving changes in our perception of sexual roles. Both women and blacks are unusual interest groups in their strong demands for rights. But both are organized as political instruments to change the institutions of society that unavoidably influence the exercise of basic rights.

The examples of black organizations and feminist groups suggest these two observations on the important interplay between rights and interests in American politics: (1) rights are less easily negotiated than interests and so, by their logic, introduce inflexibility into political issues; and (2) the securing of rights in the political world requires adjusting interest-oriented items like income, an adjustment that typically involves the usual political tactics of persuasion, pressure, compromise, and so on. Thus rights are unlike interests, but often depend on interest items for their successful realization.

THE "FREE RIDER" PROBLEM

Perhaps the most serious challenge to standard interest-group theory is the rationality of a *"free rider"* option. If interest-group theory does not fit a variety of interest groups, amendments to the theory are in order. The emphasis on rights in the black and women's movements, for example, can be accommodated with changes here and there in group theories. But the free-rider problem challenges the *logic* of interest-group theory, not merely the theory's correspondence with actual events. As a logical challenge, it offers an alternative method for explaining the origin and operation of interest groups.

Let us review briefly. Interest groups form, according to standard theories of groups, because it is to the advantage of individuals with shared attitudes to organize as an interest group. The elderly in American society, for example, can protect and maximize their interests if they form organizations that make demands on other groups and on the political system in general. If a group of people has a reason to organize to protect its interests, then it also seems to follow that each and every individual in that group has a reason to support that organization. After all, the organization is working in the interests of each person in it. This gives us a neat explanation for the formation and operation of interest groups: shared interests lead people to form interest groups, and these interests are incentives for each individual to support the group's efforts to secure these interests.

This picture of how interest groups form and operate has been challenged (Olson, 1971). The charge is specifically this: that there is a fallacy in thinking that the reason for organizing an interest group is also a reason for supporting its efforts once it is organized. We can easily imagine all sorts of irrational motives for not supporting group efforts. A senior citizen may think he can be an effective lobbying force on his own. (Unless he has considerable resources, he cannot be.) Or members of a group may be ignorant of the efforts of their organization, thinking that the group is not securing their interests. Conversely, individuals may have good rational reasons to drop out of a group—the group's efforts may in fact *not* protect or maximize their interests.

The free rider challenge, however, is interesting precisely because it assumes, first, that the individuals in a group are acting rationally, and, second, that the group is in fact acting in the interests of each and every one of its members. The challenge is this: under certain circumstances it is rational for an individual *not* to participate in group efforts even when the group's efforts are in his interests.

How can this claim be supported? Let's state a rationality calculation this way (Riker and Ordeshook, 1973):

$$B_i - C_i > B_k - C_k$$

The interpretation of this formula is very simple. The letter B stands for "benefits." The letter C stands for "costs." The smaller letters, i and k (in the equation as subscripts), represent alternative actions. So, if the benefits minus the costs of one alternative (i) is a figure greater than ($>$) the benefits minus the costs of another alternative (k), then the first alternative (i) is preferable to the second (k). It is then rational to do i rather than k.

$$i > k$$

Let's now transfer this simple cost-benefit equation to interest group theory. First, the theory provides us with the calculation on whether to organize an interest. The elderly will rationally set up interest groups if the benefits minus the costs of organizing are greater than the benefits minus the costs of remaining unorganized. Let us assume that this is in fact the case. Second, we have the calculation, or decision, made by each individual on whether to support the organization's efforts to secure these interests. Again, each individual as a rational creature decides to support the group's efforts only if the benefits-minus-costs amount of supporting is greater than the benefits-minus-costs amount of not supporting.

The second decision contains the joker *if* the outcome of group effort is a public good. Let's review again. One of the important features of a "public good" is that it is "nonexcludable," meaning that if it is available to anyone, then it is available to everyone. A good example is a defense policy against nuclear attack. If there is protection at all, everyone is protected. Public goods are unlike divisible, or competitive, goods, which can be distributed to some and denied to others. Retirement plans are examples of divisible goods.

The key feature of a public good is that an individual can consume it whether he has contributed to the efforts of producing it or not. If, for example, you do not pay your taxes, you are still as protected from nuclear attack as all those people who do pay taxes. On the other hand, if you do not make regular contributions to a retirement fund, you can be excluded from its benefits. Suppose now that an interest group is producing a public good. It follows that an individual can get the good without effort, for the good is nonexcludable. Such a person is a "free rider"; he benefits from the outcomes of group efforts without contributing to the costs of producing the good.

The free rider is acting unfairly, of course. He is getting what other people have worked to obtain. But while unfair, the free rider is eminently rational on simple benefit-cost calculations. He is getting the benefits of group action, the good that is produced, without incurring any of the production costs. So, in our equation, if an action, i, joining in group efforts to secure a benefit, is compared to another action, k, getting the same benefit without the cost of participating in the group efforts, then i will always be preferable to k. One problem with such a calculation, of course, is that if each individual carries it through, no joint effort will occur. So, on the assumption that the outcome of a group effort is desirable, rational decisions by enough individuals to become free riders leads to an irrational outcome—failure to produce the maximum benefits possible through joint efforts and, in extreme cases, failure to produce any benefit whatsoever.

WHAT MAKES THE FREE RIDER OPTION AN IRRATIONAL CHOICE

The free rider option is neither rational nor possible in all groups. If groups produce divisible goods, then those who do not participate can be excluded. Sometimes a good is consumed exactly as payment is extracted, as occurs on toll roads. With other goods, such as retirement plans, only those who contribute at some point can receive the benefits. But even with nonexcludable goods, like nuclear defense, the rationality of the free rider option varies with group size (Olson, 1971).

Imagine for a moment a group of only one hundred people. Let us say that they fulfill, in small scale, the conditions for the formation of an interest group. They share interests that will be better promoted in concert than in separate actions. As a result, they organize into an interest group. Let us also say that the outcomes of their joint efforts are public goods. A fanciful situation can illustrate this argument. Our hundred people form a mutual protection society, organized to keep hoodlums from attacking their neighborhood. Their method is to hire several armed private policemen to patrol the area.

The good produced by the joint effort, protection and perhaps even security, is nonexcludable. Unless we expand the fanciful features of the example to include sanctions against noncontributors, we can assume that all one-hundred residents living in the neighborhood are protected. (Crooks are not allowed to steal from anyone on the street, regardless of contributions.) All the same, the rationality of a free rider choice by any of the hundred organizers is severely qualified by the very size of the group. The smallness of the group makes these differences:

1. The contribution of any one individual in the group amounts to a substantial proportion of the group efforts. Any small number of individuals may even be decisive for production of the good. If, for example, even ten of our hundred-member group withdraw their support, it might be financially impossible for the rest to hire a system of private policemen.

2. The organization costs of small groups are lower than those of large groups; coordination and communication efforts are less difficult in a small group. (Three people can more easily arrange a committee meeting than thirty.) So our hundred-member group may not have to provide for substan-

tial participation costs (actual administration or the cost of hiring full-time administrators) that members of large groups do. Perhaps a few phone calls will satisfy the group effort. In short, the free rider choice may save so little in organizational costs as to be meaningless when calculated on that basis.

3. Although the production (not organizational) costs of goods may be larger in small groups, the benefits can also be greater. If our hundred-member group hired ten full-time quality private policemen to patrol the area, then the ratio is one policeman per ten individuals. That's pretty good protection—virtually blanket coverage. It is also likely to be expensive. But the same protection ratio over a million-member group may be impossible to achieve. (Are there one hundred thousand *quality* private policemen available for full-time work?) If the same number of policemen is hired for double or triple the number of people, the arrangement becomes less expensive if the costs are distributed among the additional people as well. But the amount of the good—the effective protection—diminishes for each member of the group. Therefore, the fact of smallness may provide a more favorable return on costs; if you get more for your money, it is less rational to withhold the money, especially if withholding jeopardizes the production of the good you want.

4. Nonparticipation may have costs, and participation may have benefits, in small groups. Choosing not to participate is probably harder in small than in larger groups. If even one person in our hundred-member group thinks he can get the protection he needs without being made to pay for it, he may be sadly mistaken. The protection itself may come his way, but not without social pressures to pay. The costs of alienating his neighbors may turn out to be more expensive than paying up in the first place. The intrinsic benefits of participation are also higher in small groups. If one's efforts can make a difference, then making a contribution can be a reward instead of merely a cost.

These four differences intrinsic to small groups can produce two forms of voluntary group action that successfully obtain desirable goods (Olson, 1971). One is the classic pattern emphasized in standard interest group theories. All, or most, members of the group join in efforts to secure a good that is, roughly, equally in the interests of everyone in the group. Each individual has calculated rationally that the gain to him of getting the good is more than the total cost, and that joining the group effort is more beneficial than not. In our example, all one hundred people voluntarily contribute the necessary money for the private protection system.

The other form of voluntary group action does not quite fit the picture provided by standard interest group theory. If the benefit from a good is so high for a few individuals that it exceeds the entire costs of the good, then these individuals will provide the good on their own, even if they have to bear such costs themselves. A few people in our hundred-member group may really need the neighborhood protected, perhaps because they have businesses that can show a profit only if they stay open all night and their customers feel secure about the area. These few people may then find it rational to voluntarily provide the security force out of their own pockets. The rest of the neighborhood cannot really be considered free riders, because they do not have such an overriding interest (as do the few businessmen) in the private police force. Perhaps they are best viewed as beneficiaries of an unbalanced system of security needs.

This second type of voluntary action, by the few rather than the many, can occur at some point in the development of potentially large groups. Take the development of the women's movement in its recent stages, for example: though in principle the benefits extended to all women, only a few women were active in its early stages because, for monetary, prestige, and intellectual reasons, the group benefits to this elite cadre were sufficiently great to override the costs of trying to provide the collective goods of the feminist movement on their own. Much of the efforts of feminist leaders, in fact, have been directed at convincing women that organizing as a group has advantages to women as a general class of participants.

Both forms of voluntary action, however, by the many or the few, depend initially on smallness. In the first case, the small size of the group increases the rational inclination for everyone to participate. In the second case, the small size of the group makes the cost-benefit ratio favorable for the vitally interested few. (If the neighborhood in our fanciful case were too large, the costs of protection would be beyond the means of just a few residents.) Smallness, in each case, leads to the *voluntary* production of the good by rational individuals.

WHAT MAKES THE FREE RIDER
A RATIONAL CHOICE

Several things happen to rational calculations when the size of a group increases.

1. No single individual is likely to make a decisive contribution in a large group. Imagine that our hundred-member group expands to a hundred thousand, each contributing to the maintenance of a security force. The withdrawal of a single member is not going to jeopardize the production of the good. The remaining contributors can still provide the security system.

2. Organizational costs frequently increase in large groups. If increase in size brings with it an increase in the differences among group members, organizational costs are even higher. Communicating and coordinating the efforts of a numerically large group can be very costly. (Just finding out what

the membership wants to do can be expensive.) If the group is heterogeneous, and the differences among members occur on institutional divisions, ideological convictions, and so on, bargaining costs must now be added to the costs figured on numbers alone. Imagine a group of one-hundred thousand *also* divided over basic strategy. Getting such a collection to operate as a group, even with shared interests, may be quite an undertaking.

3. The share of good provided may diminish with increased size. Again, a system of private policemen may not effectively provide security for one-hundred thousand people. The ratio of cost to benefit may thus be unfavorable, even though costs per member are lower than those paid per member in a small group.

4. The costs of not participating in large groups can, all other things equal, be avoided if participation is on a voluntary basis. Escaping detection when not complying is probably easier in large groups, and the escape avoids the social costs of group pressure. Conversely, the intrinsic benefits of participation, especially when created by a sense of efficacy, are missing in large groups. If one's actions have little important effect on the success of the group effort, it is hard to get excited about contributing to this effort.

The four results of increased group size outlined above make the free rider option more rational in large than in small groups. The rational individual discovers that one can have the good produced by the group without contributing to the group's efforts, and the contribution is more cost than benefit anyway. No one will miss the contribution; one individual doesn't make a real difference. The benefits do not outweigh the costs when looked at closely. No wonder that the free rider option appeals in large groups.

THE FREE RIDER AND INTEREST GROUP THEORY

Standard interest group theories assume that a latent group will transform itself into an actual group if it becomes rational to do so. The key to this assumption is that if a group has a reason or incentive to organize its interests, then rational individuals in that group will have reason or incentive to support the organization working in their interests. The rationality of a free rider option, however, suggests that large groups do *not* provide general rational incentives for voluntary participation in group efforts *even when* it is rational for each individual to have the good that the group can provide (Olson, 1971). As a result interest groups may never form on a voluntary basis, for the general appeal of trying out the free rider option will cause organizations to collapse for want of support before they can become established, or even after they are established.

What is the solution? Two methods of resolving the free rider problem suggest themselves.

ETHICAL

Since the free rider is acting unfairly, ethical appeal is appropriate. One form that ethical appeals take is to point out the right (or moral) thing to do. Logic can be part of such an appeal. The generalization argument, for example, could be outlined to the free rider: think of what would happen if everyone did that. This argument, known to us since we were children (in every generation), can unfortunately be turned inside out by smart thinkers attuned to rational self-interest. Yosarian in Joseph Heller's novel, *Catch 22*, is asked by officers to consider what would happen if everyone refused to fly bomber missions (as he is doing). He quite sensibly replies: "Then I'd be a damn fool to feel any different."

The strength of an ethical appeal to the free rider is finally internal. Doing the right thing must be desirable even if all others do the wrong thing. Is such an appeal intelligible? One is entitled to a certain amount of skepticism on the effectiveness of ethical appeals. But the skepticism can be muted if the internal rewards of doing the right thing can be viewed as participation benefits. When internal, or psychological, rewards are introduced, participation is no longer merely a cost (Riker and Ordeshook, 1973). The rewards of joining in group efforts can be an intrinsic benefit regardless of whether others give approval and independent of any efficacy toward outcomes. The *ethical* individual thus cannot choose the free rider option without losing the psychological benefit of acting fairly that participation itself provides, however large the group. Whether a sense of fairness is sufficient incentive to alter benefit-cost calculations is, of course, an open question.

COERCIVE

The coercive method is generally favored by recent students of politics. If a person chooses to be a free rider, he will be made to pay certain penalties. The individual who, for example, does not pay his income taxes is subject to fines and imprisonment. Coercion increases the costs of noncompliance. The rational individual can no longer assume that he will receive benefits and save costs if he becomes a free rider. It now becomes expensive *not* to participate in the group's efforts. With effective detection and stiff penalties, the free rider option is no longer rational.

The additional calculation of the costs of not participating that a coercive remedy introduces tells us much about how interest groups form and maintain themselves. Large groups are effective interest groups not only because they obtain desirable goods, but also because they act directly on their members to insure participation. The labor movement is a good example of these *byproduct* actions. A worker can get the benefits of union activity—better working conditions, higher pay, and so on—whether he belongs to the union or not; by not belonging he saves the cost of union dues. These almost perfect conditions for a free rider option were altered by union leaders. Using such devices as a closed shop, social pressure, and outright violence, the labor movement sharply increased the costs to each worker of not participating in labor unions.

The standard theories of interest groups are revised by the free rider possibility with the addition of byproduct actions. Interest groups make demands upon other interest groups and on society in general. But the free rider problem also requires that they make demands, and generally act upon, their own members as well. The free rider problem suggests that coercion in large groups is not only rational, but necessary to insure that members of the group realize their interests. That the effectiveness of voluntary action diminishes with size is also an important idea in understanding the use and justification of coercion by the modern state: any large society, the free rider theory implies, must use coercion on its citizens in order to provide even those goods that the citizens rationally want and need. The rationality of the free rider option demonstrates how people can have common goals, yet lack an incentive to cooperate until the political system actively alters the natural schedule of benefits and costs, either through ethical appeals or coercive methods.

SUMMARY

An understanding of *groups* and *elites* is important to understanding political life. Both, in their own way, express the tendency of individuals to act politically through associations of various sorts. The important points made in this chapter can be summed up as follows.

1. Politics is often, perhaps typically, the interaction of *groupings* of people.

2. *Groups* represent a lateral division of society; *elites* represent a vertical division.

3. Differences in elitist theories of American politics can be explained in terms of differences in (a) the concept of *power* and in (b) what counts as evidence for each theory.

4. Black and women's organizations in American society present interesting variations on standard interest group theories, including the addition of *rights* to the concept of *interests*.

5. The *free rider* problem introduces the need for internal coercion in large groups, replacing the emphasis on voluntary participation found in standard interest group theories.

6.   The need for internal coercion suggests that what is rational for the individual (that is, to become a free rider) may not always be rational for the group in which he or she is a member.

FOR FURTHER READING

Again, the references that follow are not intended as an exhaustive listing. They were selected for relevance and helpfulness on the topics considered in these chapters.

GROUPS

BENTLEY, ARTHUR, *The Process of Government*. Evanston, Ill.: Principia Press, 1949.
GOLEMBIEWSKI, ROBERT T., *The Small Group*. Chicago: University of Chicago Press, 1962.
———, *Men, Management, and Morality*. New York: McGraw-Hill, 1965.
HUNTER, FLOYD, *Community Power Structure*. Chapel Hill, N.C.: University of North Carolina Press, 1953.
LATHAM, EARL, *The Group Basis of Politics*. Ithaca, N.Y.: Cornell University Press, 1952.
LOWI, THEODORE, *The End of Liberalism*. New York: Norton, 1969.
TRUMAN, DAVID, *The Governmental Process*. New York: Knopf, 1971.
ZIEGLER, HARMON, *Interest Groups in American Society*. Englewood Cliffs, N.J.: Prentice-Hall, 1964.

ELITES

BACHRACH, PETER, *The Theory of Democratic Elitism: A Critique*. Boston: Little, Brown, 1967.
———, and MORTON BARATZ, "Two Faces of Power," *American Political Science Review* 56 (Dec. 1962), pp. 947–952.
———, "Decisions and Nondecisions: An Analytical Framework," *American Political Science Review* 57 (Sept. 1963), pp. 632–642.
———, "Power and Its Two Faces Revisited: A Reply to Geoffrey Debnam," *American Political Science Review* 69 (Sept. 1975), pp. 900–904.
CONNOLLY, WILLIAM, *Political Science and Ideology*. New York: Atherton Press, 1967.
———, "Theoretical Self-Consciousness," in *Social Structure and Political Theory*, ed. Connolly. Lexington, Mass.: D. C. Heath, 1974.
DAHL, ROBERT, "The Concept of Power," *Behavioral Science*, July 1957, pp. 201–215.
———, *Who Governs*. New Haven, Conn.: Yale University Press, 1961.
———, "Further Reflections on 'The Elitist Theory of Democracy,'" *American Political Science Review* 60 (June 1966), pp. 306–326.

————, *Polyarchy*. New Haven, Conn.: Yale University Press, 1971.
DEBNAM, GEOFFREY, "Nondecisions and Power: The Two Faces of Bachrach and Baratz," *American Political Science Review*, 69 (Sept. 1975), pp. 889–899.
————, "Rejoinder to 'Comment' by Peter Bachrach and Morton S. Baratz," *American Political Science Review* (Sept. 1975), pp. 905–907.
GIBSON, QUENTIN, "Power," *Philosophy of Social Science*, 1971, pp. 101–112.
GOLDHAMER, H., AND E. SHILS, "Types of Power and Status," *The American Journal of Sociology*, 1939, pp. 171–182.
LUKES, STEVEN, *Power: A Radical View*. Atlantic Highlands, N.J.: Humanities Press, 1975.
MARCUSE, HERBERT, *One Dimensional Man*. Boston: Beacon Press, 1964.
MILLS, C. WRIGHT, *The Power Elite*. New York: Oxford University Press, 1957.
SCHATTSCHNEIDER, E. E., *The Semi-Sovereign People*. New York: Holt, Rinehart & Winston, 1960.
SIMON, HERBERT, "Notes on the Observation and Measurement of Political Power," *The Journal of Politics*, 1953, pp. 500–516.
SKINNER, QUENTIN, "The Empirical Theorists of Democracy and Their Critics," *Political Theory*, Vol. 1, No. 3 (Aug. 1973), pp. 287–306.
WALKER, JACK, "A Critique of 'The Elitist Theory of Democracy,'" *American Political Science Review* 60 (June 1966), pp. 285–295.
————, "A Reply to 'Further Reflections on the Elitist Theory of Democracy,'" *American Political Science Review* 60 (June 1966), pp. 391–392.

THE BLACK MOVEMENT

BROWN, CLAUDE, *Manchilde in the Promised Land*. New York: MacMillan, 1965.
GESCHWENDER, JAMES, ED., *The Black Revolt*. Englewood Cliffs, N.J.: Prentice-Hall, 1971.
HOWARD, JOHN, "The Making of a Black Muslin," in *The Black Revolt*, ed. James Geschwender, pp. 449–458.
KEECH, WILLIAM, *The Impact of Negro Voting*. Chicago: Rand McNally, 1968.
KING, MARTIN LUTHER, "Letter From Birmingham Jail," in *Nonviolence in America: A Documentary History*, ed. Staughton Lynd. Indianapolis: Bobbs-Merrill, 1966.
LANG, KURT, AND GLADYS LANG, "Racial Disturbances as Collective Protest," in *The Black Revolt*, ed. James Geschwender, pp. 257–263.
LITTLE, MALCOLM, *The Autobiography of Malcolm X*. New York: Grove Press, 1966.
MATHEWS, DONALD, AND JAMES PROTHRO, *Negroes and the New Southern Politics*. New York: Harcourt, Brace & World, 1966.
MEIER, AUGUST, AND ELLIOT RUDWICK, *Black Protest in the Sixties*. Chicago: Quadrangle, 1970.
MUSE, BENJAMIN, *The American Negro Revolution: From Nonviolence to Black Power*, 1963–1967. Bloomington, Ind.: Indiana University Press, 1968.
OBERSCHALL, ANTHONY, "The Los Angeles Riot of August 1965," *Social Problems* 15 (Winter 1967), reprinted in *The Black Revolt*, ed. James Geschwender, pp. 264–284.
WALTON, HANES, JR., *Black Politics: A Theoretical and Structural Analysis*. New York: J. B. Lippincott, 1972.

THE WOMEN'S MOVEMENT

BEAUVOIR, SIMONE DE, *The Second Sex*. New York: Knopf, 1953.
BERNARD, JESSIE, *Women and the Public Interest*. New York: Aldine-Atherton, 1971.
CHAFE, WILLIAM H., *Women and Equality: Changing Patterns in American Culture*. Oxford: Oxford University Press, 1977.
FREEMAN, JO, *The Politics of Women's Liberation*. New York: David McKay, 1975.
FRIEDAN, BETTY, *The Feminine Mystique*. New York: Norton, 1963.
HOLE, JUDITH, AND ELLEN LEVINE, *Rebirth of Feminism*. New York: Quadrangle, 1971.
HOWE, LOUISE KAPP, *Pink Collar Workers: Inside the World of Women's Work*. New York: Putnam, 1976.
JONG, ERICA, *Fear of Flying*. New York: Signet, 1973.
MAILER, NORMAN, *The Prisoner of Sex*. Boston: Little, Brown, 1971.
MILLETT, KATE, *Sexual Politics*. Garden City, N.Y.: Doubleday, 1970.
SEIFER, NANCY, *Nobody Speaks For Me! Self Portraits of American Working Class Women*. New York: Simon & Schuster, 1976.
WERTHEIMER, BARBARA MAYER, *We Were There: The Story of Working Women in America*. New York: Pantheon, 1977.

THE "FREE RIDER" PROBLEM

CHAMBERLIN, JOHN, "Provision of Collective Goods as a Function of Group Size," *American Political Science Review* 68 (June 1974). (One of many articles attempting to revise Olson's conclusions, this one maintaining that in certain conditions a perfectly non-competitive good's production will *increase* with an increase in group size.)
FROLICH, NORMAN, JOE A. OPPENHEIMER, AND ORAN R. YOUNG, *Political Leadership and Collective Goods*. Princeton, N.J.: Princeton University Press, 1971.
OLSON, MANCUR, *The Logic of Collective Action*. Cambridge, Mass.: Harvard University Press, 1971.
RIKER, WILLIAM, AND PETER ORDESHOOK, *An Introduction to Positive Political Theory*. Englewood Cliffs, N.J.: Prentice-Hall, 1973, pp. 45–77.
TAYLOR, MICHAEL, *Anarchy and Cooperation*. New York: John Wiley, 1976. (For a discussion of the rationality of *non*-coercive cooperative strategies in groups, using a Prisoner's Dilemma format.)

RIGHTS AND INTERESTS

BARRY, BRIAN, *Political Argument*. New York: Humanities Press, 1965.
OKUN, ARTHUR, *Equality and Efficiency*. Washington, D.C.: Brookings Institution, 1975.

the people in policy
positive and
negative participation

4

THE REFERENDUM AS A DECISION-RULE

On June 8, 1976, in California the people were asked to vote *yes* or *no* on Proposition 15. Proposition 15 was a measure to curb nuclear plant construction unless (1) the $560 million ceiling on nuclear accident liability was raised by Congress or waived by the industry and (2) the safety of each plant could be clearly established in comprehensive tests and affirmed by a two-thirds vote of the state legislature.

Both supporters and opponents of Proposition 15 waged an intense, even bitter, campaign. Proposition 15 was supported by, among other groups, the Sierra Club, Friends of the Earth, the Union of Concerned Scientists, and Project Survival. (The titles of the groups suggest their orientation.) The measure was opposed by the nuclear industry, California utilities, the state's Energy Commission, and regional chapters of national physics, chemical, and nuclear societies. Each side had its share of Nobel Prize winners and its share of support from public figures. The outcome of the vote, however, was lopsided. Proposition 15 was defeated by a two to one margin.

Referendums are devices that enable the public to express a view on policy. Policy decisions can be made by means of several different types of rules. Decision-rules can include chance (the toss of a coin), one-man decree, contests (trial by combat in medieval times, winner-takes-all tennis matches today), technological discovery, majority vote, and much more. The issues resolved by Proposition 15 could have been decided, at least in principle, by having Jesse Unruh, former Democratic legislative leader, hand-wrestle ex-governor Ronald Reagan. (In medieval times jousts between knights were used to settle general disputes.) Today, however, the referendum is the traditional mechanism for allowing the people to make policy decisions directly.

Justifications of the referendum have a long history. First, there is the argument from ethics: people who are to be affected by a decision ought to be consulted in making the decision. (Rousseau, for one, made this argument.) Second, the quality of a decision is sometimes said to be improved by allowing the people to speak out and influence the decision. (John Stuart Mill valued the free "marketplace of ideas" because the *best* opinion would prevail in open debate.) Third, if people join in making decisions, the costs of implementation are reduced as opposition is co-opted. (One honorable way to handle one's opponents is to get them to join you in making policy.)

Two of these three reasons for having referendums applied to the California vote on Proposition 15. Since the dangers and benefits of nuclear plant construction would affect all people, it seemed only right to have as wide a decision-group as possible deciding on the issue. And certainly the public debate on Proposition 15, and the involvement in the campaign of so many people from so many different areas of life, helped to clarify what is at stake in nuclear plant construction (though critics said a lot of obscurity was achieved as well). The last reason, co-opting the opposition, is less easily applied to the referendum. Since 1.8 million people voted *yes*, and thus lost, the seeds of a political problem may have been planted: why should the losers accept the results when at least half the experts saw something like doomsday following a negative vote on Proposition 15?

Even when all three reasons apply to an issue, however, it is not common to have the people make policy directly. Why not? Partly because of time, partly because of general convenience, the people have traditionally been satisfied to have representatives of one sort or another make policy decisions. But even when referendums are not used to decide policy, the policy process often does involve a wide range of people; frequently the public participates in ways less formal than referendums.

In this chapter, we will look at both *positive* and *negative* participation in the civil society. Positive participation will refer to the standard behaviors of civic-minded citizens: voting, signing petitions, running for office, and the like. Negative participation will refer to all types of criminal behavior, where the citizen is no longer being civic-minded but instead is violating (actively or passively) the legal rules of society. At first glance, the assignment of positive or negative charges to "participation" may seem misdirected. But let us see the assignment as a device to approach some intriguing topics, a Jekyll-Hyde metaphor to manage at one and the same time the good citizen and his criminal counterpart.

Two physical metaphors will provide the instruments to arrange the ideas of the chapter. The first is a wide-angle lens with a zooming device, to help us see participation by focusing on a few or broadened to take in the many. (Our lens had better be wide-angled where referendums are concerned.) The second is a high-tension wire, with *rationality* explanations located at one end of the wire, *sociological* explanations at the other. The tension between these two explanatory models has been felt since chapter 2. But as explanations for participation in politics—or crime—these models produce some interesting views on deterministic versus freely-decided courses of action.

Specifically, we will discuss in this chapter some of the explanations for why people do and do not participate in politics and in crime, and how applying certain background (or environmental) causes bypasses rationality explanations in both positive and negative forms of participation. Our case study will focus on the negative side of participation, criminal behavior. In our wide-angle scan of multiple policy agents, we will also encounter two interesting paradoxes of "voting" as a decision-rule for policy. One is *logical*, the other is *moral*. Both can present serious difficulties in elections of all types, and a resolution of the second gives us a clue as to why the 1.8 million losers in California may have a reason to abide by the outcome of the vote on Proposition 15 instead of opting for civil disobedience, a form of negative participation.

TYPES OF SITUATIONS FOR POLICY DECISIONS

Let's turn back to the decision-theory literature for a moment to set our sights on a narrow view of a policy decision. Then let's let this narrow view expand to the wider horizons of a general participatory model of policy. Graham Allison (1971) has introduced a helpful typology (amended slightly here) that allows the expansion from authorities to the people to be developed clearly.

RATIONAL ACTOR

The narrowest kind of policy decision is the rational-actor type. Here the decision-maker is unitary, either a single person or a group with a single voice (for example, the Politburo in Russia). The rational-actor policy situation is closely related to our old friend, the "classical" model of rationality. Goals are consistently articulated, perhaps even ranked in importance, and decisions are made in conditions of full information. Policy, in the rational-actor situation, is a single solution of a problem presented by the social world. Both solution and problem are static: *a* single choice is made rather than the many partial choices found in the strategy of disjointed incrementalism.

ORGANIZATIONAL PROCESS

Expand the scope of the rational-actor situation and one encounters the surrounding organization in which policy authorities typically act. Decisions, with this broadened perspective, can now be seen as the output of organizations, not just unitary actors. Indeed, as we look at the operations of most governments, what we see are multiple organizational units with varying effect on policy decisions. Problems of any size or complexity are factored out among organizational units. Welfare policy, for example, is currently set by veterans administrators, specialists on gerontology, poverty agencies, and agriculture committees. Many different groups have a say in the decisions because the problem is so comprehensive that it simply extends across otherwise separate organizations.

Problems factored out in this way are also problems where the power to resolve them is fractured along organizational lines. No one group has control of any problem, nor even, in many cases, a satisfactory understanding of what is at issue. President Jimmy Carter, in a candid speech early in his administration, admitted that welfare was an extremely complicated area of policy, difficult to understand and control. Joseph Califano, Jr., Secretary of Health, Education, and Welfare, said in May 1976 that his study of the area had led him "to appreciate that any welfare reform proposal must rest on excruciatingly difficult choices on which opposing views are often intensely held." In short, welfare is a package of measures, often determined and administered by widely separated government agencies.

How is policy made along organizational lines? In pieces, as the saying goes. The *organizational-process* model comes closest to the *disjointed incremental* way of making policy decisions. Put simply, policy is the outcome of separate organizations operating with "standard operating procedures." Goals are sequentially pursued, and they function to set levels of acceptable performance for members of organizations. Uncertainty is avoided by concentrating on procedures, like budgetary traditions and limits. *Routine* is one key word, *self-protection* another; for example, FBI agents related during the Watergate investigation that they were informally instructed, above all else, to make sure that they would not be blamed when things went wrong. Leaders pick programs within an established repertoire, and perhaps trigger routines in new contexts. No individual can be held responsible and no one is in control. It is, as Charles Lindblom put it, the "science of muddling through" (1959).

BUREAUCRATIC POLITICS

Expand the viewing equipment again and a wider picture emerges. Policy can also be the political result of compromise, conflict, and bargaining amid public officials in a collection of overlapping interactions. This third type of policy situation is a rough combination of *exchange* and *gaming*, outlined in Chapter 1. Public officials are now players, acting out official roles and injecting their own personalities onto the field. The rules of the game are constitutions, conventions, statutes, cultural constraints, and so on. The prize is success. The stakes are power. Policy is the outcome of the strategy and tactics. A simple example: the internal struggle between Secretary of State William Rogers and National Security Advisor Henry Kissinger in the first Nixon administration, a struggle in which Kissinger was victorious, led to policy outcomes *as a result* of the Kissinger victory, for example "shuttle diplomacy"—a Kissinger trademark.

These three policy situations help us to see the enlarged scope of policy making. The third view of policy removes even the necessity of a "decision," for in bureaucratic politics, policy is a *result* of interacting players who may occupy a stage of international dimensions. Policy can be made by a complicated network of policy changes. Any sophisticated look at Washington, D.C., quickly reveals that policy figures may not be government officials. An informal network of columnists, lobbyists, staff workers, as well as government representatives and civil servants, are usually influential in policymaking. Though the players may change with the policies, and the success–power conjunction may be too dramatic a depiction of their interactions, policy is often a patchwork measure reflecting how a wide array of figures affect one another.

Let's expand our perspective even more. If all manner of important, though not necessarily governmental, figures in and around the nation's capitol can contribute to policy formation, then can the people also contribute? To Allison's three-fold classification, a fourth category is worth adding.

POPULAR INTERVENTION

The general public fills the viewing screen in some public policies. Sometimes the public influences policy through the formal device of a referendum, as we saw with Proposition 15. At other times, the activities of a social movement are decisive in policy decisions. Both the black and the women's movements produced, as we have seen, a wide range of public policies. A social movement does not "vote" on policies; it acts in other, less well-defined ways. For example (Freeman, 1975): (1) It affects public opinion, creating expectations, opportunities, sympathies for various policy options. (2) It provides resources for friendly government figures, resources that include information, skilled and unskilled help, and grass-root support. (3) A social movement also can confer legitimacy on an issue, as the fact of widespread endorsement made the pursuit of civil rights in the early 1960s a respectable line of action even in parts of the South.

The relationship between popular action and the government is a two-way process. The government can provide or deny a political arena for policy issues. A sympathetic senator, for example, can fuel concern for a policy area by opening hearings on a relevant issue. Or a president can create a public agency, staffed with sympathetic personnel, to explore policy alternatives. Or, conversely, the government can do none of these things, which might effectively kill a budding social movement. Sometimes, however, a friendly but moderate policy can preempt a social movement, leaving it with half a success. The Carter administration's 1977 bill restricting governmental authority to wiretap, for example, slowed the momentum of many opposed to all forms of wiretapping while giving them only a piece of the restrictive package they sought. A hostile government, on the other hand, may strengthen the resolve of a social movement. The implacable opposition of the Johnson and Nixon administrations to the anti-Vietnam War movement strengthened the support the movement had among the young.

The people do not often act to influence policy. In community studies, the public is invariably depicted as apathetic on most policy issues, rising to effectiveness only when elites divide over some popular issue (Dahl, 1961). But that the public participates effectively on occasion is an established fact. Any reasonably complete account of the policy process must include the general public as well as elite figures.

PARTICIPATION AS A RATIONAL DECISION

Let's maintain the metaphor of a wide-angle lens, or scenes stretched to their fullest across a large viewing screen. Now zoom in quickly to the scriptwriter responsible for showing the *reasons* or *motives* for action and ask him: Why do people (elite *or* mass) participate in politics? Why must the viewing equipment sometimes stretch to full length, at other times contract to only a few activists?

If the scriptwriter is knowledgeable in political science, he may be able to point to a distinction we recognized in Chapter 2: *rational* versus *sociological* factors in participation. First, let's review a basic rationality equation:

$$B_i - C_i > B_k - C_k$$

interpreted as alternative i is preferable to k where B = benefits and C = costs. (Riker and Ordeshook, 1973). A rational explanation of participation can be stated very simply in terms of this equation: where participation is i and non-participation is k, a person will have a rational motive to get on the screen of political action.

One basic truth in participation is this: the restrictions provided by the social system have an important effect on rates and types of participation. One reason the Politburo is a unitary policy authority is that effective access to the decision-making machinery is severely limited. Blacks in the South began voting more heavily as electoral restrictions were lifted in the 1960s. Restrictions of the political system can be internalized by rational actors as limits on the *efficacy*, or individual effects, of their actions. If some outcome, X, is infinitely preferable to an alternative Y, yet nothing we do will affect the success of X or Y, then there is no rational motive to act on a consideration of X and Y. Other motivation may be provided, for example, by the threat of imprisonment for *not* voting found in certain authoritarian regimes. But with negative incentives, our benefit-cost calculation has moved to considerations other than efficacy.

Restrictions of the social system do not exhaust all rational considerations in participation. Efficacy, for example, can also include (1) the importance of an issue, (2) the number of people affected by an issue, (3) the simplicity and convenience of participation, and (4) the possibility of affecting an issue on the basis of marginal actions. For example, an election that (a) is on a crucial issue, (b) bears on the interests of many people, (c) involves both simple and convenient voting arrangements, and (d) is close enough to be influenced by a small number of voters, is an election with rational factors favoring participation (Riker and Ordeshook, 1973).

One problem with all rational explanations of participation is that what counts as a *cost* and as a *benefit* can vary notoriously from one society, or even one individual, to another. For example, two candidates may both value the *goal* of winning an election, but assign different values to the *means* of campaigning to achieve that goal. One may love the campaign trail, regarding contact with strangers as an intrinsic good (Hubert Humphrey at one time was like this). The other may loath social gatherings and value private moments (Richard Nixon was said to be like this). Participation in a political campaign obviously can have different benefits and costs for each candidate.

Even the reference for benefits and costs may be different. Some people may operate from a strictly self-interested perspective: if an action doesn't pay off personally, don't do it. Others may use an other-concerned value system: do it if other people will benefit. Self-interested political actors define costs and benefits in terms of their own interests. Actors concerned with others consider the effects of actions on others besides themselves. If our two candidates are self-interested, then the one who hates campaigning may drop out if the costs of the campaign to him are not worth the benefits of winning the election. If the candidates are other-concerned, then the reluctant campaigner may view campaigns as a cost to be borne because of the more important consideration of how his actions may affect his supporters. The eager campaigner, on the other hand, may not count his own enjoyment so heavily as a benefit in his decisions to participate.

The variable view of benefits and costs can be a handy device to avoid some problems that rationality calculations present. From a narrow view of benefits–costs rationality, voting is almost always an irrational act. If, for example, we measure the expected utility, or benefits, of voting by calculating costs against individual efficacy, then the costs will almost always outweigh the benefits (Tullock, 1967). Ordinary citizens grasp the negative utility of voting quite readily when they complain that one vote (theirs) more or less will make no difference in most elections. Why shouldn't they stay home and avoid the costs to the car and the loss in time of going to the polls?

One way to answer this question is simply to rearrange the schedule of benefits and costs in voting (Riker and Ordeshook, 1973). The utility of voting may not only be in how one affects the outcome of an election; voting can also have intrinsic benefits. People can rationally expect returns on merely being active, feeling like a citizen, perhaps showing off to the neighbors. Traditional democratic theory emphasized the more serious benefits from participation, stressing the educational returns for citizens in a participatory democracy. If voting has intrinsic benefits, then it becomes rational to vote even if one's vote counts little *in itself* in deciding the outcome of an election.

The variability of defining *benefits* and *costs* leads quickly to *sociological* factors in political participation. If we cannot tell what a person, or a society, counts as a benefit or a cost until we sketch in what the person or society is like, then we must turn to social facts in general to get a working knowledge of rationality equations.

PARTICIPATION AS A SOCIOLOGICAL EVENT

Our wide-angle lens is essential to focus on *types* of participation in politics. Public policy can be influenced by many different sorts of political action. *Voting* is an important kind of action, but it is also the least exact instrument to influence policy. Votes for particular representatives are difficult to interpret as votes for or against policy issues. Were those who voted for Richard Nixon in 1972, for example, expressing a rejection of George McGovern's economic policies? Were they affirming Nixon's policies in Vietnam? Or what? Because of the variety of issues in most campaigns, voters have mixed, or little, influence on policy. Referendums sharpen the instrument. The voters in California had the opportunity to vote a key provision of energy policy, expressed in Proposition 15. But referendums are expensive and time-consuming.

Less formal types of participation also influence public policy. Campaign activity, for example, is a more finely calibrated instrument in its effect than voting. Lobbying, talking or writing to members of government, taking part in social movements—the variety of participatory forms stretches from the narrow screen of in-government pressure to the wide scope of social movements. What do we know about the realities of such varied participation?

WHO PARTICIPATES

A series of studies on the political systems of Western democracies has produced a composite picture of the active citizen. Among these works are the important voting studies conducted by the Survey Research Center at the University of Michigan (Campbell, Gurin, and Miller, 1954; Campbell, Converse, Miller, and Stokes, 1960; 1966). The active citizen has been found to be well educated, of high social status, and (at least in the 1960s in America) identifies strongly with a major political party. Also, men tend to participate in politics more than women, and whites more than racial minorities. (Blacks, however, either stay out of politics completely, or participate at extremely high levels; while the median of participation is low for blacks as a population, the deviation is substantial.)

The general point is this: those who participate in politics are not randomly distributed among the population of any political society, but are grouped under certain characteristics and not others. Certain *types* of people are active in politics, and the types of people who participate are *not* representative of their communities (Verba and Nie, 1972). Participants differ from non-participants in (1) the issues or problems they consider important, and (2) the solutions they prefer for these issues and problems.

CITIZEN CAPACITIES

Study after study of American voters has shown that people know little about their political system, and what they believe is often self-contradictory. Surveys have shown that fewer than half of the people in many Congressional districts know who either candidate for Congress is (Miller and Stokes, 1963); that less than half the general public knows at any given time which party is controlling Congress (Lane and Sears, 1964); that the American voter is ill-informed on the issues, has a low conceptualization of how issues relate to each other, and tends to vote on surface considerations of style and slogans (Campbell et al., 1960). Although later studies suggest more sensitivity to issues, gross limitations on the possibilities of rational participation are the rule rather than the exception. Generally, people seem to operate with limited information and conceptual inconsistency.

THE RESPONSES OF LEADERS

How public authorities respond to the wants or needs of the people is mixed. In one famous study (Miller and Stokes, 1963), it was determined (on a narrow data base) that the influence a constituency has on its representatives in Congress varies with the issue. When the policy domain was divided into (a) social welfare, (b) foreign involvement, and (c) civil rights, the relationship between a representative and his constituency differed in each of three areas. The first area, social welfare, corresponded to a responsible-party model; representatives act in accord with a national rather than local constituency. The second, foreign involvement, suggested (inconclusively) a Burkean model of representation, emphasizing *interest* rather than *will* (or demands). Only the last area, civil rights, conformed to an instructed-delegate model, with the representative carrying out the wishes of his constituents. The instructed-delegate model may not be the only warranted form of representation (Pitkin, 1967). But from the point of view of the individual trying to influence his representatives it is a fact to be reckoned with that only one of the three policy areas considered in this study seemed open to citizen influence.

A more general study (Verba and Nie, 1972) concluded that community leaders are more responsive to participants than to nonparticipants, and are more likely to concur in the agenda and views for resolving an issue of participants. Leaders are also more responsive to communities with high participation rates. But the responsiveness is not to the whole community, only to its activist stratum, which is not a representative group. If, however, the community is characterized by high consensus, especially consensus between participants and nonparticipants, then the leaders will respond more strongly to the community at large. The inactive in active communities, however, still receive more attention than the inactive in inactive communities, so long as some consensus is shared by participants and nonparticipants. If strong dissonance occurs between the active and inactive, then the leader becomes less responsive. So participation pays under certain conditions, even (marginally) to the inactive in active and consensus communities.

CONDITIONS FOR AND AGAINST
EFFECTIVE PARTICIPATION

Whether the rules of a political system permit authentic (as opposed to coerced) participation is an obvious condition for participation. But other less obvious social conditions are also important. One determining condition is the *size* of a community. Generally, the larger the unit of politics, the less effective an individual citizen can be; the smaller the unit, the more effective the individual (Verba and Nie, 1972; Dahl and Tufte, 1974). Even issues are affected by their references to size: local issues are more readily influenced by individuals than national issues (Verba and Nie, 1972). The relative homogeneity of a society is another factor: A society that is more nearly uniform, or internally similar, in such typical categories as age, group membership, and ideology is a society where the individual citizen can effectively influence the political system, all other things being equal. On the other hand, a homogeneous society is also one where dissent is more difficult, in part because it's more difficult to enlist allies so helpful to effective dissent in homogeneous surroundings. So consent politics is facilitated by homogeneity but dissenting politics is not (Dahl and Tufte, 1974).

SOME CONCLUSIONS ON EFFECTIVE PARTICIPATION

Empirical studies are notoriously fragile: this year's truth is next year's false hypothesis. But the broad picture that emerges, at least at this time, has mixed implications for popular participation on public policy. There are, first, the very real fruits to be gained from participation. Activists fare better than nonactivists in eliciting positive responses from leaders, as do active communities with high vertical consensus. But the conditions required for effective participation constrain success. Large communities and heterogeneous social conditions make it more difficult for individuals to influence their political systems. Then there are limitations of capability, which are more difficult to assess. Obviously those with certain characteristics are active participants. But the lack of such characteristics cannot be regarded as a limitation on participation unless the characteristics themselves cannot be altered.

There are interesting reasons, however, for thinking that the social characteristics of activists are not completely deterministic. (1) Some characteristics, like education (strongly associated with participation), can be self-determined to an appreciable degree. People can, for example, raise their educational level if they make efforts to do so, thereby acquiring one of the characteristics of activists. Thus even if education is a necessary condition for participation, it can be acquired. (2) Other characteristics of activism, like sex and race, are obviously not selectable. But, on the other hand, we have no reason to think that their relationship to participation will not change. Activism among blacks has varied dramatically with changes in the American electoral system, and cultural changes in the status of women could conceivably invert the activist ranking of the sexes.

The constraints provided by *size* and *heterogeneity* seem more important limitations on effective participation, for they are less tractable to either individual choice or reasonable social change. An individual cannot, for example, as easily change the size or social makeup of the community as he can alter his own educational level (though he can choose to live in a different, smaller, and more homogeneous community—insofar as any are available). Nor can we as easily visualize the world, or any part of it, spontaneously reverting to simpler social arrangements. The energy crisis can lead us to speculate on whether, over the long run, Western culture will revert to more pastoral and local political arrangements (see Chapter 8). But short of a general catastrophe, it is easier to imagine a woman President and an active female elite than to imagine contemporary society breaking up into small and uniform political units. If, as seems likely, large social units and complexity are here to stay, at least in the immediate future, then we are faced with more fixed limitations on effective participation than the current associations of certain characteristics (male, white, and so on) with high participation rates.

But such thoughts are themselves speculative. We can safely conclude only that both the social characteristics of citizens and general social conditions suggest limitations on the rates and effectiveness of popular participation in public policy.

OBJECTIVE CAUSES OF PUBLIC POLICY

It seems almost axiomatic that public policy originates with people, either in mass or in more narrow forms of participation. But introducing such social factors as age, income, system features, and so on as criteria and conditions for rational decisions leads to some interesting thoughts. We might look at social factors as objective *causes* of public policy, operating at a more basic level than the decisions that flesh-and-blood people make on public policy alternatives.

A *benefit* and a *cost* are important ingredients in rationality calculations. But we don't know how to fill in the details, how to say what *benefits* and *costs* mean, or what kinds of conditions *limit* rationality, unless we know something about people and society. Then, when social factors are introduced, we find that they operate as explanations, or as limitations, on whether people participate at all in politics, and whether participation is effective in influencing public policy. This would be the "modest" combination of social and rational factors.

The "hard" combination of social and rational factors is to take a long jump to social factors (at the other end of our tension-wire metaphor) at the expense of rationality. Here we maintain that how people rationally decide things fades into insignificance compared to the background social factors that *cause* their behavior and, ultimately, determine public policy.

Several recent theories of public policy and its determinants stress "environmental" variables over political variables. Traditional studies of politics emphasized the relationship of electoral variables, like party competition and voter participation, to public policy. For example, states with a competitive party system and high voter turnouts were found to have higher levels of taxation, public spending, and general social services. Thus, a *causal* chain was accepted between certain *political* factors and public policy outcomes.

Political ——————————————▶ Public Policy	
(a) party competition	(a) education spending
(b) voter turnout	(b) welfare benefits, etc.

In the early 1950s, however, this causal connection was questioned. Several scholars explored the possibility that economic factors lay behind the political variables, and that these economic factors were the true determinants of policy outcomes. One initial study (Fabricant, 1952) suggested that per capita *income* in states accounted for more variation in state and local government spending than any other variable. A later study (Sachs and Harris, 1964) identified a strong relationship between federal grants-in-aid to states and state welfare expenditures. (In effect, the federal government had supplanted the states' own resources—for example, per capita income—in welfare policy.) Other state and local policies, however, remained dependent on per capita income.

Later studies expanded the linkages between wealth and *levels* of public spending. Property taxes, for example, are important resources for school budgets; the income derived from property taxes is obviously closely related to the value of local property, which in turn is one measure of the general wealth of a community. But wealth is not the only determinant. Educational level is a particularly strong determinant of public policy: in general, the higher the educational level of a community, the higher its total public spending, especially for education. Urbanization and, especially, industrialization, are declining in importance, probably because a state-by-state comparison is more difficult on these two variables as all states become uniformly urban and industrialized. Even these two environmental factors, however, still weigh heavily in the determination of policy outcomes.

One important study (Dye, 1966) determined that four environmental (nonpolitical) variables reflecting the level of economic development—urbanization, industrialization, wealth, and education—had more effect on public policy than four prominent political factors—Democratic or Republication control of state government, degree of interparty competition, level of voter turnout, and extent of malapportionment. In effect, recent studies have suggested that economic variables are more important determinants of public policy than political factors. Economic factors seem to affect policy directly:

Economic ——————————————▶ Public Policy

. and through their effects on the political system, seem to shape public policy indirectly:

Economic —————————▶ Political —————————▶ Public Policy

For example, per pupil expenditures in educational policy seem *directly* related to levels of income and urbanization; on the other hand, Aid to Families with Dependent Children welfare benefits seem (in part) *indirectly* affected by income levels, which affect political factors first (Dye, 1975). We can conclude that, in general, studies of environmental variables suggest deeper and more fundamental causes of policy outcomes than traditional studies of politics have recognized.

ENVIRONMENTAL DETERMINISM: WHAT IT ALL MEANS

Students of politics may decide to switch to economics after digesting the importance of economic variables on public policy. Some initial alarm at these findings was in fact expressed among political science faculties, it being harder (one might suppose) for teachers to change professions than for students to change majors. But reassurances of the value of political science were quickly expressed. Some authorities (Keech and Prothro, 1968) pointed out that political scientists are interested in the dependent variable, politics, and must entertain any and all possible explanatory causes for political events. Others (Dye, 1975) agreed, maintaining in addition that correlation among variables still does not explain how the dependent variables work: to say that economic factors cause public policy still does not explain how the political system operates *even as* a dependent system in the formation of policy.

All of this is very professional, of course. It would not wear well to hint at vested interests in one type of explanation versus another. But the main significance of the elevation of environmental over political variables may lie elsewhere. To go back to our metaphor of high-tension wire, with environmental variables we have located a different *type* of explanation for public policy: it is now not simply a question of *who* or *how many* participate in making policy, but of *what* is behind public policy. *Conditions* determine public policy, not *decisions*.

Let's set up the two extremes again to make our point. At one extreme is an explanation of public policy by means of rational decisions—by one, a few, or the many. At the other extreme is an explanation of public policy by determining conditions. At the first extreme, policy originates in *choice* or *decision*. At the other extreme, policy is *determined* by objective conditions partially or completely outside the area of rational control. The elevation of environmental variables to preeminence leans policy toward the second extreme, away from the first. At the least, such factors as the wealth of a community, as limiting conditions, constrain the decisions leading to policy levels. At the most, such factors produce policies in the best traditions of economic determinism.

The more balanced judgment is, of course, the more reasonable. Though we can no longer expect (if we ever did) public policy to be solely a matter for rational decisions, a fully deterministic model of policy is also unlikely. For one thing, some policies (like tax levels) are affected at least secondarily by political factors (legislative professionalism, in this case). For another, some environmental factors can, at least in principle, be manipulated by political effort (for example, level of education), thus providing for the possibility of political control over the determining cause of policy outcomes. (Don't forget the feedback loop outlined in Chapter 1.) Though we are, fortunately, a long way from Elizabethan views on the voluntary origins of economic conditions, it is still not unreasonable to view individual human effort as at least partially effective in influencing economic factors.

This balance between rational decisions and economic determinism is approximately what all reflective political scientists accept. Let's explore the parameters of the balance with our Dostoevskian case study for the chapter, crime and punishment. Why crime and punishment? We are looking at participation in the political society throughout this chapter and crime is the ultimate in negative participation, the dark underside of society's efforts in joint pursuits.

The choosing of crime as a case study for theories of participation should not be interpreted as suggesting that criminals are either high or low participants, or that crime and participation are related in any cause-and-effect way. The key to understanding the case study is the duality of *positive* participation (legal political activity) and *negative* participation (stealing, assault, drug abuse, and so on). Standard (non-political) criminal behavior is negative in one of two ways: either as an active rip-off of social benefits or as a passive withdrawal from society (for example, the drug addict's "nodding off"). In both types of behavior, crime is a violation of the legal rules that modify and constrain the positive participation of the good citizen. Let's not be too civic-minded about the virtues of social life until we look at the reverse participation that *crime* describes.

NEGATIVE PARTICIPATION: CRIME AS A CASE STUDY

The regulation of criminal behavior has always been an important issue in public policy. At least one strong tradition in political thought, the contract theory of the state developed by Hobbes, views the maintenance of civil order as *the* purpose of the political society. *Regulatory* policy, as we have seen (Chapter 1), is a category of public policy covering a variety of vital institutions in contemporary society.

Perhaps because of its importance, crime is today a complex and unsettled issue. Almost everyone has an opinion on the subject, and many have had a personal brush with crime. The complexity of the subject begins with what the term *crime* means. At the most general level, a crime is any action that breaks the rules stated in the criminal or civil statutes of a society. Like most general propositions, this one becomes interesting only when it is pressed to yield more details: defining criminal behavior by type tells us more about the problem of crime than does the general idea of rule-breaking.

Basically, crimes are divided into felonies and misdemeanors. Misdemeanors are not serious social problems. Parking violations, jaywalking, littering—a host of minor offenses are rule-breaking actions, but are not really considered criminal behavior unless the "minor" infractions are related to more serious offenses. If, for example, it were shown that litterbugs developed into muggers, then littering would become important as a prior condition leading to street crime. The example, though far-fetched, is more plausible in the area of drug offenses. Some evidence, though far from conclusive, shows that abuse of some nonnarcotic drugs, amphetamines for example, can create the social setting for use of such "hard" drugs as heroin (Hughes and Crawford, 1972).

Felonious crimes can be classified in a number of ways. One helpful scheme is the following:

VIOLENT

The crime of most concern to the ordinary citizen is that which causes injury (physical or mental) to a victim. Predatory crimes, those committed for gain at the expense of a victim, are common violent crimes in modern societies. Robbery, burglary, larceny, and auto theft are today the most frequently committed predatory crimes. Murder, both calculated and impassioned, is obviously also a violent crime. Murders are frequently byproducts of predatory crimes, as, for example, when victims get killed in the course of a robbery. Murders can also be highly personal crimes; a murder victim is often a friend or relative of the murderer.

Polls have repeatedly indicated that violent crime is of great concern to Americans (Wilson, 1975). Nor is it hard to understand why. Personal assaults are frightening events, either to experience or to contemplate. They rob victims of a sense of security and even of community (Wilson, 1975). They affect people directly in their immediate, day-to-day life. Foreign exploitation may be more unjust on some absolute scale, but the threat of robbery, rape, or burglary is a chronic and personal worry for many city

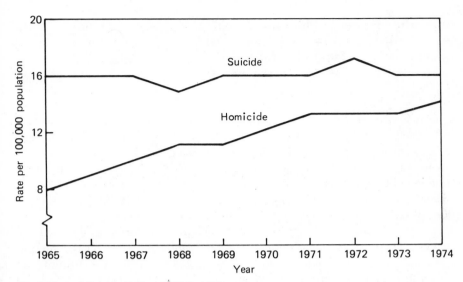

Homicide and Suicide Rates: 1965 to 1974.

Source: Chart prepared by U.S. Bureau of the Census. Data from U.S. National Center for Health Statistics. Reprinted from *Statistical Abstract of the United States, 1976.* (Washington, D.C.: U.S. Government Printing Office) p. 150.

dwellers. What can disrupt daily life is obviously more threatening to many people than remote disturbances, however severe or evil.

WHITE-COLLAR

Of less concern tò the ordinary citizen is *white-collar* crime. Embezzlement, income tax fraud, consumer deception, medical malpractice, antitrust violations—all are instances of white-collar crime. Violence is not a standard part of such crime, although there are victims. Often, the victim is the general public. When consumers are misled through false advertising, for example, the public is bilked of substantial sums of money. White-collar crime does not arouse public opinion to the extent that street crime does, possibly because of its absence of violence and its indirect, often obscure, effects. Although systematic fraud and exploitation can do as much in the long run to disrupt a community, the fact that the consequences are not immediate also makes them more ambiguous.

There are exceptions to these observations. The publicity given Medicare and Medicaid fraud has brought public outrage at each new revelation. Medical malpractice suits have increased dramatically in recent years, which may indicate (among many other things) a lowering of public tolerance for professional negligence. When high public officials commit white-collar crimes, public disapproval peaks. President Richard Nixon's income tax irregularities hurt him in his battle for public sentiment in the impeachment maneuvers of 1973/74. Still, violent crime more consistently concerns Americans than white-collar crime.

VICE

Another category of crime can be called, in line with police tradition and television categories, *vice* crime. It is distinguished by the possible absence of a victim. The word *possible* must be stressed, for illegal vice sometimes (not always) does victimize its consumers and even its perpetrators. Prostitution, gambling, the use of certain drugs, pornography—these are vice crimes where illegal. (Prostitution is legal in parts of Nevada.) Violence, while not an integral feature of vice, is not an uncommon side effect.

Vice crimes are among the more controversial forms of criminal behavior. They intersect with different moral codes and bear on the complicated relationship of morality to law. Many maintain that prostitution, for example, ought to be legal because there is no victim: it is, in the euphemism of an earlier generation, an act between consenting adults (or, less euphemistically, a cash transaction). Those who maintain this view can still regard prostitution as immoral (as is, say, adultery), but not appropriate for *legal* regulation. Those who favor legal regulation of vice point out that frequently there *is* a victim—to take the example of prostitution, if not the paying customer then the prostitute who plies her or his trade. The discovery in New York City of a pornography ring using child actors was a *cause celebre* in criminal investigation in 1977 and provided powerful ammunition for groups urging legal regulation of vice.

What is considered illegal vice has changed radically since the early 1970s. Traditional restrictions on pornography have been relaxed, although other vices, like gambling, are still carefully controlled. Even the liberalization of pornography laws has been uneven, however. The U.S. Supreme Court in *Miller* v. *California,* 1973, has permitted local standards to prevail even in the midst of general changes in pornographic statutes. The close relationship of vice laws to moral codes sometimes gives them a fluid status, changing with shifts in community norms on what is moral and on what types of immorality the law ought to punish.

POLITICAL

A type of crime often overlooked in U.S. statistics is the *political* crime, defined here as any action aimed at changing or maintaining political practices when such action is *both* illegal and in violation of accepted decision-rules in the political system. Assassinations, for example, are political crimes. They are unlike murders in that they claim political figures as victims; yet, they are acts in violation of state statutes against murder. The Symbionese Liberation Army (SLA) is (or was) a group bent on eradicating certain institutions in American society by violent means. The SLA is not playing by the political "rules of the game" *and* it is also acting illegally. Political criminals are like standard criminals in the actions they take, unlike them in the political goals they seek.

The abuse of political power is at times in violation of criminal statutes, at other times not. President Nixon's misuse of executive privilege, for example, was a crime when it obstructed justice. At other times it was not—for example, when he improperly concealed information on foreign affairs from Senate and House committees. To call all abuses of political power *crimes* is not accurate, though any abuse of political power can do damage to due process of law. When the abuse of power intersects with criminal law, as did the government-authorized burglary of Daniel Ellsberg's psychiatrist's office, civil and criminal penalties are appropriate. When abuse of power is merely a violation of accepted practices, as the "dirty tricks" some candidates use during a campaign, the appropriate remedy is political: remove the person from office.

Each of these four types of crimes presents different social problems. All, however, represent (in widely differing ways) a form of negative participation in social life. People who commit crimes are, for a variety of reasons, breaking the rules of their society.

CRIME: HOW MUCH AND WHY

All knowledgeable people agree that crime is increasing in the United States. Crime statistics are notoriously unreliable. Changes in the figures may represent changes in the reporting techniques, the inclinations of victims to report crimes, or the zeal of police. (It is a constant outrage to liberals that those with a vested interest in inflated crime figures, the police and the FBI, are also the primary sources for crime statistics.) Sometimes crime statistics from different sources conflict. The FBI, for example, published statistics showing a substantial increase in violent crime from 1974 to 1975. (The FBI report relied, as it always does, on the number of crimes *reported* to state and local law enforcement agencies.) The Law Enforcement Assistance Administration, using census data, reported for the same period of time "no meaningful change" in the rates for assault, burglary, motor vehicle theft, and commercial robbery. Yet even if we admit an "inflation" in crime statistics and some general confusion over data sources, still the severest critics of the figures will concede that crime rates are growing, and growing fast.

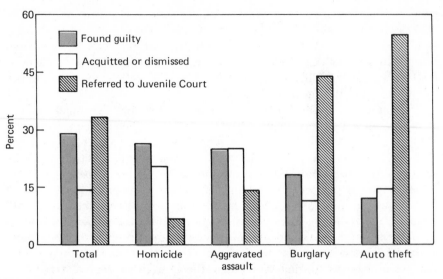

Persons Charged with Crimes and Outcome of Charges: 1974

Source: Chart prepared by U.S. Bureau of the Census. Data from U.S. Federal Bureau of Investigation. Reprinted from *Statistical Abstract of the United States, 1976.* (Washington, D.C.: U.S. Government Printing Office) p. 150.

The FBI figures on reported crimes are impressive. From 1960 to 1975, there was a 199 percent rise in total crimes against persons, and a 178 percent increase in total crimes against property. In 1960, the murder rate was 5.1 per 100,000 population; in 1975, it was 9.6 per 100,000. Robbery rose from 60 to 218 per 100,000 in that fifteen-year period, an increase of 263 percent. Forcible rape increased 174 percent. Although some decrease in crimes against persons (especially the homicide rate) was reported by the FBI in the late summer and fall of 1977, the overall trend of recent history is dismal. If the figures are even approximately correct, we have been facing an epidemic of crime in the United States. In fact, the only crime that has not increased dramatically in recent history seems to be that of political assassinations and assaults (see Table 4.1).

In addition to crime figures, statistics on guns sold in the United States are worth mentioning. The production and import of all civilian firearms in America increased 217 percent from 1960 to 1975. The largest increase, 312 percent, occurred in the production and import of handguns. The number of handguns produced and imported legally in the United States in 1975 totaled almost 2.5 million—an impressive figure, even in a Godfather movie. Whether guns cause crime or are merely the instruments to carry out crimes caused by other factors is an issue of considerable dispute between the National Rifle Association and those who support stronger government regu-

Table 4.1
POLITICAL ASSASSINATIONS AND ASSAULTS IN THE UNITED STATES

Period	Number
1835–1864	3
1865–1894	43
1895–1924	12
1925–1934	3
1935–1944	4
1945–1954	11
1955–1972	6

Source: National commission on the causes and prevention of violence, *Task Force Report on Assassinations,* 1969.

lations of guns. But certainly we can conclude at least this: if people in America are inclined to violence for whatever reason, they do not lack for weapons to carry out their inclinations.

Why is crime increasing? We have two basic models to explain the occurrence and rise of crime: *rational* and *sociological.* These two old friends, introduced in the second chapter, and used earlier in this chapter to explain positive participation, are once more useful, this time as alternative explanations for criminal behavior. Let's try a rationality explanation first. Crime, we might say, is a rational attempt by some citizens to maximize their utilities through illegal efforts. They choose a life of crime, or at least episodes of criminal action, because they have rationally calculated that the expected returns are worth the costs and risks. Criminals, on this basis, are

Table 4.2
CRIME RATES—BY TYPE (PER 100,000 POPULATION)

Year	1960	1965	1970	1975	Percent Increase 1960–1975
Murder	5.1	5.1	7.9	9.6	88
Forcible rape	9.6	12.1	18.7	26.3	174
Robbery	60	72	172	218	263
Aggravated assault	86	111	165	227	164
Burglary	509	663	1,085	1,526	200
Larceny-theft	1,035	1,329	2,079	2,805	171
Motor vehicle theft	183	257	457	469	156
Total crimes against person	161	200	364	482	199
Total crimes against property	1,726	2,249	3,621	4,800	178

Source: U.S. Federal Bureau of Investigation, *Uniform Crime Reports for the United States,* annual.

Table 4.3
CIVILIAN FIREARMS DOMESTIC PRODUCTION AND IMPORTS
(NUMBERS IN THOUSANDS)

Year	1960	1965	1973	1975	Percent Increase 1960–1975
Handguns	603	1,013	2,033	2,486	312
Rifles	871	1,035	2,025	2,289	163
Shotguns	689	1,073	1,700	2,078	202
Total	2,163	3,121	5,758	6,853	217

Source: U.S. Bureau of the Census, Statistical Abstract of the United States, 1976, p. 160.

free riders taken to the ultimate extreme—they rationally rip off the society for gain while contributing nothing by their actions.

A rationality explanation of crime has some validity with certain types of crime. Some white-collar crime, for example, originates in rational decisions. Embezzlement of bank funds by a low-paid teller is the model crime for a rationality explanation. Political crimes also have a high rationality quotient. The carefully designed image projected by the Black Panthers in the 1960s reflected a rational design (albeit one which backfired as the police responded firmly). Some ethnic crime, the Mafia being an outstanding example, can be seen as a rational response, however deplorable, to economic deprivation.

But rationality models are clearly inadequate to explain either the bulk of crime or the recent increases in criminal behavior. If a rationality model were generally valid, then we would expect the poor (with more to gain and less to lose) to be systematically more inclined to criminal behavior than the more prosperous. Studies of crime do not bear this out. The rapid increase in crime during the 1960s came at a time of rising prosperity in America and during the great social experiments to eliminate poverty. Several studies have shown with more specific data that "poverty as such is not an important cause of crime" (Sutherland, 1966). Nor, incidentally, is racial discrimination unambiguously associated with crime rates. Although blacks have a high crime rate, Japanese-Americans do not (Sutherland and Cressey, 1966). Finally, many types of crimes do not even logically fit a rationality model. So-called crimes of passion—husbands murdering wives in a jealous heat or vice versa, child-beating, rape—obviously many crimes do not originate in any sort of rational decision.

So we turn to *sociological* models to explain crime. In this type of explanation, we should recall, our efforts are directed at identifying the social *causes* (rather than, as with rationality models, the reasons) for whatever we are trying to explain. What, then, are the social causes of crime? Here the absence of any reliable association between poverty and crime helps to destroy a favorite sociological theory and to discredit rational explanations of crime. In the 1960s, many social scientists and government administrators believed that an important "root cause" of crime was poverty. (The phrase alone moved James Q. Wilson, 1975, to observe that "Stupidity can only be dealt with by attacking its root causes.") Many scholars today (for example, Wilson) doubt the presence of *any* root causes, and doubt specifically the relationship of poverty to crime.

Theories on what causes crime point elsewhere today. One major theory, that of "differential association," maintains that criminals learn to behave criminally from those they admire and associate with closely (Sutherland and Cressey, 1966). The criminal is responding to the values of those he respects. Unfortunately, these values are contrary to the general norms of the society. The "crime-by-association" model is particularly good at explaining heroin use. Surveys among addicts have consistently shown that users start with drugs given to them by friends who are users. This "contagion" model of heroin use discredits the myth of the pusher told to school children: a slightly sinister stranger dispensing goodies. The drug distributor is invariably a close friend, as are those who introduce novices to crime in general.

The "differential association" model still does not tell us why some individuals respond to peer group pressure toward crime while others do not. Another important theory on the causes of crime helps fill this gap. Evidence is strong that crime among the young is explained more completely by family conditions *in conjunction with* peer group association than by any other set of variables. The picture, drawn roughly, is this. The absence of family stability, parental affection, and discipline provide the "trigger" conditions for crime. Peer pressure pulls that trigger.

Two observations are important on this causal theory. First, the idea of "root causes" doesn't easily fit the theory. There is no underlying network of causes to unearth. A "chemical balance" is the better metaphor: crime is the product of a mixture of factors, family inadequacy and criminal peers, that reach some critical mass when combined in the right amounts. Second, eradication of crime by democratic governments is difficult, if not impossible, if these latest theories are correct. Poverty could conceivably be rooted out and eliminated. But manipulating the nuclear family and controlling who people associate with could create oppressive conditions more dangerous than crime itself (Wilson, 1975).

WHAT TO DO ABOUT CRIME

It is reasonable to think that society in general has an interest in curtailing, even eliminating, crime. Yet "crime" was a political football during the 1960s in America. The Republicans neatly appropriated the issue in the 1964 presidential election. Barry Goldwater, Republican candidate for president, attacked the incumbent Democrats for ignoring "crime in the streets." In the late 1960s, "law and order" became the slogan for conservative Republicans, including Richard Nixon, and maverick Democrats like George Wallace. Liberals interpreted the "law and order" call as a racist slogan aimed not so much at street crime as at riots and demonstrations by blacks and anti-Vietnam War activists. One peculiar outcome of this interpretation was that the Democratic Party found itself on the defensive on the crime issue throughout the late 1960s, trying hard to come out against crime without seeming also to oppose their black constituents' demands for equal opportunity.

The partisan status of crime began to fade in 1970. The Nixon administration tried again to label the Democrats as "soft on crime" during the Congressional elections of that year, but the strategy failed. Since then, the Democratic party has opposed crime with more political success. Every politician must oppose criminals. How can anyone running for office be *for* crime? Yet because of the racist overtones of "law and order" slogans, only by the mid-1970s did black candidates come out strongly against crime. "They finally figured out," said James Q. Wilson, "that crime was an important question and that it was their constituency—blacks and union members—who were being victimized in the cities" *New York Times*, 5/17/77). The natural opposition to crime is now virtually uniform in American politics.

But the bipartisan status of crime does not remove political differences in coping with it. If we want to eradicate crime more than we want any other value in society, then we can transform the social system into a garrison and totalitarian state. But most people will stop short of such a solution. At what point they will choose to stop is what divides political authorities who otherwise agree in their opposition to crime.

The first question to ask in settling on social methods to cope with crime is—what works? Well, total control of the family and friendship associations would probably work, but this is unreasonable in a society that values freedom. The social programs of the 1960s were largely ineffective in controlling crime. What's left? The police, of course—and the courts. Here is where the political divisions begin.

Several studies suggest that some types of increased police forces are effective in preventing crime (summarized in Wilson, 1975). Greater numbers of policemen on foot in heavily populated areas can reduce such street crimes as muggings and auto theft. More frequent police patrols in marked police cars does not seem to affect the incidence of crime. Local experiments linking police more closely to a community—patrolmen attending neighborhood meetings to discuss crime, one team of policemen (familiar to the residents) handling almost all calls in the area, and so on—offer promise of reducing local crime. Strategies developed by attack-force police to concentrate on specific crimes have not yet been adequately tested and evaluated.

To date, the results of innovation in police functions are mixed and tentative. Some evidence suggests that the effective patrolling of one neighborhood may simply shift crime frequency to a less well-patrolled neighborhood. Then there is the cost. As municipalities struggle to get out from under heavy expenses, an increase in police is frequently unaffordable. Even with a demonstrated need for more policemen to control crime, budgetary constraints often dictate cuts, not increases, in police forces. Finally, in spite of some changes in the way the police function is viewed ("Pigs," an epitaph for policemen used in the 1960s, is no longer bandied about), many civil libertarians object to increased police use to control crime, preferring instead to attack crime at its source rather than its actual occurrence.

From apprehension tactics (police functions) we move to social techniques aimed at the criminals who *are* caught. One controversial attempt to control crime was the District of Columbia Court Reorganization and Criminal Procedure Act of 1970, a Nixon administration effort to set up model procedures for enforcement across the country. Among other things, the act authorized (1) "no-knock" search and arrest warrants, (2) pretrial detention of up to sixty days for defendants judged dangerous to the community, and (3) life sentences for felons convicted a third time and minimum five-year sentences for a second conviction of a violent crime. These and other provisions of the act have been debated at length. Critics contend that these measures don't work in controlling crime and that they are in violation of the Fourth and Eighth Amendments to the U.S. Constitution. Supporters stress the hard treatment of "veteran" criminals and emphasize the rights of society to protect itself against criminal behavior.

An interesting argument for more systematic detention has been drawn up by James Q. Wilson. In *Thinking About Crime* (1975), Wilson points out that most people arrested for a serious crime have been arrested before (one estimate sets the figure at 87 percent). This figure alone suggests that an increase in police is not the answer to crime. Criminals *are* being apprehended, and re-apprehended. Re-arrest statistics also cast doubt on rehabilitation efforts. Those sent to prison generally come out as criminals about to commit more crimes. Wilson quotes policemen as stating, "We operate the revolving door."

If recidivism is an outstanding feature of criminal behavior, it follows that keeping known criminals isolated from society will dramatically reduce the crime rate. Wilson suggests, among other things: (1) mandatory penalties, however brief, for every conviction for a nontrivial offense; (2) the use of nonprison detention centers; and (3) increased, and still certain, deprivation of liberty for subsequent offenses. One study cited by Wilson (Shlomo and

Shinnar, 1974) estimates that the rate of serious crime would be only *one-third* what it is today if every person convicted of serious crime were imprisoned for three years. The estimate is based on the reasonable assumption that most serious crime is committed by a small number of repeaters. In effect, Wilson urges taking convicted criminals, the main source of crime, out of circulation for moderate periods of time.

Wilson's proposals have generated predictable criticism. Some have maintained that his program is irreversible: if it doesn't work as a method to reduce crime, it will lead to longer, not shorter, sentences for serious crimes. The question then is, what criteria ought we to use to limit sentences? Here an important issue is raised. Generally, studies have recognized two quite different justifications for punishment. One is *utilitarian*, the other *retributive*. A utilitarian approach justifies punishment in terms of its effect on the general welfare of society. Wilson's proposals are, in general, utilitarian. He supports set periods of incarceration precisely because they will benefit society by removing veteran crminals from social life. Critics of Wilson's proposals endorse retributive justifications for punishment. They see punishment as warranted because it gives criminals their just desserts, apart from the effects of punishment on the general welfare (von Hirsch, 1976).

Differences between "utilitarian" and "retributive" theories of punishment can be miniscule or profound. If, for example, giving criminals sentences deserved by the crimes they commit will also act as a deterrent to other would-be criminals, then social utility and retributive justice are both served by the same treatment. But sometimes what is deserved and what is most useful for society are *not* the same. Plea bargaining, for example, is a device useful for society when court dockets are full and judges cannot, for want of time, give every defendant a trial. But it may not be just to allow defendants to plead guilty to a lesser offense simply to save the community money. The conflict between the socially useful and the requirements of retributive justice can be even sharper. The forced detention of Japanese-Americans in the Second World War was defended in terms of social utility of the strongest sort: national security. Yet the imprisonment of innocent people can never be justified on a retributive theory of punishment. (The innocent justly deserve freedom from incarceration.)

Critics of Wilson do not accuse him of making ominous threats to freedom with his proposals. The main line of criticism is simply that retributive *justice*, not social *utility*, should be the bench mark to measure how much punishment to mete out. It is also interesting to note that retributive theories operate with a different idea of success. When a criminal gets what he deserves in the way of punishment, then *rehabilitation* and *deterrence* are unimportant. Utilitarian theories, on the other hand, must calculate success in terms of social outcomes. Do convicts repeat criminal behavior (or have they been rehabilitated)? Is crime deterred? Has the crime rate been reduced? Only a utilitarian theory of criminal justice actually copes with the *social* problem of crime. Retributivist theories merely insure that the criminal gets his just desserts.

No discussion of criminal justice is complete without mention of the court system. Reform, all acknowledge, is desperately needed. Sentencing is uneven and sometimes just arbitrary. One study in Wisconsin (Babst and Mannering, 1965) reported that 63 percent of adult males convicted of a felony between 1954 and 1959 who were second-time offenders were merely placed on probation. Plea bargaining increases in direct proportion to crowded court calendars, producing the irony that more arrests for more crimes result in a *decrease* in sentences. Most proposals for coping with crime also contain suggestions for more judges, greater efforts to control the corruption of the court system, and a more efficient and equitable system of sentencing.

CAPITAL PUNISHMENT

Societies have not always reserved the death penalty for only the most serious offenses. Unfortunately, capital punishment historically has been meted out for crimes like pickpocketing, blasphemy, witchcraft, and hundreds of other offenses we would consider minor or mythical today. The types of crimes currently punishable by death are much fewer in American society. Two main categories of crime bring capital punishment: (a) major assaults upon persons (murder, kidnapping, rape, bombing, and arson), and (b) major political crimes of espionage and treason. Some twenty special crimes, like train robbery and aircraft piracy, are also punishable with death (Fortas, 1977).

In recent years, the death penalty has been in legal and intellectual turmoil. On June 29, 1972, the U.S. Supreme Court, in *Furman* v. *Georgia,* ruled the death penalty unconstitutional for the first time in history. The Court reasoned that the capital-punishment statutes of three states violated the "cruel and unusual punishment" clause of the Eighth Amendment *because* these states gave the jury complete discretion to decide whether to impose the death sentence or a lesser penalty in capital cases.

Chief Justice Warren F. Burger, in a dissent to the *Furman* decision, said, "The future of capital punishment has been left in an uncertain limbo." He was right. Thirty-six states proceeded to adopt new death-penalty laws designed to avoid the objection expressed by the Supreme Court. Beginning in 1974, the number of people sentenced to death began to rise dramatically. In 1975 alone, 285 people were sentenced to death, more than double the number for any previous year. But in July 1976, the Supreme Court, in a series of decisions, in effect said that the state legislatures had misunderstood its 1972 ruling.

The 1976 Court decisions have not resolved all of the legal issues in capital punishment (Fortas, 1977). They attempted to strike a balance between complete jury discretion and laws that absolutely require the death sentence. The Court (1) rejected "mandatory" statutes that automatically impose death sentences for defined capital offenses, but (2) approved statutes that set out "standards" to guide the jury in deciding whether to impose the death sentence. The Court also observed that capital punishment is "an extreme sanction, suitable to the most extreme offenses"—a remark that reflects the modern rather than the traditional use of the death sentence.

Public response to the death sentence has been inconsistent, though generally favorable. In 1966 an opinion poll found 42 percent of Americans in favor of the death penalty, 47 percent opposed, and 11 percent undecided. Gallup and Harris polls taken in 1972–73 showed 57 to 59 percent in favor of the death penalty. More recent polls point to even greater public support. Especially dramatic executions, like that of Caryl Chessman in the late 1950s and Gary Gilmore in 1976, galvanize emotions and sharpen the national debate over capital punishment. A total of twenty-seven states now permit the death sentence, although in many of these states laws are in a state of confusion because of the 1976 Supreme Court rulings. The strong feelings elicited by capital punishment are reflected in the views expressed by governors of California and New York. Both Jerry Brown and Hugh Carey stated flatly in 1977 that they would automatically commute any death sentence passed in their states. (Governor Brown later changed his mind and, though still personally opposed to the death penalty, decided to defer to the will of the California legislature—which *did* favor capital punishment.)

Arguments for and against the death penalty are framed on both *utility* and *moral* considerations. One of the oldest supporting pillars for capital punishment was a claim for its deterrent effect on others. However, recent studies have presented at best a mixed case on the deterrent effects of capital punishment (Erlich, 1975; Bowers and Pierce, 1975; Peck, 1976; Passell, 1975; etc.). One reason is the spare use of the penalty. Since 1951, the death sentence has been carried out no more than 100 times per year, although the number of homicides in death-sentence areas has ranged from 7,500 to 10,000 per year in the same period of time. The execution of Gary Gilmore in 1976 was the first execution in the United States since 1967. It does not take a trained statistician to see that the chances of suffering the death penalty for murder are infinitesimal, something less than one percent (Fortas, 1977).

Of course the death penalty does effectively resolve the problem of recidivism. Those who are executed, to put it bluntly, sin no more (at least in this world). But the very extremity of the penalty is used by opponents of capital punishment. First, executing a human being is above all else an irrevocable action. If mistakes are made, they cannot be rectified. (People cannot be brought back from the dead, though they can be released from prison and restitution made if sentenced wrongly to a term in jail.) The chances of executing an innocent person are probably quite small, especially in view of the low number of executions carried out in the United States. But if executions come back into legal fashion (they are, after all, on the books of several states), then the probability of executing an innocent person will also go up. That it can happen at all, however, is enough for some people to oppose capital punishment. An important statement in existentialism opposed the death penalty on the grounds that we can never know guilt with the certainty required for irrevocable actions (Camus, 1961). We can frame the issue in more familiar terms—an incrementalist logic would likely rule against anything so absolutist as taking life on legal evidence.

Second, opponents of the death penalty maintain that its severity makes it an unlikely sentence in actual practice. Judges, they argue, are reluctant to impose a sentence of death, juries are hesitant to find a person guilty of a crime that can bring the death penalty, and prosecutors do not usually ask for the death penalty, either because of expected resistance from juries or because of the relative ease of plea bargaining to a lesser, more certain, penalty. Also because of the severity of the death sentence, the legal system provides numerous opportunities to escape it, from appeals on slight technical errors to commutations of death by governors. Only a very unfortunate person suffers the death penalty unless, like Gary Gilmore, he actively seeks it. The result is often no punishment, or inappropriate punishment, for capital offenses. Critics maintain that the abolition of the death penalty would, in actual practice, produce harsher penalties for capital crimes.

The problem with capital punishment, perhaps at the root of legal and moral confusion over the issue, is that it cuts across our ethical landscape. The Judeo-Christian tradition is repelled by killing, holding that all life is inviolable. Yet freedom of choice seems to require at least giving felons convicted of capital offenses the right to choose death over the agony of a life sentence. (Hence the public anguish over Gary Gilmore.) Also, the very sanctity ascribed to life fuels our revulsion over crimes that brutally take life. Here the sense of justice is confused: the right to life is unabridgable, yet retributive justice seems to demand a punishment commensurate with the crime. Even as the constitutional problems in capital punishment are resolved, the moral complexities of the death penalty are likely to persist indefinitely.

CIVIL DISOBEDIENCE

A type of "political crime" that does not easily fit into discussions of criminal behavior is *civil disobedience*. A person engaging in civil disobedience is breaking a law, consciously and intentionally. But his motive sets him apart from other types of criminals: the civil disobedient does not act for personal gain; he acts because he believes the law he is breaking to be unjust. Frequently, the civil disobedient accepts the legal punishment for his illegal behavior. Nor is a civil disobedient a revolutionary, who is trying to overthrow the entire political system. Civil disobedience is usually limited to breaking only a few laws singled out as unjust within a legal system that, on the whole, may be acceptable.

Civil disobedience was prominent in the 1960s and early 1970s. Resistance to legal segregation in the South and to the Vietnam War mobilized large numbers of people in mass demonstrations against laws and policies they regarded as unjust. The success of civil disobedience varies with (1) the numbers of people willing to act illegally for the sake of justice, and (2) the general sympathies of the rest of the social system to appeals based on justice. A few civil disobedients in an authoritarian society indifferent to justice will probably end up in jail without having had much effect on the system. The civil rights movement in the South was more successful in its appeal to the conscience of the country, although the appeal was strongest in the northern latitudes unaffected (at first) by the proposed reforms.

The central problem in civil disobedience is that of determining the principles that justify deliberately breaking a law. Most people would recognize that there are some laws which, if passed, they could not possibly obey. Nazi Germany, for example, is an extreme case of a system legal on internal rules, but grossly unjust on any reading of human rights. But is it merely the following of one's *conscience* that justifies disobedience of society's laws? If so, we are in trouble, for the dictates of conscience are frequently random and unreliable. Are principles of natural law available to guide our judgments? Philosophers from the beginning of time have claimed such laws exist, but do not always agree on what they are. If those trained to discover them cannot agree, how then is the ordinary citizen to determine what they are?

Proponents of civil disobedience generally recognize several guidelines for deciding when and how to disobey a law. The first rule is "fidelity to law." The person deciding to disobey select laws does so on the premise that law itself, and his own legal system, are generally to be obeyed. Thus, only important breaches of justice are to affect the normal obligation of citizens to the law, not trivial inconveniences or simple disagreements over policy. The second rule is "peaceful dissent." Civil disobedience cannot involve injury to other persons, and can involve damage to property only in the most unusual circumstances. (Thus, the "days of rage" conducted by the Weathermen in the late 1960s, when property was systematically destroyed, count as criminal or revolutionary actions, not as civil disobedience.) Finally, the civil disobedient must be willing to accept the proper legal punishment for his actions, including going to jail if the law requires it.

These rules still do not tell us exactly when we ought to disobey the law—and it would be surprising if they did. The absence of hard and fast criteria for civil disobedience is part of what makes decisions to disobey the law so difficult and, often, uncertain. Civil disobedience is one of the most troublesome commitments a citizen can make. We must allow for it, for no one can say flatly anymore that all laws ought to be obeyed no matter what. But deciding to disobey select laws is never easy. Once that decision is made, the general guidelines of civil disobedience describe the proper limitations.

We will look again at some rational considerations for and against civil disobedience later in this chapter when we return to California's referendum on Proposition 15. As an issue in the general area of crime, civil disobedience obviously presents different problems to law enforcement authorities than does straightforward criminal behavior, or even other types of political crime. Civil disobedients, in general, are peaceful, prepared to be apprehended, and willing to accept legal punishment. On the other hand, if civil disobedience is carried out by substantial numbers of people, civil functions can be disrupted. Many police units are more adequately trained now in handling mass disobedience of laws, so that the dogs, cattle prods, and hoses employed by some local police in the 1960s are almost never used today.

Still, massive illegality is not an easy problem for police to handle. The law has always depended upon its general acceptance by the people to be effective. When large numbers of people disobey the law, neither the police nor the jails can easily accommodate them. But the most difficult problem for society may not be in the effective handling of civil disobedients. It may lie in the moral issue civil disobedients present. Since the motive for civil disobedience is to protest an unjust law, the nagging question for civil authorities and the general public is: what if the civil disobedients are right and the law is wrong?

CRIME AND PUBLIC POLICY

The same types of explanatory models we use in understanding why and how people participate in a positive way in politics can also explain criminal behavior. First, we may explain some small amount of crime as originating in rational decisions. So, too, we may explain political participation as a rational decision. Second, we may turn to sociological variables to explain crime, arranging such factors as age, residence, income (poverty), family background, peer group associations, either as influential conditions on decisions to commit crimes or as environmental causes of criminal behavior. Similarly, studies of political participation may combine rational decisions with sociological variables as conditions that limit rationality decisions, or see sociological variables as environmental determinants of public policy.

The fabric that covers both crime and political participation begins to tear and come apart, however, when each is seen as an issue in public policy. Crime is an immediate and unavoidable problem for any society. It must be managed, consciously treated *as* a problem. The explanations offered for crime are important in determining how a society handles criminal behavior. If an important amount of crime is traced to family inadequacies, for example, the possibilities for successful treatment of crime by democratic governments are severely limited. That crime is an unavoidable public issue even affects the types of explanations sought. Some students of crime maintain that only explanations that produce policy solutions should be explored (Wilson, 1975).

Participation in politics, or its absence, is not so immediate an issue in public policy. That voter turnout is chronically low in the United States, for example, is a problem. But it is not the type of problem that the government is obligated to resolve in the short run. In the long run, low rates of participation may be more insidious than crime to the stability and general value of the political system. But it is an open question whether the government ought to treat the problem as an issue for public policy. The relative distance of positive participation from the heat of policy issues makes more deliberate study of political participation an indisputably valuable undertaking. The recent studies of voting, for example, are important, regardless of their contribution to public policy. Unlike crime, positive forms of participation are proper topics for reflection without the pressures of immediate policy needs.

A LOGICAL PARADOX IN PARTICIPATION

Public participation in the formation of public policy is the happy reverse of criminal behavior and is generally considered good (certainly better, in any society, than the negative participation of crime). We have seen that both rational considerations and sociological factors can produce participation, and on occasion impede it. But now let us assume that both rational and sociological impediments to participation were removed. Could we then expect a direct line between citizen preferences and public policy?

Cynics would say *no*, arguing that authorities would most likely frustrate popular will anyway. But even if optimism were to win out, and even if those in authority earnestly wanted to see the people govern, two curious paradoxes could still obstruct the translation of popular preferences into public policy. One is *logical*. The other is *moral*. Let's take them each in turn.

Imagine, for a moment, the people voting on a number of policy alternatives. Let us label these alternatives with standard notations a, b, and c. Now let us suppose that the people are asked in an election to rank the alternatives, a, b, and c, in order of their preferences. The outcome of such an election will likely present no logical problems. Either *a*, *b*, or *c* will end up a preferred alternative. But sometimes the voters in such elections will group their support in such a way that a logical paradox will occur, with the result that a majority decision is rationally impossible.

The simplest grouping that leads to a voting paradox occurs when one-third of the voters prefer a ranking of *a*, *b*, *c*; another third prefer *b*, *c*, *a*; and the final third prefer *c*, *a*, *b*. Notice what happens: (1) Alternative *a* is preferred to *b* by a majority; (2) *b* is preferred to *c* by a majority; and (3) *c* is preferred to *a* by a majority. Sound strange? It is. Let's look at it again in outline form.

1st group	2nd group	3rd group
a	*b*	*c*
b	*c*	*a*
c	*a*	*b*

Again: groups one and three prefer *a* to *b*; groups one and two prefer *b* to *c*; and groups two and three prefer *c* to *a*. (The preference ranking is from top to bottom.) So among our voters, a majority of two groups (one-third plus one-third of the voters) prefers, in each case, *a* to *b*; *b* to *c*; and *c* to *a*. But this ranking is not rational. It violates one of the logical conditions of rationality outlined in Chapter 2: *transitivity*. Remember, if *a* is preferred to *b*, and *b* is preferred to *c*, then *a* must be preferred to *c*. In our hypothetical referendum, however, *a* is preferred to *b*, *b* to *c*, but then *c* to *a*. Thus the voting paradox: though each one of our three groups of voters logically and rationally arranges a preference order among *a*, *b*, and *c*, the collective result of the voting is a logical paradox. Put another way, the individual groups are rational in their expression of preferences, but the social outcome of these expressions of preferences is irrational (because it is intransitive).

The possibility of voting paradoxes has been known since Condorcet publicized them in the eighteenth century. They have received prominence recently in a number of works, especially Kenneth Arrow's *Social Choice and Individual Values* (1966) and the growing secondary literature commenting on Arrow's use and development of the paradoxes. The important lesson of the voting paradoxes is that even if all social limits on popular participation in policy-making were avoided, the numerical combination of preferences could still be irrational if certain groupings occur in the voting population.

THE FREQUENCY OF VOTING PARADOXES

How frequently can voting paradoxes be expected? Are we merely playing games with numbers? Or are voting paradoxes common impediments to the expression of popular preferences?

Several attempts have been made to determine the probability that a paradox of voting will occur using majority-rule as the method of decision-making (partially surveyed in Riker, 1961; Riker and Ordeshook, 1973, pp. 95–109). The soundest of these studies have concluded that, on conditions of equi-probability (conditions where it is as likely that voters will prefer one alternative as another), the chances of a paradox will increase as (1) the number of voters increases, and as (2) the number of alternatives is increased. When, conversely, the number of voters and the number of alternatives are small, the chances of a paradox occurring are relatively small (Riker and Ordeshook, 1973).

If the curious student presses forward, however, he will discover that the assumption in most of these studies of voting paradoxes, that of equi-probability, is as unlikely in the real world as is the probability of intelligent life on Mars. The world (*our* world) is filled with probability assignments of varying weight, from consumer tastes to traffic patterns to the inclinations of world leaders. One important source of varying probabilities is the *desirability* of the paradoxes. Suppose, for example, that policy *a* is a clear winner in some voting population over policy *b*. Let us further suppose that *a* is a policy that would bring in some new law, while *b* would maintain the status quo. Those who support policy *b*, if they are rational activists interested in winning, will try to devise a strategy to defeat *a*.

One attractive and well-worn strategy available to supporters of policy *b* is to "divide and conquer." If the *b* people can introduce a third alternative, call it policy *c*, which will divide the supporters of policy *a*, then the supporters of *b* may win. Let us suppose that policy *c* is introduced and gains the support of one-half the people previously supporting policy *a*. If originally two-thirds of voters had been for *a* and one-third for *b*, then the shrewd introduction of policy *c* by the supporters of *b* has changed the outcome. We now have the classic voting paradox: one-third of the voters prefer $a > b > c$; one-third prefer $b > c > a$; and the newly splintered group (formerly supporters of *a*) prefer $c > a > b$.

The outcome of the vote is intransitive, thus with no rational winner among the three alternatives. But wait. If no decision can be reached, then the status quo is maintained. Policy *b*, representing the status quo, wins by default. A voting paradox can itself be preferred, and developed as a strategy, because (a point not clear from looking at the technical components of the paradox) a "no-decision" outcome maintains things as they are. Thus, the paradox can be the rational preference of those who endorse the status quo.

It takes no special insights to see that such an outcome may be quite common in politics, and common at important historical junctures. One prominent theorist, for example, has demonstrated how such a strategy delayed the Seventeenth Amendment for nearly ten years (Riker, 1965). So we must view equi-probability assumptions with some skepticism. Not only do people have uneven preferences for alternatives, but the voting paradoxes themselves can be brought about by design, as well as chance (Riker and Ordeshook, 1973). The paradoxes are hardly just mathematical curiosities (though they are that). They are important political strategies in winning the battle for alternatives in voting. (See Appendix C for a more extended discussion of the voting paradoxes.)

A MORAL PARADOX IN PARTICIPATION

The second paradox of participation is *moral*, not logical (Wollheim, 1962). Let's go back to the vote in California on Proposition 15. Focus the lens of our viewing equipment on a single individual voting *yes* on Proposition 15. Suppose that this individual has a strong moral commitment to Proposition 15, feeling that the issue of safety for nuclear plants goes to the heart of survival for the human race. (Not so farfetched, really—many voters feel deeply about the morality of safety requirements for nuclear energy development.) The election takes place and Proposition 15 is defeated. The complication begins. Our sample voter is also morally committed to democracy and feels obligated to accept the outcomes of elections. Here is the paradox: He endorses a *yes* on Proposition 15 because of a moral commitment to world survival, yet as a believer in democracy he must also endorse the *no* on Proposition 15 because of a moral commitment to the democratic system. The voter is torn between two contrary moral obligations, *yes* and *no*, in a situation where only *yes* or *no* is acceptable.

A moral paradox does not present the voter with illogical outcomes. It presents him with alternatives that cannot both be chosen on *moral* grounds. The moral paradox of participation arises because of simultaneous commitments to (a) a policy outcome and (b) a decision-rule for producing policy outcomes (Weiss, 1973). The flip of a coin can as easily produce the paradox. If I feel I should serve first in tennis, agree to abide by the outcome of a coin flip to settle the matter, and then lose, I am mildly torn between my conviction about serving first, and my agreement to accept the results of the coin flip.

The conflict between outcome and decision-rule becomes interesting when (1) moral principles underlie both outcomes and decision-rules, and (2) a substantial number of people are confronting the paradox. If even a small proportion of the 1.8 million losing voters on Proposition 15 felt moral commitments to its passage, then California had a substantial number of citizens brooding over how they could morally accept the results of the referendum.

Anyone who has faced such a paradox knows that the commitment to the policy outcome is sharper, more direct. We go along with the outcomes of decision-rules because they are *valid*, because we have previously endorsed the decision-rule. But the commitment to the "right" policy is direct, with nothing intervening between our commitment and the policy. It is hard to be a loser, especially in a conflict invested with moral values. The negative outcome on Proposition 15 was no doubt acceptable to many voters on the losing side only as a "piggy-back" commitment, one that was a rational consequence of accepting voting as a decision-rule.

Could the California voters who lost have refused to accept the outcome of the referendum? Of course. The moral imperative of the policy outcome might have overridden their commitment to the decision-rule of voting. It might be both rational and moral to prefer the survival of the human species to the maintenance of a decision-rule (if that is what the alternatives amounted to). If so, the citizens of California could have resisted the election results in any of the standard ways, from civil disobedience to outright revolutionary activity. But in deciding to resist the outcomes of a legitimate decision-rule, several considerations must be closely examined.

Let us say that the broad alternatives facing our would-be resistors were these: (1) Proposition 15 is passed (a *yes* vote); (2) Proposition 15 fails to pass (a *no* vote); (3) the decision-rule in use (elections) is maintained; (4) the decision-rule in use (elections) is overthrown. Supporters of Proposition 15 obviously prefer the first alternative to the second. But they may also prefer the second to the fourth: better the failure of Proposition 15 than the chaos a rejection of the electoral process might bring. The second alternative may not always be preferred to the fourth, for issues may be so basic that they are worth supporting no matter if the whole political system must fail in order to keep them alive. (Revolutions do occur, after all.) But the very moral principles behind a particular policy may favor accepting the losing outcome to maintain the decision-rule (Weiss, 1973).

The supporters of Proposition 15, for example, might still think that the best bet to see their cause triumphant in the long run is to keep elections as the decision-rule to settle disputes. They might try again in a different election, perhaps placing the measure on the ballot for general elections at some later time. (The "Yes on 15" committee decided that such a move in the immediate future would not be cost-effective.) This thought, that losers can become winners on some other occasion, has historically justified support for elections as a stabilizing decision-rule. Or, more generally, the supporters of Proposition 15 might decide that they can more effectively further their aims by using the electoral machinery to pursue a variety of alternative policies or tactics.

Supporters of Proposition 15 have pointed out that, though they lost the election, they won the campaign by (a) focusing national attention on the issue, and (b) helping to bring about three nuclear power bills that were generally considered as moderate alternatives to Proposition 15. (The fact that these bills, mandating safety requirements but exempting existing nuclear plants from coverage, passed into law just before the referendum was considered a factor in the defeat of Proposition 15.) For a specific measure to fail while its underlying principles succeed is a common long-range outcome in American politics. (Witness the failure of the Populist movement to elect a candidate, and the subsequent adoption of its main principles by the major political parties.) Larry Levine, a spokesman for the "Yes on 15" committee, echoed the sentiments of minority political factions in American history when he said after the election: "Our constituency won't go away. We'll watchdog the legislature and the State Energy Commission. We'll be ready to go back on the ballot in California, if necessary." If "watchdog" activity is effective under a decision-rule, we have a reason to maintain the decision-rule even in the face of unfavorable *direct* outcomes (losing an election).

The weighing of moral principles against the utility of a decision-rule to realize these principles is as fundamental a calculation as any that can be made in politics. At the center of the scales is the issue of anarchy versus the political society. Very close to the center is the question of which decision-rules are good, which are not. (*Are* referendums the best way to decide energy issues, for example?) The citizen who rationally decides to oppose valid outcomes of decision-rules has weighed the results of resistance against the long-run desirability of working with the established system, and come down on the side of resistance. In the language of Chapter 3, the resistor has rejected the rules of the game in favor of open opposition.

What justifies opposition to valid policy outcomes? A judgment, first, that one's moral principles are worth realizing, and, second, that they have a better chance of realization in active opposition to established decision-rules. But as we said in the earlier discussion of civil disobedience, furnishing instructions beyond these guidelines is difficult. The prospect of civil disobedience presents citizens with a choice between the two themes of this chapter: positive versus negative participation. If the society is just (see Chapter 7), the decision for resistance is less easily made. But though we all must make such judgments, no single scale may be just right for all of us. What is clear is that the mere fact of losing a contest over policy is never in itself enough to justify opposition to established decision-rules. Choosing illegal resistance, or negative participation, is only rational on a calculation of outcomes extended over time. The 1.8 million losers in California may have been eminently rational in adopting that peculiarly political slogan, "Wait until next time," even when attached to the deepest of moral principles. Or they may not have been. They, and all the rest of us, can only wait and see.

PARTICIPATION AND PUBLIC POLICY

In George Orwell's *1984*, Winston and Julia make a commitment to participate politically against the state:

"You are prepared to give your lives?"

"Yes."

"You are prepared to commit murder?"

"Yes."

"To commit acts of sabotage which may cause the death of hundreds of innocent people?"

"Yes."

"To betray your country to foreign powers?"

"Yes."

And so on to Winston's later regret.

For Orwell's fictional characters, and for any revolutionary tradition, meaningful political activity is criminal by the rules of the state, and sometimes by the rules of morality as well. But what counts as a "crime" is one thing to revolutionaries, another to the authority they are opposing. We have in this chapter operated with a single coin, positive participation on one side and negative participation on the other. The use of a single coin, however, is one item in a single denomination within the rich currency of "politics" and "crime." The existential crime of a Raskolnikov is one remove from politics; revolutionary crime is extreme "political" opposition. In between and surrounding these two poles are numerous variations, including the concession that what counts as "crime" may itself have a political origin. The continuum we have high-stepped across here is, by contrast, a single theme—that the two basic models to express participation in politics, rational and sociological, are useful to express participation in crime; and that at least one impediment to effective political participation, the moral conflict between a decision-rule and outcomes produced by its employment, offers to any political figure the rational alternative of illegal opposition to the political order.

In succeeding chapters, the ethical components of public policy will be explored more fully; and, though crime will not be used as a case study for the remainder of the discussion, the later exploration of ethics and justice cannot help but remind us of the underground alternatives to positive participation in the body politic.

SUMMARY

1. The referendum is a decision-rule allowing the people to influence policy directly. It is justifiable (a) ethically on the requirement of prior consultation with those affected by a decision, (b) as a device to find and test the best policy alternatives, and (c) as a means to co-opt possible opposition.

2. The general types of policy "situations" include Allison's (a) rational-actor, (b) organizational-process, and (c) bureaucratic-politics, to which can be added (d) popular intervention (where the people decide).

3.   Participation in politics can generally be viewed as originating in a rational decision where the benefits of participation are greater than the costs.

4.   Sociological factors affect, and perhaps determine, kinds and rates of participation. These factors include (a) such individual characteristics as income, age, and education, and (b) social conditions, such as community size and heterogeneity.

5.   Some studies suggest that "external" variables determine policy outcomes, bypassing people as originators of public policy.

6.   Crime can be viewed as a form of negative participation. Criminal behavior includes (a) violent crime, (b) white-collar crime, (c) vice, and (d) political crime.

7.   Although crime is increasing in America, what causes crime is not known. Some combination of family neglect and peer group pressure seems to provide the most useful explanation currently. Managing, or eradicating, crime is difficult in a democracy if family conditions are, in fact, an important contributing factor in crime.

8.   Justifications of punishment for crime take two forms: (a) retributive justice and (b) utilitarian consequences for society. The death penalty does not seem to be an effective deterrent (though the evidence is incomplete), but some people justify it on retributive grounds. Civil disobedience is a "crime" presenting special problems for society not easily solved with theories of punishment.

9.   Positive participation by the people in elections can produce logical paradoxes under certain conditions. These paradoxes frustrate the translation of popular will into public policy.

10.   A moral paradox faces voters who support a policy alternative on moral grounds, yet find that the outcome of a decision-rule, which they have accepted, produces a policy opposed to their moral principles. The moral paradox can be resolved on the calculation that the long-run consequences of maintaining the decision-rule are morally preferable to illegal opposition to the rule.

FOR FURTHER READING

Having established selection standards in the last two chapters, I will say no more about the advantages and limitations of these reference lists.

PARTICIPATION DECISIONS

DOWNS, ANTHONY, *An Economic Theory of Democracy*. New York: Harper & Row, 1957.

OLSON, MANCUR, *The Logic of Collective Action*. New York: Schocken, 1968.

PITKIN, HANNA, *The Concept of Representation*. Berkeley, Calif.: University of California Press, 1967.

REIMAN, JEFFREY, *In Defense of Political Philosophy*. New York: Harper & Row, 1972.

RIKER, WILLIAM, AND PETER ORDESHOOK, *An Introduction to Positive Political Theory*. Englewood Cliffs, N.J.: Prentice-Hall, 1973, pp. 45–77.

TULLOCK, GORDON, *Toward a Mathematics of Politics*. Ann Arbor, Mich.: University of Michigan Press, 1967.

WOLFF, ROBERT PAUL, *In Defense of Anarchism*. New York: Harper & Row, 1970.

EMPIRICAL THEORIES OF PARTICIPATION

CAMPBELL, ANGUS, GERALD GURIN, AND WARREN MILLER, *The Voter Decides*. Evanston, Ill.: Row, Peterson, 1954.

CAMPBELL, ANGUS, PHILIP E. CONVERSE, WARREN E. MILLER, AND DONALD E. STOKES, *The American Voter*. New York: John Wiley, 1960.

——, *Elections and the Political Order*. New York: John Wiley, 1966.

DAHL, ROBERT, AND EDWARD TUFTE, *Size and Democracy*. Stanford, Calif.: Stanford University Press, 1974.

LANE, ROBERT, AND DAVID SEARS, *Public Opinion*. Englewood Cliffs, N.J.: Prentice-Hall, 1964.

MILLER, WARREN, AND DONALD STOKES, "Constituency Influences in Congress," *American Political Science Review* 57 (March 1963).

VERBA, SIDNEY, AND NORMAN NIE, *Participation in America*. New York: Harper & Row, 1972.

SOCIOECONOMIC AND POLITICAL VARIABLES

DAWSON, RICHARD, AND JAMES A. ROBINSON, "Inter-Party Competition, Economic Variables, and Welfare Policies in the American States," *Journal of Politics* 25 (May 1963), pp. 265–289.

DYE, THOMAS, *Politics, Economics, and the Public: Policy Outcomes in the American States*. Chicago: Rand McNally, 1966.

——, *Understanding Public Policy*. Englewood Cliffs, N.J.: Prentice-Hall, 1975, pp. 277–305.

FABRICANT, SOLOMON, *Trend of Government Activity in the United States Since 1900*. New York: National Bureau of Economic Research, 1952.

KEECH, WILLIAM, AND JAMES W. PROTHRO, "American Government," *Journal of Politics* 30 (May 1968), pp. 510–538.

LEWIS-BECK, MICHAEL, "The Relative Importance of Socioeconomic Variables and Political Variables for Public Policy," *American Political Science Review* 71 (June 1977), pp. 559–566.

SACHS, SEYMOUR, AND ROBERT HARRIS, "The Determinants of State and Local Government Expenditures and Intergovernmental Flow of Funds," *National Tax Journal* 17 (March 1964), pp. 78–85.

CRIME AND PUNISHMENT

BABST, DEAN, AND JOHN MANNERING, "Probation Versus Imprisonment for Similar Types of Offenders," *Journal of Research in Crime and Delinquency* 2 (July 1965).

BALDUS, DAVID C., AND JAMES W. L. COLE, "A Comparison of the Work of Thorsten Sellin and Isaac Ehrlich on the Deterrent Effect of Capital Punishment," *Yale Law Review* 85, No. 2 (Dec. 1975).

BOWERS, WILLIAM J., AND GLENN L. PIERCE, "The Illusion of Deterrence in Isaac Ehrlich's Research on Capital Punishment," *Yale Law Review* 85, No. 2 (Dec. 1975).

CAMUS, ALBERT, "Reflections on the Guillotine," in *Resistance, Rebellion, and Death*. Ndw York: Alfred E. Knopf, 1961.

COHEN, MARSHALL, "Civil Disobedience in a Constitutional Democracy," in *Ethics and Public Policy*, ed. Tom Beauchamp.

EHRLICH, ISAAC, "Deterrence: Evidence and Inference," *Yale Law Review* 85, No. 2 (Dec. 1975).

FORTAS, ABE, "The Case Against Capital Punishment," *The New York Times Magazine*. Jan. 23, 1977.

HIRSCH, ANDREW VON, "Giving Criminals Their Just Desserts," *The Civil Liberties Review*, Vol. 3, No. 1 (April/May, 1976).

HUGHES, PATRICK H., AND GAIL A. CRAWFORD, "A Contagious Disease Model for Researching and Intervening in Heroin Epidemics," *Archives of General Psychiatry* 27 (Aug. 1972).

PASSELL, PETER, "The Deterrent Effect of the Death Penalty: A Statistical Test," *Stanford Law Review* Vol. 28, No. 1 (Nov. 1975), pp. 61–80.

PECK, JON K., "Comments—The Deterrent Effect of Capital Punishment: Ehrlich and his Critics," *Yale Law Review* 85, No. 3 (Jan. 1976).

RAWLS, JOHN, "The Justification of Civil Disobedience," in *Ethics and Public Policy*, ed. Tom Beauchamp. Englewood Cliffs, N.J.: Prentice-Hall, 1975.

SHINNAR, REUEL, AND SHLOMO SHINNAR, "A Simplified Model for Estimating the Effects of the Criminal Justice System on the Control of Crime," School of Engineering, City College of New York, 1974. Unpublished.

SUTHERLAND, EDWIN, AND DONALD CRESSEY, *Principles of Criminology*. Philadelphia: Lippincott, 1966.

TAO, L. S., "Beyond *Furman* v. *Georgia*: The Need for a Morally Based Decision on Capital Punishment," *Notre Dame Lawyer* 51, No. 4 (April 1976).

WILSON, JAMES Q., *Thinking About Crime*. New York: Basic Books, 1975.

Yale Law Review, "Statistical Evidence on the Deterrence Effect of Capital Punishment" (Editor's Introduction), Vol. 85, No. 2 (Dec. 1975).

LOGICAL PARADOXES OF VOTING

ARROW, KENNETH, *Social Choice and Individual Values*. New York: John Wiley, 1966.

———, "Values and Collective Decision-Making," in *Philosophy, Politics, and Society*, eds. Peter Laslett and W. G. Runciman, Third Series. Oxford: Basil Blackwell, 1969.

BLACK, MAX, *The Theory of Committees and Elections*. Cambridge: Cambridge University Press, 1958.

BUCHANAN, JAMES, AND GORDON TULLOCK, *The Calculus of Consent*. Ann Arbor, Mich.: University of Michigan Press, 1962. (The classic defense of logrolling.)

FISHBURN, PETER, "Paradoxes of Voting," *American Political Science Review* 68 (June 1974), pp. 537–546.

HOOK, SIDNEY, ED., *Human Values and Economic Policy*. New York: New York University Press, 1967, especially the essays by K. Arrow, K. Baier, R. Brandt, and P. Samuelson.

RESCHER, NICHOLAS, *Introduction to Value Theory*. Englewood Cliffs, N.J.: Prentice-Hall, 1969, pp. 99–110.

RIKER, WILLIAM, "Voting and the Summation of Preferences," *American Political Science Review* 55 (Dec. 1961), pp. 900–911.

RIKER, WILLIAM, AND STEVE BRAMS, "The Paradox of Vote Trading," *American Political Science Review* 67 (Dec. 1973), pp. 1235–1247. (The authors argue that "rational trades by all members (may) make everyone worse off" when externalities are considered—thus a more pessimistic view of logrolling than the one adopted in Appendix C here.)

RIKER, WILLIAM, AND PETER ORDESHOOK, *An Introduction to Positive Political Theory*. Englewood Cliffs, N.J.: Prentice-Hall, 1973, pp. 78–115.

SEN, AMARTYA, *Collective Choice and Social Welfare*. San Francisco: Holden-Day, 1970.

STROM, GERALD, "On the Apparent Paradox of Participation: A New Proposal," *American Political Science Review* 64 (Sept. 1975), pp. 908–913.

USLANER, ERIC, AND J. RONNIE DAVIS, "The Paradox of Vote-Trading: Effects of Decision Rules and Voting Strategies on Externalities," *American Political Science Review* 69 (Sept. 1975), pp. 929–942.

MORAL PARADOXES

BARRY, BRIAN, *Political Argument*. London: Routledge & Kegan Paul, 1965, Chap. 4, Sec. 3.

——, "Wollheim's Paradox: Comment," *Political Theory* 1 (Aug. 1973), pp. 317–322.

HARRISON, ROSS, "No Paradox in Democracy," *Political Studies* 18 (Dec. 1970), pp. 514–517.

PENNOCK, ROLAND, "Democracy is Not Paradoxical," *Political Theory*, Vol. 2, No. 1 (Feb. 1974).

SCHILLER, MARVIN, "On the Logic of Being a Democrat," *Philosophy*, 1969.

WEISS, DONALD, "Rejoinder," *Political Theory* 1 (Aug. 1973), pp. 323–328.

——, "Wollheim's Paradox," *Political Theory* 1 (May 1973), pp. 154–170.

WOLLHEIM, RICHARD, "A Paradox in the Theory of Democracy," in *Philosophy, Politics and Society*, 2nd Series, eds. Peter Laslett and W. G. Runciman. Oxford: Basil Blackwell, 1962.

organizational decisions and public planning

5

POLITICS AND THE ENVIRONMENT

High up in the atmosphere is a layer of ozone, a byproduct of oxygen, that protects life on earth from the searing effects of ultraviolet sunlight. In the last several years, scientists have identified a growing number of human products that may threaten the existence of the ozone layer. These products include such common items as fluorocarbon aerosol spray, supersonic transports (SSTs), and nitrogen-rich fertilizer.

What will happen if the ozone layer is reduced? Scientists say that cancer of the skin will increase, especially among people with lighter skin. Some also speculate that increased ultraviolet light may destroy microorganisms in the sea, including plankton, thus disrupting the oceanic food chain with disastrous consequences for the whole biological world. The National Academy of Sciences, recommending a ban on the use of fluorocarbon gases, estimated that fluorocarbons alone might eventually deplete the ozone layer by between 2 and 20 percent, with 7 percent most probable. A 7 percent reduction is thought to be enough to increase markedly the rates of skin cancer.

The problem of ozone depletion exhibits many of the standard features of an environmental issue in politics. First, both the effects of the problem and the costs of resolving it are at first uneven, bearing more on some people than others. Although the more severe effects of ozone reduction may endanger all life on earth, modest reductions will cause greater incidence of cancer among lighter-skinned rather than darker-skinned people. Eliminating the causes of ozone depletion will also affect people unevenly. Obviously

145

those with an economic interest in the products that cause the reduction of ozone will be more severely hurt by social efforts to restrict the products. (Whether the originators of environmental problems *ought* to bear dispro-portionate costs for resolving them is an issue to be taken up later.)

Second, like other environmental problems, ozone depletion can reach a crucial stage where everyone is affected. The ozone layer is required for the maintenance of all life. If it goes, we all go together. So the uneven distribution of costs at the beginning is equalized as the problem reaches critical proportions.

Third, resolving the problem of ozone depletion requires joint effort. No one person can prevent the manufacture and use of products that threaten the ozone layer. (Nor can one country effectively act alone on this problem.) Concerted efforts are required. The groupings of people discussed in Chapter 3 are not only back with us, but the coordination and communica-tion efforts of *organized* activity are necessary for any real hope of success.

Fourth, the information that identifies the problem, and on which activ-ity to resolve the problem will be based, is grossly imperfect. We *think* we know what is happening to the ozone layer around the earth: it is being reduced, say distinguished scientists. But other equally distinguished scien-tists disagree. They point to the number and complexity of chemical reac-tions in nature's daily cycle of ozone breakdown and replenishment. They stress the normal changes in atmospheric ozone, and doubt the accuracy of predictions about man-caused reduction. The problem is familiar: uncertain knowledge and high risks.

One standard method to compensate for uncertain knowledge and high risk is *organization.* Organized activity can have several advantages over unorganized activity. First, an organization can develop procedures that represent cumulative wisdom, in effect a codification of what we learn over time. Second, reliability of performance can be increased as practices are standardized in organizational units. Third, various parts of an organization can, if we are lucky, correct each other, minimizing error. Environmental issues like the problem of ozone depletion are excellent case studies for organized activity. In fact, the uncertain knowledge (some would say down-right ignorance) and high risks characterizing environmental issues stretch the planning capacities of recent organized efforts almost to the breaking point (as we shall see in a moment).

With these thoughts in mind, the discussion in this chapter will concen-trate on (1) the nature and role of organizations in policy, recognizing that organized responses are increasingly required for handling environmental issues; (2) the types of rational planning recently used in federal organiza-tions, again with our thoughts leading to rational planning toward the envi-ronment; and, more directly, (3) the environment as a case study of social problems that face policy authorities now and in the coming years.

ORGANIZATIONS: STRUCTURAL FEATURES

When we think of groupings of people, our first thought is how people are *organized*. Organization is almost a litmus test in practical politics: those who appreciate its importance are the professionals; and those who do not are exposed as amateurs. Along with the practical importance of knowing how to organize, the concept of "organization" is a powerful tool to help us understand politics.

Modern organization theory originated with Max Weber, who stressed the *structural* features of organizations. Weber was particularly concerned with *authority* as an organizing principle. He identified three types of authority: *traditional*, legal-rational or *bureaucratic*, and *charismatic*. *Authority* is not synonymous with *power*. *Power* relations exact compliance without consent; *authority* relationships (for Weber) are based on the consent of those who are directed or controlled. Authority can be seen as *legitimate* power, power exercised in terms of values that authorize its use. The three types of authority, then, represent the three general ways of making power legitimate.

Each type of authority provides a principle of organization. A collection of people can be organized in a traditional way, legitimacy of rule being bestowed because it corresponds with the way things have always been done. Or people can be organized in terms of rational or bureaucratic arrangements, where rules govern. (A legal system, for example, is, usually, a rational type of organization.) Or people may accept power because of an emotional attachment to a leader, a psychological connection we are all familiar with on a limited scale. Each of these types of authority describes what we earlier called the "glue" of social arrangements: they state principles which legitimately bind people together as aggregate units. We can round out Weber's typology by inserting the coercive form he recognized: that people can also be held together through the exercise of naked power, against their will but organized nevertheless through effective force.

A FUNCTIONAL VIEW OF ORGANIZATIONS

Structural features, whether legitimate or representing unadorned power, emphasize the static arrangements of aggregates. Although the arrangements are not "static" in the sense of being permanent fixtures of social units, structural features do describe aggregates much as a photograph describes a scene: here are the trees, the lawns, a parked car, and so on.

Now imagine how one's description would change if a sense of *process* were introduced to the scene. Since trees and lawns are involved in growth processes, shift your emphasis to the parked car. If you were asked to describe the car, you might mention its color, its size, the number of doors, the make and model, and so on. But if you were asked to describe the car in terms of what it *does*, you would probably emphasize its top speed, its cornering ability, its braking capacity, and so on again. Many features would overlap in the two descriptions, but a different "picture" would emerge. The first description would be like a photograph; the second, more like a movie film.

To describe an organization in "moving picture" terms, the first natural feature we would emphasize is *goals:* what they are and how organizations acquire them. Goals can be identified as: internal and external. We might simply take as authentic internal goals of an organization whatever some segment of its membership or its constitutive rules say are goals. For example, a yacht club may be formed for the purpose of sailing, a purpose understood and endorsed by its membership. But a keen observer of the social scene might focus on external goals and correctly observe that the preening and strutting about of the club's members reveal another implicit goal: maintaining the social status of those who join the club.

We can talk about an organization's goals, then, much as we describe a car in terms of what it can do on the road. We can identify the components of the organization that help or hurt the acquisition of the goals; from there it is but a short step to the assessment of performance levels both for the organization itself and for its component parts. The *structure* of the organization becomes one component among several in a goal-oriented description of the organization. And when we broaden the description to include both types of goals, internal and external, we are in effect describing an organization as a *system of actions*, a term we should be familiar with by now.

Organizations as systems are described through their (a) performance, (b) environment, (c) resources, (d) components, and (e) management (Churchman, 1968). For example, a systems description of a business firm concentrates on net profit (performance); constraints on capital, product prices, demand, technological level (environment); money and personnel (resources); product bylines, or the subsystems that produce and market products (components); and decision-making on the amount of resources to make available to each product line (management). The structure of the organization has been submerged, in such a description, to the more general concern with the functions of the organization as a system of activity.

ORGANIZATIONAL FORMS AND MEASURES

One of the more comprehensive, yet simple, frameworks for studying organizations has been offered by Allen Barton (1961). Barton distinguishes between *external* and *internal* characteristics. External characteristics are of three types: (1) *inputs*, (2) *outputs*, and (3) the *environment. Inputs* cover such items as the kind of personnel an organization recruits, the economic resources available to it, and its physical facilities. *Outputs* cover its physical production, its effects on people, and the general consequences of its activity (both intended and unintended). *Environment* includes where the organization is located and its relationship with the general public and with other organizations.

Internal organizational characteristics are divided into three basic categories: (1) *social structure*, (2) *attitudes*, and (3) *activities*. The *social structure* of an organization, more specific than Weber's typology, includes the formal authority structure, the power structure, communication and job contact structures, informal social relationships, the division of labor and departmentalization, and the size of the organization. *Attitudes* refer to organizational goals and values, norms concerning organizational roles, perceptions of organizational characteristics, and satisfactions with roles or with the organization itself. *Activities* extend to individual role behavior, collective behavior, and administrative devices.

We can measure organizations in several ways. To get a clear understanding of measurement in organization theory, let's step away from Barton's categories for a moment and try to see organizations as parts collected together to form a whole.

Let's start with a simple physical cluster of units, say ten dice on a table. The easiest and most direct way to see the units as a whole is to count them. The dice may be seen as a *numerical* whole consisting of the ten units added together. Trivial as this exercise may seem, it illustrates a common method for arriving at social wholes. The gross national product, for example, is the *sum* total of goods and services produced in a society in any given year. On a simpler level, an angry crowd is nothing more than the summation of anger felt by each individual in the crowd. Hobbes' state of nature is a numerical whole, as is the electorate (votes are *counted*, remember?). Wholes, as numerical clusters, happily fulfill the cliche that "the whole is never more than the sum of its parts."

Look at the dice again. Concentrate on their arrangement. For elegance, let's line them up on the surface of the table in three lines of two, three, and five dice. We can now describe the ten dice in terms of the three-line arrangement, what might be called a *structural* whole. Plato's *Republic* is a structural whole, as is Marx's society of economic classes. The arrangement of society into any of the standard vertical or horizontal groupings—class, interest group, association—is a structural whole. Structural wholes do not consist of the *sum* of their parts, but rather consist of the *arrangement* of their parts. An angry crowd is a summation of individual angers. A *dense* crowd is not a result of addition. No individual in a dense crowd is dense. It is the arrangement of the individuals (high concentrations in fixed space) that makes the crowd dense.

Concentrate on the dice one last time. Can the ten dice be arranged in such a way that the whole can be described as "independent" of its parts? It doesn't seem so. Without the parts we have no whole. Yet it is a peculiar fact about social theory that arguments for independent social wholes were seriously advanced for a long time. Rousseau, for example, maintained a corporate whole in the General Will, which is independent of individual wills. Durkheim, whom many consider to be one of the forerunners of empirical social science, developed strong arguments for "social facts" that are not dependent on individual units. Are all versions of such theories hopelessly wrong?

The ten dice on our table top are physical units roughly equal in relevant respects. They can thus be grouped as elements in a set, something that can be done with all equal units. For example, houses, cats, dice—each type of unit can be placed in a set, ten houses, ten cats, ten dice. Whatever the value or sense of each of these different items (houses, cats, dice), only one equivalence relation holds among sets containing the same number of members. A set of ten (houses) equals a set of ten (cats) equals a set of ten (dice). And so on.

But now sweep the ten dice off the table (and the houses and cats as well). Let's put another type of item on the table. Suppose that we have pieces of gold, or amounts of coffee or water in front of us. The first thing we would notice is that many of these items require containers, for they sprawl across the surface in not even roughly uniform parts. We had ten dice. But we do not have ten golds, ten coffees (unless cups), ten waters. We have *amounts* of these items—pounds, quarts, and the like. The difference between these items and the dice is that these items do not form parts without the use of some method of measurement. The importance of the difference is this: the comparisons of the groupings of the later items *varies with the measure*. A pound of gold, for example, is not equal *in volume* to a pound of coffee. In short, there are no natural *sets* of these items, nor even natural individuals. Unlike a litter of cats or a neighborhood of houses, gold, coffee, and water do not break up into parts unless we break them up with some method of measurement.

Philosophers call such groupings as gold, coffee, and water *mass* nouns (Cartwright, 1970). They are not wholes independent of parts. Nothing is, really. But, unlike dice, mass nouns do not naturally reduce to constituent parts, nor are they produced naturally by adding or arranging their parts. They have no parts unless they are arbitrarily broken up by applying one measure or another (like pounds or quarts). Perhaps some social wholes are like this—not divisible into units that fit sets of items, but rather composed of rougher chunks or pieces of smaller items. Let us call such wholes *mass*, after the noun they parallel.

Now let's clear the table, take a clean sheet of paper, and outline a typology of wholes from these examples.

Numerical: Parts are added to arrive at the wholes, and the parts are discrete units that can be grouped together in logical classes. Examples: Hobbes' state of nature (where atomistic agents are at war, all against all), the gross national product in economic theory, and all angry crowds.

Structural: Parts are arranged to arrive at the whole, and the whole is described in terms of the arrangements among units, not the units themselves. Examples: Plato's *Republic*, Marx's theory of classes, and all dense crowds.

Mass: Wholes are arrived at directly, and they do not separate into discrete units that can be seen as elements in a set. Examples: Rousseau's General Will, Durkheim's "social facts," and any pure public good.

Let's turn back now to Barton and use this typology to understand how we can measure organizations. (1) A numerical whole is formed by *additive* measures: individual attributes are added or averaged. (2) A structural whole is produced by two types of measurement: (a) distributional or (b) relational patterns. A distributional measure is the degree of sameness, variation, or correlation among individual units in an organization. For example, if we compare organizations on their homogeneity, we might ask whether their membership is truly mixed in terms of race, education, or other characteristics, or whether the members are fairly uniform. A measure of relational patterns concentrates on such items as the relationships between pairs of individuals, the average frequency of interaction of group members, and the clique structure or communication nets. For example, we might view our yacht club in terms of the ratio of in-group friendships to those where one of the friendship pair is outside the group.

(3) Mass wholes seem most appropriately accommodated by *integral* measures. An integral measure, in keeping with the logic of mass nouns, is one based on organizational attitudes, not on data from individual members. Integral data come from such sources as programs, general outputs of the organization, possessions of the organization as a whole. For example, most private universities have endowments, which are owned by the university as a social unit, not by any of its members. Generously endowed universities can be made up of monetarily poor teachers, students, even administrators. With integral measures we are measuring the "mass" holdings of an organization.

If Barton's framework for studying organizations seems complicated, perhaps the chart on the following page will give us a comprehensive perspective on organizations.

The *process* character of the earlier systems model (see Chapter 1) is clearly present here. We are viewing organizations in terms of the functions

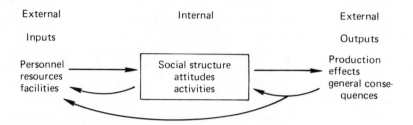

| External | Internal | External |
| Inputs | | Outputs |

Personnel resources facilities → Social structure attitudes activities → Production effects general consequences

they carry out and the means they use to carry out these functions. The typology of wholes, and the accompanying methods of measurement, can be seen as formal variations on the shape and nature of the internal characteristics (the middle box).

Types of Wholes		*Measures*
numerical	— — — —	additive/averaging
structural	— — — —	distributive/relational
mass	— — — —	integral

This schematic presentation completes the more theoretical account of organizations. Any of us can quarrel with this or that component (and probably will). But the important thing is to realize that we are now studying units that are greater in scope, and perhaps different in kind, than individuals. Perhaps the best way to continue the discussion of organizations is to turn to some practical examples in public policy expenditures, since all organizations, past and present, have to grapple with the problem of securing enough money to stay in existence.

PUBLIC SPENDING AND GENERAL PLANNING

One of the major activities of political systems past and present is the extraction of moneys from their memberships and the use of these moneys in public projects. All of us feel the bite of this activity, though who feels it most and how sharply has always been a major political issue. However the issue is resolved at any time, those responsible for spending public moneys are in effect exercising their powers of reasoning on one of the more vital, and visible, functions of governments everywhere. One might think that the visibility, if not the vitality, of this activity would have brought about a consensus on budgeting methods by now. Nothing could be further from the truth. We argue among ourselves not only on the scope and depth of taxation, but also over the rational methods for spending tax revenues. Whether the persistence of such dispute is healthy or pathological is unclear. What is clear is that the divisions over budgeting practices are deep and, probably, will always remain so.

The formal process of forming the budget is well known. The Office of Management and Budget (OMB), established in 1921, is the executive agency responsible for preparing and overseeing the national budget. Budget preparations begin more than a year before the fiscal year for which the budget is designed. OMB sends each major federal agency goals and guidelines and follows up with numerous conferences and bargained adjustments. The final budget represents an agreement between OMB and the various agency heads; the president adjusts and approves the document in its final stages before submitting it to Congress.

The legislative branch, traditionally the controller of money in Great Britain and America, must authorize and appropriate all expenditures. Since 1974, the Congress has relied on two committees, one in the House and one in the Senate, plus a Congressional Budget Office, to review the budget. Congress approves the budget by passing appropriation bills, sent to the executive branch for the President's signature or veto. Once appropriations are approved, the responsibility for the expenditure of money returns to the executive branch of government, where funds are made available by the Bureau of the Budget to the various federal agencies.

Such is the simple picture of the budget. In practice, the budget process is extremely complicated and often divisive politically. Money is a basic consideration in every organization. Even Aristotle recognized the importance of a material base for good and intelligent politics. Many a politician has found the absence of funds a death knell to even the most lofty and profound of goals. If agencies are not funded, they cannot operate. So the allocation of moneys is vital to all interests in the federal goverment and elsewhere. The budget, we might say, is the start and often the final resolution of politics and policy; how the moneys are appropriated becomes a framework for almost all other ideas of government.

Students of the budgetary process generally agree on the following description of federal budgeting.

1. It is, as we would expect, an intensely *political* contest, involving some of the more fundamental interests in American politics. Many an issue is settled by decisions on funding. The decision in June 1977 by the Carter administration to develop and deploy a new generation of more powerful and accurate nuclear warheads atop its fleet of Minuteman III intercontinental ballistic missiles was a policy rich with security implications for U.S. society and the world. The decision also had important consequences for powerful constituents in the defense industries. Yet the *form* of the crucial decision by the President was simply not to remove from the defense budget funds for continuation of the deployment process.

2. The budgetary process is, by definition, *conservative*. Budgets generally are based on funding from previous years. Policy authorities work within narrow limits of expansion and contraction (hardly ever more than 10 percent) of the previous year's budget. Except for proposals of "zero-based" budgeting (to be taken up in a moment), the budget in any given year is bulky with accumulations from past years.

3. The budget is made in a *fragmentary* way, with decisions parceled out among competing agencies and committees. Historically, the budget has been considered in separate pieces by separate groups, not as a whole by a single group. (Critics maintain that the budget's natural inconsistency in policy implications requires piecemeal treatment.)

4. Yet recently, the budgetary process has also been characterized by efforts toward greater systematic treatment. The Planning, Programming, and Budgeting System (shortly to be discussed) and the 1974 Budget Act created a Congressional rival to the OMB in an attempt to plan the budget as a single, seamless web of funding. As a consequence, the budget has become the object of a tension between (a) the natural fragmentation that competing government bodies produce and (b) rational efforts to bring the pieces of the budget together as a systematic whole.

Let's look at the recent attempts to plan the budget from a central perspective. Not only do these attempts revive again the earlier distinctions between comprehensive, or classical, rationality versus incremental rationality, but also public budgeting efforts in recent years helpfully illustrate general ideas of organizational planning.

THE LOGIC OF PPBS

The most famous recent introduction of a comprehensive approach to budgeting is the Planning, Programming, and Budgeting System (PPBS) established in 1961 by Secretary of Defense Robert S. McNamara. The type of planning represented by PPBS was an attempt to manage the entire budgetary process on a rational, centralized basis. In 1965, President Lyndon Johnson ordered that PPBS be adopted by all civilian agencies of the federal government. Although today even the staunchest supporters of PPBS would admit that in practice the system did not work quite the way it was supposed to, PPBS was the darling of program planners in the federal government during its early tenure. Even today PPBS functions in mixed fashion in the government; fragments of PPBS, "zero-based" budgeting for one, continue to be endorsed by some public figures (especially those running for office). Candidate Jimmy Carter, for example, stressed zero-based budgeting in his successful bid for the White House in 1976.

So we can profit greatly by (1) looking at this actual attempt to budget moneys comprehensively in the federal government, (2) paying attention as we do so to the alternatives to PPBS, and (3) trying to understand why PPBS ran into troubles in the American political system.

THE BUDGET DOLLAR

Fiscal Year 1978 Estimate

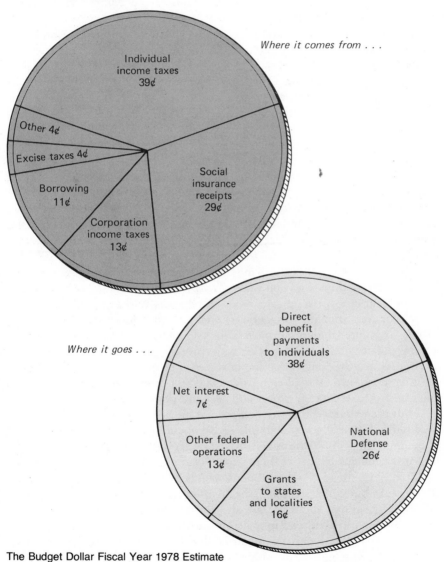

The Budget Dollar Fiscal Year 1978 Estimate

Reprinted from *The Budget of the United States Government, 1978* (Washington, D.C.: U.S. Government Printing Office, 1977), p. M2.

What *is* PPBS? Many a department head in the federal government asked that question rhetorically in the 1960s. Let's try to answer it seriously here. The PPBS approach attempts to look at each segment of the budget process in terms of the whole budget. The activities of each department are placed in the larger context of major areas of government action. The major areas are examined in terms of *goals, outputs,* and *values.* The goals of government action are roughly equivalent to the things leaders set out to accomplish; the outputs are roughly what is in fact accomplished; the values express what ought to be brought about by government. Goals can be evaluated both by output (how successful are goals realized) and by values (how do goals measure up to what government ought to do). Outputs, in turn, should reach or exceed goals and values under normal conditions. And values are themselves accountable to "ideal" concepts of government activity.

For example, a major government activity is defense policy—maintaining the external security of the society. We can set out to specify (a) the goals of agencies operating in the general area of defense, (b) the outputs of those agencies, and (c) the values identifying the best production for this type of government activity. Then the operations of each department, or institution, involved with national security are scrutinized in terms of these goals, outputs, and values. Let us call this scanning a *lateral* comprehensiveness; because it extends across departments and agencies.

PPBS also measures governmental programs by examining costs and benefits extended over several years. Traditionally the budget has been seen as a one-year enterprise, a calculation of revenues and expenditures for the fiscal year just arriving (projections) and just completed (conclusions). In PPBS, goals and values are projected for several years; outputs are calculated for the past several years. In this way, proponents of the PPBS approach attempt to see the long-range implications of government activities. Let us call this scanning a *vertical* comprehensiveness. It extends across time to set goals and secure data on promise (goals) and performance (outputs).

But the extended time frame does not mean that program decisions can necessarily be justified by a simple sense of cumulative arrangements. One of the ingredients of PPBS is zero-based budgeting, a type of budgeting that requires agencies to justify their expenditures from scratch each year. For example, if the head of a department spends $7 million in one year, and has developed a budget of $8 million for the next year, he or she must defend not only the $1-million increase but also the original $7 million. Among the devices a department head may use to justify a budget would be the long-range nature of the departmental goals, thus the importance of the extended time frame. But figuring a budget over several years does not, in PPBS, mean that expenditures in one year can be assumed in a subsequent year *just because* a previous budget was acceptable.

In addition to lateral and vertical comprehensiveness, PPBS examines costs and benefits from as wide a perspective as possible. Again, a traditional calculation of costs and benefits might concentrate on *internal* considerations. For example, when figuring the costs of a cross-city highway system, we would calculate the expenses of labor, materials, land—all the things we would look at when deciding whether to spend money privately on a project. In calculating the benefits, we might include the advantages to motorists of getting across the city in less time, reduction of traffic on city streets—again the same kinds of items included in a private budget.

But public budgets also provide *external* costs and benefits. An external cost of our highway system might be the ruinous effect of a high-speed roadway on the neighborhoods it crosses. An external benefit might be the psychological satisfaction of citizens who feel such construction is "progressive" (a feeling probably more frequent at the turn of the century than now). The PPBS approach attempts to look at the wider net of *external* costs and benefits, not just the narrower *internal* considerations.

PPBS enlarges the viewing equipment through which we perceive public policy. First, the PPBS approach expands the criteria of examination: laterally (more comprehensive scanning of government functions, information, and alternatives); vertically (greater time span incorporated in planning); and through an expanded sense of values ("ideal" goals and outcomes; external costs and benefits). Second, and as a corollary of more expansive criteria, a greater range of issues can be handled in a coordinated way. National defense, for example, can be seen not as an isolated policy area, but as a component in a *system* of policy extending to such seemingly disparate areas as civil rights. Thus the efforts of the military to secure integrated public housing even in off-base facilities is a legitimate comprehensive use of the policy machinery. The expanded viewing equipment will also look at the appropriation processes of government, not just expenditures.

The PPBS approach does not lead to a single plan or fixed set of values. It simply locates existing policies in a comprehensive network of planning, a network that extends beyond the administrative scope of any single set of program categories (Schultz, 1968). Financial and managerial control are achieved through what can be called "strategic" rather than "tactical" planning.

THE JUSTIFICATION OF PPBS

What is the justification of PPBS? Were we able to choose, all of us would like a broader perspective rather than a narrower one. Executives in either business or government can act more rationally if they can see beyond particular programs, if they can see how programs fit into a general budgetary picture. The president of the United States in particular cannot make decisions solely on the basis of individual programs. He must frame a budget for all programs in order to tie specific requests into the appropriation structure of the federal government. So the initial, and perhaps most important, source of support for PPBS is the desire for rational decisions—not only rational in the minimal sense, but fully rational from a comprehensive perspective (Schultz, 1968; Gross, 1969).

The initial desire for maximum rationality in planning is easily transformed by PPBS supporters into a brief for *basic* rationality requirements in governing. First, it is easy to see that many public policies have boundaries that overlap existing government agencies. Welfare, to take just one policy area, is in itself sufficiently comprehensive—covering health facilities, Medicaid, retirement benefits, unemployment compensation, and so on—to outstrip the natural limitations of any single agency. Unless such a broad policy area is viewed comprehensively, proponents of PPBS argue, the result will be a proliferation of uncoordinated agencies. Wasteful duplication and uneven efforts will be inevitable. A PPBS approach to budgeting addresses *areas* or *functions* of government activity that a program orientation to public policy cannot.

Second, the fundamental requirement of even a marginal rationality in planning is that we know how actions lead to consequences. Supporters of PPBS maintain that their approach is an effort to make this linkage of action-to-consequences as precise as possible over as complete a range of policy areas as possible. The systematic orientation of PPBS tries to establish such a linkage in two ways (Schultz, 1968).

1. General values are "operationalized" into specific objectives, which can then function as standards to measure actual performance. One general value of our society is the goal of full employment. Unless we specify what we mean by "full employment" and how it can be measured, then we cannot evaluate the specific policies that attempt to realize it. To operationalize a term like full employment we must identify the classes of people we are prepared to count as employable (will we count students, the ill, those looking for part-time work?) as well as the activities we will count as employment (summer jobs, substitute teaching?). Then we must determine the research techniques we will use to secure the figures for the indices of "full employment." Until we specify indices (what counts as employable and employment) and data-gathering plus data-inferring techniques, say proponents of systematic analysis, we cannot tell whether we have succeeded with any policy or not. Without operational exercises we have no idea either of what would constitute success or of what our policies have accomplished.

2. A systematic analysis of policy, as conducted in PPBS, attempts to determine the social practices and institutions that transform values, information, and effort into policy outcomes across a spectrum of politics.

This determination is conducted on two levels. First, the institutions necessary for certain values are identified in a general way. For example, maintaining internal freedom requires such institutions as voting, elected committees to monitor intelligence agencies, and an established system of law. Second, specific agencies are ranked as to their effectiveness in realizing certain policies. For example, the success up to now of social security might be linked to its development by federal rather than state agencies. (So might its recent financing problems.) In each level, general and specific, the social arrangements either required by, or optimal in, transforming values and policies to social outcomes, are stated as clearly as possible in order to assess the action-to-consequences equation.

The PPBS approach thus requires as part of routine budgeting the installation of systematic review procedures *in* all departments and a comprehensive overview *of* all departments. Whether such an ambitious system can work, and what changes are required to make it work, will be discussed below, for the case study of this chapter, environmental issues, clearly revives the arguments for and against the comprehensive planning represented by PPBS.

ENVIRONMENTAL RESOURCES: A CASE STUDY

Environmental resources, when we consider how they are used, are clearly public goods. The *ecosphere*—the living space for all creatures—provides resources that are, in a phrase introduced earlier, nonexcludable. Imagine for a moment a small group of people in a ship moving through both time and space (Commoner, 1971). Some of the items on this craft, such as clothes, bedding, perhaps utensils, can be privately owned. Other items, however, are held in common—such resources as the air the travelers breathe, the pathways they walk through to get to different parts of the craft, the protective devices insuring that the spaceship survives a meteor hit. It would be impossible or uneconomical to own such resources privately. Many, though not all, of our environmental resources on earth are like those held in common on such a spaceship.

The fact that resources are used jointly, however, does not preclude the possibility of conflict over their use. People can overcrowd the aisles of the spaceship, cook lunches on hotplates that dirty the air in the next cabin, even play radios that interfere with the electronic devices guarding against meteors. The supply of such resources may also be reduced by consumption. Too many people breathing can reduce the air supply; too many people trying to use the spaceship aisles at once will hopelessly clog the access routes. However, common use of resources does not rule out distributive patterns of consumption, especially if the supply of the commodity is reduced: those cabins, for example, nearer the air-supply source might get a larger share of breathable air if the delivery capacity of the atmospheric system were under strain.

Common-use items may also have to be produced to be available. We would have to construct the transportation system of our spacecraft, make and install the oxygen bottles for the atmosphere, invent and maintain the electronic devices deflecting and absorbing meteor hits. If we were lucky, some common-use items would be natural byproducts of the living conditions in our craft. Shipping lanes on the earth's oceans, for example, were not made by man, but were discovered. But for common-use items that must be produced, costs and benefits will be unevenly distributed among those who populate the spacecraft. Common-use items need not be produced in common: a class of manufacturers may provide items that are held and consumed by everyone uniformly.

Common-use resources may be used in two ways: by consumers and by producers. Those who breathe the air of the spaceship are consumers, obvious beneficiaries of the common-use item. But the fact that everyone may use items like air means some may use these items to produce other goods, even goods that will be privately owned. The enterprising space traveler who makes luxury clothing with a miniature production plant that burns "free" oxygen in the atmosphere for fuel and emits carbon dioxide is using commonly held resources to produce private goods. This person competes for the available supply of the environment to profit him in his business.

Both uses of environmental resources, consumptive and productive, can lead to that event we call an *externality*. An *externality* is any activity by one or several people that affects others who cannot control that activity (Dorfman and Dorfman, 1972). If, for example, I breathe the air of the spaceship and, by doing so, reduce the supply for you, then my action has the external effect of reducing your air supply. The ambitious manufacturer of space clothing is causing external effects on other inhabitants of the vessel with both his commercial use of oxygen and resultant carbon dioxide emissions from his operations. The crowding of spaceship aisles results in mutually effective externalities from each user to all others. Generally, an externality in the use of environmental resources is important for public policy only as it affects the welfare or productive functions of other people.

The issues that occur in the use of environmental resources can be illustrated with examples from the spacecraft. First, if the resource is not a natural one (occurring as part of the ecosphere), then we must decide *how* to produce the item and *how much* of the item to produce.

Second, we may have to decide on how the resources are to be *used*, a question of distribution. Distribution of environmental resources is less of a problem than distribution of competitive goods; public goods, as nonexcludable items, either cannot physically be made available to some while denied to others, or distributing them would be extremely uneconomical.

For example, the ozone layer gives earth roughly the same protection as the meteor-protection device gives our hypothetical spaceship, except that the ozone layer is a natural, not a produced, item. Neither the ozone layer nor the meteor device can be made available to some but not to others. Distribution is almost inconceivable, certainly impossible in fact. Private breathing devices, on the other hand, would be physically possible both on earth and on our spaceship, but grossly impractical when compared to the economy of a common-use atmosphere. Such are the characteristics of nonexcludable goods.

But if a resource diminishes with use, as does the spaceship air, we may have to decide whether all uses of the resource are equally warranted. The breathing of air would probably be given a higher priority than the burning of air to make luxury clothing. Or if undesirable externalities occur, then we may want to legislate the activities that produce the externalities. Even natural transportation networks can get so overcrowded that finally all are denied useful access to the resource.

We may also have to modify the activities that affect the successful use of resources that are not diminished by consumption. We cannot physically allocate safety or security on our spacecraft, but we can modify the activities of people on the basis of security needs: for example, we can forbid radio-playing at certain hours or at a certain frequency if the music jeopardizes the electronics of the meteor-protection device. On earth, everyone benefits from the ozone layer. But to insure those benefits we ban fluorocarbon aerosols because of their effect on the ozone in the stratosphere. Thus, even physically nondistributive goods, like security, can require rules that have a distributive effect on social practices in other than security areas of policy.

Third, we have to decide *how* to resolve the problems of production (if relevant) and use. Let's review. An environmental resource is a public good in its nonexcludability. Problems can arise in producing it or using it. Production problems are typically issues of how much, by whom, and by what method. Usage problems are (1) diminishing supply (as in consumption of fossil fuel), (2) externalities (mutual interference, as on transportation systems; undesirable effects, as in polluting the air), and (3) establishing practices that do not jeopardize the good (as in ruling out fluorocarbon spray cans). The issue then is what methods to adopt to effectively handle these problems.

Two methods can be ruled out immediately by the nature of environmental problems. Private ownership is one. The problems of diminishing supply and the maintenance of practices can sometimes be effectively handled if people own the goods in question. They can charge for use and install their own protective practices as part of costs covered by revenue. (Externalities are not so resolvable; they are neither costs nor risks to the owner of the good.) But the nonexcludable character of environmental resources makes private ownership frequently absurd. How can an item that can be used by anyone be owned?

The nonexcludable status of resources can change. American Indians often entered treaties in the nineteenth century that ceded much territory to white settlers; they assumed that the land could not be owned any more than the air could. Events proved otherwise. Perhaps even the air we breathe will be economically excludable someday and thus desirable to own privately. But the physical and economic considerations in nonexcludability rule out the private ownership of many environmental resources. They must be used in common or not at all. Even a cursory examination of those environmental resources that are privately utilized in production does not seem to encourage private ownership as a solution to the problem. The coal mine owner who profits privately from the earth's resources is precisely the type of rational agent who creates obnoxious externalities (in air and water pollution) and diminishes supply. So private ownership seems either not possible or not a method for resolving environmental problems.

Individual action of almost any sort is the other method that will not work. We all know Ralph Nader, but we should also keep in mind that he works with numerous "raiders"; and then, to be effective, he must enlist the support of Congress or the courts. Individual direct action is usually impotent in resolving environmental problems simply because the problems are created by *joint* actions, and so must be relieved by joint actions. One person can refrain from using a congested roadway, or do without spray cans, or refuse to burn the leaves raked up from his yard. But none of these singular actions, laudable though they may be on ethical grounds, has any appreciable effect on the ecological problems they purport to address. The *usage* problems of environmental resources are caused by multiple, or aggregate, use; only those methods aimed at modifying aggregate actions can hope to resolve them.

It is well to keep the spaceship analogy alive in our thoughts. Many of our environmental problems will make more sense if we think of earth as limited in space and resources, with a population dependent on its environmental possibilities, and moving through time, if not space.

THE ENVIRONMENT: PROBLEMS

All three types of usage problems have become important in recent years for occupants of the earth. We face, first, a serious diminution in our fossil fuel supply. This condition has been a potential threat since Western civilization developed a technology dependent on coal, natural gas, and oil. But its acute state, complete with a projected expiration date for fossil fuel supplies, has only recently been known and appreciated. The Arab oil boycott in 1973 dramatized the politically explosive problem of uneven distribution of oil deposits under the earth's surface. The boycott emphasized that long before the available supply of fossil fuel is exhausted, its natural distribution in some parts of the world and not in others will create a volatile political, and even military, situation.

A second major problem in the use of environmental resources is the growing seriousness of unpleasant, even toxic, externalities. In fact, *externalities* is a euphemism for outright pollution. The industrial firms that have produced so much, in Hobbes' phrase, "commodious living" in the last century of Western life either directly polluted the air and water, or produced commodities (like automobiles) that pollute. Nor is the problem any longer aesthetic, if it ever was; rather, it is potentially lethal, affecting those very environmental resources necessary to sustain life on the planet. When chemical companies dump Mirex (a poisonous chemical linked to cancer) in waterways, the "keep America beautiful" or anti-litter campaigns of the 1960s are reduced to irrelevance. (This chemical was discovered in the Oswego River and other New York waterways in late 1976.)

The third major problem of environmental resources today is the growing list of human activities that seem to threaten the basic security arrangements of the *ecosphere*. We have already mentioned the actual effects of aerosol sprays and the possible effects of SSTs on the protective layer of ozone in the upper atmosphere. Also threatening is the increasing production of heat as a byproduct of industrial civilization, a thermal increase with potentially disastrous effects on climatic conditions and ocean levels (Ayres and Kneese, 1972). The population explosion has been well publicized and, though population figures shift like sand under tidewater, some demographic studies still maintain that the worst effects of population increases will be felt at the turn of the century (Frejka, 1973). Then there is the threat of other types of explosions, increasing in risk with the proliferation of atomic capability. It is easy to slip into a permanent state of gloom in looking at these growing risks, a gloom that would make Malthus seem an optimist. But this, what can be called the *jeopardy* problem, is dismaying enough without histrionics.

Production problems in environmental issues today seem more a part of the larger *usage* problem: how best to use our natural resources. Even specific production issues reflect such a question. The awareness that fossil fuels are both limited and unevenly distributed beneath the surface of the planet has occasioned such production questions as where to drill or mine for fuel, how to retrieve and market fuel (the question of authorizing the Alaskan pipeline, for example), whether fuel industries should be more heavily subsidized. Pollution problems have raised issues of control for industrial plants, issues of whether and how to substitute one type of product for another (substitutes for fluorocarbon in aerosols, for example), and issues of whether to maintain or change the structure of basic products (the internal combustion engine, for example). Jeopardy problems have required comparisons of basic types of power plants (conventional versus nuclear, for example) and even called into question the industrial base of Western civilization (Heilbroner, 1974). Without exaggeration, the basic question of environmental policy today, cutting across more narrowly conceived productive and consumptive issues, is how best to use the natural resources of our planet.

POLLUTION: SOME ATTEMPTS AT SOLUTIONS

Public policy in the United States has attempted to manage all three types of environmental problems—diminishing fuel supplies, pollution, and jeopardies—but the concentration through the early 1970s was on the second problem, pollution, for several reasons. Pollution problems were the most visible for many years. Dirty skies and waters can be seen, felt, even tasted, by the general public. Only later did Americans become aware of the seriousness of the other two problems: diminishing fuel and the dangers of modern technology. The fuel shortage received dramatic attention during the Arab oil boycott of 1973, but even this sudden sense of urgency diminished as tension relaxed in the Middle East. Jeopardy problems are like cigarette smoking: the risks are long run and, as a consequence, seldom heeded in the short run. We also are less certain about what threatens the environment than we are even about the risks of smoking cigarettes. Little wonder that pollution stood out as a major problem.

Three reasonable, plausible methods are available for resolving pollution problems.

Regulation. The social system can attempt to stop pollution by regulating the production or disposal of products that pollute the environment. Products or actions judged as deleterious to the environment can be made illegal.

Rational Incentives. The social system can provide rational incentives for polluters to change their bad habits. This method would normally involve the use of tax penalties and rebates to make it economically desirable for industries, and even consumers, to stop polluting the environment.

Access Control. Finally, the social system can control *who* is allowed to pollute and *how much* pollution is allowed by both individuals and aggregates. To do so, the society can adopt either (a) neutral decision-rules (for example, a lottery system) or (b) a system of justice establishing limited rights to pollute. Access control generally involves government selection of productive and consumptive functions, a measure of control in excess of managing the existing economy through either (1) legal regulation or (2) rational incentives.

THE REGULATORY APPROACH

The American social system has opted in recent history largely for the first method, the *regulation* of production and disposal by law, with some measure of the second method, rational incentives, thrown in as a carrot to modify the legislative stick. Laws against water and air pollution have been passed with increasingly stringent requirements in recent years.

In 1948, the federal government passed the first comprehensive legislation on control of water quality, an issue that had previously been regulated by the separate states. The 1956 amendments to the 1948 Water Pollution Control Act tightened federal law and increased federal assistance: enforcement actions were aimed at individual dischargers of waste and federal funds were made available for construction of waste treatment plants. The 1972 Water Pollution Control Act Amendments again enlisted both the stick and the carrot, but the stick carried the way. The Amendments call for (a) the elimination of pollutant discharge by 1985, (b) the establishment of "an interim goal of water quality" by 1983, (c) the issuance of permits to municipal plants and industries based on the attainment of the effluent limits, and (d) the establishment of heavier fines, provisions for legal remedies, and an emphasis on research and education to increase and distribute the technologies of pollution control.

Changes in the Clean Water Acts passed by Congress in late 1977

Table 5.1
FEDERAL BUDGET OUTLAYS: NATURAL RESOURCES, ENVIRONMENT, AND ENERGY (IN MILLIONS OF DOLLARS)

	Actual	Estimated	Estimated	Estimated
Year	1976	1977	1978	1979
Energy	2,385	4,115	6,094	6,892
Pollution control and abatement	3,067	5,196	5,913	6,043
Water resources and power	3,600	4,790	4,895	4,743
Conservation and land management	1,245	1,464	1,370	1,352
Recreational resources	895	1,237	1,381	1,512
Total (includes miscellaneous)	11,282	17,050	19,748	20,619

Source: The Budget of the United States Government 1978, p. 103.

introduced new complexities to government regulation of water quality, dividing even environmentalists over the desirability of the new provisions. Among the provisions are: (1) a one-year extension of the July 1, 1983, deadline for the use of "best available technology" to clean up such "conventional" pollutants as solid waste (with a recognition that the cleanup of some "nonconventional" pollutants may be delayed until 1987); (2) "user charges" for industries based on actual use of water treatment systems rather than on the assessed value of the industry; (3) an extension of liability for oil spill cleanups to 200 miles off the coast (from the old 12-mile limit); (4) an 18-month moratorium on "industrial cost recovery" requiring an industry to pay back extra costs on sewage systems created by its discharges; and (5) power given to the Environmental Protection Agency to control toxics used or produced by industry *prior* to their discharge into the water supply. The Chamber of Commerce labeled the amendments "reasonable, rational." Environmentalists decried the extension of deadlines for cleaning up water, but praised the new taxes, increased liabilities for oil spills, and new governmental power to control toxics.

Federal regulation of air quality stresses even more strongly the enforcement element of policy. The 1955 Air Pollution Control Act authorized federal action on air pollution control, and the 1963 Clean Air Act gave the federal government power to enforce air quality standards. The 1965 Motor Vehicle Air Pollution Control Act gave the Department of Health, Education, and Welfare (HEW) power to prescribe emission standards for automobiles. The Air Quality Act of 1967 required states to establish air quality standards; it also set federal standards for automobile emissions. But it is the 1970 slate of Clean Air Amendments that marked the strong role of the federal government in setting air quality standards. Among other requirements, the Amendments mandate specific standards for automobile emissions, including a 90 percent reduction in hydrocarbons and carbon monoxides by 1976. That the year at issue has already passed and the standards have been accordingly relaxed is itself indicative of the difference between carrying a big stick and using it.

The U.S. Congress in August of 1977 extended for an additional two years, until 1980, the existing tail pipe exhaust standards for hydrocarbons, carbon monoxide, and nitrogen oxide. States were also granted options to obtain waivers on air pollution restrictions to permit the construction of power plants (this provision being aimed at permitting the construction of Intermountain Power Project in central Utah, a plant designed to use low sulfur coal in providing power to 25 communities). Also, cities were given ten more years to clean up air. Supporters of the bill pointed out that the extension on auto emission deadlines avoided a threatened shutdown by the automotive industry.

Attempts to combat both air and water pollution have followed a common pattern (Kneese and Schultz, 1975). At first, little or nothing is done,

Table 5.2

OUTLINE OF MAJOR FEDERAL LEGISLATION ON AIR AND WATER POLLUTION CONTROL[a]

Date of enactment	Popular title and official citation	Key provisions
Water		
March 3, 1899	1899 Refuse Act (30 Stat. 1152)	Required permit from Chief of Engineers for discharge of refuse into navigable waters.
June 30, 1948	Water Pollution Control Act (62 Stat. 1155)	Gave the federal government authority for investigations, research, and surveys; left primary responsibility for pollution control with the states.
July 9, 1956	Water Pollution Control Act Amendments of 1956 (70 Stat. 498)	Established federal policy for 1956–70 period. Provided (1) federal grants for construction of municipal water treatment plants; (2) complex procedure for federal enforcement actions against individual dischargers. (Some strengthening amendments enacted in 1961.)
October 2, 1965	Water Quality Act of 1965 (79 Stat. 903)	Sought to strengthen enforcement process; provided for federal approval of ambient standards on interstate waters. (Minor strengthening amendments enacted in 1966 and 1970.)
October 18, 1972	1972 Water Pollution Act Amendments (86 Stat. 816)	Set policy under which federal government now operates. Provided (1) federal establishment of effluent limits for individual sources of pollution; (2) issuance of discharge permits; (3) large increase in authorized grant funds for municipal waste treatment plants.
Air		
July 14, 1955	1955 Air Pollution Control Act (69 Stat. 322)	Authorized, for the first time, a federal program of research, training, and demonstrations relating to air pollution control. (Extended for four years by amendments of 1959.)
December 17, 1963	Clean Air Act (77 Stat. 392)	Gave the federal government enforcement powers regarding air pollution, through enforcement conferences similar to 1956 approach for water pollution control.
October 20, 1965	Motor Vehicle Air Pollution Control Act (79 Stat. 992)	Added new authority to 1963 act, giving the Department of Health, Education, and Welfare power to prescribe emission standards for automobiles as soon as practicable.
November 21, 1967	Air Quality Act of 1967 (81 Stat. 485)	(1) Authorized HEW to oversee establishment of state standards for ambient air quality and of state implementation plans; (2) for the first time, set national standards for automobile emissions.
December 31, 1970	Clean Air Amendments of 1970 (84 Stat. 1676)	Sharply expanded the federal role in setting and enforcing standards for ambient air quality and established stringent new emission standards for automobiles.

Reprinted from Allen Kneese and Charles Schultz, *Pollution, Prices, and Public Policy* (Washington, D.C.: The Brookings Institution, 1975), pp. 31–32.

even when problems are recognized in their early stages. Second, government agencies conduct surveys on pollution, with enforcement largely the preserve of state governments. Third is a growing centralization of authority in the federal government with considerable emphasis on voluntary action by polluters to remedy the problems. Finally, federal legislation with "teeth" in it is passed, aimed at regulating economic activities that cause pollution. At this latter stage also appear the problems the enforcement method encounters as a social policy.

ENFORCEMENT PROBLEMS

The problems with enforcement as a means for resolving pollution are: (1) those associated with specific legislation, and (2) those general to the enforcement approach.

The first type of problem can be found in both the water and air programs established by the federal government. The water-quality and air-quality legislation were both handicapped by the delays allowed to violators in realizing stated quality goals. Some delays were based on honest assessments of technological difficulties. Others were characteristic of general failures in the American system of regulatory agencies, primarily chronic problems of overlapping interests (such agencies are often staffed by former members of the industry they regulate). Moreover, federal agencies have largely depended in the past on the violators of water and air quality to provide data on their discharges. Sometimes the data were accurate, other times not. It is almost a political truism to observe that accurate information is best secured by disinterested, not partisan, investigators.

But each area of pollution policy, water and air, also exhibits its own characteristic problems related to specific legislation. The greatest deficiency of early water-quality programs is now generally acknowledged to be their failure to have built instructions for *region*-wide management of waterway quality (Kneese and Schultz, 1975). We are rapidly discovering that even what seems to be local pollution has geographically wide-ranging roots, and that only programs covering wide areas of the country will have even a moderate chance of success. Moreover, many of the water statutes were expressed in ambiguous language, which permitted loopholes for violators. Two chronic examples were the phrases "best practical technology" and "best achievable technology," offered as limiting conditions on water-quality enforcement. Reasonable as such qualifiers seem at first glance, the phrases can too easily become principles allowing unanticipated delays in reaching water quality goals. Since laws qualified by such language had, finally, no precise meaning, enforcement was rendered more difficult than it would have been with less ambiguous legislation.

Air-quality legislation also has a set of problems peculiar to its own goals and characteristics. Soon after the passage of the stricter air-control bills, it became apparent that a fundamental conflict exists between emission control and fuel economy. The catalytic devices installed on automobiles, for example, cut exhaust emissions, but at the price of fuel economy. Using "cleaner" oils and gases for heating is both more costly and extravagant, for example, than burning dirtier, though more plentiful, coal. The conflict between air quality and economy is not categorical. New forms of transportation, heating, even production, could make the two compatible. But with existing plant and home facilities, efforts at controlling air emissions have faced a trade-off with the vital issue of fuel conservation.

Legislation against automobile emissions has, in effect, required modification of the existing internal combustion engine. The severe time limits set for attaining air-quality standards may have unwittingly contributed to the delay in developing an alternative power plant: car manufacturers had no choice but to tinker with the present type of engine. But, whatever the role of time constraints on alternative power forms, the fact is that the internal combustion engine seems limited in its capacity to both restrict emissions and conserve fuel. Therefore, legislation aimed at simple regulation is bound to fall short of enforcement goals because of the limitations of the machines being regulated.

In addition to those problems specific to water and air policy, the enforcement model has general problems originating with its method of treating environmental issues. Many of the specific enforcement problems can be corrected without discarding the regulative approach: ambiguous language can be made more specific, regional development can be encouraged, even the emission control versus fuel economy issue can be solved (public transportation can be mandated, for example). But more general problems cast doubt on the capacity of enforcement methods to control pollution successfully.

(a) Available information seems *essentially* inadequate. Assigning neutral agencies to collect data can of course improve the quality of the information. But, as we know by now, information is not free; it costs money and time. If the government is to get the information it needs to legislate against pollution, the costs of legislation go up, sometimes prohibitively. It is also far from certain that completely adequate information can be gathered by government agencies. Current pollution problems frequently originate in areas so technologically complex that only specialists can understand their significance. Unless the government hires experts for each type of problem, some dependence on industry expertise will probably be needed both for collecting and interpreting data. But polluters do not ordinarily self-regulate when it is not in their interest to do so. Therefore, legislation must originate with those who are "outside" of the pollutant industry to make any enforcement sensible. But to the degree that it is from the outside it may lack an adequate base of information.

(b) Regulation, especially in the form of laws, seems the crudest of methods to attack pollution. A law is a form of rule, applicable in the same way to a wide range of situations. Naturally, laws can be sufficiently general to permit local interpretation. But the teeth in the law's bite come from firm and clear provisions rigidly enforced, not provisions accommodated to each situation. The 1970 Clean Air Amendments could be effective because they meet such requirements.

The trouble with such laws is that, while they avoid the ineffectiveness of ambiguous or decentralized policies, they cannot make the complex discriminations among firms and situations that a least-cost method requires (Kneese and Schultz, 1975). Pollution problems vary in important ways from industry to industry, and a blanket regulation makes it difficult to resolve particular problems on an individual basis. General regulations also offend equity considerations. Burdens may be unfairly distributed: meeting a law's requirements may be easy for a large business, impossible for a small firm. Worse, the total costs of cleaning up may simply be passed on to the consumers (a shift in burden possible in rational-incentive methods as well).

(c) Finally, enforcing regulatory laws on pollution is difficult even without some of the troubles already mentioned. Polluters of the environment constitute major portions of American society; they include not only industrial complexes but also ordinary consumers. Economic units are powerful lobbyists in the political system, often capable of blunting even the sharpest of laws. But such ordinary events as general population shifts and expansions (for example, migration to the Sunbelt States) also cause regional pollution problems. How can such an activity as freedom of movement be controlled with regulatory methods in a democracy? What we find in pollution issues are problems caused by the most fundamental of our social practices and values. If a way of life is the problem, it is difficult to solve it by passing and enforcing laws. The enforcers, after all, are also finally the perpetrators, which is to say—all of us.

THE RATIONAL-INCENTIVE APPROACH

No sensible person would give up regulatory methods entirely if the social problem to be resolved were serious enough. But because of the specific and general problems identified here with regulatory approaches, many social critics have urged that rational-incentive programs be expanded beyond present use. Mainly, their suggestions stress a tax on discharges, an approach that, in the stock phrase, "internalizes the externalities": it raises the cost of polluting. The "pollution-tax" approach has several advantages over the regulatory method (Kneese and Schultz, 1975).

(a) It is not arbitrary; it applies to all polluters at the same time, yet can also be adjusted to the amount and kind of pollutant discharged into the air or water. It is generally applicable, yet can be adapted to particular levels of pollution. A taxing method is also basically just—it provides penalties roughly proportionate to offenses. It does not, however, address the problem of who eventually pays the penalty, the manufacturers or the consumer (in raised prices).

(b) A taxing system yields revenues. Policing any industry, whether to insure that laws are obeyed or taxes paid, is costly in time and personnel. But if money is collected, then a net dividend is secured. This revenue could then, at least in principle, be used to develop alternative technologies to help resolve pollution problems.

(c) Incentives are provided for cleaning up beyond the standards set by regulations. Unless a law sets standards of absolute purity, some minimum amount of pollution will always be allowed. If, however, each and every unit of pollution discharged into the water or air is taxed, then it pays to reduce pollution as close as possible to zero. There will always be limits on reduction efforts, for cleaning the water and air is subject to increasing marginal costs: the closer to zero-pollution one gets, the greater the cost of each increment of reduction. Also, with existing technology, zero-pollution is not always physically possible, at least if certain industrial and consumer practices are to be maintained. Whereas a regulatory approach sets limits that often turn out to be arbitrary (as did the clean-air standards set by Congress) a taxing method forces a more natural reduction in pollution to the rational limits of economic and technological constraints.

(d) Finally, taxing methods shift the burden of collecting information from the government to the polluters. The government must still monitor effluents and taxes must be collected on pollution units. But the information required in a tax system is restricted to counting units of output. It is not necessary to determine standards of purity, the impermissibility of industrial and consumer practices, locations for industrial concerns—all stipulations requiring highly expert information in the regulatory approach. Decisions on how and when to stop polluting can be left to each individual firm and group. A tax on units of pollution simply makes it rational to eliminate, or at least minimize, pollution. In effect, a rational-incentive model alters the conditions of a game—producing and consuming—so that it is rational to limit discharges in the most efficient way possible, with those in the business of polluting making the decision on what is most efficient.

A rational-incentive model also has disadvantages. First, some kinds of pollution must be absolutely prevented by regulation because of their extreme danger to the human species. Among these are Mirex and PCBs (polychlorinated biphenyls) in the water supply, both of which, among other dangers, are strongly suspected of having cancer-causing properties. Potentially lethal units cannot be taxed, for whether it is rational or not for polluters to eliminate them from discharges on an incentive scheme, it is still rational for the general society to prohibit them completely. Other effluents, detergent phosphates, for example, are better targets for a rational-incentive approach. So the rational-incentive model, however advantageous, must be supplemented with regulatory measures against extremely toxic substances.

Second, a rational-incentive model must be sensitive to maintaining current environmental quality. President Nixon, for example, proposed in 1972, and again in 1973, a tax on emission of sulphur to the atmosphere, but used as a base for air quality the 1975 standards set by Congress. Since the air quality in many areas of the country already exceeded the standards, Nixon's proposal made it rational for industrial firms to move their plants to "virgin" air zones, an action that would have resulted in lowering existing air quality in these regions. The moral is that a rational-incentive model can *increase* pollution if it is not carefully developed to anticipate all possible payoffs. Hippocrates long ago urged doctors at least to do no harm to the patient as a result of treatment. The same rule can reasonably apply to public policy attempting to curb pollution.

AN UNUSUAL METHOD: ACCESS CONTROL

The third method for handling pollution problems, *access control,* has not been tried extensively in American society, for fairly obvious reasons. Any method that directly controls the industrial or consumer practices of a society, however fairly, limits both political and economic freedoms. Certainly such measures are inconsistent with the basic tenets of capitalism. Whether the freedom of action characteristic of American society is possible with the environmental problems some foresee in the latter part of this century is an issue we will take up in the last chapter. For now we can see that the third method involves a modification of American institutions generally not yet acceptable to either producers or consumers, although some will argue that such modifications may yet be necessary to survive the graver threats to the *ecosphere* now facing the human race.

One area where access control likely will be exercised in the near future, however, is in *land use.* The growing urbanization and general exploitation of physical space has already moved many people to think seriously about government control of development rights, environmental zoning, selling or granting of permits to use land, and perhaps even some social control of basic industrial and consumer practices after permission has been granted to acquire land. The town of Ramapo, New York, for example, uses a program of timed release of permissions for land development. Generally, the chronic problems of flooding, pollution, depletion of land resources, and overall misuse of land may make land-use policy the initial test of access control on a large scale.

ENVIRONMENTAL DILEMMAS

Any method adopted to handle pollution, however, must face one general melancholy condition: even the best information is often inadequate simply because there is much about pollution we do not understand. The recent reports (New York Times, 10/10/76) on pollution in the Great Lakes is an excellent case in point. A generation or more ago the capacity of the five Great Lakes—Superior, Michigan, Huron, Eric, and Ontario—to absorb waste was exceeded by the deposits into them from some 47 million people and hundreds of industrial plants. The lakes, starting with Erie, began to go bad, to stagnate.

Major efforts were launched to stop pollution of the Great Lakes. The United States and Canada spent billions of dollars to install elaborate facilities for cleaning up fluid wastes before they reached the lakes. A United States-Canada International Joint Commission reported in 1976 that over 90 percent of the population on the Canadian side and 60 percent on the American side are now provided with adequate sewerage facilities. Unfortunately, the lakes are still severely polluted. Now the broader dimensions of the problem are beginning to be perceived. A more recent study has revealed that up to 18 percent of the phosphorous and almost 50 percent of the PCBs deposited in Lake Michigan came from rain and snow, not from pipes leading out of industrial complexes and bordering communities. So the *air* is an important source of contamination for the lakes, and the air, carrying pollutants to the lakes from distant sources, cannot be controlled by the recently completed municipal and industrial sewerage facilities.

No one would say that the enormous efforts to halt pollution of the Great Lakes represent failure. Many parts of the lakes, once polluted, are now clean. But the problem has escaped the full solution because of new information, which itself may reveal only one more side of a still greater problem. Those studying pollution problems often find the experience like the reverse of the Chinese box: each opening reveals a larger container to be opened. Because of the chronic inadequacy of information an incremental model may be called for. But the problem requires synoptic approaches if it is to be treated at all.

Efforts to acquire information on the environment are rapidly approaching international dimensions. The United Nations Conference on the Human Environment in 1972 endorsed a proposal to set up a global environmental monitoring system to gather data on harmful and beneficial substances in air, land, water, and all living organisms; measure solar output, air transparency, and soil chemistry; record generally harmful and beneficial effects on life; and keep an inventory on indexes of climate change. Even this data, comprehensive though it would be, is viewed by experts as only a necessary, not a sufficient, condition to understand our environment. This, finally, may be the ultimate irony of environmental problems: they require almost categorical commitments of time and money while yielding only partial glimpses of their full complexity.

POLICY PLANNING ON ENVIRONMENTAL ISSUES

Environmental issues are joint concerns: they are caused by collections of people concentrated in societies with developed technologies, they affect us all, and they can be resolved only by joint efforts. Resolving the problems of our environment requires policies that may alter basic ways of life in Western societies.

Let's apply our concepts in organization and planning to understanding environmental policy.

1. The typology of wholes helps us to see environmental problems. Pollution, all other things equal, is caused by *numbers* of people. The recent shifts of population to the state of Florida, for example, have brought about ecological problems unknown when the state was more sparsely settled. But numbers alone do not cause problems; rather the numerical concentration of people in a geographical area, the *density* of a population (a *structural* term), leads to problems. Not only density, but certain social *practices* (a *structural* or a *mass* term) produce pollution. The modern way of life in industrial Western civilization is responsible, in the most general way, for the strain we put on the ecosphere. Because environmental resources are public goods, they are an aggregate in the *mass* sense; the ultimate effects of usage are relatively uniform across social differences (all of us are being poisoned together).

2. The simple solution to environmental problems is (a) to reduce numbers, (b) to rearrange structures, and (c) to mobilize mass attitudes. But the efforts required to accomplish these general goals may themselves favor, or even require, one type of organization over another. The most general type of numerically-based policy, *voting*, may not produce the radical reforms needed to resolve environmental problems. An organization of rigid structures, or a tightly controlled mass society, may be needed to effect policies that run contrary to popular demand. Certainly a *process* view is required in environmental policy, where long-term outcomes are considered at least as carefully as static, or short-term, considerations.

3. Planning may have to be centralized and comprehensive. Environmental issues are wide-ranging problems, not local or piecemeal ones; as a result (as we have seen) they are not amenable to fragmented approaches. The PPBS model of planning is thus the appropriate choice for environmental policies. But to understand the implications of such a choice, let's re-examine the use of PPBS in the federal government during the 1960s.

First, what did PPBS replace as alternative models for making policy?

Two models, both familiar to us by now: disjointed incrementalism and bargaining. Let's briskly outline the main differences between PPBS and its prime rivals in policy-making to see clearly what is at stake.

(a) *PPBS versus disjointed incrementalism:* The PPBS approach stresses comprehensive information and overall central coordination of policy; disjointed incrementalism assumes limited information and favors policies fragmented along local lines of authority. PPBS assumes that the costs of full information and central coordination pay off in greater efficiency; incremental models view the costs of such information and control as prohibitive. PPBS accepts systematic analysis as required even for the basic rationality of an action-consequences equation; incrementalism maintains that consequences can be known accurately only *through*, not *before*, action, and that means and ends can be adjusted as the consequences become known. PPBS plans in advance over time; incrementalism modifies goals, and even means, as policy is implemented.

Generally, as we saw in Chapter 2, the differences between the two approaches come down to (1) the certainty or uncertainty of what we can know, and (2) the costs of acquiring our information.

(b) *PPBS versus bargaining:* The PPBS approach emphasizes effectiveness or efficiency criteria in policy actions; bargaining relies on consensus criteria. PPBS relies on central coordination; bargaining grants each person an effective veto over policy proposals. PPBS stresses coordination among policy agents on the basis of *prior* planning, but bargaining is an adversary process that leads to coordination only as a *result* of political transactions. PPBS consists of advocacy for effective or efficient operations; bargaining agents advocate their differing interests.

Generally, PPBS is an arrangement for planning on rational criteria formed before the political process begins, while bargaining is a system for reaching decisions on policy as an outcome of transactions among parties adjusting their demands to each other.

If environmental problems require a type of policy planning similar to PPBS, then it also would be helpful to understand how PPBS was actually used in the federal government. How did PPBS work in fact, not in theory?

CENTRAL PLANNING IN THE REAL WORLD

The installation of PPBS in the 1960s was an effort to replace the mixture of incrementalism and bargaining that generally characterizes the American policy process (Lindblom, 1968; Dahl and Lindblom, 1953). If we see PPBS in the context of that form of politics, several conclusions can be drawn about PPBS in practice.

(a) The immediate result of PPBS was to introduce yet another partisan into the policy process, the advocate of PPBS (Schultz, 1968). Several policies of the 1960s can be considered nonincremental in scope, among them the 1964 tax cut, the poverty program, and Medicare. Yet careful inspection of each policy will reveal that their comprehensiveness was not framed or carried out in terms of the strict systematic analysis of PPBS. The reason for this is so simple as to be a political truism: the introduction of efficiency criteria on a systematic scale still must accommodate the political realities of an entrenched method of doing things. Short of a revolution, the PPBS approach must contend with its rivals. So the advocate of PPBS, trying to get the system adopted by often hostile bureaucrats and legislators, finds himself in the ironical—even paradoxical—position of a partisan struggling, even bargaining, for his point of view.

(b) In small measure, PPBS strengthened the hands of some figures in the policy process at the expense of others (Schultz, 1968). For department heads in the federal government, the help came in the form of that aphorism, "Knowledge is power." The introduction of systematic methods to acquire information benefited those who received the information; these people tended to be the department heads rather than lower-echelon people. So in developing budgets the planning could, indeed *must* in PPBS, be formulated at the top. Put simply, those who know the most are in the best position to control policy; PPBS provided information for such control.

But PPBS is not supposed to encourage this *differential* allocation of information. Instead of increasing power divisions by favoring some factions, PPBS is supposed to introduce the *general* rationality principles that govern indifferently: efficiency ought to favor the entire system and, thus, smooth over factional divisions. That on the whole it did not shows once more what can happen when general methods of planning are introduced to political realities.

(c) The PPBS approach seemed more successful with some types of policy conditions than others (summarized from Schultz, 1968). First, where the policy involved the production of a public good rather than what we have called here a competitive good, PPBS worked better. A pure public good, let us recall (Chapter 1), is any good that is (a) nonexcludable, that is, consumable by everyone if available at all, and (b) supply-irreducible, that is, consumption does not diminish supply.

Few, if any, actual public goods are pure public goods. Even clean air, for example, is often distributed unevenly: clean-up efforts favor those living in certain neighborhoods, or at a higher elevation. But the idea of a public good can categorize those polices that more or less approximate the pure standard. At the other end of the continuum can be found competitive goods, those that are typically consumed in a distributive pattern and where supply is directly reduced by consumption. Between these two extremes are quasi-public goods—public education or public works projects—that are unevenly consumed and that are not directly reduced by consumption.

A	pure public good	quasi- public good	competitive good	B

First two things happen as one moves toward A on the graph above. (1) The market system is *less* able to produce the goods located in the region of A, because production and consumption decisions cannot be made if supply and demand are not related. (2) The PPBS approach is *more* successful with goods in the A region (though critics still contend that even A-region success was mixed, even doubtful, in actual trials).

Second, PPBS was more successful with policy requiring technical decisions to produce an outcome than with policy that was heavily involved with political issues. (To distinguish: *technical* issues would require expertise on the policy issue itself and *political* would require consent from authoritative groups or the general public.) For example, in March 1977 President Carter announced a review of nineteen major water-development projects already passed by Congress and signed into law. Many environmentalists applauded the review on *technical* grounds, calling the projects unnecessary and even harmful to the land. But Congress objected. Water projects have long been at the center of that pork-barrel, log-rolling tradition of jobs and contracts that is a *political* necessity from a legislator's point of view. The president gradually reversed his course, although the technical arguments against the projects were still valid. A policy satisfactory on technical grounds, in short, may not satisfy political needs. The PPBS approach was found more successful in technical than in political policies.

Third, PPBS was more effective in new rather than established programs. The various efforts to eradicate poverty prominent in the 1960s were more amenable to PPBS than were, say, the education programs with longer tenure and established personnel and procedures. The success in newer programs has an ironic twist: older programs typically have a more thorough data base drawn from their history of trying things out, thus more nearly complete information on relevant policies. Newer programs, on the other hand, are just beginning to secure information because of their naturally experimental status. But PPBS, which rationally requires comprehensive information, was more easily put into operation in programs with a lower quantity and quality of information.

What made for the relative success of PPBS in these three conditions? If we look at them closely, we can see that all share an interesting feature: PPBS seems to have been successful where individuals or groups were *not* competing for outcomes, where policy decisions could be made in a way rationally indifferent to the people the policy affected. A pure public good is not a market item competed for by consumers; a technical decision is valid independent of people's interests; and a new program does not involve the rearrangement of an established bureaucracy. This curious feature of PPBS provides a dual sense of "success": the satisfaction of systematic norms of effectiveness or efficiency (PPBS) versus the satisfaction of interests or demands in the political system.

If we turn back to the typology of wholes introduced earlier, we can get a fuller sense of what the PPBS approach to policy requires. The PPBS approach seems to assume that people can be rationally grouped in *mass* terms, with effectiveness or efficiency the principle binding them happily together. The incremental and bargaining models, on the other hand, view people in *structural* terms, societies divided, not uniform, and requiring either piecemeal strategies or bargaining transactions to reach policy outcomes. Perhaps, though, people are just people, *numerical* units associated for brief moments to bring about some joint social effort.

Let's not argue what kinds of wholes social units *really* are. It is enough to understand that, to the degree that social conditions are not what a model of policy assumes—fragmented rather than uniform for PPBS; uniform rather than fragmented for incrementalism; harmonious rather than contentious for bargaining—then that particular model is not going to fit these social conditions.

CENTRAL PLANNING TOWARD THE ENVIRONMENT

What do these outcomes of the PPBS experiment mean in the context of environmental problems?

One of the fixed features of public policy at any given time in American politics is its inconsistency. No institution seems immune. The U.S. Supreme Court, for example, in 1977 (a) had forbidden, as an invasion of states' rights, the application of the federal minimum-wage law to local government employees whose work affected interstate commerce *and* (b) had affirmed a federal conviction of a man for mailing obscene material from one city to another in a state with no restrictions on the distribution of such material. Constitutional lawyers had their usual field days pointing out the inconsistencies between (a) and (b), not for the first time in American judicial history.

Also, ordinary students of logic could point to (a) the federal government's campaign against smoking (with warning labels on cigarette packages and equal-time on television for antismoking commercials) and (b) federal subsidies to tobacco farmers. Then, in the saccharin flap of 1977, the federal government banned saccharin from general use because of its carcinogenic nature, yet allowed cigarettes, at least as strongly linked to cancer, to be sold with the proper warnings. Advanced students of logic could no doubt discover different reasons for each policy, which might remove the more glaring inconsistencies. But to the man in the street, public policy must often display neither rhyme nor reason when taken as a whole.

Any student of the federal government can list similar examples. Public policy is notoriously fragile when logic is brought to bear on it. The reasons for inconsistencies are well known. The fragmented body of institutions responsible for policy produces a package satisfactory on local requirements while inconsistent as a single whole. The saving grace of such an arrangement is also well known. Policy that is inconsistent as a single whole may yet be implemented consistently one piece at a time. Or, what cannot be done logically all at once can be feasible when extended over time. Remember the voting paradoxes discussed in Chapter 4: the intransitive ordering of preferences requires counting votes all *at the same time.* Preferences expressed in piecemeal fashion, with a time lag between them, need not be compared on logical grounds (see Appendix C).

The main influence of environmental problems on policy may be to remove this buffer against logical requirements through the contraction of time. We may not have a long and leisurely time span to solve the problems of the environment; we may have to solve them now, all at once. If so, the normal contradictions of policy, tolerable over extended time, will have to be resolved. Logical inconsistencies are also real-world impossibilities: a paradoxical policy cannot by definition be successfully implemented all at once. Since rationality requires that all institutions responsible for a body of policy be coordinated, then the tendency to central planning on environmental issues is self-evident.

One way to see this tendency is to revive the different types of aggregates outlined earlier. Structural or differentiated institutions, the source of public policy in the American political system, will face pressure to become uniform, either as mass or numerical arrangements. Organizations conceived on integral measures may be the only tolerable form for policy-making. The designation in the 1970s of an energy czar, a post first occupied by James Schlesinger in the Carter administration, reflects this growing pressure for central coordination. It is a standard change in American politics when the press of time and circumstances requres policies rational all at the same time.

Environmental problems will also bring pressure for technical rather than political solutions. Nature is notorious for being indifferent to popular demand. The problems of the ecosphere may require solutions painful to the most influential constituencies in American politics. Business in general may not, however, be among the losers. Pollution control is very profitable. In 1976, Americans spent $16 billion to clean the environment and dispose of waste. Among those reaping profits are some of the biggest names in industry, including Corning Glass (which makes the glass for catalytic converters). New pollution-control businesses are rapidly joining the ranks of the nation's largest companies. One loser in pollution control may be the taxpayer. The federal government, for example, pays 75 percent of the cost of sewage treatment plants. But whoever loses, the gravity of environmental problems may force government to adopt policies that are correct, whether or not they are popular.

What these pressures from environmental problems, especially the energy shortage, may do to democratic institutions will be discussed in Chapter 8. The outlook for rational planning, however, is clear in both outline and detail: the rational model central to PPBS may be the choice forced on policy authorities dealing with the environment. And, along with all of the advantages and limitations of the model disclosed by its trial period in the 1960s, these authorities will confront the additional problem of inadequate information characteristic of so many environmental issues.

If comfortable practices are to be radically altered, however, evaluative questions are sure to be raised. Cleaning up the environment and conserving energy may require a radical redistribution of income. President Carter's energy program presented to Congress during his first year in office involved taxes on gasoline and oil, combined with price increases for natural gas. Rebates to the consumer were designed to soften the bite of increased energy costs. These are all budgetary decisions and policies. But the changes such proposals require in our basic way of living slides the budgetary issues over to more fundamental questions of fairness and efficiency.

Environmental pressures thus bring renewed emphasis on more traditional inquiries and concepts. Is a certain policy in the public interest? Are social arrangements just? We will turn to questions like these in the next two chapters.

SUMMARY

1.   Aggregates of people, an idea central to our understanding of politics and public policy, can be arranged in three basic forms: (a) numerical, (b) structural, (c) mass.

2.   Organizations can be described in a systems framework specifying the input-output dimensions of aggregate action. The measures used to arrive at organizational attributes correspond to the aggregate typology: (a) additive, averaging—numerical whole; (b) distributive, relational—structural whole; (c) integral—mass whole.

3.   The Planning, Programming, and Budgeting System (PPBS) attempts to plan aggregate expenditures on a synoptic basis. The success of PPBS seems to be greater in noncompetitive and uniform conditions. Approaches competitive with PPBS—incrementalism and bargaining—seem to flourish in fragmented, contentious social conditions.

4.   That environmental resources are common-use items is one important source for ecosphere problems: many of the things of nature can be used
without internal costs, although undesirable externalities typically occur.

5.   The main problems in environmental concerns are (a) fossil-fuel
depletion, (b) pollution, and (c) practices that seem to jeopardize the security
of the human race.

6.   The attempts in American society to handle pollution problems can
be separated into three general methods: (a) regulation, (b) rational incentives, (c) access-control (little used). Although each of these methods has its
advantages and disadvantages, the absence of complete success in their use
sometimes is symptomatic of general difficulties in environmental policy: the
need for comprehensive planning on inadequate understanding.

7.   Environmental problems may renew pressures for central, rational
planning of public policy, though standard budgetary matters may be transformed into basic evaluative issues covered by the public interest and justice.

FOR FURTHER READING

As will be clear to anyone familiar with the literature bearing on this
section, three books figure with special prominence in my thoughts on the
PPBS and environmental sections. So let me list them first to acknowledge
my debts before listing other works worth reading on the topics of this
chapter.

THE BIG THREE

DORFMAN, ROBERT, AND NANCY DORFMAN, EDS., *Economics of the Environment*.
    New York: Norton, 1972. (All the essays are solid, though the Introduction
    alone is worth the price of the book.)
KNEESE, ALLEN V., AND CHARLES SCHULTZ, *Pollution, Prices, and Public Policy*.
    Washington, D.C.: Brookings Institution, 1975.
SCHULTZ, CHARLES, *The Politics and Economics of Public Spending*. Washington,
    D.C.: Brookings Institution, 1968. (A minor classic on the subject.)

ORGANIZATIONS

BARTON, ALLEN, *Organizational Measurement*. Princeton, N.J.: College Entrance
Examination Board, 1961.
CARTWRIGHT, HELEN, "Quantities," *Philosophical Review*, Jan. 1970.
CHURCHMAN, C. WEST, *The Systems Approach*. New York: Dell, 1968.
ETZIONI, AMATAI, *A Comparative Analysis of Complex Organizations*. Glencoe, Ill.:
Free Press, 1961.

————, *Modern Organizations.* Englewood Cliffs, N.J.: Prentice-Hall, 1964.
MARCH, JOHN, AND HERBERT SIMON, *Organizations.* New York: John Wiley, 1958.
SIMON, HERBERT, *Administrative Behavior.* New York: Free Press, 1959.

PUBLIC BUDGETING

CRECINE, JOHN P., *Governmental Problem Solving.* Chicago: Rand McNally, 1969.
FENNO, RICHARD, *The Power of the Purse: Appropriations Politics in Congress.* Boston: Little, Brown, 1966.
GROSS, BERTRAM, "The New Systems Budgeting," *Public Administration Review* 29 (March-April, 1969).
SCHICK, ALLEN, "The Road to PPB, the Stages of Budget Reform," *Public Administration Review* 26 (Dec. 1966).
SHARKANSKY, IRA, *The Politics of Taxing and Spending.* Indianapolis: Bobbs-Merrill, 1970.
WILDAVSKY, AARON, *The Politics of the Budgetary Process.* Boston: Little, Brown, 1964.
————, "Rescuing Policy Analysis from PPBS," *Public Administration Review* 29 (March/April 1969), pp. 189–202.

THE ENVIRONMENT

ANDERSON, WALT, ED., *Politics and the Environment.* Pacific Palisades, Calif.: Goodyear, 1975.
AYRES, ROBERT, AND ALLEN KNEESE, *Economic and Ecological Effects of a Stationary State,* Resources for the Future, Reprint No. 99, Dec. 1972.
BARTELS, ROBERT, ROBERT D. HENNIGAN, AND ROBERT M. L. BELLANDI, EDS., *The Severe Restriction of Development.* Syracuse, N.Y.: State University of New York, 1977. (Conference Proceedings and selected articles on land use that touch on what I have called "access control.")
BISH, ROBERT, L., *The Public Economy of Metropolitan Areas.* Chicago: Rand McNally, 1971. (The author discusses pollution "rights" or franchises.)
COMMONER, BARRY, *The Closing Circle.* New York: Knopf, 1971.
Environmental Quality - 1976. Washington, D.C.: U.S. Government Printing Office, 1976.
FREJKA, TOMAS, "The Prospects for a Stationary World Population," *Scientific American,* March 1973.
HEILBRONER, ROBERT, *An Inquiry into the Human Prospect.* New York: Norton, 1974.
MEADOWS, DONELLA, DENNIS MEADOWS, JORGEN RANDERS, AND WILLAIM BEHRENS III, *The Limits to Growth.* New York: New American Library, 1972.
MESAROVIC, MIHAJLO, AND EDUARD PESTEL, *Mankind at the Turning Point.* New York: New American Library, 1974.

public policy evaluation

6

THE EVALUATION OF "POLITICS"

Though we all make value judgments from time to time, only recently has evaluation become acceptable—even honored—in the study of politics. Until a few years ago, the fiction of neutrality was maintained in the intellectual marketplace on the assumption that values can and ought to be suspended for the sake of "objectivity" (Weber, 1949; Brecht, 1959). Dispassionate, even neutral, inquiry was not only considered the soundest approach to any professional work, but also the supporting form for true (read: means–ends) rationality (Simon, 1947).

Exactly how events produce and condition ideas is not always easy to say. But no one who has lived through the last decade can maintain a neutral view of values. Not only has the possibility of value-neutrality itself been challenged effectively (Taylor, 1967), but the demands of our institutions have required the systematic entrance of evaluations. Impact studies by both governments and businesses routinely require evaluative criteria, demand equity as well as efficiency. Teachers must unearth value assumptions and examine ideological proposals as part of the day's activities. Policy study centers grow in numbers. Even such weighty ideas as "the public interest" and "justice" have become reasonable topics for students of public policy. One of the standard graffiti of the 1960s was "God exists—He just doesn't want to get involved." Now we know that even if God is indifferent to values, human beings cannot afford to be.

Evaluating political life is both like and unlike other kinds of evaluations. To evaluate anything, generally we assign it a value based on criteria

183

we have adopted. But because things vary from one another in important ways, so too must our criteria. Determining what makes an apple good requires one set: a juicy taste, a crisp texture, perhaps a nice color. Determining what makes a political system good calls for quite another set, not always as easy to identify but certainly not juiciness, crispness, and good color. When we assign value to things, our assignments are conditioned by the nature of the things themselves.

Determining the nature of "politics" is difficult, in part because the term has been extended to so wide and heterogeneous a cluster of human activities (see Chapter 1). But we can assume that at least the *policy* side of "politics" is involved with aggregates of people, and that when we evaluate political life, we are evaluating joint, not singular, action. Even this mild assertion is packed with implications for ordinary evaluations. A value assigned to one thing may be modified if the thing valued is multiple. A collector who believes he possesses a rare coin may assign it less value if the market becomes flooded with identical coins.

Many of the evaluative concepts in political discourse take on their peculiar characteristics because of the aggregate or group nature of political experience. The five that will be discussed here and in the next chapter at some length—*equity, efficiency, Pareto Optimality, the public interest,* and *justice*—weigh and compare the arrangements people have with one another. They are strong only as comparative concepts, and are generally used to evaluate multiple social units. Our case study for this chapter is *welfare policies,* a public policy area that offers a strong test for the evaluative power of these five concepts.

POLICY VERSUS "PURE" RESEARCH

We have not only evaluations *of* "politics" but also evaluations to be used *for* "politics." Political action (as mentioned in Chapter 1) is a strong *directive* type of action. People seem continually to be trying to get others to do things, to change or maintain social arrangements, to increase their interests or values—what some (Marshall McLuhan, for one) would call "hot," not "cool," activity. Often this heat spills over to the intellectual world and research contracts are assigned to study the needs for, and the paths of, political activity. Policy evaluation is thus frequently the arm of politics, not just the judge or spectator.

The "contractual" status of some evaluations does, moreover, make a difference. Policy-motivated research marches to a different drummer than "pure" research. Let us distinguish carefully between the two. Research motivated by policy concerns is directed toward specific social issues, intended to offer insight into resolving those issues, and commissioned by activists in the social process.

An excellent example of policy research at the highest intellectual level is the study of education directed by James Coleman, *Equality of Educational Opportunity* (discussed in Chapter 2). The U.S. Congress appropriated funds for the study, stating that the Education Commissioner "shall conduct a survey and make a report . . . concerning the lack of availability of equal educational opportunities . . . ." The resulting Coleman Report was research motivated by policy.

"Pure" research, on the other hand, is not motivated by policy, though it may have implications for social issues. The voting studies discussed briefly in Chapter 4 are good examples of research that (1) is not directed toward special social issues, (2) does not offer recommendations for policy nor aim at providing information to guide policy decisions, and (3) is not commissioned by activists in the social process. The conclusions of the voting studies are rich with implications for policy, but the policy implications are the consequences of the research, not the motivations.

The ways in which policy-oriented research differs from pure research reflect the different motivations for each, differences persuasively described by James Coleman (1975).

1. If action is required, if delay is costly or inconceivable, then partial information is better than no information at all, and even better than complete information that is not available until after the time for action has passed. Political conditions have a way of demanding immediate responses. Unlike such placid games as chess and bridge, politics is at times analogous to fire-fighting: some form of action is required just to avoid the loss of standing by. Information pointing to the best course of action is useless after the fire has done its damage. Even a few clues on how to proceed before the damage is done is better than well-documented theories about fire-fighting after one's house is demolished. *Timely* knowledge is what policy-motivated research reaches for. Pure research may proceed indifferent to immediate societal needs.

2. Policy-oriented research aims to produce a social policy modified or conditioned by the results of the research. Pure research produces conclusions supported by theory and data. Policy-oriented research is not concerned with contributing some original theory to the world of scholarship; it's not necessarily concerned with any theory. Its aim is to work out a satisfactory policy by means of research that meets standards of reliability. Pure research, on the other hand, aims at scholarly contributions with no pressing need to relate the scholarship to social policy.

3. Because of the different products of policy-oriented and pure research, different standards of adequacy guide each approach. In policy-oriented studies, trial-and-error methods can suffice: in pure research, theoretical propositions must be verified. Coleman uses the example of artillery fire to make this point. The trajectory of a cannonball in the eighteenth century could have been calculated by (a) using Newtonian equations on

projectile and wind velocity, angle of fire, distance, and gravitational pull, *or* by (b) using the trial-and-error method of raising and lowering the barrel of the cannon after each shot. The first, theoretical, calculation is of course more elegant, and the conclusions drawn from such calculations exemplify pure research: they are well supported by theoretical propositions. But the second, trial-and-error calculation may meet the needs of the policy-oriented researcher just as well as, and even better than, the first calculation. It is not as elegant, and perhaps lacks any theoretical base whatsoever, but it is pragmatically as good as the theoretical method *in the way that it works*. The trial-and-error method gives approximately correct results with high reliability, while the theoretical calculation is likely to be grossly wrong much of the time because of the difficulty of estimating all of the variables. So, though the first method is theoretically sounder, the policy-oriented research can be eminently satisfied with trial-and-error as a method for supporting policy proposals.

4. The policy researcher is interested in uncovering the conditions of social problems that can be cured, not causes that resist solution. James Q. Wilson (1975) laments the confusion of *causal* analysis with *policy* analysis, maintaining that policy research does not want to discover ultimate causes of crime so much as to discover what will reduce crime. Coleman (1975) urges a distinction between two kinds of independent variables, controllable and uncontrollable. The *policy* variable is controllable. Uncontrollable variables are *situational* in policy research. Pure researchers are interested in both kinds of independent variables (controllable *and* uncontrollable). Policy researchers are concerned primarily with policy (controllable) variables.

Policy research cannot totally ignore situations beyond their control. If family problems contribute to crime, this fact cannot be dismissed just because modifying family life is difficult in democratic societies. But if a social problem is brought about by multiple variables (as often happens), the policy researcher is more inclined to put his research money toward trying to understand those variables that can be changed rather than those that cannot.

5. Policy researchers have clients, pure researchers do not. Policy scientists, unlike pure researchers, thus must translate the needs of their client into research language, sometimes a tricky task. Coleman (1975) relates how his staff had to discover both the intent of Congress in the 1964 directive and the interests of various groups experiencing the unequal educational opportunity marked off in the directive. Then the concept of "inequality" had to be specified. The staff identified five different measures of the concept:

(a) Community input, such as per-pupil expenditure, school plants, libraries;

(b) Racial composition of schools;

(c)   Intangible characteristics, such as morale, expectations, interests;

(d)   Consequences of schools for individuals with equal backgrounds and abilities; and

(e)   Consequences of schools for individuals of unequal backgrounds and abilities.

The Coleman Report focused primarily on measure (d) above, but also provided information on the other four interpretations of inequality. The reasoning that led the staff to focus on the consequences of schools for individuals with equal backgrounds is exactly what we would expect from policy-oriented research: the results of such a concentration were deemed to be more readily translatable into policy than outcomes focused on the other four senses of inequality (Coleman, 1975).

POLICY-ORIENTED EVALUATIONS

The main complaint about policy research is that values have too tight a hold on research itself. Critics often relate some version of the following story: If we go to the doctor for a routine physical examination, we expect him to check all pathological problems, not just those that are curable. He would not focus his attention on a hangnail instead of a cancer of the liver simply because he could cure the former and could not cure the latter. Certainly therapy is sensibly directed where it can do the most good, though even here we might prefer a little improvement on a serious problem to a great improvement on a minor problem. Initiating radiation therapy of lymphoid cancer, though not a "sure cure," is still more desirable than ignoring the condition to concentrate on nervous tension. Even if treatment is only marginally successful, avoiding immediate death seems infinitely better than attending to less pressing needs.

The point critics make is that the seriousness of a problem is a factor, quite apart from its malleability, or general responsiveness to therapy, whether we are discussing medical treatment or social policy. Taking a page from the book on pure research, the proper sequence might be: (1) establishing the full range of conditions that cause problems, *then* (2) ranking methods for resolving these problems. Critics stress that the danger in policy-oriented research is that the sequence is frequently inverted, at the expense of (1): the methods of treatment are allowed to set the priorities in researching the causes of social problems. With such an inversion we risk practicing the absurdity exhibited in the medical example above: letting the possibility of cure influence the treatment of disease.

Critics also point out that pure research may, in the long run, have more lasting impact on policy precisely because it is theoretically sound. The voting studies carried out in the last two decades by the Survey Research Center at the University of Michigan (see Chapter 4 for references) are types of (roughly) pure research. The Coleman Report was policy-oriented research. Yet which has had more important consequences for the political system is an open question. Both have been used by political activists for social change and maintenance. Both have altered our basic understandings of the social system. One might argue that the voting studies have furnished more reliable information for public policy, even though they stand primarily as contributions to ongoing scholarship rather than to public policy. Certainly the bare fact of policy orientation has not made the Coleman Report a more reliable guide, and may even have contributed somewhat to its uneasy status in both the scholarly and policy worlds.

Finally, it is costly to experiment with social programs. The great sums of money poured into many social measures of the 1960s, for example Head Start Programs, sometimes produced only great social headaches instead of remedies. The trial-and-error approach, critics say, may be fine for cannon trajectories, but is prohibitively wasteful when used in public policy.

However strong a case critics build against policy-oriented research, the stress of time, the fact of a client commissioning the study, the pull of solutions bearing on aggregates of people—all these factors operate to push social values deeply, perhaps irretrievably, into the research process. The pure researcher simply does not have to cope with these pressures. The critics of policy research are often right. Values that motivate research, especially when in the form of policy needs, can distort the identification of valid causes for social problems. But the need to resolve policy problems is also among the important functions of research into policy. So the risk of distortion in policy research is taken for the best of reasons: improving social life here and now.

TRADITIONAL CONCEPTS
IN THE EVALUATION OF POLITICS

Any attempt to improve social life, whether in the short run or long run, must operate with some concept of the "good society." Though the phrase may sound today like a political slogan, philosophers from the beginnings of Western history have seriously worked with concepts to evaluate societies as good or bad. Many of these long-standing concepts are basic to political theory today and help illuminate fundamental issues in political activity.

Consent versus Worthy-of-Consent.   One of the oldest elastic scales in political theory is the one extending from consent to any number of principles that govern consent. At one end of the scale some political theorists have maintained that a good political system is one based solely on *consent*. Theorists at the other end of the scale have maintained that certain principles of political rule are good whether they are in fact desired or not. Such principles are said to be *worthy of consent*. Those on the "consent" end of the scale maintain that the people know what is good for them. Those on the "worthy-of-consent" end of the scale claim that some things are good for the people whether they want them or not.

Like most political concepts, the two represented here—consent and worthy-of-consent—are a mixture in actual practice. Most consent political systems insulate certain rules and values from simple consent. Constitutional principles, for example, are not valid in the United States because the people do, or would, consent to them at all times. Some, like electoral machinery, are conditions for the expression of consent, not objects of consent. Conversely, most worthy-of-consent political systems operate with some people consenting to the principles that govern. Even in Plato's *Republic*, an extreme case of a worthy-of-consent system, the philosopher-kings at least recognize and assent to the ruling principles.

Though mixed in actual political systems, the two concepts of "consent" and "worthy-of-consent" still provide contrasting views on the good political system, and on the kinds of decision-rules one will favor for resolving political disputes. A consent proponent, for example, would likely consider it good to decide political issues through referendums; a worthy-of-consent proponent, on the other hand, would likely favor more narrowly based decisions made by experts qualified to understand the principles that ought to govern.

The Scope of Government Action.   Another long-standing device to evaluate political systems is the extent to which government is accepted as the instrument to resolve social disputes. At one extreme are political philosophers like Hobbes and John Stuart Mill. Hobbes viewed the state as concerned only with the maintenance of order. Mill allowed that the government was justified in acting only if a person's actions resulted in harm to another. At the other extreme of governmental scope are political philosophers like Aristotle, who invested the political order with the responsibility for promoting the good life, and even inculcating virtue in its citizens.

Disagreements over the scope of government are found today in evaluations of American politics. Conservatives are prone to see government as the problem, not the solution to social ills (a Ronald Reagan phrase). Liberals are more inclined to extend government into many areas of social life. Even the sharpest of ideological differences, for example socialism versus capitalism, turn substantially on differences over the extension of government action. To one favoring restricted government, a good political system is one of limited government activity. To one favoring an expanded scope of government, the best political system is one that governs extensively.

Legitimacy. Perhaps the most overarching evaluative concept in traditional political thought is "legitimacy." Whether a political system is legitimate is usually settled only when secondary evaluative criteria are introduced. We have seen in Chapter 5 how Max Weber, for example, interpreted "legitimacy" in three ways: charismatic, traditional, and legal. A political system was, for Weber, legitimate only if it was justifiable on any one of these three interpretations. But the concept of legitimacy is an umbrella that covers many more interpretations than those outlined by Weber. If, for example, we firmly endorse *consent* and/or *restricted scope* as warranted grounds for good political systems, then we can stamp as legitimate those systems that fulfill these standards. Legitimacy is that which stamps approval on politics after a number of other evaluative criteria have been fulfilled.

Traditionally, distinctions between *power* and *authority* have been argued under the rubric of legitimacy. When, for example, a group seizes control of a political system through violence and the duly elected leaders are forced to flee the country, many people will view the exiled leaders as the "legitimate" government (having *legal authority*), while recognizing that the new rulers have effective *power*. (Such a distinction was at the heart of America's "China policy" toward Mao Tse-tung's regime for over two decades.) Abuse of power, where accepted rules of governing are broken, as with President Nixon during the Watergate episode, is an issue in legitimacy.

"Legitimacy" is not the final evaluative word in politics. Governments may be both legitimate and bad—for example, on grounds of gross inefficiency. But legitimacy is among the more powerful and comprehensive of evaluative concepts in political theory.

SIMPLE COST-BENEFIT CALCULATIONS

Recent evaluations of politics have drawn concepts from economic theory. Among the more famous of economic ideas is the cost-benefit calculation we have discussed at various points in this book. Let's review again, to keep our memory fresh:

$$B_i > C_i - B_j > C_j.$$

When the benefits (B) of an action (i) minus the costs (C) of the action (i) are greater than the benefits (B) of an alternative action (j) minus the costs

(C) of an alternative action (j), then—on simple cost-benefit calculations—the action (i) is preferable to its alternative (j). If, for example, the benefits-minus-costs of playing tennis are greater than the benefits-minus-costs of playing golf, then tennis is preferable to golf—at least on a cost-benefit analysis.

The reason why we are careful to insert the label "simple" in front of this calculation is not to denigrate the cost-benefit method of evaluation nor to insult its supporters. It is only to suggest that difficulties occur when the bare bones of the formula are transferred to social policy. These difficulties are so grave as to transform "simple" cost-benefit calculations into calculations so complicated that they barely warrant the same title. These problems are a combination of (a) specifying *what* a *cost* and a *benefit* are (discussed in Chapter 4), and (b) *measuring* costs and benefits once we have settled on what they are.

Tennis and golf, for example, both cost time and money to play. But such easily quantifiable costs do not exhaust actual costs. Some people, indolent by nature, find tennis a pleasurable but physically demanding sport, while golf better suits their internal rhythm. Such people count the physical demands of tennis as a cost. Others may find it embarrassing to don shorts; since such attire is a requirement at many tennis clubs, such people would count this as another minus factor for tennis. But factors like physical and psychological strain are notorious for being *not* quantifiable. Of course, we can assign scales to the emotions and even measure physical stress. What we cannot do, however, is say with assurance that we are scaling or measuring objectively what a person *feels*. Even, for example, though he exhibited the same blood pressure and heart beat in two different sports, a person could be experiencing different emotions of stress.

The same difficulty occurs with benefits. Economists use monetary units to reflect value. A willingness, for example, to part with twelve dollars from limited monetary resources suggests the value we assign to tennis. Perhaps then the dollar amount is a means to measure the benefit we accrue from tennis in a market system. But, again, even the monetary expenditure does not necessarily measure the benefit on a scale providing comparisons among activities. We cannot even be sure that dollar expenditures reflect true benefits, since a person may part with hard-earned cash for things that harm him (like cigarettes). Also, the willingness of a person to spend money on tennis rather than golf varies with the fortune he has, while the benefits of each activity may not. If a person wins the New York State Lottery, then doubles the money he spends on tennis, it does not necessarily mean the value he assigns to tennis has doubled. He may simply have more money to spend.

The problem with cost-benefit calculations is that psychological considerations too easily enter our specifications of costs and benefits; once they have entered, measuring such factors on an objective scale providing comparisons among activities (for example, tennis versus golf) is extremely difficult.

SOCIAL COSTS AND BENEFITS

The problem of comparing activities of a single individual is paralleled and compounded when we move to cost-benefit calculations for groupings of people.

1. The initial problem is finding a formula that will allow benefits and costs calculated for one individual to be compared to the benefits and costs calculated for any other individual. Unfortunately, this problem—long known as the impossibility of making interpersonal comparisons of value—has not yet been successfully resolved. The sticking point is the absence of a common cardinal scale across individual calculations of costs and benefits. Even if individuals can assign a numerical value to benefits and costs, we have no way of knowing if they are using the same zero point or the same size increments in their measurements.

The absence of a common cardinal scale is the social version of the quantification difficulties found in comparing two or more activities from the perspective of a single individual. In the social version, each person may be using a different scale to assign a value to *his* benefits and costs. To try to compare benefits and costs for two or more individuals without assurances of a common scale would be something like comparing the weights of various items by comparing the numerical values assigned to the items without knowing whether the numbers stood for grams, pounds, or some other unit in yet another weighing system altogether.

2. A second problem in social cost-benefit calculations is the tendency of actions to have consequences on people who are not directly involved. This is the problem of *externalities*. The cost-benefit calculation of a single individual on, say, whether to burn leaves in his backyard, is a strict weighing of the benefits minus the costs of burning leaves versus not doing so (choosing instead one of a number of alternatives). But when we look at the same equation from the more general perspective of everyone's benefits and costs in the community of those affected by the leaf-burning, then different considerations enter the calculation. We have to look at benefits (a reduction in leaves) minus costs (smoke polluting the air) for the whole community.

3. Once we turn to such *aggregate* considerations in cost-benefit calculations, other criteria intrude. Look again at the leaf-burning incident. Not only are we faced with the two earlier questions that can be raised on individual cost-benefit calculations—*what* is a benefit or cost and how do we *measure* benefits and costs—but we also have now the additional problem of

distribution. Since the leaf-burning has benefits and costs for a range of people, and the benefits and costs vary with different people, the question is, how do we distribute the benefits and costs in the best possible way. Notice that the issue of distribution is not found in individual calculations. Only as other people are involved do we encounter the issue of how best to arrange things for the general absorption of costs and the enjoyment of benefits.

At this point the important evaluative concepts used today in the study of politics make their entrance. These are concepts dealing with social *arrangements;* in the most general sense they are questions of interest and fairness. We may want to introduce these larger evaluative matters, stand by for the applause, and then come back on stage with cost-benefit formulas. But we should at least be aware that other concepts now begin to be dramatized, concepts that give central meaning to evaluative exercises in politics in general and public policy in particular and that may in the end displace at least simple cost-benefit calculations altogether.

CASE STUDY: WELFARE AND HEALTH

One area of public policy that seems both inspired in part by some lofty vision of the good society and, at the same time, hopelessly confused as to purpose and method is that of welfare and health policies in the United States.

The idea of *welfare* has long had a pungent status in American society. Taking something without contributing in return offends Western notions of fairness. Welfare also goes against the grain of the work ethic, a belief that working is a good in itself and—with its Calvinistic overtones—that a person cannot be good in other ways without giving evidence of hard work. This linkage of goodness and work developed fully in the capitalist system of American life. Capitalism emphasizes production, the role of each individual in expanding and developing the economy. Seen from this perspective, a welfare recipient seems to be shirking his responsibility, a "free rider" benefiting from the efforts of others.

This view of welfare was supported with comprehensive theories of how the world operated. The most important of these theories in the nineteenth century was Social Darwinism. In 1859 Charles Darwin published the Origin of Species, and in the book introduced with impressive evidence the basic ideas of evolution that are commonly accepted today. But evolutionary ideas also had a short but sensational life in *social* theory. Herbert Spencer developed the view that man is also subject to evolutionary development, and maintained that those who survive are not only more *adaptable* but also *superior* (an evaluation Darwin resisted in his study of the animal world). It was but a short step from the superiority claim to the view that the poor are inferior by virtue of not having succeeded economically, and thus they should be allowed to perish so as to insure the "survival of the fittest." Welfare, on such a view, disrupts the evolutionary development of a better mankind.

Ethical assumptions also contributed to antiwelfare feelings in Western society. If we combine the moral idea of individual responsibility with the capitalist notion that anyone can be successful if he but tries, then we must conclude that the poor are poor because they have not made any real effort to succeed. If it is true that the poor are at fault for their condition, then once again we come out against welfare. Why help those who won't help themselves? This harsh judgment was tempered somewhat by the idea of *noblesse oblige* prominent in both English and American society: the well-to-do have an obligation to take care of the unfortunate. But such care was always voluntary, carried out by the wealthy on their own initiative. It reinforced the belief that the poor really are inferior creatures.

Work was even the mark of mental well-being. Freud defined mental illness as the incapacity to love—and to *work*, to function productively in society. The biblical observation that the poor will always be with us may have been accepted in nineteenth century society, but not the more charitable thought that the poor are also blessed. Even today, going on welfare is a terrible experience for many American citizens. It is no wonder, given the legacy of ideas hostile to poverty and to welfare for those not at work in the society.

The rich supply of theories against welfare as a social *policy* began to lose their effectiveness in this century. Social Darwinism began to lose its lustre in the face of powerful counterarguments. We know now that genetic change is remarkably slow at the species level, and we also have a more complex picture of superior traits in the human race. Simple dominance, even economic success, can be intimately paired with loathsome characteristics. The fascist call for racial superiority did much to discourage theories that linked competitive success with desirable human traits. That titillating picture of the world in Social Darwinism, "nature red in tooth and claw," is not even uniformly true for the animal world as we understand it today, much less for human societies. Cooperation, we know now, is at least as desirable and common a condition as simple competitiveness.

Our views on the needs of capitalist society have also altered considerably. Since the general acceptance of Keynesian economic theory, the importance of consumption in a productive society has been generally perceived. The poor may not be productive members of a capitalist system, but unless they are given the resources to exercise purchasing power, the system will falter in its capacity to sell products. Businessmen may still view the poor with distaste, but now they have an economic reason to accept some form of welfare: it is good business to have consumers who can buy goods even if the consumers are poor and out of work. The productive emphasis of capitalism has turned to reveal a need for welfare on purely economic grounds.

Moreover, the thought that the poor are always responsible for their plight did not survive the Great Depression of the 1930s in the United States. Marxist theory had always claimed that the *system* is at the root of human misery, not the inclinations of individuals to avoid work. It did not take even a half-hearted Marxist in the 1930s to see that the system of capitalism was at fault for the unemployment figures. Part of this awareness was due to sheer numbers: when fully 25 percent of the work force is out of work, which was in fact the case during the Depression, it is difficult to charge laziness or moral turpitude. But also the Keynesian economic doctrines had revealed the structural inadequacies of pure capitalism to maintain full employment without government effort. The plain fact is that jobs were not available in the Depression, and the individual could hardly be blamed for not working if work was not available.

As a result of changed ideas and dramatic economic problems, the federal government entered the economic sphere in the 1930s in two ways. First, the government made efforts to manage the economy, efforts which today are taken for granted in our expectations that the political system ought to act to maximize employment and minimize inflation. Second, it began to install a system of social welfare, protecting individuals from those states of illness and poverty that were largely taken for granted just a century earlier.

TYPES OF WELFARE

Elizabethan attitudes toward the poor, dating from the Poor Relief Act of 1601 enacted by the English Parliament, encouraged punitive as well as therapeutic treatment of the poor. Those able to work were sent to workhouses: those not (widows, aged, orphans, and such) were sent to poorhouses. Private charities distributed food and clothing to those institutions. This combination of a punitive society and occasional private generosity was dramatized by Charles Dickens in *Oliver Twist*. It seems a world far removed from ours, yet some vestiges of this earlier approach are present in present welfare policies.

The basic distinction in types of direct welfare policies in the United States today is between (a) a generalized form of *public assistance*, and (b) a complicated form of *social insurance*. "Public assistance" types of welfare limit benefits to those who can establish need and generally require the recipients to disclose their income and resources in order to qualify. Though the Elizabethan spectacle of a poorhouse is missing, many of the suspicions and hostilities that administering officials feel toward the poor receiving public assistance resemble Dickensonian dramas. Especially Elizabethan is the Aid to Families with Dependent Children (AFDC) public assistance programs: at one time welfare workers would stage late-night raids on apartments of husbandless women to see if a lover was sharing the welfare mother's bed. The effect of the program, demanding as it did the absence of a husband, was to penalize stable families.

"Social insurance" types of welfare do not single out those who receive benefits in terms of need. A "social insurance" program distributes welfare across wide segments of the population, supporting those with and without need. Social insurance policies represent the important shift in the 1930s from Elizabethan approaches to welfare to some institutional arrangement of forced savings as insurance against various sorts of calamities, including illness, unemployment, disability, and aging. The Social Security Act of 1935 is the clearest beacon of change in welfare approaches. The act established Old Age and Survivor's Disability Insurance—a clear instance of compulsory insurance—and induced the states (successfully) to set up unemployment compensation programs through a payroll tax on employers.

The government today also deals in indirect ways with the candidates for welfare. Fiscal and monetary policies to reduce unemployment obviously affect the number of those on welfare lists, primarily by providing jobs. The government also has developed a number of programs to make the poor better qualified for work. As a result of the Economic Opportunity Act of 1964, society now provides a number of remedial programs for those below the official poverty line. Among these are the Job Corps, aimed primarily at teaching skills to young unemployed people; the Comprehensive Employment and Training Act, providing on-the-job training for workers otherwise unemployed; Federal Work-Study Programs that provide matching funds at a 60–40 ratio for students coming from poor families; Community Action Programs, developing resident participation in antipoverty efforts; and various free services for the poor in the areas of legal advice, family planning, and so forth. Many of these remedial efforts are obviously still inspired by the work ethic, the assumption that the poor are best helped by putting them back to work.

Among all of the forms of welfare, the area that has expanded most rapidly and brought on the most intense controversy is that of *public assistance*, especially in the broad area of health care. The federal government began two comprehensive health care plans in 1965. One, known today as *Medicare*, set up a compulsory health insurance plan to cover medical costs for the aged, financed through social security funds. Medicare also includes a voluntary program that pays doctor bills and additional medical expenses, a program financed through a combination of contributions from aged participants and general tax revenues. The other health program, known as

Medicaid, provides federal funds to enable the states to guarantee medical services to all recipients of public assistance (unemployed, handicapped, families with dependent children, and so forth).

With two exceptions, other public assistance programs are not as expensive and controversial as Medicare and Medicaid. The titles of the other major programs describe their activities: Old Age Assistance (cash for the needy aged), Aid for the Blind, Aid for the Permanently and Totally Disabled, and the myriad of programs for veterans under the Veterans Administration Office. The two exceptions, programs that are growing in size and controversy at a rate similar to the two health plans, are the Food Stamp Program and the already mentioned AFDC. In the Food Stamp Program, over five billion dollars are allocated annually to help the poor. The assistance takes the form of food stamps redeemable at markets, sold by the government to the needy at below their redemption value. The difference in selling price and redemption value represents a grant by the social system to those receiving food stamps. AFDC grants money to families with dependent children but no employable person living at home.

Even this brief description of welfare policies and programs reveals that American society has come a long way from the antiwelfare attitudes of the last century. Some of those attitudes, of course, persist, both in the work-ethic nature of many programs as well as the public opposition to welfare. In a 1977 New York Times/CBS news poll, 58 percent of the respondents disapproved of government-sponsored welfare programs and 54 percent agreed that "Most people who receive money from welfare could get along without it if they tried." This opposition, however, may be keyed on the term "welfare." When "welfare" was dropped from the wording, 81 percent approved of the Government "providing financial assistance for children raised in low-income homes where one parent is missing," 81 percent favored the Government "helping poor people buy food for their families at cheaper prices," and 82 percent approved using taxes to "pay for health care for poor people." Though the poll was not a study-in-depth, it suggested an antipathy to the welfare slogan which *might* be consistent with a sympathetic view of welfare philosophies.

Since the 1960s, the federal government has officially endorsed a growing variety of welfare policies unknown to Western institutions a century earlier. Whether we have come too far or not far enough is one of the more divisive social issues of our times.

ISSUES AND PROBLEMS

Few doubt today that welfare policies in the United States are plagued with difficulties, though they may disagree over how to resolve these difficulties. Let us set aside for the moment the larger evaluative questions—does welfare work, is it good or equitable—and instead sort out some of the more visible internal difficulties with welfare policies as they operate today.

EXPENSE

The overriding concern with welfare at least in the popular mind is the growing *expense* of the various programs. A good case in point is social security, the landmark policy of recent welfare programs. Originally launched as a form of social insurance, social security is now financially in the red even on a pay-as-you-go basis. Total revenue from the social security tax (the second largest source of income for the federal government) was in the neighborhood of $82 billion in 1977. All of this revenue is allocated in social security benefits. These benefits exceeded revenues by about $5 billion in 1977. The largest expenditure of the federal government, now even greater than defense spending, is in welfare and social security.

What the revenue-expenditure imbalance means for social security is that the present generation is now paying for the benefits accruing to those who worked in the last generation. In effect, the "insurance" concept is no longer valid. This generation of workers is not setting aside funds to cover their benefits when they are eligible. The *next* generation will pay for this generation's benefits on then-current taxes. Further, the system has features that slant it toward greater rather than lesser benefits in the future. The payments for retired workers are now tied to a cost-of-living formula, making increments automatic. Also, in spite of the fact that Congress has been generous with increases in benefits (an increase in total benefits of almost 600 percent since 1960), the average monthly benefit in 1976 for a retired couple was still in the vicinity of $360. Since this figure was less than $60 per month above the accepted poverty level, social security benefits are at worst inadequate, at best a supplement to other retirement programs.

Table 6.1
SOCIAL SECURITY BENEFITS (AVERAGE MONTHLY BENEFIT, 1976 DOLLARS)

Year	1960	1970	1976
Retired workers	$144	173	225
Retired worker and wife	242	291	361 (in 1975)
Disabled workers	174	192	245
Wives and husbands	76	86	108
Widowed mothers	115	127	160
Widows and widowers	113	149	207

Source: U.S. Social Security Administration, *Statistical Abstract of the United States, 1977,* p. 328.

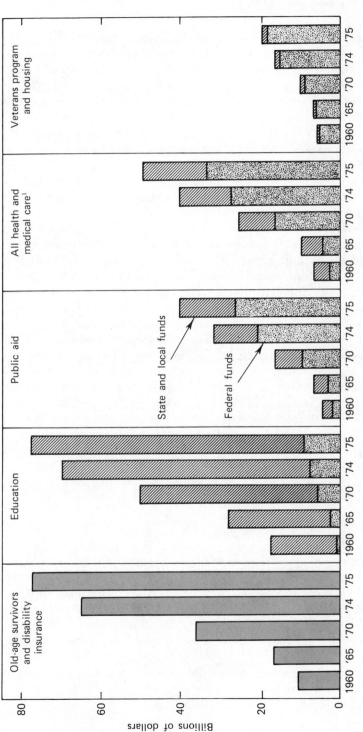

Social Welfare Expenditures Under Selected Public Programs: 1960 to 1975.

[1]Includes all medical services provided under programs for social insurance, public aid, veterans, and other social welfare.

Source: Chart prepared by U.S. Bureau of the Census. Data from U.S. Social Security Administration. Reprinted from *Statistical Abstract of the United States, 1976* (Washington, D.C.: U.S. Government Printing Office), p. 292.

Recent reforms of social security have increased taxes to finance the program into the next century. Under a measure passed by Congress in late 1977, the maximum tax increased to 6.13 percent on $22,900 of earned income for 1979, 7.15 percent on the first $42,600 of income by 1987. The new law almost triples the payroll taxes of persons paying the maximum, from $1,143.45 (the 6.05 percent rate on the first $18,900 in effect before the 1977 law) to $3,045.90 in 1987. Critics contended that the act was at the same time inflationary in pressuring businesses to offset their tax increases by raising prices, and economically depressing in reducing the purchasing power of the workers who are taxed. Supporters of the new law maintained that if social security is to be saved without using general revenues, then higher taxes are inevitable.

Since social security was for years the most successful of welfare policies, the growing cost is disturbing. But the costs of other programs are in general rising even more rapidly. The food stamp program, aid to families with dependent children, and Medicare and Medicaid, are growing especially fast, expanding both in the numbers of those eligible and in actual costs in an inflationary economy. Over eleven million people were receiving welfare in 1977. Additional financing is a problem. Again, examining social security, still the soundest of the welfare programs, suggests some of the difficulties. The social security tax is extremely regressive and any increase affects lower income groups more than the more affluent. (The tax is on wages, not income.) Today, more than one-half of all government expenditures are for welfare, an increase from $77 billion in 1965 to $330 billion in 1976. The Census Bureau reported a six-fold increase in federal government spending for welfare programs from 1960 to 1976. Even roughly similar increases in the future could not be adequately financed without a general reform of the tax structure.

ABSENCE OF EFFECTIVE COORDINATION

A second problem in welfare policies is the *absence of effective coordination* among the various programs. The problem is a simple one: the institutional arrangements of the federal government do not correspond exactly to the functions of the various welfare programs. At the moment, the Department of Health, Education and Welfare (HEW), Housing and Urban Development Administration (HUD), the Department of Agriculture (USDA), and the Veterans Administration (VA) all have a piece of welfare. But many programs, such as the Food Stamp Program, cut across some or all of these departments.

The Economic Opportunity Act of 1964 was an attempt to coordinate at least the antipoverty programs. But even this effort has been fragmented along departmental lines and between federal and local levels. One of the more volatile issues of the 1960s was who would control welfare policies: federally authorized agencies at the local level or the local poor themselves. The Office of Economic Opportunity (OEO), notoriously disorganized during the 1960s, in effect presided over programs that contradicted each other at the level of implementation.

Let's look at an oft-told story in the 1960s: A local community action agency is established, with a white majority, to allocate poverty funds. The OEO also grants money to prepare the poor, usually black, to participate in the antipoverty efforts. The black poor, now organized, displace the white majority on the community agency board, usually with much rhetoric, threats of violence, and bad feelings on all sides. Since the white majority previously on the board is part of the political establishment, local politicians bring pressure on Congress to cut off, or at least review, poverty funding. Meanwhile, the local antipoverty efforts flounder, marked by general ineffectiveness and, often, financial scandals. Conclusion: great promise and chaotic results (Moynihan, 1969).

DYSFUNCTIONAL CONSEQUENCES

Many of the welfare programs also seem to have *dysfunctional consequences* for the larger institutions of society. Two such consequences are most frequently noted by critics. First, welfare benefits often provide a negative work-incentive. One study estimated that an urban family of four can get up to $11,000 per year in social services if no one in the family is employed (*The Future of Social Programs*, 1973). Obviously only a well-paid job would rationally tempt anyone in such circumstances to get off the public assistance rolls. And since most welfare recipients are poorly trained for work, *not* working often pays better.

If wages had only a partial effect on welfare benefits, the negative incentive would be weakened. But in most states getting a decent job means that assistance checks are drastically reduced and often stopped altogether. Earning even modest wages also makes a welfare client ineligible for a host of other services such as food stamps, Medicaid, and public housing. Even social security payments provide monetary incentives against working. Earnings in 1978 that exceeded $4,000 resulted in a forfeiture of $1 of social security payments for every $2 earned above $4,000. If work is a valuable activity for both the willing individual and his society, as it is generally regarded today, then supplying negative work-incentives is irrational.

Second, many welfare programs have a lethal effect on the family. The effects of unemployment on the head of a family are difficult enough by any standards. But Aid to Families of Dependent Children undercuts the very family role that an unemployed man may be trying desperately to maintain. Until very recently, the presence of a man in the household, whether he was working or not, meant that the children in the house were no longer considered dependents of society and thus were not qualified for AFDC aid. Thus it paid a family to break with the unemployed male head of the household rather than keep the family intact. The rules are more relaxed now, but fatherless families still fare better than united families in securing public assistance. This rule on dependency, like many others in welfare policies, is rational in origin: the state does not want to pay for children who are the responsibilities of resident wage-earners. But the unintended consequences of the rule are dysfunctional; the rule helps break up one of the stabilizing institutions in American society, the nuclear family.

FRAUD

Finally, there is the problem of *fraud* in the administering of many welfare programs. Several sensational Medicaid scandals have been discovered, where both doctors and patients have charged for services that were not performed, or overcharged for routine therapy. Unnecessary medicines and treatments are often prescribed only because they are substantially or fully funded under welfare provisions. The fraud is costly. Senator Frank Moss estimated in 1976 that one-fourth to one-half of the $15 billion being spent on Medicaid each year is being wasted through fraud, poor quality of care, and provision of services to ineligible persons. Richard Horan, New York State welfare inspector general, judged in 1976 that approximately $1 billion is wasted annually in New York State alone through various abuses of the welfare system and agencies. Joseph A. Califano, Jr., Secretary of Health, Education and Welfare, estimated that nearly $440 million was misspent in the first half of 1977 alone in the AFDC program (New York Times, 1/16/78). Most of these erroneous payments went to persons who were ineligible. Fraud is not only an unneeded expense in already overburdened welfare policies, but the attendant publicity often increases an already existing hostility to welfare on the part of the general public. Unfortunately, the chronic persistence of fraud may suggest a structural problem that cannot be erased without wholesale reform of basic welfare approaches.

EVALUATING WELFARE

The identification of internal problems—expense, coordination, dysfunctional consequences, fraud—merely lists things that have gone wrong with welfare policies. Such problems lead to that popular political judgment that welfare is "a mess." A reform of welfare, like reform everywhere, could profit from a broader look at the policy area. Specifically, it would help to know by what criteria we are evaluating welfare as "a mess" and what proposals will remedy the apparently sad state of the programs.

To begin such an evaluation, let us set out some important evaluative concepts particularly appropriate to politics: (1) equity, (2) efficiency, (3) Pareto Optimality, and (4) the public interest. These concepts are not exactly on a par logically, and some overlap among them can be tolerated and sometimes is even helpful. But taken sequentially they reveal a lot about evaluation in politics and may indicate how to evaluate welfare policies. Using a thorny area like welfare as a case study should also illuminate the advantages and limitations of the evaluative concepts.

EQUITY

Equity is an idea with roots in Aristotle's philosophy. Basically, it means fairness. In law, it is often used to accommodate general rules to particular cases, allowing differences among cases to justify different treatment not reflected in rules that would ordinarily call for the cases to be treated uniformly. A handy rule-of-thumb that explains equity is: treat like cases in like fashion, unlike cases in unlike fashion (a rule also basic to rationality models).

One would think that equity considerations go to the origins of modern welfare policy. Once we establish that the poor are not to blame for their plight, then we can quickly conclude that it is not fair to leave them stranded economically; some redistribution of society's resources must be arranged. But after so justifying welfare, the particular arrangements to redistribute resources can also be evaluated on equity criteria. We might ask, are current welfare policies *fair*?

Here the picture is mixed. If the social system is at fault for the undesirable economic state in which many people find themselves, then any welfare is fairer than none at all. No one has a right to keep all gains or a duty to suffer all losses if the outcomes are determined by social conditions rather than by individual effort. On the other hand, the progressive distribution of social resources can cut unfairly into gains fairly made by industries, individuals, and groups.

It has been estimated, for example, that a further redistribution of resources would be extremely difficult, largely because any substantial increase in benefits would require intolerable tax rates on *all* American families (Browning, 1975). Still, the larger question of equity depends to a great extent on the kind of society one is prepared to accept. If single-family homes, private transportation, personal art collections, and a host of other accoutrements of American society are regarded as unfair, then a much more drastic redistribution of social wealth is both possible and desirable. It should be clearly understood, however, that such views require for their realization a substantial rearrangement of current institutions, a rearrangement approaching revolutionary proportions.

We can, however, point out other features of current welfare policies that are inequitable on more modest grounds. The most important of these is the exclusion of the working poor from welfare benefits. Though defining poverty is a difficult problem, it is generally accepted that the millions of people on welfare rolls do not include nearly all the poor in America, primarily because many, some say most, of the poor are *working* poor. They hold low-paying jobs that place them in the poverty category (below $5,815 for a non-farm family of four in 1976), but because they have jobs they are ineligible for welfare assistance. We have already pointed out the irrationality of negative work incentives; penalizing the working poor also seems inequitable. In this case, the rule in operation stresses a secondary criterion, *unemployment*, at the expense of the primary criterion implied in welfare philosophy, *inadequate income*. One reasonable conclusion: unfair treatment.

EFFICIENCY

Whether or not an action is efficient can be decided on many different grounds. Discharging workers who are not needed to do a job is, from the employer's point of view, efficient. From the worker's point of view (the satisfaction of his economic needs) it is hardly efficient to be fired. From the perspective of the economic system, it might be more efficient to keep workers on the job even when not needed so as to maintain their purchasing power without adding to welfare rolls. But the multiple reference points for efficiency can be handily arbitrated in a particular policy area by asking: Is the policy successful in terms of its own goals? Does the policy effectively accomplish what it sets out to do? Do welfare programs meet the needs of the indigent? Has poverty been reduced? Are people better off as a result of welfare benefits? Is there a better way to get the same, or superior, results?

These questions are some of the things that must be asked in judging the efficiency of welfare policy. They do not exhaust all questions under the heading of efficiency; these few questions cannot even be answered exhaustively here. But the questions do represent the evaluations many people are beginning to make today of welfare programs and policies.

1. If we ask the recipients of welfare benefits if their needs are met, we would likely get a resounding *no*. To begin with, it is still an indignity to have to "prove" economic need, and harrassed, greatly overworked welfare workers do not make this easier. Welfare mothers are such an agitated class that they have already reached cult status: Lily Tomlin has lampooned them in a satiric character sketch. ("We *built* this country," says Tomlin's welfare mother.) Yet many people currently on welfare rolls would be destitute without welfare. One thinks especially of the aged and handicapped, not well enough off now but desperate without some form of welfare benefit.

2. Whether poverty has actually been eliminated in the United States is an open question. Census figures show that the number of poor declined

from 1959 to 1973 (39.5 to 23.0 million), but has increased of late (to 25 million in 1976, a 9 percent increase from 1973)—unless the transfer payments of welfare are counted as income (see below). The census also indicates that income differences are declining, but very slowly and unevenly. If, however, poverty is defined as *relative* deprivation, then all these figures go out the window; only a perfectly equalitarian society can eliminate poverty on these terms.

By all historical and current standards the poor in America live affluent lives. But by American standards they are badly off and, what is more important, they perceive themselves as badly off whatever the figures prove. This relative poverty is not attacked by welfare policies, which primarily aim to bring people above some predetermined poverty line through redistributions of wealth. We could fault welfare on the relative-poverty score only by expecting a revolutionary change toward absolute equality, an unlikely prospect.

One problem in assessing the effectiveness of welfare programs toward the poor is that the measurement of poverty is a difficult and controversial task. The Census Bureau counts only *cash* income in determining who are poor. Family assets are not counted in; special classes of people who are not poor in spite of low income (such as students) are not filtered out. Even worse, say some economists, transfers in *kind* (nonmoney income) are not counted. Food stamps, housing subsidies, and Medicaid, to name but three such transfers, do not figure in census data on poverty. But obviously $1000 worth of food stamps is income to a poor family. A study by the Rand Corporation, counting cash, goods, and services, reported that in 1974 an average welfare family of 3.3 persons in New York City received the equivalent of $6,000, or roughly $1,000 above the poverty line for a family of four.

Table 6.2
POPULATION, BY CATEGORIES, WITH INCOME BELOW POVERTY LEVEL, 1959–1976

	Number below Poverty Level (in Millions)			Percent below Poverty Level		
	1959	1970	1976	1959	1970	1976
All persons	39.5	25.4	25.0	22.4	12.6	11.8
White	28.4	17.5	16.7	18.1	9.9	9.1
Black and other races	11.0	7.9	8.3	56.2	32.0	29.4
Black	not available	7.5	7.5	not available	33.5	31.3
In families with male head	29.1	14.3	13.6	18.7	8.2	7.8
In families with female head	10.4	11.2	12.3	50.2	38.2	34.6

Source: U.S. Bureau of the Census, *Current Population Reports,* Series P-60, No. 106 and 107.

Professor Edgar Browning (1975), also counting transfers in kind, maintains that

> "the average poor family in 1973 had an income that was approximately 30 percent *above* the poverty line. In terms of the average income of officially poor families, there is practically no poverty—statistically speaking—in the United States today, and indeed there has not been for several years."

It seems that if we count the transfers of welfare policy as income, then welfare has indeed had a decisive effect on poverty in American society.

3. Are welfare policies, as currently set up, the most efficient when compared with alternative measures? Most people—politicians, voters, even welfare recipients—condemn some or all current welfare programs. But deciding what to support as a replacement is not easy. In 1970, President Nixon proposed a "family assistance plan," a bill that incorporated features of the negative income tax (NIT) long urged by some economists. NIT begins with cash, rather than "in kind" transfers to the poor. Under one scheme, for example, a family with no income would receive $2,500 a year in (nontaxable) transfers from the state. At progressively higher incomes the cash transfer diminishes until at, say, $5,000 no cash transfer is made. In an NIT program, some minimum income is guaranteed, an amount that pro-

Table 6.3
MONEY INCOME–PERCENT DISTRIBUTION BY FAMILY (ALL FAMILIES)

Year	1950	1960	1970	1975
Under $2,000	24.7	13.0	4.6	2.1
2,000–2,999	17.8	8.7	4.3	2.4
3,000–3,999	20.7	9.8	5.1	3.4
4,000–4,999	13.6	10.5	5.3	4.1
5,000–5,999	9.0	12.9	5.8	4.1
6,000–6,999	5.2	10.8	6.0	4.2
7,000–9,999	5.8	20.0	19.9	12.8
10,000–14,999	—	10.6	26.8	22.3
15,000–24,999	3.3	2.8	17.7	30.3
25,000–and over	—	0.9	4.6	14.1

Source: U.S. Bureau of the Census, *Statistical Abstract of the United States, 1976,* p. 404.

gressively diminishes as nontransfer income (from employment) increases until some breakeven point is reached.

The surface advantages of NIT programs are clear (Browning, 1975). First, assistance is given without proof of need, only proof of low income (thus removing some of the indignities suffered by the poor in getting welfare). Second, the amount of assistance is directly correlated with need as determined objectively through income, not scaled on subjective factors. Third, cash is given, not services or tokens, thus allowing welfare recipients greater freedom to purchase what *they* value most highly. Fourth, NIT programs should be easy to modify, for the rates of cash transfer, the breakeven point, and the amount of assistance are monetary units that can be altered on a moment's notice.

Unfortunately, the disadvantages of the NIT are also considerable, as the Nixon administration quickly discovered with its "family assistance plan." First and foremost the cost can be prohibitive. It was estimated that Nixon's program would have at least doubled, and perhaps tripled or more, the costs of welfare. Second, income, while an objective measure of need, can still be a grossly inadequate measure (assets, for example, ought to be relevant). Third, NIT proposals, along with other welfare programs, still do nothing to alleviate the *causes* of poverty—the fact that the poor are unskilled, uneducated, generally unprepared for work—and may even continue the negative work-incentive when the costs (clothes, transportation, and such) of going to work are considered. Fourth, even the freedom to use cash has a double edge, for while such freedom is consistent with democratic views, the low education of the poor makes it unlikely that they will spend money wisely and economically even for food. (This paternalistic attitude, though repugnant, has been supported in studies that show a direct relationship between education and smart buying habits.)

Conclusion: while welfare programs are generally viewed with good reasons as inefficient, the major alternative to current policies—programs organized around the negative income tax—has major disadvantages as well.

PARETO OPTIMALITY

Pareto Optimality is an evaluative criterion that states this: a social system is optimal (in its best state) if no one person can be made better off without making at least one person worse off. Thus, a policy that makes one or several persons better off without hurting anyone else is desirable under this criterion. A policy that helps some at the expense of others is, accordingly, undesirable.

Two features of Pareto Optimality make the criterion appealing. First, it resolves, by ignoring, the problem of interpersonal comparisons of value.

We do not, with the Pareto criterion, have to judge whether one person is better or worse off than another, but only whether the person is better or worse off than previously. Second, it provides, in fact exclusively advertises, improvements that do not require losses. What could be more attractive to policy authorities than a social gain without a social loss?

Welfare policy, however, does not fare very well under Pareto Optimality. Welfare is, in essence, social *transfers*. Some are made better through the distribution of social resources, and distribution (unless totally absorbed by production gains—which does not happen with welfare) requires making some poorer by taking their wealth to make others better off. Does this mean that welfare always—by definition—fails the Pareto Optimal test?

Let's look at welfare from a broader, and more controversial, perspective. Some have maintained that the real purpose of welfare is to reduce civil disorder (Piven and Cloward, 1971). It is argued, for example, that giving relief is designed primarily to serve the larger economic and political order by insuring social stability and only secondarily to give relief to the recipients. Supporting this argument is the fact that welfare policies *are* typically installed during periods of potential social disorder—for example, during the high unemployment of the 1930s and the civil unrest of the 1960s. Also, some retraction of welfare programs usually follows when the social turbulence passes.

But, the general validity of this argument aside, *if* we view welfare in terms of a conflict-management purpose, then Pareto Optimality sanctions the distribution: the wealthy gain by preserving social stability, the poor gain by getting assistance. Each class also loses, of course: the wealthy lose money, the poor are fixed more firmly in the system of prevailing inequities. But one could also maintain that each class receives a net gain, thus remaining true to Pareto Optimality.

We don't have to discuss either the narrow or broad perspective on welfare any further to see that Pareto Optimality is a loose and uneven evaluative criterion. Not only is it notorious for "freezing" inequitable systems—the harshest inequalities might be reformable only by causing some people to gain at the expense of others—but the multiple perspectives available on gains and losses allow us to judge the same policies as Pareto Optimal or not depending on the gain-loss perspective we endorse.

THE PUBLIC INTEREST

For generations, students of politics have denigrated the concept of "the public interest." Many have felt that the concept is empty, without meaning or reference. Others have noted its rhetorical function in practical politics: no politician can come out against the public interest, though this often means very little in practical terms. We also have attractive theories of politics that make no reference to the concept of a public interest. Interest group theory, as we have seen, operates with competing groups that ultimately produce a public policy of mutual adjustment. There is no *general* public interest, only a splicing together of partial interests.

Careful analysis, however, reveals that the concept of the public interest helps us understand and, especially, evaluate political activities. An examination of the public interest also reveals that it is a multiple, not a single, concept. Let's reintroduce the types of aggregates outlined in Chapter 5 in order to understand several *procedural* methods for expressing the public interest.

Numerical Public Interest.   Perhaps the easiest way to arrive at the public interest is to count the interests of each member of the society. A preponderance of such interests then counts as the public interest. Almost any factor can in principle be counted to arrive at a numerical public interest. An objective characteristic like low income can be tallied to demonstrate a public interest case for higher income. Generally, however, the democratic bias in numerical versions of the public interest is to count preferences, usually through votes and sometimes through polling. Preference counting would be favored as a method for getting to the public interest by those who endorse "consent" political systems. Those who favor "worthy-of-consent" systems would favor objective factors for determining the public interest.

Two features of a numerical public interest are important and interesting. First, a summed public interest can always run counter to at least some individual interests. Short of unanimity, some in the society will always fall outside the sum of preponderant preferences. Certainly voting almost always produces at least one losing alternative with its unsuccessful supporters. Even objective properties are usually counted up to the exclusion of those who don't have the property (high-income people when low-income people are counted). To say that some policy or program is in the public interest *numerically* expressed is not to say that it is in everyone's interests, only that it is a preponderant interest of the society (Held, 1970).

Second, whatever is used as a measure or indicator of interests—preferences or some objective property—there is never a perfectly comfortable fit between the measure and the public interest. Preferences are notoriously poor as a definition of interests. Which electorate has not regretted at some time or other its choice of a candidate, seeing later that the summed expression of preferences was *not* an accurate reading of interests—that X was preferred, but Y *really* represented the interests and therefore should have been chosen. Objective properties are similarly prone to error. Low income, for example, may be dropped as new information appears in favor of health needs as a measure of public interest policies. No specification of *what* is to be counted may ever be a final indicator of the public interest.

Structural Public Interest.   Another way to conceive of the public interest is in terms of social structures or general practices. Those who see the public interest as bound up with certain institutions may oppose an otherwise good policy because it jeopardizes these institutions. For example, a person who views capitalism as a fundamental interest in modern society may oppose welfare policies because they undermine the work ethic so vital to capitalism.

A structural view of the public interest also provides for a conflict between individual interests and the public interest. A person may find it in his interests, for example, to oppose a social rule. Yet the rule may still be viewed as in the interests of society to maintain. The driver who cuts briefly (and safely) across a one-way street in the wrong direction to get home earlier may be fulfilling his (limited) interests, but it is in the interests of society to prosecute him so as to insure that motorists will not begin ignoring one-way signs.

A national telephone number is now available for youthful runaways to call and get sometimes desperately needed assistance. The success of this arrangement depends on maintaining the anonymity of the runaway and *never* calling the youth's parents or the authorities. Social workers sometimes find that it would be better in some individual cases to notify the parents. Both the youth and his family would be served by calling his home. Yet it would be against the interests of the assistance *system* to violate anonymity. To call one set of parents would jeopardize the entire setup. In such cases, the interests of the *individual* require one thing, the interests of the social *arrangements* require the opposite.

Sometimes we call this a conflict between acts and rules; the interest or utility of each is set against the other. Here we will recognize such conflicts as structural versus individual interests, where structures can represent public interest considerations.

Mass Public Interest.   The public interest may also be formed on (a) those features every member of the society has *in common*, or (b) ideals. For an example of (a), the public interest might require defending a society from foreign attack because each and every member of the society has an interest in being secure against aggressors. No need to count interests or focus on structures. The interest of the individual, *all* individuals, is identical to the public interest. Or, as an interpretation of (b), we might work with some Platonic truth, or natural right, or God's law, to say what the public interest is for each and every person in the society. Members of the Hare Krishna sect, for example, have no trouble visualizing the public interest as a mass conversion to their view of religious consciousness.

With a *mass* public interest no division can occur between any individual interest and the public interest. They are, by definition, the same. But there can still be conflicts between different values falling under a mass public interest. Both freedom and security are excellent candidates for mass public interest: all people have an interest in freedom and security, or they ought to. Yet it is well known that the two values can conflict. In conditions of war, for example, freedom sometimes is traded off for security. The devisiveness of the public interest can therefore still occur among the values the concept covers even when it does not occur between the individual and his society.

The attentive reader has noticed by now that each of these senses of the public interest—numerical, structural, mass—are only technical devices to focus our attention on different ways of seeing society and its interests. We still have not established the *values* that tell us what exactly society's interests are. Is it freedom? Security? Something else? We can count factors, concentrate on social practices, or look to common or ideal items. But unless we know *what* to count, *which* practices or items are in the interests of society, we have only a skeleton public interest, interesting as a cadaver to students, but of little help in evaluating public policies.

One helpful approach to the public interest is the theory of *primary goods*, which does try to put values into the concept of a public interest.

THE PUBLIC INTEREST AND PRIMARY GOODS

Let us begin by establishing a distinction between primary and secondary goods. One of Hemingway's characters asked from life only for "a clean, well-lighted place." It is instructive to know that the man in the short story was old and tired. Most of us want that from life and a bit more. Theories of primary goods are built on a distinction between the basics of life and that bit more.

Some of life's goods are necessary for life itself; food and security probably top this list. Other goods are necessary as a means of obtaining other things. Education, for example, is required to get most other goods in life; even following a healthy diet—rationally consuming that primary good, food—seems to depend on some rudimentary instruction. Still other goods, while not necessary, contribute to a full and civilized life: concerts, paintings, convenient modes of transportation, comfortable housing (clean, well-lighted, *and* aesthetically pleasing).

Some would rank these unnecessary goods as basic. Many argue from time to time that art is more important than life (arguments more seductive in youth than later). But theories of primary goods generally are concerned with life, on the quite reasonable grounds that in the absence of life no art or anything else is possible. So a primary good can be defined as one (a) necessary for the maintenance of life (food, basic clothing, minimal housing, security), *or* (b) necessary for the acquisition of other goods (education). A good, then, that is neither (a) nor (b) is a secondary good (single-family homes, stylistic clothing, private automobiles).

One of the strongest reasons for having social arrangements is that many primary goods can only be secured through joint efforts, and many others, though obtainable by individuals acting on their own, are still *best* achievable through social actions. The production of food or the maintenance of security, for example, is almost impossible for an individual to obtain acting alone. One can imagine extreme cases, the armed and solitary farmer, but even his purchasing of arms and farm implements is dependent on other people. Education can be conducted within a single family. But the range of training required to educate children effectively makes education a social enterprise if it is to be done well. This need to bring about primary goods is one important rational justification for society in general.

The theory of primary goods also holds the evaluative seeds of the "public interest." Primary goods are, by definition, desirable. They are valued because they are needed to maintain life or acquire secondary goods. Only social efforts can get them, either at all or effectively. It follows that it is in the public interest, indeed vital to the rationale of social arrangements, to provide such goods. If society does not provide them, then the rational grounds for having society in the first place are undermined. The value component of the public interest is thus introduced with the recognition of primary goods that can only, or best, be obtained through joint efforts.

Notice, however, that the recognition of primary goods at the heart of the public interest still says nothing about the appropriate social forms for getting these goods. One basic choice of social forms important today is between government action and the market mechanism. Some primary goods can only be obtained through the political system. Security seems clearly to be one such good. Though imaginative journalists and bored civil servants occasionally speculate about turning over national defense to private enterprise, even perhaps to the Mafia, the government remains the best arrangement to secure society's defense.

Other goods are not so clearly located within the province of the political system. Education seems a mixed bag, in practice and assessment. Both public and private schools exist in American society and, at least at the college level, a case can be made for either approach. Still other primary goods are best secured through the market mechanism; food production is one of these. To say that a primary good is in the public interest does not determine in itself how to go about obtaining it. The right social mechanism depends to a considerable extent on what type of good is at issue.

That an item is a primary good requiring social effort does, however, give it a priority status with the political system. It is reasonable to think that one function of the political order is to guarantee primary goods. At least, many people today view the government in this way, a view supported with the thought that society must provide primary goods in one way or another in order to justify its existence. Therefore, the government is understandably active even when primary goods are obtained through market production. The political system, for example, often operates to insure the required *conditions*, such as fairness, for effective market actions. (Example: The Securities and Exchange Commission as it attempts to regulate the stock exchange.) Also, the market often produces *externalities* that can only be effectively controlled through government action. Thus even the use of a market mechanism to produce primary goods still can require efforts by the political system.

The government does not, however, always represent the public interest when it acts. Many public policies have nothing to do with primary goods, indeed sometimes seem detrimental to their effective acquisition. Certainly those who argue classic free enterprise doctrines feel that way about many government fiscal and monetary policies, though at least as many view these government policies as absolutely necessary for minimal economic success. The state may also actually represent itself as a self-interested agent in an adversary relationship with other social agencies. When the government goes to court to protect governmental procedures, such as executive privilege, the government is a partisan subject to legislation, often on the basis of public-interest considerations. The public interest is, ultimately, a concept to evaluate the political system, not its exclusive property.

Also, an item that is in the public interest by virtue of its being a primary good is not necessarily a public good. A *public good*, let us recall, is available to all if available at all. Security policies are public interest items *and* public goods. To defend a society today, at least against something as comprehensive as nuclear attack, can only be done uniformly: protection for everyone in the society if any protection is provided at all. Education, on the other hand, is a public interest item, but not a public good. It can be made available to some and denied to others; whether it is in the public interest to make education uniformly available or not can itself be debated.

Because some public interest items are not public goods, we can see that *how* to distribute primary goods is a subject for public-interest discussion. With public goods like national defense, availability is not an issue (though provision can be—who will get the defense contracts). But if the good can or must be distributed, then that cliche question of politics reappears: who gets what, when, and how. Dialysis machines, for example, are primary goods for people with kidney failure; until a transplant can be arranged, they can be kept alive in no other way. But suppose, as can easily be the case, there are not enough dialysis machines to service those who need

them. Then although we have agreed that a primary good is at stake, deciding who is to use the machines is a vital question. The public interest can be
involved not only in *providing* primary goods, but also in *distributing* them.

WELFARE AND PRIMARY GOODS

Do welfare policies meet the primary-good criterion of the public interest? To this question, we can give a typical "political" answer: *yes* and *no*. On
the *yes* side, welfare is *basically* concerned with providing at least some
primary goods. Items like health, housing, and food are all prime candidates
for primary-good status. Again, the logic of social arrangements requires that
primary goods be made available. Older societies provided them by a combination of voluntary charities and rewards for individual efforts; society felt
that those who failed to get the needed goods failed by virtue of their own
deficiencies. More lately, with the general recognition that the free market is
inadequate to provide at least certain primary goods, welfare policy has
become the means of providing them. So *yes*, welfare policies are justified in
the public interest because they furnish needed items of life, which it is in
the public interest to provide.

But arguments exist on the *no* side. Welfare programs, critics say, go
beyond providing primary goods. Basic needs in health, housing, and food
are met and then some. Single-family housing, for example, is not required
to maintain life. The difficulty, they say, is that the affluent standards of
living in American society are used to interpret primary goods, not the
minimum standards that can in theory be applied. Also, primary goods can
compete with each other. If welfare programs are so expensive as to jeopardize the productive institutions of society, and these institutions are viewed
as vital to the attainment of other primary goods (like security), then it is in
the public interest to choose among these goods. There is no guarantee that
welfare will win out in such a choice.

Finally, even if we agree that the social order should provide the goods
that it currently does provide through welfare, it does not follow that welfare
programs as they now exist are in the public interest. At this point rationality
models supplement such evaluative concepts as the public interest. Agreed:
evaluative criteria require society to provide primary goods for its members.
But an agreement on the best or most optimal arrangements to provide such
goods is a question for rationality criteria. Although the market mechanism
has long been discarded as a fully satisfactory solution, any number of governmental forms, from local to federal, can be used to provide the primary
goods covered under welfare.

The endorsement of primary goods leaves open the question, once
more, of which type of government action can best secure the goods. Also, if

the goods are scarce, if not enough houses, health facilities, and food are finally available for all the needy, then hard decisions must be made on alternative distribution. These decisions go considerably beyond the agreement that providing primary goods is society's responsibility.

SOME CONCLUSIONS ON THE PUBLIC INTEREST

Applying the evaluative factor in the public interest—primary goods—to welfare policies tell us a lot about both the public interest and welfare. Here are some conclusions.

1. *Public interest* is still inadequate as a general concept to evaluate public policy. True, it legislates for and against fundamental justifications for many policies. Once we accept the theory of primary goods, we cannot condemn welfare as totally irrelevant without accepting an unrealistic view of the market's capacity to make primary goods available. On the other hand, we cannot select optimal government agencies and distributive formulas for goods using public interest criteria alone.

2. The inadequacy of the public interest criteria holds for all procedural versions: numerical, structural, and mass. Whether we sum individual interests, look to social practices, or resort to common interests or ideals, the political problem remains—how do we translate the value of the public interest, developed here in terms of primary goods, into desirable institutions? Which *structures* provide the best social arrangements is precisely the problem which the concept has so much difficulty solving. Primary goods are obviously good for everyone, all human beings, and so are *mass* versions of the public interest. But the twin problems of scarcity and optimal social arrangements make structural issues the aching concern of public interest evaluations.

3. Two versions of the public interest, structural and numerical, may each produce policies opposed to an individual's interests. A *numerical* public interest may be contrary to an individual's interest when the preponderance of interests is against him: he is in a numerical minority. A *structural* public interest may work against an individual's interests by placing a social practice or institution against him: to maintain some structures may require a sacrifice of some individuals (it may be necessary to fire employees to avoid bankrupting the business, for example).

A *mass* public interest is, on the other hand, consistent with the interests of each and every individual in the society; securing primary goods is in the interests of each and every member of the human race. But, although such interests are harmonious, the implementing of even mass interests may operate against an individual's interest. The social machinery to distribute scarce goods and develop optimal social arrangements may work against the interests of some individuals or not favor all people equally when put into practice. Those who, for example, would profit more from a free market do not have an interest in welfare mechanisms, though they share an interest in primary goods with welfare recipients. For those who do not get needed dialysis machines on a lottery system, a different method of distributing the machines would be in their interest, though again the basic interest in having machines available is common to both winners and losers. So although people may have a joint interest in providing primary goods they may disagree over the social mechanisms selected to provide these goods.

THE PUBLIC INTEREST AND JUSTICE

The public interest stands as an important concept to evaluate public policy and social arrangements, even though it is only partially effective. We have suggested how *efficiency* criteria both complement and on occasion supplant the public interest in determining optimal social arrangements to secure even primary goods. But even the heady combination of the public interest with rationally supported social arrangements does not complete the evaluative picture. We might still ask—are the arrangements *just*? Sometimes they are not.

Consider the following hypothetical cases.

1. The country is at war. The draft must be reinstalled to bring the armed forces up to fighting strength. Even worse, the conflict is a particularly violent one, with a high casualty rate expected among the new inductees. An issue arises on who to draft and what system to use. Some people favor deferments for those who can contribute in important ways to the society *and* who possess unique or rare skills, such as certain types of research physicians and nuclear physicists. Others argue for a "blind" draft system, inducting people without regard to their characteristics: a lottery method, for example, that selects draftees indifferently.

2. After long debate in Congress, a bill is passed authorizing *and* federally financing all "abortions-on-demand." Legally and economically, any expectant mother can now secure an abortion up to six months after conception. Proponents of the measure based their arguments on the moral, or natural, right of women to control their own bodies. To the surprise of everyone, for and against the bill, the new law leads to an astounding number of abortions. Studies are hastily made. It is reliably concluded that the abortion rate is so high that the population of the country in the near future will be reduced by more than one-half, a population too small to maintain the industrial and farm base of the society. People begin efforts to repeal the law. Others oppose these efforts, maintaining that a moral right cannot vary with the number of people who choose to exercise this right.

Those in favor of repeal point out that the very existence of the society is at stake.

3. On a lonely country road in a small community, an entire family is brutally killed one night. The senselessness and sheer violence of the murders—the victims have obviously been tortured—and the family being one of the kindest in the community combine to generate an unprecedented rage among the local residents. Since the evidence shows that the murders were committed by someone living in the community, the residents are tearing each other apart with suspicions and accusations. Vigilante groups are formed to ferret out the murderer. The local sheriff knows that as the vigilante activity escalates from hysteria to frenzy, which it will do unless the murderer is caught, many innocent people will die and the community will finally destroy itself. He knows who killed the family; he had the physical evidence to prove it, but a careless lab technician accidentally destroyed the evidence. Some of the sheriff's deputies urge a public lynching party to kill the murderer and preserve the community. Others point out that the rules of law require a fair trial even if the guilty go free and the community is destroyed.

4. A cancer epidemic begins sweeping the United States. It turns out that toxic substances in the environment are far more lethal than previously thought by any but the most pessimistic scientists. Almost one in every three people can now expect to develop one or another form of cancer. Therapy resources are obviously scarce in the face of such demand. A national committee is formed to determine selection criteria for treatment. As expected, a variety of suggestions are made. Some on the committee, fresh from arguments over the draft system, push for a lottery system. Their opponents argue for the criteria of social utility—who will help society most if their lives are prolonged. But new proposals also appear. One callous conservative proposes that only those who can pay the stiff costs of treatment should receive therapy. Others argue *need* as the criterion—who has the largest family to support and so on.

Each of these four examples is different in important ways from the other three. But they all point to a distinction between the interests of society, in effect the public interest, and the requirements of justice. Sometimes the distinction is drawn on the considerations that support the various, often conflicting proposals. Interest-oriented considerations seem to be more concerned with survival, both for the individual and the society. Justice-oriented considerations seem more concerned with need. But the main difference between the public interest and justice that the examples underscore is between *social utility* and *fairness*. The public interest, defined as that which benefits society, can be served with (1) a selective draft excluding individuals important to society, (2) the reduction of access to abortion as the number of abortions increases, (3) the lynching of the guilty

218 Public Policy Evaluation

party, and (4) the application of cancer therapy to the socially useful. Justice in each case favors an opposing alternative.

We may legitimately demur at the utility of some of these measures, especially the lynching, on the grounds that justice has its own social utility. And so it does. Justice is frequently in the public interest. Communities pacified by extralegal sacrifices do not rest easily on a confident social conscience. (Additional troubles frequently follow.) But justice can easily conflict with public interest requirements as well. Each of the examples can be redescribed to show how injustice, or indifference to justice, actually benefits society. (Add child hostages held in starvation by the murderer in case three, then weigh the desirability of torturing him to reveal their location.)

We need not turn even to these mildly esoteric examples to see the possible social disutility of justice. A social system that practices racial discrimination in order to maintain high productivity and consequent stability is unjust; making it just could be the most painful and socially disruptive process possible. But justice is not satisfied with simple utility. Social arrangements must be fair, though the society may crack open at the mere thought of what realizing fairness means. It is to this more demanding evaluative concept of justice that the discussion turns in the next chapter.

SUMMARY

1.   Politics can be both the subject of evaluation and its motivation. Policy-oriented research is unlike pure research in its pragmatic, as opposed to theoretically rigorous, orientation. The danger in policy-oriented research is that social needs can obscure valid causes of social problems.

2.   Simple cost-benefit evaluations encounter complicated issues when applied to groups, in particular (a) making interpersonal comparisons of value, (b) weighing externalities, and (c) deciding how to distribute costs and benefits.

3.   Today's welfare policy represents a fundamental change in attitudes toward the causes of poverty, shifting responsibility from the individual to the social system. Direct welfare policies include two types, public assistance and social insurance.

4.   Among the numerous problems in current welfare programs are (a) exhorbitant, and growing, expense; (b) the absence of effective program coordination; (c) dysfunctional consequences; and (d) fraud.

5.   Four concepts are helpful in evaluating public policy: equity, efficiency, Pareto Optimality, and the public interest.

6.   Welfare policies are weakly inequitable in that they do not cover the working poor. Whether they are efficient presents a mixed case: welfare programs, though grossly inefficient from many points of view, (a) may have contributed to the elimination of poverty if transfers in kind are counted and (b) are less costly than at least those major alternatives based on the negative income tax.

7.   The public interest as procedure can be separated into *numerical, structural,* and *mass* considerations. But the concept requires a theory of primary goods for its evaluative component. Even primary goods, however, require decisions on optimal social arrangements to provide the goods, decisions that simple public interest cannot specify.

8.   Welfare programs are weakly justified because they guarantee primary goods. But they are not necessarily justified by the public interest when they provide more than primary goods. Nor are the social arrangements that implement welfare necessarily justified by the theory of primary goods.

9.   The public interest, even when optimally carried out, may still conflict with the requirements of justice.

FOR FURTHER READING

POLICY RESEARCH

BRECHT, ARNOLD, *Political Theory.* Princeton, N.J.: Princeton University Press, 1959.
COLEMAN, JAMES, "Problems of Conceptualization and Measurement in Studying Policy Impacts," in *Public Policy Evaluation,* ed. Kenneth Dolbeare. Beverly Hills: Sage Publications, 1975.
SHARKANSKY, IRA, *Policy Analysis in Political Science.* Chicago: Markham, 1970.
SIMON, HERBERT, *Administrative Behavior.* New York: MacMillan, 1947.
TAYLOR, CHARLES, "Neutrality in Political Science," in *Philosophy, Politics and Society,* 3rd Series, eds. P. Laslett and W. G. Runciman. New York: Barnes & Noble, 1967.
WEBER, MAX, *The Methodology of the Social Sciences.* Glencoe, Ill.: Free Press, 1949.

WELFARE AND HEALTH

BOWLER, M. KENNETH, *The Nixon Guaranteed Income Proposal: Substance and Process in Policy Change.* Cambridge, Mass.: Ballinger, 1974.
BROWNING, EDGAR K., *Redistribution and the Welfare System.* Washington, D.C.: American Enterprise Institute for Public Policy Research, 1975.

DOWD, DOUGLAS, *The Twisted Dream*. Cambridge, Mass.: Winthrop, 1974.

FEAGIN, JOE, *Subordinating the Poor*. Englewood Cliffs, N.J.: Prentice-Hall, 1975.

HARRINGTON, MICHAEL, *The Other America: Poverty in the United States*. New York: MacMillan, 1962.

JOINT ECONOMIC SUBCOMMITTEE ON FISCAL POLICY, *The Future of Social Programs*. Washington, D.C.: Congressional Quarterly, 1973.

MOYNIHAN, DANIEL PATRICK, *Maximum Feasible Misunderstanding: Community Action and the War on Poverty*. New York: Free Press, 1969.

PIVEN, FRANCES FOX, AND RICHARD A. CLOWARD, *Regulating the Poor: The Functions of Public Welfare*. New York: Random House, 1971.

————, *Poor People's Movements: Why They Succeed, How They Fail*. New York: Pantheon Books, 1977.

RESCHER, NICHOLAS, *Welfare: The Social Issues in Philosophical Perspective*. Pittsburgh: University of Pittsburgh Press, 1972.

STEINER, GILBERT, *The State of Welfare*. Washington, D.C.: Brookings Institution, 1971.

WILENSKY, HAROLD, AND CHARLES LEBEAUX, *Industrial Society and Social Welfare*. New York: Free Press, 1965.

THE PUBLIC INTEREST

BARRY, BRIAN, *Political Argument*. London: Routledge & Kegan Paul, 1965, pp. 207–285.

BENDITT, THEODORE, "The Public Interest," *Philosophy and Public Affairs*, 2 (1973).

BRAYBROOKE, DAVID, "The Public Interest: The Present and Future of the Concept," in *The Public Interest NOMOS V*, ed. Carl Friedrich. New York: Atherton, 1962.

CONNOLLY, WILLIAM, *The Terms of Political Discourse*. Lexington, Mass.: Heath, 1974, pp. 45–83.

FLATHMAN, RICHARD, *The Public Interest*. New York: John Wiley, 1966.

HARSANYI, JOHN, "Cardinal Welfare, Individualistic Ethics, and Interpersonal Comparisons of Utility," *Journal of Political Economy*, 63 (Aug. 1955) (for Harsanyi's "solution" to the problem of interpersonal comparisons of value).

HELD, VIRGINIA, *The Public Interest and Individual Interests*. New York: Basic Books, 1970.

OPPENHEIM, FELIX, "Self Interest and Public Interest," *Political Theory* 3 (Aug. 1975).

RAWLS, JOHN, *A Theory of Justice*. Cambridge, Mass.: Harvard University Press, 1971 (for the discussion of "primary goods" as necessary means to other desired things, on pp. 90–95).

RESCHER, NICHOLAS, *Distributive Justice*. Indianapolis: Bobbs-Merrill, 1966.

STEINER, GEORGE, "The Public Interest and the Public Sector," in *Public Expenditures and Policy Analysis*, eds. R. Haveman and J. Margolis. Chicago: Markham, 1970.

ethics, justice, and public policy

7

POLITICAL ETHICS

Following the Watergate scandals American politics was filled with renewed emphasis on ethics in government. How could it be otherwise? The American people had witnessed the resignation under fire of a president and the jailing of his three top associates and many lesser figures. Many felt that Richard Nixon had himself evaded prison only because of the pardon tendered by President Gerald Ford. The Watergate scandal came to be viewed as one of the most corrupt episodes in American history.

Closer studies of Nixon's predecessors revealed something even worse. The abuses of power in the Nixon presidency were part of a pattern extending through several past administrations. Misuse of the Internal Revenue Service and the FBI occurred in the Kennedy-Johnson years as well as during Nixon's tenure in office. The development of an Imperial Presidency seemed to have immunized the Oval Office from ordinary ethics. Nixon even claimed in one of the later David Frost interviews on television that presidential authority could make illegal acts legal (for example, robbery in the name of national security).

In the years immediately preceding and following Nixon's resignation, several scandals also rocked Congress. Several Congressmen were indicted for a variety of offenses, including conspiracy (conflict-of-interest), bribery, mail fraud, perjury, extortion, campaign violations, and failure to file income tax returns. Fourteen Congressmen and two congressional aides were indicted during the years from 1968 through 1977. In 1976, the efforts of the South Korean government to "buy" Congressmen became a public issue.

Envelopes stuffed with money, paid junkets and charge accounts, and liaisons arranged with members of the opposite sex, were said to be part of the tactics used by South Korean officials to insure Congressional good will. Sexual misconduct in general seemed commonplace in Congress. The most sensational event involved Representative Wayne Hays' assignations with Elizabeth Ray, who charged that she was paid with federal funds to be Hays' mistress.

The sting of these scandals, from abuses of power to sexual adventures, moved each branch of Congress to adopt a code of ethics in early 1977. The final push toward reform came with a 29 percent pay raise Congressmen had voted themselves shortly before the ethics bill came to the floor. Many legislators were afraid to vote against the code of ethics so shortly after rewarding themselves with handsome salary increases. Both House Speaker Tip O'Neill and Senate Majority Leader Robert Byrd tied their support of the big pay boost to the understanding that the code of ethics would also be adopted. It was, 402 to 22 in the House and 86 to 9 in the Senate, though not without some bitter criticism by the legislators.

Both House and Senate codes were similar. The important provisions were these: (1) a requirement that legislators disclose their financial standing (income, investments, property, and so forth); (2) a limitation on outside earned income of 15 percent of their Congressional salary; (3) a bar on accepting gifts valued at more than $100 from persons having an interest in legislation; (4) the abolishment of unofficial office accounts, known as "slush funds"; and (5) a host of restrictions on mailing privileges, travel expenses, fund-raising by staff aides, and a ban on discriminatory practices. During debate, the ethics code was variously called a "milestone" (by Senator Gaylord Nelson) and "an unfortunate April fool's joke" (by Senator Barry Goldwater).

Those supporting the code stressed the importance of an open government and the need to restore confidence in the American political system after the series of shocks in the years preceding the code's adoption. Those opposed to the code attacked the limitation on outside income as unfair, since it banned *earned* income without restricting *unearned* income from investments, such as stock dividends, and family-owned farms and businesses. Many legislators also opposed the financial-disclosure requirement, on the grounds that it was an invasion of privacy (among other, perhaps less savory, reasons).

Do ethics codes work to make government better? Optimists see an ethics code as at least a needed step toward government reform. Weary cynics see such codes as impossible to support because of the nature of politics and as perhaps causing more problems than they solve.

We will, in this chapter, avoid the posturing of either the optimist or the cynic. Instead, we will direct our efforts (as usual) toward understanding limits and possibilities in politics. We will explore as full a range of ethical issues in politics as space permits, beginning with ethical conduct and ending with the just society. At least the complexity of ethics and politics can be illuminated, if not the solutions to each problem the topic raises.

TYPES OF ETHICAL ISSUES IN POLITICS

Being a "good guy" is usually more appealing politically than being a "bad guy." Also, bad guys sometimes go straight to jail from their political offices. But the definition of a good guy, someone ethically straight, is not always clear. Nor is it always understood that the system itself may be the ethical issue, not the people running it.

Let's outline, for clarification, several types of ethical matters that bear on politics.

PECCADILLOES

The Catholic Church distinguishes between mortal and venial sins. There is no reason why we can't start with a similar distinction to grasp the realities of political ethics. Government authorities, like all of us, sometimes do things that, while they are unethical, are not matters of extreme gravity for the law or their individual conscience. Now, the sensitivity of the conscience can vary greatly from one individual to another, so that one person's veniality may be another's road to damnation. But some things are trivial to almost anyone. Jack Anderson, in a column published on September 17, 1976, solemnly related the story of the National Endowment for the Arts official who forgot her luggage containing official papers when she flew from Washington to Los Angeles on official business. The suitcase was quickly flown to her, prompting Anderson to intone that "All told, the misplaced suitcase cost the taxpayers $42.75." This incident, to almost anyone other than Jack Anderson, is venial, not mortal.

There are many who would classify sexual misadventures in the peccadillo category. That a Congressman keeps a mistress may be a matter between him, his wife, and his religion, but not a grave political matter. Wayne Hayes' main undoing was that he (1) put Elizabeth Ray on the government payroll (when, on her own admission, she could neither type nor even answer the telephone), and that he (2) lied (like John Profumo in the Christine Keeler scandal in Britain a decade earlier) to his legislative colleagues about the affair. In the Hayes-Tilden presidential campaign a century earlier, it was claimed that candidate Hayes had sired an illegitimate son and that Tilden had been touched by political corruption. The voters put Hayes into office and sent Tilden back to private life, a judgment historians applaud on grounds of appropriateness: Hayes was honest in public life,

Tilden impeccable in private life. The Hayes of a century later mixed his sexual affair with public money and testimony, to his own misfortune.

Establishing a peccadillo category for political ethics obviously requires a distinction between public life and private ethics. But some ethical issues, though nominally private, are either relevant to politics or so vital in themselves that they slide over to public performance. A person who chronically lies in private life, for example, may not be someone to whom we would give unexamined trust in public matters. (Honesty is a private *and* a public virtue.) Or sexual activities that involve kinky, sadistic-masochistic sex may reflect character disorders that could overlap with political judgments. To be classified a "peccadillo," an ethical offense must be both trivial and separate from political performance.

OFFICIAL MISCONDUCT

More important politically are those ethical offenses that bear directly on political office. Influence-peddling, absence of candor (issuing misleading statements), outright demagogery—actions like these may not be illegal, but they are still unethical in the political sense. A candidate, for example, who deliberately misleads the public to his own advantage by concealing damaging information is acting unethically, though he may be breaking no law. Ironically, Richard Nixon, in his famous "Checkers" speech in 1952, set up just such standards for himself in addressing charges that he had accepted a slush fund from California businessmen: not just that the acceptance of the fund was legal, but that it was ethical as well. The U.S. Senate's reinvestigation of Bert Lance in 1977, when he was still head of the Office of Management and Budget, came back again and again to ethical, not legal, issues in Lance's banking career.

Ethical codes in political life are typically aimed at defining and penalizing official misconduct. House and Senate codes, for example, specifically regulate the use of political money (either government or private funds) and require disclosure of financial resources. Sometimes the legal system addresses official misconduct as well. All states have passed in one form or another a "sunshine law" requiring that meetings where public business is conducted be open to the public. Though these laws differ in important ways from state to state, all are based on the premise that secrecy in government is bad, public access is good, and the open meeting is less vulnerable to political chicanery and misconduct than the closed meeting.

ILLEGAL ACTIONS

Public officials can also break the law, a form of behavior that is often both unethical and illegal. The office-holder who, for example, accepts payment from a business firm to quash a regulation the firm finds undesirable, who fails to report the payment on his income tax return, and then lies to a grand jury investigating the incident is in trouble that goes far beyond official misconduct. He has broken at least three laws—those against bribery, income tax fraud, and perjury.

Not all types of criminal behavior are appropriate considerations for political ethics. The public official who occupies his spare time by robbing liquor stores in the District of Columbia is a criminal, but his robbery is not a political crime (see Chapter 4). The issue of "illegal political actions" arises when ethical misconduct of a political nature (conflict-of-interest, for example) intersects with the law (bribery, for example). The remedy for illegal political action is standard: indictment and trial in the legal system.

UNJUST ACTIONS

The last category covers the ethical status of policies in the political system and the ethical state of the system itself. Discussions of political ethics frequently involve the sins and omissions of politicians. Do they take graft? Are they padding votes? More significant matters for discussion are the ethical qualities of policies and systems. Is a law or a policy ethical? Do the rules and practices of a society fulfill the requirements of justice? President Carter's emphasis early in his first administration on "human rights" addressed one of the ethical issues this category covers. The difficulties that Carter's emphasis encountered also reveal some of the more basic problems of ethics and politics (to be summed up at the end of the last chapter).

Appraising the justice of policies and social arrangements is an exercise as old as political theory itself. The concepts of appraisal are familiar ones— equality, fairness, rights. We will turn to these concepts throughout this chapter as we concentrate on the points of intersection between ethics and social justice.

EQUALITY

How do social arrangements satisfy ethical requirements? An idea with powerful ethical appeal is equality. Aristotle maintained that men who are relevantly equal should be given equal treatment, a thought that reveals Aristotle's views on "equity" and even politics itself, which he saw as an activity among equals. Like the rule, "treat like cases alike," the Aristotelian idea is basic also to current models of rationality (Chapter 2). More recent views on ethics, as expressed in the Declaration of Independence, for example, accept human equality as the foundation of social justice. George Orwell in *Animal Farm* reminded us that some men are often viewed as more equal than others, but he was describing the harsh realities of politics rather than its ethical ideals. Generally, the concept of equality for all, regardless of race, creed, sex, or national origin, is used as the initial ethical standard for judging social arrangements.

Even the strongest proponents of equality, however, would readily agree that absolute equality is not only impossible in fact, but can produce ethical distortion as well. Aristotle was quick to add that relevantly unequal persons should, in proportion to their differences, be treated unequally. The doctrine of equality, stated as a rational principle (treat like cases alike), is also notoriously deficient in establishing justice. Since people differ from one another in seemingly infinite ways, what determines a *relevant* difference is an ethical issue itself.

In a famous referendum held in Dade County, Florida, in June 1977 voters were asked to repeal or uphold an ordinance that barred discrimination against homosexuals in employment, housing, and public accommodations. In effect, voters were being asked to single out, by putting into law, the express *irrelevance* of sexual preference in the three areas of employment, housing, and public accommodations. The voters repealed the amendment, though whether the negative vote represented an endorsement of the *relevance* of sexual preference in the three areas listed (thus approving discriminatory treatment), or merely expressed a feeling that sexual preference ought not to be singled out for explicit legal protection against discrimination, was difficult to say.

Aristotle, no enemy of homosexuals, condoned slavery, though only for those who were not Greeks (they were, to Aristotle, "relevantly" unlike Greeks) and excluded women from politics (they were supposed to have unfilled cavities in the backs of their heads where men had additional brains). If we disagree with Aristotle and maintain that national origin and sex are irrelevant considerations in judgments of equality, or if we take a stand on ordinances barring discrimination against homosexuals (as the Dade County voters did), then we are involved in a dispute that will not be resolved by the rational concept of equality: it is precisely what to count in determining equality that is the moral and policy issue.

We have two ways of filling in rational or "procedural" equality to resolve the problem of *relevance*.

1. The oldest is to claim that natural rights exist which compel us to treat all people impartially because they are human beings. Eighteenth-century political philosophy, especially that part of it which influenced American politics in this country's origins, emphasized rights to life, liberty, property (Locke), or the pursuit of happiness (the Declaration of Independence). Naturally one may always accept such rights, then claim that certain people are not really human beings, as many defenders of slavery did in the nineteenth century. But today the ascription of nonhumanness is not easily made, both for good anthropological and ethical reasons. So natural rights

seem to compel equal treatment on matters of freedom, opportunity, maintenance of life, and so on, toward all people regardless of their differences because all people have these rights in the natural order of things.

Several problems occur, however, in applying natural rights to all issues of equality. The first, and more general, problem is that disputes might occur over what the list of natural rights should include. A favorite eighteenth-century ploy was to claim "self-evident" status for natural rights: any rational person would see what they are. But this does not help if otherwise rational people disagree about whether, say, property is a natural or an artificial right (as they frequently do).

Second, even when they agree on a list of natural rights, people may disagree over their application in specific cases. It is a depressing fact of political history that the language of natural rights has been used to justify anything and everything, which the vagueness of terms like "liberty" permits. Locke seemed to feel that disputes in areas covered by natural rights simply would not occur—but then he did not live in our century.

Third, even basic rights can conflict with one another. Freedom, for example, can on occasion be counter to property rights. Reference to natural rights will not resolve such a conflict, because the conflict is *between* natural rights.

Finally, the assumption of natural equality among all people, helpful though the idea is when its internal problems are avoided, still says nothing about the ways in which people are justifiably treated as *unequal*. Sometimes unequal treatment is required on the basis of distributive justice. Those who, for example, are impoverished may be said to have a claim on greater social stakes than those who are well off. We do not, to put it more bluntly, divide the social pie equally when one of those at the table is starving and the others are already sated—at least not without wondering if there is not more to social justice than simple equality.

2. The second way to give content to procedural equality is to introduce social practices into the idea of *relevance*. We may say that the type of rule covering an activity provides the criteria of relevance in determining whether people are to be treated equally or not. For example, if we are admitting people to law school, then relative scores on law board exams allow us to favor some applicants (high scorers) against others (low scorers). But we may not favor redheads against blondes, men against women, tall people against short people, whites against blacks—because such differences are not relevant to performance in law school. Notice that allowing the rules of a social practice to govern equality not only effectively resolves the "relevance" problem—if women score well in law boards (which they do), then Aristotle would not be able to keep them out on the basis of the head-cavity argument—but also allows for the unequal treatment that relevant inequality justifies.

The main problem with the "practice" interpretation of equality is that the practice itself may contribute to the inequality the social rule tries to measure. Low scores on law boards, for example, are sometimes attributed to the historical tendency of the tests to keep certain minorities out of law school; and without the upward mobility that such institutions as law schools provide, future generations of minority groups are not given the opportunity to grow up in those culturally advantaged homes and schools that do contribute to high performance on entrance exams. The circle, in short, may be seen as a vicious one: the system of social practices may effectively reinforce, and even create, the inequalities it is supposed to reflect indifferently.

Also, the criteria of relevance found in many social practices may be questioned. At a narrow level, data like performances on law boards are sometimes said *not* to correlate decisively with success in law. Other criteria, like faculty recommendations, may be as important and may favor groups other than the high-scoring candidates. But, more generally, the basic criteria can be challenged. Some argue that those social practices that base unequal treatment on *ability* ought really to base unequal treatment on *need*. With this fundamental shift in criteria, law schools would admit, at least in part, those who could most benefit from a law degree rather than only those who could best practice law. However one views criterial change of this sort, the "practice" interpretation of equality has itself become the issue rather than the solution of relevant equality when such questions are raised.

Equality, even if all of these problems could be resolved, is also at best only a partial concept in our ethical evaluations of the best society. Equality may conflict with productive criteria, for example. Consider a three-man society (A, B, and C) with the following distributive characteristics (as outlined in social arrangements I, II, and III). The numbers in each cell of the matrix represent units of value and a higher number is better than a lower number.

	A	B	C
I	100	60	40
II	10	10	10
III	200	10	5

On a strict equality criterion, society II is best: it is by a considerable margin the most equalitarian. (Members A, B, and C each have ten shares.) But most people, including especially the members of the society (A, B, C) would prefer society I: though less equal than society II, all of the members are better off because the society has a greater amount of goods to distribute.

Notice, however, that a purely productive criterion won't be sufficient as an evaluative standard either. Society III, though possessing a greater amount of goods than I (a total of 215 versus 100), is too unequal to be desirable. What we have in our evaluations are both *productive* and *distributive* criteria, or the twin principles of that utilitarian formula, (a) the *greatest* good for (b) the greatest *number*. Equality alone won't suffice.

Critically inspecting the concept of *equality* seems to lead to this conclusion: our ethical evaluations must specify a balanced distribution of society's goods, not simply require equality. The task of a social ethics, then, must be to describe the arrangements that legitimately reflect the inevitable inequalities among human beings.

REVERSE DISCRIMINATION: INEQUALITY AS COMPENSATION

One of the more volatile social issues in American society is how to redress unfair inequalities that have existed over a period of time. Let us assume what is generally acknowledged as fact: several groups—blacks, Indians, Mexican-Americans, women—have been discriminated against throughout most of this country's history. They have been treated unequally on irrelevant differences when they should have been treated equally. Having conceded this, the question of social ethics now is, what do we do about it?

The elimination of long-standing discrimination typically takes the form of progressively active policies to insure the representation in social units of the excluded group (summarized from Nagel, 1973). The first step is obviously to eliminate deliberate barriers that deny access to minorities. Often this first step involves changing the rules of an institution to end overt discrimination. Law schools, for example, that have implicit or explicit procedures that exclude minority candidates would have to change these procedures as a first step in ending discrimination.

A second step is to eliminate hidden bias in the access routes to institutions. Even with perfectly fair (or "blind") admittance procedures, those responsible for admitting law students may still maintain a bias against minorities in their application of the procedures. So a second step would require the self-conscious scrutiny of minority candidates to insure fair treatment. Special attention to minority qualifications might avoid implicit discrimination.

The third step introduces compensatory measures to affect *system* bias. Many critics of American institutions have concluded that the bias against minorities in the United States goes deeper than procedures and the attitudes of "gatekeepers" (for example, admittance officers). Bias, some maintain, is reflected in the basic institutional arrangements of society; because bias is so fundamental, it affects the ability of minorities to take advantage of fair access routes when competing with those who have had a more advantageous start. On this assumption is based the reasonableness of compensatory programs like special training centers, additional financial help, remedial education—all of those measures aimed at bringing minorities up to a competitive level with groups that have historically *not* been discriminated against.

A fourth step is to extend compensatory measures to the point of, in effect, reverse discrimination. In this fourth step, disadvantaged groups are allowed increased access to institutions by admitting more than would have been admitted through competitive performances. A law school, for example, would admit some minority candidates because they are members of a minority group, not merely because they have competitively superior qualifications on law board exams, faculty recommendations, grade averages, and so on. This fourth step frequently reflects a failure of compensatory programs to bring minority group members up to a successful competitive level. The choice, then, is whether to accept the unbalanced representation of minorities in institutions or to extend compensatory measures to the access routes. Those favoring this fourth step support the extension.

Finally, the fifth step is to provide representation of minorities in institutions proportional to their numbers in the general population. Law schools, for example, would have to admit enough minority applicants to reach a prearranged distribution in the student population.

This fifth step is obviously the most controversial measure to combat discrimination. Its controversial status is largely a product of a fundamental shift in criteria: from *merit* to *reform* or *desert*. Those endorsing this fifth step often maintain that the institutions of society must be used to remedy the effects of discrimination by favoring the disadvantaged (reform measures). Sometimes the more radical step is taken to a desert criterion: the rewards of society ought not go simply to those who have more ability; they must also go to those who deserve them because of their immediate needs or because they are due compensation for previous unjust treatment. In the law school example, admission policy would then discriminate in favor of minorities, either because minorities need greater access to professional schools or because the social system must make amends for past injustice, or both.

THE LAW AND REVERSE DISCRIMINATION

In his senior year at the University of Washington (1970/71), Marco DeFunis, Jr., applied for admission to the University of Washington School of Law in September 1971. This law school employs a common, but intriguing formula for evaluating applicants. For a preliminary ranking, each applicant's junior-senior undergraduate grade average is combined with his or her test scores on the Law School Admissions Test to produce a Predicted First-Year Average (PFYA). DeFunis' PFYA score was 76.23. From previous experience, the law school marked off those applicants with a score of over 77 as the most promising group. Applicants with a PFYA below 74.5 were judged not very promising as potential law students.

Applicants with a PFYA above 77 were admitted, unless the admissions committee felt their PFYA score was misleading on the basis of such other considerations as faculty recommendations or relative difficulty of course work. PFYA applicants with scores below 74.5 were generally rejected, but two kinds of exceptions were made. First, those applicants previously admitted to the law school but inducted into the armed forces were routinely allowed to re-enter after completing military service. Second, and pertinent to the issue at hand, minority candidates were given special consideration and some with relatively low PFYA scores were admitted so as to achieve reasonable representation of minority groups in the law school.

A total of 275 students were admitted to the law school in the year that DeFunis applied. DeFunis, not a veteran and white, was rejected. Of the accepted applicants, 74 had lower PFYA scores than DeFunis did. In this group of 74, 36 were minority applicants, 22 were returning from military service, and 16 were applicants the committee judged to be better than their PFYA scores indicated. Twenty-nine applicants with a higher PFYA score than DeFunis were rejected. Several of the minority applicants admitted had PFYA scores so low that they clearly would have been rejected immediately had they been white.

Marco DeFunis challenged the denial of his admission in court. On the grounds that race was a decisive factor in his rejection by the law school, he sued the University of Washington for admittance under the equal protection provisions of the state and federal Constitutions. In *DeFunis* v. *Odegaard,* the court (in the initial disposition of the case) ruled in his favor. DeFunis was admitted to the University of Washington law school in the fall of 1973 under a court injunction.

On appeal, the lower court decision was reversed in the Washington Supreme Court, where it was decided that the university was legally warranted in considering race as a factor in selecting law students. DeFunis appealed to the U.S. Supreme Court, meanwhile remaining in law school on the intervention of Justice William Douglas during the appeal period. The Supreme Court finally found the case mooted because of DeFunis' imminent graduation from law school in 1974: no decision was rendered by the highest court on the merits of the case.

The issues that the DeFunis case raises obviously did not disappear when the U.S. Supreme Court refused to make a decision. Since the issues go to the heart of social remedies for discrimination, they will reappear again and again. The two lower court decisions represent basic contrasting attitudes toward discrimination. The initial decision followed the standard of what can be called formal impartiality. Relying on *Brown* v. *Board of Education*, the Supreme Court of Washington maintained that the state could not permit the consideration of race as a criterion in an admissions process: the equal protection clause of the Fourteenth Amendment is colorblind, requiring states to treat all races alike.

The Washington Supreme Court, in reversing the initial decision, allowed racial considerations in alleviating a racial imbalance. The majority argued that even the *Brown* decision held that only "invidious racial classifications—i.e., those that stigmatize a racial group with the stamp of inferiority—are unconstitutional" (*DeFunis* v. *Odegaard*, 1973). Where the purpose of racial classification is to bring together, rather than separate, the races, or "to undo the effects of past segregation," then such classification is constitutional. The court concluded that the classification used in the law school admissions policy was necessary to realize a compelling state interest, increasing minority representation in the legal profession, and thus was justified. The court further declared that the case did not raise the issue of whether the Fourteenth Amendment *requires* affirmative action to eliminate de facto segregation. The only issue is "whether the Constitution *permits* the law school to remedy racial imbalance through its minority admissions policy." The court answered *yes*.

A second important case in the area of reverse discrimination is *Regents of California* v. *Allan Bakke*. Allan Bakke, a white, blue-eyed blond of Norwegian ancestry (almost the prototype physical specimen to test racial issues) achieved an A− grade average while majoring in engineering at the University of Minnesota. After graduation, he entered the Naval Reserve Officers Training Corps, and later became a captain in the Marine Corps in Vietnam. Then, while an engineer for a space-agency laboratory near Palo Alto, he began working with physicians studying the effects of space on the human body. This work inspired him, at age 32, to become a doctor.

Bakke applied to eleven medical schools in 1972, one of which was the University of California at Davis. Davis, like most medical schools at that time, had a two-track system of admissions: eighty-four of its one hundred places were to be filled by open competition; the remaining sixteen places were reserved for "disadvantaged" applicants (in effect, blacks, Mexican-Americans, and Asian-Americans). Bakke scored 468 out of 500 in the combined subjective and objective test scoring used at Davis, a score that normally would have gained him admission. But due to illness in his family he withdrew from competition until only a few of the 84 slots were still open. When he re-entered competition, he was rejected at Davis and at ten other medical schools, primarily because most of the slots were filled. Davis, in the meantime, had admitted no minority students in open competition, but had admitted six blacks, eight Chicanos, and two Asians under the lowered standards of the special disadvantaged track.

Bakke tried again the following year. This time, a new admissions officer gave him a conspicuously low score on the interview (he had in the interim threatened legal action against Davis' minority program) and, in a close contest, he was denied admission again. Bakke then brought suit against the university, claiming racial discrimination on the grounds that the minority program deprived him of equal protection under the Fourteenth Amendment.

The California Supreme Court ruled six to one for Bakke, the majority arguing that the university could not now discriminate *for* minorities, having never discriminated *against* them. The court ruled that a program for the disadvantaged was acceptable only if available to all races and not, as in the Davis program, if based on a racial quota. The court also maintained that race-conscious admissions plans are justifiable only if there is a compelling state interest that could be served by no other means.

The U.S. Supreme Court heard arguments in the Bakke case in October 1977. Over 50 friend-of-the-court briefs were filed in the case. The Justice Department urged a narrow ruling against Bakke, upholding the principle of giving preferences to minorities in university admission policies to compensate for past discrimination. The government maintained that race is an important factor even in determining ability, for a numerical score on an entrance exam earned by a black might be effectively equivalent to a higher score earned by a white (if, as seems true, earlier deprivation can distort test scores downwards). Other groups, for example the Young Americans for Freedom, argued that the Constitution is color-blind and preferential treatments of one race are illegal. The Supreme Court, after months of deliberation, finally ruled for Bakke, on the grounds that the University of California had used a quota system. But the Court advised that race could be a relevant consideration in university admissions policies on a different set of procedures. The Court did not address the broader issues of reverse discrimination, including whether race is a legal consideration in other equal-opportunity areas, like housing and jobs.

SOME ISSUES IN REVERSE DISCRIMINATION

Several issues that will likely be discussed in public policy for some time are raised by the DeFunis and Bakke cases.

1. How do we identify the disadvantaged in society? Whatever criteria are used, we must realize that the groups covered will change with status changes in society. Jews, Irish, and Italians, for example, were disadvan-

taged groups in American society early in this century. Now they are rarely included in lists of the disadvantaged. More serious is the problem of over-lapping characteristics. Once we begin filling in our disadvantaged criteria with specific properties, like being black, poor, uneducated, and so on, we have the problem of uneven mixes: poor whites, rich blacks (Hughes, 1968). Justice William Douglas, dissenting from the mootness decision of the Court in *DeFunis*, argued the even stronger thesis that there is no precise defini-tion of "disadvantaged": however the term is specified, if blacks are so labeled, then Appalachian whites, for example, must also be so labeled.

Whether one wants to go as far as Justice Douglas in maintaining that "disadvantaged" is a hopelessly elusive term, it must be admitted that the concept is complex. Those arguing the logic of affirmative action, however, can turn to the history of *official* discrimination in American society: al-though alienation of many minority groups is common in the United States, only black Americans and American Indians have been singled out in dis-criminatory legislative, executive, and judicial pronouncements. Those op-posing affirmative action, in turn, can still point out that categorical treat-ment of minority groups by race alone ignores the fact that some members of disadvantaged minorities are eminently successful and do not require fa-vored treatment. At the very least, the progress of minority groups to advan-taged status will signal an early need for additional distinctions in the idea of "disadvantaged."

2. Should our "professional" institutions, our law schools and medical schools, be used as instruments to bring an end to the effects of discrimina-tion? No matter how desirable the goal, this issue raises the spectre of possible dilution of quality as professional schools shift from pure *merit* criteria to *reform* or *desert* criteria. If, for example, minority applicants with low qualifications are admitted to law schools, critics maintain that lower-quality lawyers will be produced. This sacrifice of professional standards, some argue, is not worth the beneficial results of racial balance: in the long run, everyone will be worse off as the quality of our professional services is diminished.

Proponents of policies favoring the admission of minority groups to professional schools on a *reform* or *desert* criterion tend to take a more skeptical view of *merit* criteria. The Washington Supreme Court, for exam-ple, pointed out in its reversal of the initial *DeFunis* ruling that objective measures of law school potential are neither conclusively reliable nor accu-rate representations of later professional ability, even when reliable. The court pointed out that the admissions committee for the law school routinely looks at more than numerical indicators, evidenced in the *DeFunis* brief by the fact that sixteen *nonminority* general applicants were admitted with test scores lower than DeFunis'. Also, the practice of law is, in the general sense, a transaction with the community. At least the *delivery* of legal services might then be amplified with minority representation: that a lawyer is black or Hispanic might give him greater *ability* to provide legal services to minority groups in the society once certain minimal standards of legal knowledge are met. Thus, *merit* can be more broadly defined to include delivery of services.

The opponents of affirmative action, in turn, stress the technical aspects of ability or merit, pointing out that at least some professions, like brain surgery, are all skill and no social transaction. Supporters of affirmative action programs then point to the wide range of professional work that does not require the pure skill represented in brain surgery.

Obviously no single answer will resolve this criterial conflict. Resolving the issue in one direction or another will depend on how narrowly or broadly one conceives of *ability*, and how reliably our testing procedures identify *merit*. Resolution also requires extensive work in defining the ability requirements of particular professions and practices, case by case rather than across-the-board.

3. Are we justified in favoring minorities at the expense of members of nonminority groups? DeFunis' suit was inspired by a practical consideration: the Washington law school had 150 openings for new students and DeFunis was convinced that the admission of less qualified minority students effectively denied him a place in law school. He maintained that he was the victim of racial discrimination in reverse. Similarly, Bakke claimed that he was effectively thwarted in fulfilling his vocation because of policies that gave minorities preference.

We can concede that reverse discrimination is unlike the older "positive" discrimination: affirmative action projects that favor minorities are aiming for racial justice, not simple exploitation. Nevertheless, there are victims—DeFunis and Bakke figures—whenever "blind" impartiality is replaced by favoritism, however nobly intended. One way to avoid harm to nonminorities is to endorse a Pareto Optimal criterion: improvement only where no one incurs a cost. In hiring the disadvantaged, for example, a simple formula of attrition might be adopted: replace nonminorities with minorities only as openings occur from retirement and voluntary departures. But it has been shown that such a use of Pareto Optimality requires an oppressive number of years to effect a desirable balance, a passage of time that the victims of a history of discrimination will understandably find unbearable.

Suppose, for example, that we have one hundred elite positions in a business, and ninety-six are occupied by white males, two by women, and two by nonwhite males. If we assume that normal conditions of growth, turnover, and retirement will open up five positions each year, and these five positions are filled on the basis of equality, then on the further reasonable assumption that the supply of candidates for these jobs includes three

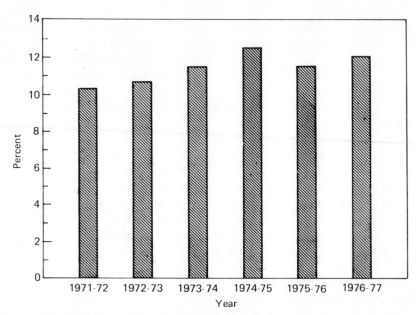

Minority Admissions to U.S. Medical Schools (Percent of total enrollment. Includes all minorities in U.S. who comprise 18.5 percent of total U.S. population)

Source: American Medical College Application Service (Reprinted *New York Times,* September 25, 1977)

white males to every two women or nonwhites, it will take 47 years for minorities to achieve equal representation (Held, 1973). In situations of fixed positions with constant competition, as in admissions to law schools, Pareto Optimality is not even relevant; some will have to be denied if others are to be admitted.

The cry of nonminority competitors is profound: let the competition be conducted impartially. But if ability to compete in "impartial" tests is impaired by past bias, then impartiality is itself biased in not recognizing the handicaps that the disadvantaged carry. Only bias in reverse would then make "blind" impartiality itself fair and make possible a future generation where special treatment is unneeded. The good of future generations is not likely to appeal to present victims, however, and this provides a more general observation: social justice may require painful sacrifices. And with sacrifices, it is imperative that what we are bringing about is in fact social justice, not something else.

Let us, then, step back for a moment from the issues in reverse discrimination and ask a larger question: on what grounds can we say that social arrangements generally fulfill the requirements of *justice*?

JUSTICE: FAIR SOCIAL ARRANGEMENTS

Let us start by regarding fairness as roughly equivalent to *some* form of *impartiality:* not making an exception for any person or favoring any particular person without good reason. Such an idea is behind the perennial attempts in political reform to prevent special interest groups from unduly influencing policy: that the best law is one that impartially regulates us all, without special favor to some. Efforts to enforce fairness are familiar in public policy; they range from court decisions to insure a "fair" balance among the races in education and employment to Federal Communications Commission requirements of "equal time" on television for all bona fide candidates for public office.

We all have ideas about fair procedures. If two people are in a dispute and their claims are equally valid, yet only one claim can be chosen, then one way to resolve the conflict fairly is to flip a coin. Both winner and loser are treated fairly: neither is favored by the procedure. Or think about another device to insure a fair distribution of some valued commodity. If we want to distribute the pieces of a pie fairly we might give the person cutting the pie the last piece after everyone else has chosen.

Obviously many occasions can be fair without procedural guarantees. It is a rare and competitive family that has to separate choice from cutting in distributing pieces of pie (though perhaps it's not so rare to flip coins over which of equally innocuous television programs the children will be permitted to watch). But social arrangements often must present the appearance as well as the reality of fairness,and procedures are often the only assurances we have that fairness requirements are being met. Ideally social arrangements would have the same guarantee against unwarranted favoritism that the pie-cutting procedure provides: the cutter will divide the pie as equally as possible to insure that his piece, the last one, will be an equal share.

We also want to distinguish between fairness of *procedure* and fairness of *outcome* that even these ordinary examples provide. A fair outcome can be merely a matter of following certain procedures, or it can be defined by criteria independent of the procedures followed. The outcomes of games of chance, for example, are fair exactly by virtue of the randomness of the procedure. The loser in a coin flip to determine who serves first in tennis may complain that flipping coins is not the appropriate way to settle the issue—as a chronic loser he may feel he deserves first service against better players—but he cannot maintain that the outcome of the coin-flip is random *and* unfair if the procedure is appropriate. The randomness of the outcome is precisely what we mean when we say a coin-flip is fair.

Sometimes, however, we judge outcomes as fair on criteria not completely satisfied by the procedure adopted to reach them. A criminal trial is considered fair if certain procedures are followed. But we also want the outcome to be fair in the sense that the innocent go free and the guilty are punished. As we all know, fair procedure and fair outcome do not always coincide. A perfectly fair trial on *procedural* grounds can still have an unfair *outcome*, and vice versa. This distinction between fair procedures and fair outcomes is provided by the possibility of settling on who did or did not commit a crime by pretrial investigation, in effect settling on *factual* guilt independent of *legal* guilt. So, unlike a game of chance, the fairness of a trial outcome is not exactly a matter of the fairness of the trial procedure.

One version of perfect justice, defined as perfect fairness, might be for procedure and outcome to coincide always (Rawls, 1971): impartial procedures leading to outcomes satisfying independent criteria of fairness. Actually, something like this happens in the pie-slicing example if we assume the goal of equal shares: the criterion of equality is satisfied when the pie-slicer gets the last piece (assuming, as we must, that he wants an equal share). But one complication (among others) that makes the world a poor model from the standpoint of perfect justice is that a happy symmetry of procedure and outcome is rarely found, even in pie-slicing: if one person at the table is dieting and another trying to gain weight after an illness, then the norm of equality is lost. The procedure no longer guarantees the perfectly fair distribution. We have, in such a case, a good reason to favor some over others.

Still, the world is where we must establish justice. Let us ask this: how can social arrangements, infinitely more complicated than pie-slicing, be judged as fair or not? What method can we use to establish the fairness standards for social arrangements in general?

THE ORIGINAL CHOICE

John Rawls' *A Theory of Justice* (1971) is generally regarded as the most important work on social justice in decades. In it, Rawls develops an alternative to utilitarianism based on a concept of justice as fairness, not social utility. The fairness of social arrangements could be established, according to Rawls, by the hypothetical fact that such arrangements are the outcome of rational choices by all individuals in society under conditions of ignorance. Thus the fact that institutions originate through rational choice is the "test" of their fairness: only if all individuals would choose certain social arrangements in special hypothetical conditions can we say that the arrangements are fair, or—to use Rawls' special term—*just*.

The special conditions in which this hypothetical "original" choice is made are obviously important. They can be described by the two features characterizing those who make the choice: (a) ignorance, and (b) rational egoism (those who choose are not selfish, choosing at the *expense* of others, but they choose principles that are in their own interests). The individuals who choose social arrangements do so without any knowledge of their social position in the arrangements or even their particular talents or inclinations. And they are motivated solely by considerations of rational self-interest, not altruism of any type.

The function of *ignorance* in original choice is easy to understand. If we do not know what position we will occupy in society, or even what ability we possess, then we cannot choose social arrangements to favor ourselves. The arrangements chosen must be impartially advantageous to all because each person who endorses them might end up in any position the institutions provide. The rule-of-thumb seems to require each person to design "a practice in which his enemy was to assign him his place" (Rawls, 1971). Fairness is thus guaranteed by the "veil of ignorance" in the original choice of institutions. Under these special conditions of ignorance, self-interest can only be satisfied by the choice of impartial social arrangements.

Why are arrangements chosen in ignorance *fair*? Because we cannot be sure that those who know their locations or abilities will choose impartially. If I know, for example, that I have the ability to be a first-rate carpenter, I will be tempted to choose social arrangements that reward carpenters highly. But such arrangements would favor my own abilities, thus not be fair. Only if I am ignorant of my abilities and ignorant of what social position I will occupy in the arrangements can fairness be assured. Let us not make the mistake of thinking that the choice of institutions is actually made in some factual social contract. We need only apply the test hypothetically: would all the members of a society choose these arrangements that do exist if they didn't know their positions or abilities?

Rawls makes some modifications on the conditions of ignorance that needn't concern us here. The only important additional knowledge relevant to our discussion is the theory of primary goods. Rational actors in the original conditions of choice do have knowledge of primary goods, which Rawls defines as goods that any rational human being would want to have (a definition consistent with our account in the last chapter). Rawls' elaboration of primary goods is worth noting. They include wealth, power, freedom of thought and conscience, self-respect, and the right of participation. Whether all of these items are universally desired by rational persons, or whether they would be wanted before anything else, is open to dispute (Barry, 1973). But unless some theory of primary goods is developed to fill in the skeletal knowledge of the rational actors, then of course they would have no idea of what their self-interest is and of what they are trying to bring about by the social arrangements they are endorsing.

Rational actors must have some general knowledge about what is good for human life of any form, though we can leave open the particular items that we would list under primary goods (though minimal food, clothing, housing, and education sketched out in the previous chapter might suffice for a theory of primary goods).

THE PRINCIPLES OF JUSTICE

Rawls maintains that rational actors would choose two governing principles in the original position. They are (1) equal rights to the most extensive basic liberties compatible with a similar liberty for all, and (2) an arrangement of social and economic inequalities that is (a) to the greatest benefit of the least advantaged consistent with a concern for the economic well-being of future generations, and (b) attached to offices and positions open to all under conditions of fair equality of opportunity.

These two principles are the standards persons would choose to regulate their relations with one another if they chose impartially. Since these regulating principles are fair (impartial), they are the principles of justice for social arrangements. Further, Rawls argues that they would be chosen in a priority relationship, with (1) to be satisfied first, then (2a), and finally (2b).

Why would rational actors choose such principles? Because it is to their advantage to do so, Rawls argues, if they are ignorant about both their particular locations in the scheme of things and their particular abilities. Liberty, the first principle, is a requirement to achieve other things, as well as a good in itself. For Rawls, it can be restricted only on the basis of other liberty-motivated considerations, for example curtailing one person's liberty to insure the liberty of another. The first part, (a), of the second principle, what has been called the difference principle, insures that the lowest stratum in society will not be exploited (one could be a member of this stratum). Part (b) of the second principle requires that social arrangements permit the opportunity to develop and use one's abilities, whatever they are. The argument maintains that these two principles represent the most rational choice of social arrangements by self-interested people operating under Rawls' "veil of ignorance."

The choice of liberty is easy to understand. To be free in the social sense is to have the ability to choose those goods we need and want. It is almost inconceivable that a rational agent would choose *not* to have liberty except under unusual circumstances (though he may well trade off liberty for other goods, contrary to Rawls' assumptions), for liberty seems almost a natural condition in being human. It may be rational to expand one's freedom at the expense of others. But if one were not sure whether he would be slave owner or slave, exploiter or the one being exploited, then it would be rational to endorse a system of mutual liberty, on the quite reasonable grounds that liberty is both an instrumental and an intrinsically valuable good.

The second principle of justice is not so self-evidently appealing, and so requires some elaboration. Let us concede that part (2b), the equality of opportunity condition, is rationally desirable. To have equal opportunity is, in the broadest sense, to have freedom in a society organized impartially in institutions. So equal opportunity is justified in substantial part by the desirability of freedom itself. But part (2a), the difference principle, is not at all connected with freedom. It says this: that inequalities can be justified only if they are of greatest benefit to those worst off in society. Rational considerations, according to Rawls, require that we choose social arrangements that maximize benefits for the lowest stratum in society, for in conditions of ignorance we must consider the possibility of occupying the lowest point in society.

Here are some illustrative arrangements using our three-man society again.

	A	B	C
I	100	50	30
II	10	10	10
III	200	150	25

A strict equality criterion would require the choice of society II, for it is the most equalitarian. Rawls' difference principle, stated in (2a), would require the choice of society I: it contains the highest value for the worst-off individual (member C in all three societies). Further, any change in the relative inequality of A, B, and C could only be justified if it raised the benefits for C.

JUSTICE-AS-FAIRNESS VERSUS UTILITARIANISM

Much of the appeal, even beauty, of Rawls' theory of justice is in what it avoids. The major moral and political philosophy of the last hundred years has been utilitarianism. Though the rich literature on utilitarianism has provided a variety of interpretations on the main theme, the central idea in utilitarian social philosophy is this: the value of an action is determined by the consequences it has for social well-being. Two components of this basic idea stand out: first, its consequentialist thesis and, second, the evaluative criteria for determining well being or social benefits.

On the first, an action is evaluated not in terms of whatever intrinsic merit it has (if there is such a thing as intrinsic merit), but in terms of its consequences. For example, admissions policies in law schools, in a utilitarian formula, would be assessed as their consequences are beneficial or harmful. Whether the policies have certain features, like fairness, is not as important as the consequences of the policies. On the second, a utilitarian social philosopher looks to the *social* benefits of consequences. Again, law school admissions must be weighed on the scale of benefits or harms to the larger society. Thus, the utilitarian question is: do the consequences of the admissions policy benefit or harm society? If they benefit, they are morally desirable; if they harm, they are morally undesirable.

What counts as social utility or its opposite (benefits/harms) has been a source of major dispute over the entire history of utilitarian thought. Some have leaned toward what people *want*, others toward some form of *ideals*, as the criterion for benefits. But whatever criterion is endorsed, a major division occurs between those who weigh consequences in terms of *total* utility and those who evaluate in terms of *average* utility.

Total utility is calculated with a formula that adds each individual's utility to arrive at a total for the entire society. Average utility is figured by dividing the total utility sum by the number of individuals in society. Total utility is more a productive criterion: if an action increases the sum of benefits, it is good. Average utility is weakly concerned with distribution: only if an action increases the average of benefits is it good.

Average utility seems preferable to total utility for one important reason: it avoids the possibility that a society of weaker benefits is preferable to one of stronger benefits just because of population figures alone.

	A	B	C	D	E	F
Society I	2	2	2	2	2	2

	A	B	C
Society II	3	3	3

A total utility formulation would make society I preferable to II (totals of 12 against 9), but only because I has more members than II. Average utility favors society II (averages of 2 against 3). Society I is a poorer society with more members. The poverty is not reflected in a total utility calculation, for the relatively weak holdings of each poor person loom large when summed and compared to a smaller society like II. Society II is richer per capita, which can be discovered only by calculating average, not total, utility. Since many policies and even social arrangements affect, and are affected by, population changes, this difference can be crucial in our evaluations. Where population is constant, the two utility calculations are roughly equivalent in setting value.

The difficulties with both utilitarian formulas are these. First, they require interpersonal comparisons of value, and thus the use of a cardinal scale when we have no satisfactory cardinal scale with which to compare individuals (see Chapter 6). Second, the calculation of social utility can tolerate distributions so severe as to sacrifice individuals in undesirable ways (as some of the dramatic examples at the end of Chapter 6 suggested).

	A	B	C
I	300	200	10
II	150	100	90
III	100	100	100

The utilitarian formula requires the selection of society I, because both total utility (510) and average utility (170) are higher than in societies II (total utility, 340; average utility, 113.3) and III (total utility, 300; average utility, 100). But the inequality operates so severely on C that many of us would prefer either of the two other societies to I (certainly C would!). If the utility sums represent life and death issues, say that anything below 50 prohibits survival, then either utilitarian formula favors a society that sacrifices some for the greater good of others.

The chronic problem in utilitarianism, which this example represents, is that societal choices are conceived to be like individual choices: as an individual will weigh gains and losses to settle on the best course of action, so a society can weigh utilities for different individuals to arrive at some optimal balance. But an individual is weighing alternative gains and losses, while the society is weighing individuals. Thus while an individual can discard C as a course of action in favor of A or B, a society sets aside C *as a human being* when the social distribution is skewed sharply in favor of A or B. This indifference to the contrasts between individual and social choice finally leads to the grim possibilities outlined at the end of the last chapter: a concern for *social* utility (the public interest) can tolerate conditions where total or average benefits are raised when otherwise innocent human beings are sacrificed totally.

The theory of justice that Rawls develops claims to avoid these two problems in utilitarian theory. First, there is no need in the choice of the principles of justice to make strong interpersonal comparisons of value. The two principles of justice are not comparative among individuals in the strong sense of *adding* utilities: we merely have to identify the worst-off person in each society. The principles state the conditions of fairness under which individuals may pursue their own definitions of utility, with one exception: the theory of primary goods sets out what any rational individual would want. But even primary goods are general objects of preference among human beings. A comparison of "objective" individual utilities is not required in the theory because we do not have to add utilities to get the greater good.

Second, the severely uneven distributions possible with a utilitarian formula, tolerating even the sacrifice of some for the greater good, cannot occur in the theory of justice. Since those choosing social arrangements would not know whether they are A, B, or C, Rawls maintains that they would not rationally choose principles which permit the severe distributions represented by society I. Instead, they would choose on the difference principle rather than on a principle that maximizes the average or total utility of a society. Since the principles chosen are fair, or impartial, they are principles of justice. But notice that the principles disallow precisely those unfair sacrifices of innocent individuals for the greater good that utilitarianism permits, and so the principles correspond to our intuitive notions of justice as well (maintaining fairness whatever the consequences for social well-being). Not knowing if one will come to be the one sacrificed, rational self-interest requires endorsing arrangements preventing the possibility of individual sacrifices for the general welfare.

SOME PROBLEMS IN THE THEORY OF JUSTICE

The growing secondary literature on Rawls' theory of justice is even now almost endless and shows no signs of diminishing in volume as time passes. Several famous criticisms are relevant here:

1. The difference principle, while preventing the unfair distributions for the sake of the greater good that utilitarianism permits, still can lead to the choice of undesirable social distributions *if* the principle is given what Rawls calls a "lexical" interpretation. The lexical version of the difference principle requires that benefits to the worst-off representative person be maximized, then to the next worst-off, and so on up the social ladder. The lexical difference principle is to be used in societies where benefits allocated to the well-off do not in fact affect the status of the least advantaged (fragmented, unconnected societies). (Rawls, pp. 82–83.) But now consider the following distribution.

	A	B	C
I	100	90	10
II	100	12	11
III	10	10	10

On the lexical difference principle, society II is preferable because the worst-off individual (member C) is better off in II than in I or III. But since B is so much worse off in II than in I, one might think that society I is more desirable. If we increase the number of members in a lower stratum, the contrast is even sharper (Rae, 1975).

$$
\begin{array}{lccccccc}
I & - & 100, & 100, & 100, & 100, & 100, & 100, & 10 \\
II & - & 100, & 12, & 12, & 12, & 12, & 11, & 11
\end{array}
$$

The lexical difference principle still forces the choice of society II because the criterion is indifferent to any comparisons except on the worst-off person in society. Society I, however, seems preferable on the number of people better off who are not in the lowest stratum. So the lexical difference principle, though concentrating on the improvement of the lowest stratum, may still favor societies where the worst-off are slightly better than in an alternative arrangement but so numerous as to cancel out the gain.

2. The "simpler form" of the difference principle produces yet another criticism. Rawls more generally uses the difference principle not in its lexical form, but as a rule which justifies inequalities as they do in fact benefit the least advantaged. Further, these benefits can occur in the long-run (Rawls, p. 199). Well, anyone who has studied economics knows that long-range expectations can justify severe inequalities in the short-run. Again, let's look at an illustrative distribution.

	A	B	C
I	100	50	10
II	50	51	11
III	300	50	11

The "lexical" difference principle requires the choice of society II, for C is better off in II than in I and B is better off in II than in either I or III. But the "simpler" difference principle might require the choice of society III *if* it can be demonstrated that the riches of A (300) are needed for the future improvement of B and C. So the "lexical" and "simpler" versions of the difference principle can force different choices. But the main point is that the "simpler" difference principle can also justify the grossest inequalities so long as these inequalities improve the long-range expectations of the worst-off. What we have here seems like nothing so much as a device for the standard defense of predatory capitalism: great wealth for a few ultimately benefits all as production increases "filter down" to the poor.

It is an interesting commentary that the "lexical" difference principle produces criticisms that Rawls' theory of justice concentrates overly much on the least advantaged at the expense of others, while the "simpler" difference principle produces criticisms that the theory is too inequalitarian in permitting severely skewed distributions of benefits in the short-run.

3. Does the maximin rule produce absurd choices? Some critics maintain it does. John Harsanyi (1975) offers a number of counter-examples which
suggest the inadequacy of maximin when compared to utilitarian decision-
rules. Remember (Chapter 2) that a maximin rule requires the maximization
(or improvement) of the worst-off alternative. Harsanyi asks us to suppose
examples like this one: A doctor is faced with the problem of being able to
treat only one of two patients because of a shortage of medicine. One is
terminally ill. Therapy will prolong his life only for a brief period. The other
is not as sick, but will be disabled for life if not treated with the medicine. A
maximin decision seems to require treating the terminally ill patient, for he
is the worst-off of the two. But on a decision-rule which maximizes utility,
the medicine would be applied where it would do the most good, in this case
helping the less seriously ill patient on the grounds that a greater net benefit
will result.

Such counter-examples strike powerful blows at the sensibility of maximin rules in ordinary life. But Rawls is careful to confine maximin to the
special conditions of ignorance in the original choice of governing principles.
These conditions exclude knowledge of probabilities, for example. (Thus
they escape those counter-examples introducing risk, for example choosing
never to fly anywhere on the slight chance that a worst-possible outcome
might occur—a plane crash.) Also, the choice of *both* governing principles,
the freedom principle and the difference principle conjoined with equal
opportunity, represents a maximin strategy—a strategy of choice rational in
the original-choice conditions but not necessarily rational in ordinary social
life of the sort in which the counter-examples occur.

More important here, however, is that Rawls' theory of justice outlines
the rational choice of basic social principles, not one-shot allocations or
small-group transactions. The difference principle (DP), for example, is justified as a rule for the permanent structure of society. The DP, as with
maximin, may produce bizarre counter-examples in more limited circumstances. The doctor-patient example highlights some of these difficulties.
But the correct issue is—would a permanent structure of society produce
such intuitively irrational outcomes? In terms of the counter-example—
would institutional arrangements which allocated medicine to terminally ill
patients at the expense of potentially healthy patients be justifiable under
Rawls' theory of justice? Here a negative answer is possible. We might
maintain, on the medicine example, that institutions which devote resources
to hopeless cases benefit no one in the long run, thus violating one of the
requirements of the DP in transforming the practice of medicine into a
hopeless enterprise. Whether Rawls' theory of justice is itself transformed
into some type of utilitarianism with long-range considerations is another,
much more complex, question. But the theory must be evaluated in terms of
its selection of basic institutions, not its production of absurd outcomes in
restricted situations.

4. Would rational persons in condition of ignorance choose social arrangements governed by the two principles of justice? Rawls maintains that they would because they do not know where they will be placed in the arrangement, and thus they would protect the worst-off positions from severe exploitation. The strategy of choice that rational actors would adopt in such ignorance and uncertainty, according to Rawls, is *maximin*. Again, the choice of the two principles of justice—as a maximin strategy—is rational *because* of the conditions of ignorance and uncertainty, conditions which also make the principles *fair* choices as well.

But look carefully at the following distribution.

	A	B	C
I	1,000	1,000	10
II	12	12	11
III	10	10	10

Would a rational person, not knowing whether he would be A, B, or C, necessarily choose society II (the maximin choice)? Obviously the choice would depend on several things, in particular: (a) whether the difference between 10 and 11 is at all significant when compared with the difference between 12 and 1,000; and (b) the number of places in A, B, and C—for if only one C-place exists and several hundred A and B places exist, one might be prepared to chance it even if the C-place is abominable.

Considerations (a) and (b) are, respectively, expected value and probability considerations (again, from Chapter 2). Rawls rules out these considerations in the original choice because if we are in conditions of true ignorance then we cannot know either the value of alternative positions or the probabilities of their occurrence. We choose on a maximin criterion precisely because we are in ignorance about values and likelihoods. But, against Rawls' assumptions, we might be inclined to risk-taking even in total ignorance of outcomes.

Suppose a person chose on a maximax criterion: maximize the *best* position in society. We might prudently point out that he might end up suffering in a worst-off position made intolerable exactly by shifting goods to the higher stratum. But if he were totally ignorant of values and possibilities, with no probabilities to lean on, he might as easily chance the high gain on the thought that he might be the winner (best-off) rather than the loser (worst-off). Whether one is willing to take risks or avoid calamities seems a *psychological* rather than a *rational* matter.

Rawls points out that, since the principles of justice are permanent arrangements that govern future generations, prudence rather than risk-taking will appeal. But we can satisfy even this expanded sense of caution by rigging our arrangements to insure against certain losses while permitting risks once the insurance has been laid down (Hare, 1973). Suppose we guarantee against certain disasters, in effect endorse a society that provides a minimum floor for the lower stratum, but then permits maximax principles beyond the minimum guarantee.

$$
\begin{array}{lllllllll}
I & - & 100, & 100, & 50, & 10, & 10, & 10 \\
II & - & 12, & 12, & 12, & 12, & 12, & 11 \\
III & - & 100, & 100, & 100, & 50, & 5, & 3
\end{array}
$$

If the figure 9 represents disasters any rational person would avoid, then society III is ruled out by the reasonably cautious man. But, having guaranteed that all members of the society would be above that level, then risk-taking may again be preferred and society I chosen. A maximin criterion, however, forces the choice of society II, for the worst-off member in II (value of 11) is better than the worst-off member in I (value of 10). The point is, however, that an insurance strategy, the social analogy of paying premiums to cover the possibility of one's house burning down, can avoid disasters without requiring the use of a maximin criterion: the government, for example, can simply guarantee a minimum income for all persons. And if disaster can be avoided while choosing otherwise on risk-taking criteria, then one of the main rational considerations for accepting a maximin criterion is defeated.

5. The fifth problem in the theory of justice comes with the implementation of its provisions. Let us allow for the moment that the two principles of justice, (1) maximum liberty and (2) the difference principle with equal opportunity, are authentically impartial and thus represent fair social arrangements. The question then is how to bring about a society governed by these principles.

One constant factor in all theories of justice is that they start with an unjust world, for otherwise there would be no reason to develop theories of justice. But an unjust world requires revisionary measures in any theory of justice: not only must we say which arrangements are just, but also we must say by what techniques and at what cost the world is to be transformed into these just arrangements.

A good case in point is the existence of discriminatory social arrangements. If institutions discriminate unfairly, they are unjust. We are obligated to change them. But recall what happens as remedial measures are taken to eliminate bias toward certain minorities. Those profiting from the existing system must suffer losses. Sometimes reforms are required that make even the blameless suffer—white law and medical school applicants are denied admittance because of affirmative action toward the disadvantaged. (White law and medical school applicants may have *profited* from the biased system, but few if any of the applicants can be said to be *responsible* for it.)

We may even find that the realization of justice leads to losses for all, advantaged *and* disadvantaged. Hypothetical situation: You are the sole director of an established industry that is vital to the economy of the entire society. This industry has operated under ancient hiring practices that exclude women and blacks from positions of authority, practices that are blatantly discriminatory. The industry is located in a conservative community with racist, sexist views—views shared by virtually all your employees except for some of the minorities who are victims of the discrimination. To eliminate the discriminatory hiring policies will with certainty disrupt the productive power of the industry and depress the general economy. What strategies of change do you, as director, adopt in order to bring about just (fair) practices?

Well, if you are interested in surviving as director, you will probably pursue some gradual policy of change, trading off fairness against the public interest in economic well-being. The point to see in such examples is not only the obvious fact that realizing justice can be painful for the advantaged, but also the harsher reality that it can lead to losses for the disadvantaged as well. The consequences of changing an unjust world can, put simply, lower everyone's level in society. These commonplace observations are not a brief for conservatism, for one may still adopt that biblical injunction, "Justice, though the heavens may fall." But the possibility of falling heavens does strange things to the concern of justice for the disadvantaged. If implementing just arrangements can victimize all persons, then the utilitarian sacrifice of a few for the general good may have been reproduced and extended in different form: a sacrifice of *all* for the sake of justice.

RIGHTS VERSUS INTERESTS

One important difference between the advantaged and the disadvantaged in an unjust society is that the former have *interests* in the arrangements while the latter have *rights* against the arrangements. We know (from Chapter 3) that interests are, roughly, things that increase opportunities to get what one wants or needs. Rights are those which are due someone by virtue of a just claim.

Imagine a situation (the example adapted from Thomson, 1971) where two brothers have been given a box of chocolates for Christmas, the chocolates for both of them and to be equally shared. Now suppose that one of the boys (the older and stronger of the two) grabs the box and starts helping himself to all of the chocolates without giving his brother any. As parents we would say that the younger brother has a *right* to his share of the chocolates, that the older brother is unjust (this pronouncement if we have read our

Rawls) in his treatment of his brother. We would likely take the box of chocolates and distribute them equally.

Now change the scene slightly. The box of chocolates has been given to the older brother, not to both brothers. The older brother again sits stuffing his mouth with chocolates and refusing to give any to his younger brother. His younger brother again sits crying and asking you, his parent, to make his older brother share the chocolates. You will no doubt accuse the older brother of being selfish, a hog even (this if he continues to eat the chocolates while you scold him), lacking kindness, and so on.

But the notion of *unfairness* is more difficult to make stick—the chocolates after all are his under the terms of the gift. You may once again take the box and give some chocolates to the younger boy, but probably not an equal share and not with the same certitude that you are doing the right thing. You may even throw up your hands and go buy the younger child his own box of chocolates rather than force a distribution. The difference is that in this case the younger brother may have a general interest in the chocolates, stemming from a rough fusion of his wants and family expectations on general sharing, but he no longer has a *right* to the chocolates.

Those who profit from unjust social arrangements, although they obviously have an interest in maintaining them, do not have a right to keep and preserve what is theirs. The disadvantaged, by virtue of the unjust arrangements, have a right to the social goods unfairly denied them. Their claim is stronger than the interest-grounded claim of the advantaged. If the disadvantaged were poorly off in a just society, they would have an interest in a larger share of goods, but no right to more goods. So justice, by crystallizing rights, carries in itself the blueprints for rearranging unjust societies on strong grounds, even though the interests of some are overridden in the change.

The difficulty, and danger, of just change is that the result may work against the interests of the disadvantaged as well. If by forcing a fair distribution of the chocolates given to both boys the box is broken and all the chocolates lost, then no one gains a thing. We can still say that since the younger boy had a right to his share, better that neither eats the chocolates than only one. But the possibility of a general loss to all also occasions that uniquely political solution of negotiating a distribution that keeps the box of chocolates together while realizing as much as possible the rights of the disadvantaged to a fair share.

ABORTION: LEGAL AND SOCIAL BACKGROUND

Whether *rights* or *interests* are involved in policy is often a vital consideration, as we saw in the study of black organizations and the feminist movements in Chapter 3. Another area where the interplay between "rights" and "interests" is especially important is medical ethics. One important public policy issue in medicine, an issue where moral, legal, political, and medical considerations are intertwined today, is abortion. Few issues strike so divisive a chord in American society or extend to so many otherwise diverse fields. A complete discussion of abortion would require expertise in philosophy, religion, medical technology, sociology, and many other areas. Some of the oldest of human questions—what is human life and when does it begin?—combine with practical questions—who is favored by different abortion policies (for example, rich or poor)? what are the psychological effects of abortion?—to produce a policy area rich with important lessons for any student of public policy.

Laws restricting abortion go back to the early nineteenth century in England. In 1803 the British Parliament forbade the administering of any "deadly" substance to bring about miscarriage. Curiously enough, the statute was designed to protect women's lives, not those of the unborn, on the reasoning that (as described in the 1832 *London Legal Examiner*) abortion "rarely or never can be (e) effected by drugs without the sacrifice of the mother's life." From 1821 to 1865, American states followed the British example by passing similar laws restricting abortion.

The development of antiseptic surgery toward the end of the nineteenth century in both Britain and America gradually invalidated the concern for the woman's life in abortions. By about 1920 both abortion and childbirth mortality rates began to decline. In time, the risk in early abortion for the expectant mother became less than in carrying the pregnancy to term. Today, abortions performed by physicians in the first trimester of pregnancy are virtually without risk to the woman's life, and even when performed after three months are still considerably less dangerous than childbirth. This improvement in medical techniques was cited by the U.S. Supreme Court in 1973 as one reason for its pro-abortion decision (U.S. Commission on Civil Rights, 1975).

Laws restricting abortion remained as statutes in the United States through most of the 1960s. However, several changes in American society provided pressures for liberalization of abortion statutes. First, sex and procreation were no longer considered divine and necessary partners. The general sensitivity to population density, the shift in the status of children from an economic blessing to one of dependence (often extending through college and beyond), the dissemination of safe and convenient methods of birth control, the sexual "revolution" itself (however puffed up)—all separate sex from the birth of children.

Though many approve contraception while disapproving abortion, not a few people also see abortion as the final means to maintain the separation between sex and procreation: "Contraception involves the first line of defense against an unwanted birth; abortion the last . . ." (dissenting opinion in *Rosen* v. *State Board of Medical Examiners*, 1970). Pro-abortion champions also have denied that intercourse constitutes a commitment to have a child: "the vicissitudes of life produce pregnancies which may be unwanted..." (Justice William Douglas in *Doe* v. *Bolton*, 1973). A denial of continuity between impregnation and birth provides the possibility of denying pregnancy as an event in itself, separate from the natural and desirable events of sexual union.

Second, social attitudes toward women and from the perspective of women had changed dramatically by the late 1960s. Pregnancy is frequently viewed today as a burden that requires relief, not as a blessing or noble obligation. Justice Douglas (in *Doe* v. *Bolton*) viewed the right to abortions as necessary means for women generally to pursue educations, careers, and their present life styles. Others have described the statutes restricting abortion as reflecting a nineteenth-century view of women as housekeepers, not as active contributors to society. The feminist movement has been firm in its belief that women have rights to control their own bodies, deciding for themselves whether to continue or discontinue pregnancies.

In 1962, the Sherri Finkbine case acted as a catalyst for the pro-abortion segments of the American public. Thalidomide, a tranquilizer thought safe for pregnant women (and used by thousands in Europe, though never approved for general use in the United States), was discovered to have terrible effects on fetuses. Ms. Finkbine, a local television personality, was pregnant and had taken Thalidomide. She was denied a legal abortion in the United States and finally flew to Sweden to have an abortion performed. The fetus she was carrying was found to be grossly deformed. The publicity surrounding her case created new pressures for liberalization of the abortion laws. The rubella epidemic in the United States in 1964 and the legal restrictions barring abortion for pregnant women who had contracted the disease further sensitized the public to the restrictiveness of abortion statutes.

LEGAL REFORMS OF ABORTION STATUTES

Changes of abortion statutes have occurred in two ways. One has been liberalization of state law. In 1967, Colorado, California, and North Carolina liberalized their laws to permit abortions to preserve the women's life and health, in rape or incest cases, and when there is reason to believe the fetus might be defective. Ten other states have passed similar laws. The most radical liberalization of abortion laws, however, occurred in 1970 when Hawaii, Alaska, New York, and Washington passed laws legalizing abortion upon demand by the woman and the consent of a physician during the early months of pregnancy.

The New York State abortion reform law was sufficiently controversial to be repealed by the state legislature in 1972; the repeal was then vetoed by

Governor Rockefeller. The law defines a justifiable abortional act as one "committed upon a female with her consent by a duly licensed physician acting (a) under a reasonable belief that such is necessary to preserve her life, or (b) within twenty-four weeks from the commencement of her pregnancy." The law goes on to allow self-abortive actions by a woman, with the advice of a physician, under the same two conditions.

Change in abortion statutes has been effected by the Supreme Court. In *Roe* v. *Wade* (1973), the Court decided that (a) a state cannot bar any woman from obtaining an abortion during the first three months of pregnancy; (b) the state can regulate abortions in the second trimester only where the law is concerned to preserve or protect the woman's health; and (c) during the last trimester the state can regulate and even prohibit abortions except those necessary "in appropriate medical judgment" to protect the woman's life and health.

The *Roe* decision in effect legalized abortion-on-demand in every state during the first three months of term. On the same day, the Court, in *Doe* v. *Bolton*, struck down a Georgia statute restricting accessibility to abortions by means of state accreditation requirements for hospitals, committee approval of abortions, and concurrence by two additional physicians on the treating physician's recommendation to abort. Also, Georgia's residency requirement for abortions was found unconstitutional.

The issue of public assistance money for abortion was later addressed by the Court. In June of 1977, the Supreme Court ruled that states have no legal duty to pay for abortions when the lives of mothers are not endangered. Thus welfare money for elective abortions may be denied by state governments without, according to the Court, abridging any constitutional right. At the time of the decision, some 300,000 women had undergone abortions on Medicaid funds, for a total cost of $50 million. Those morally opposed to abortion applauded the Court's 1977 decision on the grounds that states have no right to spend tax money to finance what they considered to be immoral actions. Critics of the Court's decision maintained that "equality under the law" had been denied, for the Court had upheld the rights of affluent women to get abortions but had in effect denied such rights for those who were too poor to pay. In late 1977 Congress passed a compromise bill allowing the use of Medicaid money to pay for abortions for rape and incest victims as well as to save a mother's life if she would suffer "severe and long-lasting physical health damage" by carrying the fetus to term.

In spite of the 1977 Supreme Court decision and the resulting state restrictions of public money for elective abortions, the 1973 *Roe* decision made abortion legal nationwide for the first time in American history. The logic of the Court rested on both medical fact and philosophical ambiguity (Moore, 1974–75). The medical fact is that the mortality rate in childbirth is greater than in abortions performed in the first three months by licensed physicians. Hence one historically important reason for prohibiting abortions—protecting the life and health of the woman—now favors the liberalization of abortion laws.

The philosophical ambiguity occurs in the difficult area of determining when human life begins. The Court made no attempt to determine the beginning point for human life and recognized the difficulties of the inquiry: "When those trained in the respective disciplines of medicine, philosophy, and theology are unable to arrive at any consensus, the judiciary at this point in the development of man's knowledge is not in a position to speculate as to the answer" (Justice Harry Blackmun, for the majority). The general principle on which the Court based its decision in *Roe* was the right to privacy, found in the Fourteenth Amendment's concept of personal liberty and the Ninth Amendment's reservation of rights to the people. The right to privacy as an independent constitutional right had been established in *Griswold* v. *Connecticut* (1965), where a penumbra of constitutional guarantees from the Bill of Rights, including the Ninth Amendment, had been involved to strike down state statutes prohibiting the use and distribution of contraceptives.

But the abortion decision, unlike the *Griswold* case, had to address the question of whether compelling state interests warranted the restriction of even the fundamental right to privacy. The issue in *Roe* is this: If there is clear evidence of a state interest in the goal to be obtained by restricting fundamental rights, then the long-established doctrine of "compelling state interests" will override the right to privacy. Two such interests in the *Roe* case were (1) the health risk to the mother, and (2) the potential for human life of the fetus. The Court decided to restrict the right to privacy, in this case involving freedom to abort, in the second and third trimesters precisely because of these two state interests, but excluded the government from abortion decisions during the first three months of pregnancy.

The difficulty with the *Roe* case is in the philosophical puzzle of life, in this case determining when it begins. Obviously if the fetus is conceded a right to life at any stage in its development, then the state must have a compelling interest in the life of the fetus at that stage, an interest that will then legitimately override the right to privacy. The Court recognized this compelling interest in the last six months of pregnancy, when the fetus "is at viability" and then "presumably has the capability of meaningful life outside the mother's womb" (Blackmun). But it denied such state interest in the first trimester, presumably on the grounds that the conditions existing in the last six months that establish a compelling state interest—viability, potential life—do not occur in the first three months. But then the Court *is* establishing a point where at least the potential for life exists, though it has acknowledged only that at "some point in pregnancy" the state interest becomes compelling and that the judiciary cannot settle the issue of when life begins.

Why differentiate between the first trimester and the last six months of pregnancy? Here the Court relied on the single biological fact that the fetus has, after three months, the capability of independent life, but presumably does not have this capability before three months of term. Unfortunately, the biological fact is only generally, not absolutely, true. At least one fetus has been known to survive to adulthood when born at the early age of twenty weeks (cited in Duin, 1972). Many fetuses aborted in the first trimester have lived for short periods of time.

The question is what period of time constitutes independent or "meaningful life outside the mother's womb." It is well known that even babies born after a full term can die quickly when neglected medically. This is even more dramatically true about babies born with some deficiency, and of course no one would argue that such babies can be allowed to die because they are unable to live independent of the womb without, say, a respirator. In fact, babies born at term who, in spite of all treatment, die very shortly after birth are still considered to have been born alive. If an aborted fetus is expelled alive, then dies shortly afterwards, has a "live birth" occurred under the law? And if so, has "viability" been demonstrated in some modest sense of that term?

THEORETICAL ISSUES IN ABORTION

The point at which human life begins is one of the oldest of our moral concerns. The Stoics maintained that birth is the starting point. Many advocates of abortion today accept live birth as the beginning of human life. The history of the common law attached greater importance to "quickening"— that point at which recognizable movement of the fetus occurs (usually between the sixteenth and eighteenth weeks of pregnancy). Aristotle developed the doctrine of "mediate animation," which was generally accepted through the Middle Ages and the Renaissance even by the Catholic Church until the nineteenth century. This doctrine states that a "person" comes into being when the fetus becomes recognizably human, occurring without question at some point between conception and birth but fixed in Christian theology as 40 days for a male and 80 days for a female.

Physicians, typically disinterested in the more subtle moral and philosophical issues, have frequently relied on the concept of "viability" to identify the beginning of human life—that point at which the fetus has the capability to live outside the mother's womb. Then there is the belief that life begins at conception, a view dogmatically held by the Pythagoreans, reflected in the Hippocratic Oath, and currently the official view of the Catholic Church.

The curious feature of the "origin" issue is that, though most civil and legal authorities recognize the difficulty of settling a dispute with such a long and conflicting history, most statutes and legal interpretations must favor one view or another. Both the newly liberalized state laws on abortion and the recent Supreme Court decision in *Roe* v. *Wade* restrict abortions in the first three months of pregnancy. This restriction makes sense only by rejecting the view that life begins at birth, though it is not always clear which of the alternative views are being accepted. (The Supreme Court, as we have seen, relied on "viability" in the *Roe* decision.)

One problem that all "origin" views share, except the one that holds that life begins at conception, is that they must find a way to handle a very difficult criticism, the "slippery-slope" argument. This argument sees pregnancy as a continuous development from conception to birth, with no important differences from one time during pregnancy to another. A proponent of the slippery slope argument adopts the following strategy. Choose any point in pregnancy to establish a relevant difference on which to develop an abortion policy. Then, the proponent maintains, I can choose a point a few hours or even days earlier and ask you to tell me what the difference is between my earlier point and the one you have chosen.

Take the first trimester difference used by the states and the Supreme Court. Suppose we have a fetus two days past the first trimester. Is there any relevant difference between that fetus and one only two days on the earlier side of the trimester period? Obviously not. Then, say those using the slippery slope argument, the first-trimester distinction is without force, as is every other point of time chosen in the pregnancy term. The strength of the argument is drawn from the fact that some qualitative difference does occur at conception, but only a continuous development seems to occur after conception until birth.

The extreme answer to the slippery-slope argument is that life begins at birth, a view that neither the states nor the Supreme Court have yet been willing to endorse. One good reason why the answer is extreme is that it can without too much difficulty force an endorsement of some forms of euthanasia and infanticide. Try thinking about the differences between a just-born baby and a just-about-to-be-born fetus. Not only can we control the timing of birth near the end of term by means of medical techniques (which makes the time of birth itself arbitrary at that point), but almost any property we can assign to the new-born baby can also be assigned to the fully developed fetus. There is only one important difference: the baby has been born and is out of the mother's womb.

Proponents of the life-begins-at-birth view of course maintain that the separation of birth is an important event, establishing relevant difference from preceding conditions. But, even conceding that birth is an important difference, some troubles still lie ahead for this view. The independence of the new-born baby is easily exaggerated. Anyone who has cared for a small baby can testify that the absence of an umbilical connection can produce more, not less, helplessness and attendant need for extensive attention. Still, the dependence is not direct, like the symbiotic relationship of the fetus to the mother, but general. The baby is, in one sense of the phrase, now "on its own" in being released from the womb.

But not all newborn babies can fend for themselves, even in this limited sense. Some are born deficient and require intensive care. Suppose a baby required the mechanical equivalent of an umbilical cord, a life-support system that assumed the role of the mother's body. True, the baby is still not within a womb. But the ideas of independence, viability, even separation as a living unit, come onto hard ground in identifying what is relevantly different about birth in such cases. Or think about older people stricken with strokes, totally dependent on elaborate life-support systems. Now quickly swing back to the healthy, fully developed fetus a few days or hours from birth, completely human but for some finishing touch and the somewhat arbitrary moment of birth. What criterion will allow us to say that a fetus of this status is a legitimate candidate for death, but the dependent child or adult on life-support systems is not?

Well, some would say with some consistency, the fact of near-total dependence warrants the imposition of death in both cases, if mother or relative desires it. But one reason the states and the Supreme Court stay away from the life-begins-at-birth view is that it opens the door for precisely such problems; as soon as mature fetuses become candidates for abortion-on-demand, then the chilling vista of relevantly similar candidates for infanticide and euthanasia comes too clearly into focus.

RIGHTS: LIFE VERSUS MAINTAINING LIFE

One novel proposal to avoid the worst of these difficulties—from the vulnerability of "quickening," "mediate animation," and "viability" views to the "slippery slope" argument or the chilling implications of the "life-begins-at-birth" view—is to accept the Catholic doctrine that life begins at conception but deny its anti-abortion conclusion (Thomson, 1971). This proposal rests on a simple thesis: that having the right to life does not mean having the right to all means required to maintain life. Suppose I am captured by the enemy during a war and the only way I can stay alive is by betraying all members of my immediate family, bringing certain death for all of them. I have, as a human being, the right to live, but not, one would think, the right to have others killed so as to realize that right.

If we take this distinction—between the right to life, and the right to the means to maintain life—and apply it to the issue of abortion, the fetus may have a right to life from conception forward but not necessarily the right to use the mother's body as a means to maintain that life. This prior right to control one's body is at the heart of the feminist view on abortion: that a woman can refuse to allow her body to be used to maintain the life of any human being, including the fetus. What makes the argument so interesting is that it accepts the strong conservative thesis that the fetus is human life at all stages of pregnancy (thus avoiding the slippery slope critique), yet manages to arrive at a pro-abortion conclusion.

The "right-to-one's-body" argument allows us to see that having a right to life may only mean having a right not to be killed *unjustly* and does not mean having a right never to be killed. Then, when the justice of killing is introduced, our attention is shifted to the kinds of considerations that warrant taking a life or allowing someone to die. Among these in the area of abortion might be the health of the mother, the origin of the pregnancy (rape, incest, carelessness, rational planning), the state of the fetus (deformed, normal), —and the right of a woman to control her own body.

Some reasons for aborting the fetus are clearly ruled out once we accept the conservative doctrine that life begins at conception. For example, the woman who wants an abortion because she has changed her mind and now wants a Caribbean vacation instead of a child is on the far side of a *no* vote. The woman who wants an abortion because physicians have established that the fetus suffers from Downs' syndrome is more clearly on the *yes* side.

Many, perhaps most, considerations are in a far murkier area, however, where the justification for fetal death cannot be established until the justifying criteria are more sharply defined. The clearest point here is perhaps the most controversial: once we accept the conservative position of conception as the origin of life, then simple, unsupported demand as a justification for abortion cannot be supported. Some other view on the beginning of human life is required for abortion-on-demand.

We should also notice that the complicated tension between *rights* and *interests* occurs again. Among the considerations that might justify abortion are the rights of the mother versus the rights of the unborn. One might argue, for example, that the right-to-life of a fully developed sentient being overrides the right-to-life of a potentially conscious being. So when either the mother or the fetus can be saved, we might easily choose the mother's life on the grounds of an overriding right. But abortion might also be justified as a social policy by interest-oriented considerations. Some societies, for example, justify abortion as an effective means to control birth rates. The interests of a generally high standard of living, or perhaps even survival in some crowded conditions, are used to justify liberal abortion laws.

If the thought of *interests* being used to justify the taking of life repels, remember that other doctrines are available for describing the fetus that do not accept conception as the starting point for life. But even with the acceptance of a life status for the fetus, it is not at all certain that *rights* will always prevail. If the *only* method of population control were abortion, and the population had reached levels that threatened the survival of the society, one might maintain that everyone's general interest in surviving overrides all rights of the unborn; for, on the Hobbesian view, no rights can be realized for anyone in the absence of the civil society.

This tension between *rights* and *interests* cannot be resolved in any final way. But describing it again here reveals the pressing needs for clarification on what, if anything, justifies abortion once we have rejected the simple formula of mother's demand and physician's compliance.

The political implications of abortion reveal yet another side to this complicated issue. Abortion ranks high on the priority list of social issues for feminist groups. At NOW meetings, for example, abortion and the Equal Rights Amendment typically draw more discussion than any other item. But abortion is, by a considerable margin, a more divisive issue than ERA. The "right-to-life" forces, those who oppose abortion, often provide opposition slates of candidates at NOW conventions. This, the moral and philosophical dimensions of abortion have direct ties to the long-run success of the feminist movement. Like few other issues, fundamental theories on life and human rights have explosive political repercussions in the issue of abortion.

POLITICIANS, POLITICS, AND ETHICS

The extended treatment we have given to social justice and the two issues discussed in this chapter, reverse discrimination and abortion, should suggest that the ethical troubles of our political world do not begin and end with politicians. The policy issues that are salient today, and the just status of social arrangements in general, are central topics in the formation of public policy. Though the Aristotelian fusion of ethics and politics is a long way off (some would say thankfully), the ideas of *justice* and *morality* are vital instruments to comprehend public affairs.

The concerned reader need not form an opinion on the ethical issues discussed here. Rather, the reader should take from these pages a *way of arguing*. The study of public policy, as should be clear by now, is too important to be left to facts alone, without values. The morality of both policy and the arrangements for making policy are fair game in today's marketplace of ideas. Unless we can use standard ethical concepts like equality, fairness, and rights, we cannot buy and sell in this exciting area. The purpose of this chapter is to develop such concepts for general use, not to teach some particular moral point of view.

Yet to be explored is the political arrangement most people today would rank as ethically desirable: democracy. We will continue our discussion of ethical issues as we explore democratic decision rules in the next chapter and we will re-open as well the difficult conditions that energy problems, among others, present to any democratic polity.

SUMMARY

1. Ethical issues in politics can be categorized as (a) peccadilloes, (b) official misconduct, (c) illegal actions, and (d) unjust actions.

2. Equality is among the oldest of our ethical standards, but is deficient in that it does not recognize the need for distributive arrangements in society.

3. Reverse discrimination is an attempt to redress unfair inequalities. The *DeFunis* and *Bakke* cases are examples of reverse discrimination. That remedial justice may require painful sacrifices makes it important to insure that it is social *justice* we are trying to bring about with such changes.

4. Justice has been developed lately in terms of *fairness*. In one important theory, John Rawls has maintained that people in an "original" position (insuring impartiality) would choose two principles to govern the relations they have with one another: (a) equal rights to basic liberties, and (b) the difference principle coupled with equal opportunity. These two principles basically define (for Rawls) the just society.

5. Justice-as-fairness has an advantage over utilitarianism in not permitting unfair distribution for the sake of the greater social good. But it has problems: (a) it permits some undesirable social distribution, (b) it does not take into full account the inclinations of some people to take risks, and (c) it does not develop a strategy for implementing justice.

6. One general theme in the area of social justice is the uneven tension between *rights* and *interests*, with no fixed solution as to which overrides the other.

7. Abortion as an ethical and social issue is highly controversial at the moment. The legal system currently permits abortion on demand of the woman with the consent of her physician during the first trimester, but only with considerations of the life and health of the woman thereafter.

8. Many theoretical issues crowd under the abortion title, including when human life begins and what types of reasons will warrant letting someone die.

9. The use of ethical concepts like equality, fairness, and rights is important to understanding public policy today.

FOR FURTHER READING

GENERAL: ETHICS AND POLITICS

ARISTOTLE, *Nichomachean Ethics*. New York: Library of Liberal Arts, 1962.
————, *The Politics of Aristotle*, transl. by Ernest Barker. Oxford: Oxford University Press, 1961.
BAIER, KURT, *The Moral Point of View*. New York: Random House, 1965.
FROHOCK, FRED M., *Normative Political Theory*. Englewood Cliffs, N.J.: Prentice-Hall, 1974.
HARE, R. M., *Freedom and Reason*. Oxford: Oxford University Press, 1965.
OPPENHEIM, FELIX, *Moral Principles in Political Philosophy*. New York: Random House, 1968.
SEARLE, JOHN, "How to Derive 'Ought' from 'Is' ", in *The Is-Ought Question*, ed. W. D. Hudson. New York: St. Martin's, 1969.
TAYLOR, CHARLES, "Neutrality in Political Science," in *Philosophy, Politics, and Society*, 3rd Series, eds. P. Laslett and W. Runciman. Oxford: Basil Blackwell, 1967.
TOULMIN, STEPHEN, *Reason in Ethics*. Cambridge: Cambridge University Press, 1960.

Two fine anthologies in normative ethics and ethics and politics, each of which contains several of the articles cited for this chapter:

BEAUCHAMP, TOM, ED., *Ethics and Public Policy*. Englewood Cliffs, N.J.: Prentice-Hall, 1975.
RACHELS, JAMES, ED., *Moral Problems*. New York: Harper & Row, 1975.

REVERSE DISCRIMINATION

BALDWIN, FLETCHER N., JR., *"DeFunis* v. *Odegaard,* The Supreme Court and Preferential Law School Admissions: Discretion is Sometimes Not the Better Part of Valor," *University of Florida Law Review* 27 (1974/75).
FISCHER, THOMAS, *"DeFunis* in the Supreme Court: Is That All There Is?" *Journal of Law and Education* 4 (1975).
HELD, VIRGINIA, "Reasonable Progess and Self-Respect," *The Monist*, Vol. 57, No. 1 (1973).
HUGHES, GRAHAM, "Reparations for Blacks?" *New York University Law Review* 43 (1968).
KARST, KENNETH L., AND HAROLD W. HOROWITZ, "Affirmative Action and Equal Protection," *Virginia Law Review* 60 (1974).
NAGEL, THOMAS, "Equal Treatment and Compensatory Discrimination," *Philosophy and Public Affairs*, Vol. 2, No. 4 (1973).
O'NEIL, ROBERT M., "Racial Preference and Higher Education: The Larger Context," *Virginia Law Review* 60 (1974).
PAULSON, MONRAD G., *"DeFunis:* The Road Not Taken," *Virginia Law Review* 60 (1974).
SANDALOW, TERRANCE, "Racial Preferences in Higher Education: Political Responsibility and the Judicial Role," *University of Chicago Law Review* 42 (1974/75).

JUSTICE-AS-FAIRNESS

BARRY, BRIAN, *The Liberal Theory of Justice*. Oxford: Clarendon, 1973.
DANIELS, NORMAN, ED., *Reading Rawls*. New York: Basic Books, 1974. (This is, from my point of view, the best collection of critical pieces on Rawls. Instead of listing the important works, I will simply recommend this anthology. Special attention, however, should be given to the articles by Nagel, Dworkin in "The Original Position," Hare, Lyons, and Hart—though most of the other selections are worth reading as well.)
HARE, R. M., "Rawls' Theory of Justice," *Philosophical Quarterly* 23 (1973).
HARSANYI, JOHN, "Can the Maximin Principle Serve as a Basis for Morality?" *American Political Science Review* 69 (June 1975).
————, "Cardinal Utility in Welfare Economics and in the Theory of Risk-taking," *Journal of Political Economy* 61 (October 1953). (For one of the first statements on an "original position," although in this case as a device to support utilitarianism.)
RAE, DOUGLAS, "Maximin Justice and an Alternative Principle," *American Political Science Review* 69 (June 1975).
RAWLS, JOHN, *A Theory of Justice*. Cambridge, Mass.: Harvard University Press, 1971.

ABORTION

BRODY, BARUCH, *Abortion and the Sanctity of Human Life: A Philosophical View*. Cambridge, Mass.: M.I.T. Press, 1975.
————, "Thomson on Abortion," *Philosophy and Public Affairs*, Vol. 1, No. 3 (1972).
COHEN, MARSHALL, THOMAS NAGEL, AND THOMAS SCANLON, EDS., *The Rights and Wrongs of Abortion*. Princeton, N.J.: Princeton University Press, 1974. (Thomson, 1971, included here.)
DUIN, VIRGINIA NOLAN, "New York's Abortion Reform Law: Unanswered Questions," *Albany Law Review* 37 (1972/73).
MEANS, CYRIL C., JR., "The Phoenix of Abortional Freedom: Is a Penumbral or Ninth-Amendment Right About to Arise From the Nineteenth-Century Legislative Ashes of a Fourteenth-Century Common Law Liberty?" *New York Law Forum* 17 (1971/72).
MOORE, ELIZABETH N., "Moral Sentiment in Judicial Opinions on Abortion," *Santa Clara Lawyer* 15 (1974/75).
MOORE, EMILY C., "Abortion and Public Policy: What are the Issues?" *New York Law Forum* 17 (1971/72).
THOMSON, JUDITH JARVIS, "A Defense of Abortion," *Philosophy and Public Affairs* 1 (1971).
U.S. COMMISSION ON CIVIL RIGHTS, *Constitutional Aspects of the Right to Limit Childbearing*. Washington, D.C.: U.S. Government Printing Office, 1975. (Includes text of U.S. Supreme Court Opinions in *Roe* and *Doe*.)

public policy and democracy

8

DEMOCRACY: WHAT DOES IT MEAN?

Pollsters in the United States have again and again confirmed what politicians know by instinct: people favor democracy as a form of government. In a survey broadly representative of later studies, Samuel Stouffer and associates discovered that democratic ideals are high consensus items (1955). Most people overwhelmingly favor free speech, majority rule, representative government—in general, the ingredients common to most forms of democracy. One would be pressed to find anyone in the world today who flatly opposes democracy. Stalin agreed to democracy for the countries of Eastern Europe after the Second World War. China has a "People's Republic" political system that claims to be a "true" democracy. The United Nations pays constant lip service to democratic values.

The joker in all these endorsements is, of course, that the meaning of *democracy* may vary as widely as the number of people who champion its virtues. We know by now that Stalin did not mean by *democracy* what Roosevelt and Churchill meant by the term. (Churchill was defeated in the 1945 election in England, a risk Stalin's perspective on *democracy* would not countenance.) The United Nations comprises many countries whose claims for democracy are notoriously unlike the democracies of Britain and the United States. China is, by Western standards, a strict dictatorship. And even those innocent souls that Stouffer and friends interviewed seemed inconsistent in their understanding of the social *practices* that democratic ideals require: while, for example, agreeing to free speech in the abstract,

263

they were ready to deny atheists and Communists the right to speak in public.

One reason *democracy* has so many meanings is that it is a partisan political term. When we describe a country as democratic today, we mean generally to praise it as well as describe it. The praising function of *democracy* is a product of recent history. Plato ranked democracies on the lower end of his preference scale. Until about the seventeenth century, democracies were widely viewed as undesirable forms of government. But recent history has favored democratic arrangements, so much so that even the harshest of authoritarian regimes today often feel obligated to label their political systems as democratic. The problem is that the political use of the word *democracy* to describe any and everything understandably obscures whatever precise meaning the term may once have had.

To get a clear picture of what *democracy* means, then, we must cut away the partisan layers of meaning the term has accumulated. Regardless of how any particular society is affected, we want to know this—what type of political system does *democracy* describe?

POPULAR SOVEREIGNTY

One of the ideas central to democracy is also the simplest: that effective political power is with the people. In shorthand, the people rule. Aristotle offered one of the oldest typologies of governing, classifying constitutions according to two criteria, (a) the size of the ruling segment, and (b) whether the ruling segment governed in its own interests (corrupt states) or in the interests of all (good states).

	Itself	*All*
One	Tyranny	Monarchy
Few	Oligarchy	Aristocracy
Many	Democracy	Polity

If we cancel out Aristotle's inclination to see democracy as invariably corrupt, we can view democratic arrangements as *rule by the many*. Then, if we use Aristotle's value scheme, democracy can be either corrupt or good depending on how power is exercised. Of course, since the ruling part in democracy *is* "all," Aristotle generally meant to judge *rule by the many* according to whether the many rule only to satisfy their wants or are governed by rules that constrain wants.

Let us, however, set aside the "good" or "bad" judgments on democracy and concentrate on the numerical consideration Aristotle intoduced: rule by the many. In democratic theory, this principle is known as *popular sovereignty*, meaning that power is with the people. Certainly a democratic political system must fulfill at least this basic principle, that the people rule. But *how* the people rule may vary greatly. The best way to understand *popular sovereignty* is to see it as a principle that can consistently provide a variety of decision-rules through which power is exercised. For example, unanimity, majority, and plurality voting all allow the people to rule. But each of these three decision-rules provides a different method to realize popular sovereignty.

We can also see popular sovereignty as an "accordion" concept, expanding and contracting with the efforts of different players (theorists). The two main traditions in American democratic thought, Madisonian and Populist democracy, represent interesting extremes. Madison was famous for his contractions of popular sovereignty, developing in his philosophy that subtle arrangement of governmental checks and balances that has survived historically as the U.S. Constitution. Both government officials *and* the people are politically restrained in Madisonian democracy. Populist democracy, on the other hand, expands the concept of popular sovereignty, encouraging the direct and full translation of popular will into public policy.

In addition to (a) the variety of decision-rules consistent with popular sovereignty, and (b) the elastic nature of popular sovereignty, various governmental forms satisfy "rule by the people." The most literal interpretation of popular sovereignty is that all, or a substantial part, of the people actually exercise political power. Direct democracy requires all the people to rule on every government measure. From this "pure" extreme one can move point by point—only a substantial part of the people rule; only most of the issues are decided by the people—until some form of representative democracy is reached. Here, through various devices, the people control those who rule. Or, as it is said, the representatives of the people rule.

Finally, the "many" who actually rule can be fractured along issue lines. One theorist, who has revived the old term *polyarchy* to stand for *rule by the many*, suggests that democracy can be *rule by revolving minorities* (Dahl, 1961). The people rule, but never as a single unit. They rule by turns, depending on the issue at stake. For example, on urban renewal one segment of the people may be decisive, on education yet another may prevail, and so on. The "many" who rule are a series of minorities. One important implication for democracy of the revolving minorities view of popular sovereignty is that decision-rules may then be suitable only for particular minorities. The minority that is decisive on urban renewal, say, may express its will more appropriately on a unanimity principle, while the education group may decide better on majority rule. Gone, therefore, may be the traditional issue of which decision-rule is suitable for an entire society organized on the democratic principle of popular sovereignty.

CONSENSUS ON THE "RULES OF THE GAME"

Traditional theories of democracy maintained that a consensus on democratic procedures is necessary to a successful democracy. This consensus was said to be logically required to avoid a paradox of democratic life: the people expressing their will in antidemocratic ways. Suppose, to take an extreme possibility, that a society unanimously voted to have a dictatorship. Democratically expressed choice would then terminate democracy. To avoid such peculiar results, democratic theorists maintained that the people must agree on the rules of the game if a democracy is to operate successfully (Mayo, 1960). Included in those rules would be the decision-rules that realize popular sovereignty (for example, *voting*, not dictatorship), as well as minority rights (to protect the exploitation of a few by the democratic many).

In traditional democratic thought, the rules of the game functioned as the background, or context, within which popular sovereignty is exercised. Such rules set aside certain items as not negotiable by popular will; they are rather conditions for a successful democracy. So, the logic ran, the people must agree to exclude such as authoritarian forms of government from the choice of alternatives in order to continue free choice. Without such a minimal consensus, democracy was said to be impossible, much as playing chess is impossible without a basic agreement on the defining rules of chess.

This view underwent a shock when the results of survey research conducted in the 1950s and 1960s became known. Consistently the American people were found to be seriously confused and ignorant about the basic rules of democracies (Stouffer, 1955; McClosky, 1964). While consensus was strong in the abstract—*yes* for free speech, for example—the translation to concrete terms was rich with confusion. Further, what might be considered fundamental knowledge of the political system—the Bill of Rights, Supreme Court decisions, even who one's Congressional representative is—was sadly inadequate. Yet the United States is generally described as a functioning democracy. How can the inconsistency be explained?

Two explanations are possible. The first is to maintain the traditional view on a required consensus and glumly conclude that the United States is not a healthy democracy. Although this first answer would have been received with scepticism throughout the quiescent 1950s, the rude awakenings of the 1960s transformed commonsense views of American democracy. The political assassinations, the black revolution, the peace marches, the general street violence, the underground political movements, and (perhaps most important) the police state mentality of many national leaders—all suggested a pathology at the center of the U.S. body politic. Perhaps the absence of a consensus on democratic "rules of the game" was (or is) symptomatic of this malaise.

The second answer, far more popular during the Rip Van Winkle time of the 1950s, is that the traditional view of democracy is wrong: consensus on fundamental rules is not necessary for a successful democracy (Prothro and Grigg, 1960). *Apathy* will do as well. To see how *apathy* can substitute for *consensus*, simply imagine a society where the people disagree substantially on democratic rules. Now if the antidemocratic factions participate in politics, then something like the dictatorship alternative becomes possible: people may vote in an authoritarian system. But if the antidemocratic factions stay at home, if they are apathetic, then the democratic system can function *as if* a consensus exists.

The functional equivalence of consensus and apathy runs into problems, however, when we think of what a democracy means: rule by the people. While apathy will allow a democratic system to operate in the face of widespread antidemocratic sentiment, which would otherwise paralyze or even destroy the system, an apathetic public is still not a ruling public. Supporters of the apathy component stress the structural features of democratic systems, in particular the *accessibility* of institutions to popular participation. In contrast to authoritarian systems, a democracy provides access to power to those who want to participate. Nonparticipation, say proponents of a functional-elite operation of democracies (Dahl, 1961), is a complicated phenomenon that can reflect many things, including satisfaction with the political system. Critics, on the other hand, argue that apathy signifies a sick democracy, for the simple reason that popular sovereignty requires rule by the *many* and not the few (Walker, 1966).

Whether a consensus on the rules of the game is a necessary condition for democratic systems clearly turns on how we interpret *popular sovereignty*. If *rule by the people* can be defined as providing *access*, not requiring participation, then apathy can substitute for a consensus. But if participation is part of the definition of *popular sovereignty*, then only agreement on the rules of the game can guard against authoritarian outcomes (dictatorship selected in an election) as people *do* generally participate in the political process.

POLITICAL EQUALITY

While the idea of popular sovereignty is central to any theory of democracy (though interpreted differently in different theories, as we have seen), the Populist movement added another component to American democracy: political equality. The rationale for this addition is persuasive enough. Politics among unequals easily produces domination, and the dominated party can lose his political power as a result. Since Aristotle, political theorists have seen the need for political equality in democratic arrangements. The issue has been: what conditions produce political equality?

The answer most political theorists give is *economic* parity. The strong ties between economics and politics have been recognized for centuries. Aristotle, to go back to virtually the beginnings of political thought, suggested a property requirement for political participation. Charles Beard, in his classic, *An Economic Interpretation of the Constitution*, maintained that the protection of property was the single most important motive and goal for the makers of the U.S. Constitution. Marx perceived a hostile, undesirable relationship between economics and politics, finally urging the abolition of private property to achieve political justice. From such rich origins, the Populist emphasis on an economic leveling to insure authentic democracy seems a mild palliative by contrast.

However mild the palliative, numerous commentators on American society have observed a concentration of wealth, which they see as ruling out effective democracy (Parenti, 1974). Economic studies have shown that three or four companies do 80 percent of the business in every major industry (Galbraith, 1967). Corporate power in America is enormous. Even the proliferation of stock ownership in corporations has taken place largely among the economic elite (Hacker, 1970). Some critics have complained that American democracy is a myth, that instead of popular sovereignty, the centralization of economic wealth has created elite rule (Mills, 1956; Parenti, 1974).

Although a conclusion on the *actual* relationship of the American political system to economics—whether public policies are the rulers, the brokers, or the servants of economic interests—will have to be assessed by exploring the books cited at the end of this chapter, the *theoretical* relationship is clear: unless some economic parity, or generally distributed control over economic power, occurs, the *political equality* many theorists regard as vital to democracy is simply impossible.

SYSTEM CAPACITY

Still another addition to popular sovereignty, though perhaps only an extension of the idea, is *system capacity*. Dahl and Tufte argue (1974) that a democratic political system comprises two components: (1) citizen effectiveness ("citizens acting responsibly and competently fully control the decisions of the polity"), and (2) system capacity ("the polity has the capacity to respond fully to the collective preferences of its citizens").

The first of the democratic components, citizen effectiveness, is straightforward enough. It is a restatement of rule by the many, or popular sovereignty. The second is a realistic correlate of the first. Unless the political system can respond to the efforts of its citizens, it is difficult to see how the citizens can be exercising effective power. Imagine having the freedom and opportunity to build your own house, then discovering that the stores are unable to sell you the equipment you need. In such conditions, you do not have effective power to build the house. The capacity of the system to respond is part of the definition of citizen *effectiveness*, so vital to democratic arrangements.

It is important, however, to avoid an easy confusion on what *system capacity* means. It does not mean either the importance of the issues a system deals with, or a system's effectiveness as such, two interpretations that are sometimes erroneously made (Barry, 1974). That a political system treats the more important issue of health care instead of the less important issue of background scenes for the latest first-class stamp may be a plus for the system, but it does not make the system any more democratic. Nor, more starkly, is a more effective political system necessarily a more democratic one. It is one of the sad themes of twentieth-century political experience that fascist states are frequently more effective than democratic systems. The punctuality of Mussolini's trains did not, however, contribute anything to the democratic status of the Italian political system.

We expect from democratic systems the capacity to respond to the preferences *of its citizens*. This is a component of democracy in the simple sense of what popular sovereignty requires, no more and no less. Thus if political system A can more effectively translate demands into policy outcomes than political system B and the demands are constant from system A to system B, then system A is more democratic (that is, there is greater power with the people).

PEREMPTORY VALUES AND FALLIBILITY

Democratic systems seem to assume fallibility in citizen claims, at least to the point where peremptory (or absolute) values are not rigidly enforced. Suppose, to illustrate this need, you know the right answer to a problem in public policy, *really* know with no chance of error. Further, your answer is the only answer; all others are wrong, categorically. Then along comes someone with an answer to the problem unlike yours. You listen impatiently to his argument, out of politeness and nothing else because he is mistaken. At the end of the conversation, or perhaps at the beginning, you overrule him (if you can). There is no intellectual point to justifying, or implementing, a wrong answer. Nor, more broadly, is there any point to using a decision-rule that arrives at conclusions through voting, or any other type of preference-aggregation. Do math instructors tolerate votes on right answers? The thing to do, it seems, when you have an absolutely certain right answer to a public policy question is obvious: impose it if possible.

This fanciful case is too extreme, of course. Not only are there few categorically "right" answers, but also prior consultation with affected parties is politically desirable to get even perfectly right solutions to public policy issues effectively implemented. Still, one strong justification for free speech and democratic rule is that there are no certain truths; the "best" alternative is the one that emerges from the free exchange of conflicting opinions. This doctrine of free speech is John Stuart Mill's, and it informs many types of democratic theory. You let others speak out because they may be right. However, if you know they cannot be right because *you* are unquestionably right, then much of the foundation of democratic practice has been washed away with your peremptory value. You are the math teacher with the right answer standing before a class holding forth in error (Smith, 1957; Thorson, 1962).

INFORMATION

Finally, we would expect that popular sovereignty can be exercised only if people have adequate information about the political system. How much information is "adequate" is not easy to say, but it is clear that the lack of information, or misleading or false information, damages the capability of people to govern themselves. To see this we only have to think of what it is like to act in ignorance. Take the example of a person building a house with no information on what houses are like. Imagine the blunders, the hopelessness of the task. Now multiply such efforts to the scale of an electorate and the picture becomes clear. A condition for any rationally effective action is that information be available. No less is needed for effective citizen rule in any political system.

DEMOCRACY: SOME CONCLUSIONS

Democratic political systems are, at the heart of things, expressions of (1) popular sovereignty. Effective political power is distributed among the people, not consolidated in the hands of a few. To realize popular sovereignty may require other conditions, among these (2) either a consensus on the rules of the game or some substitute condition like apathy. Also, (3) political equality, and its requirement of economic parity, may be needed to avoid dominance by a few. To insure effective rule by the many may also require (4) a political or social system with the capacity to respond to citizen preferences. Then, (5) the absence of peremptory, or ultimately overriding, values insures the ready translation of popular preferences into public policy. Finally, (6) information must be available to the public for effective popular rule.

This capsule summary of democratic political arrangements should help us to understand the possibilities and problems of public policy in democracies.

THE NIXON YEARS: WATERGATE IN PERSPECTIVE

Many of the political events in American society during the late 1960s and early 1970s are now viewed as strains on the political system, threatening stability and the democratic character of American institutions. Let's look at these events from the perspective of our capsule summary of democracy.

Although the decade of the 1960s seemed to be ushered in politically with the end of the Eisenhower years and the inauguration of John Fitzgerald Kennedy, the more accurate character of the period was revealed on November 22, 1963. The assassination of President Kennedy on that day began the domestic violence and unrest that seemed to culminate in the resignation of Richard Nixon from the presidency in disgrace during the summer of 1974. Assassination became a dramatic part of the violence. Martin Luther King and Robert F. Kennedy were murdered in 1968. George Wallace was permanently crippled and nearly killed in 1972. Few other periods in American history were so hazardous for prominent leaders.

The 1960s were also times of mass unrest. The civil rights movement (as we saw in Chapter 3) took to the streets, with mass demonstrations and frequent confrontations between black leaders and the white power structure. Ghetto riots began in Watts in 1965, were repeated in Newark and Detroit in 1967, and erupted again in still more cities after King's assassination in 1968. Mass movements also formed to oppose the Vietnam War. The Democratic National Convention in 1968 was marked by days of antiwar protest and police violence in Chicago. In May 1970, National Guardsmen dispatched to Kent State University to restore order among antiwar demonstrators fired their weapons into a crowd of students, killing four and wounding nine. Sixty thousand people gathered in Washington, D.C., that same May to protest peacefully against the war. Guerilla groups like the Weathermen fought with police and randomly destroyed property. Bombs were set off periodically by various underground groups.

The Vietnam War also split the Nixon administration. Although the appearance of unity was maintained, several high officials began "leaking" information to the press in attempts to change U.S. policy on Southeast Asia. Daniel Ellsberg, a former Defense Department expert, sent the "Pentagon Papers" to the newspapers. These highly classified documents, published by the *New York Times* and the *Washington Post* in 1971, showed the development and implementation of U.S. foreign policy in Southeast Asia. Although the Pentagon Papers were easily the most dramatic information leak of the period, they were but one example of government "secrets" flowing to the press. Newsmen obtained and published the most closely guarded information, culminating with the revelations that destroyed President Nixon politically.

Against this background of violence, civil unrest, an unpopular war, elite disagreement, and media access to sensitive government documents the Nixon administration began the espionage efforts that eventually brought the president and his associates down. Wiretaps were installed in 1969 in an attempt to find out who was leaking information to the press. In the following year, more extensive measures were taken in reaction to the increased domestic violence. At the direction of President Nixon, the directors of the FBI, the CIA, the Defense Intelligence Agency, and the National Security Agency prepared a report urging expanded domestic intelligence efforts, including electronic surveillance, reading of private mail, burglaries—all aimed against American citizens. The plan was not implemented because FBI Director J. Edgar Hoover objected—on the grounds that the FBI should control all the efforts.

Other extraordinary security measures, however, were undertaken. After the Pentagon Papers were published, President Nixon created the special investigative unit known later as "the plumbers." The plumbers, operating independent of most of the official intelligence units in the government, conducted numerous investigations, often illegal, including the burglarizing of Daniel Ellsberg's psychiatrist's office to get confidential information on Ellsberg. H. L. Hunt and Gordon Liddy, two of the chief plumbers, later went to work for the Committee to Reelect the President (CREEP) in the 1972 campaign. Soon the security people in CREEP began espionage anew. In the summer of 1972, James McCord, Hunt, Liddy, and some other associates were apprehended while burglarizing the offices of the Democratic National Committee headquarters in the Watergate Hotel complex.

THE COVER-UP

It seems, in retrospect, that the decisive *political* mistake of the Nixon administration was to deny any knowledge of the Watergate break-in. Immediately after it occurred, Press Secretary Ron Ziegler dismissed it as a third-rate burglary, unworthy of attention and having nothing to do with the presidency. When investigations into the Watergate burglary continued and began to bear fruit, then began also the unfortunate efforts of the Nixon administration to conceal the facts of the case (including the complicity of high officials) and to smother the investigation with a national security cloak. Eventually, President Nixon's own efforts to manipulate the intelligence agencies exploring the Watergate burglary, his subsequent denials of involvement, and the final revelation that he had lied in his denials, destroyed the last support he had in Congress.

One problem the Nixon administration couldn't resolve satisfactorily was how to separate national security from clearly illicit and unneeded domestic surveillance. In 1973, President Nixon defended, as he would through the moment of his resignation and afterwards, the security measures he instituted in response to civil disorders and government leaks. He maintained, in a statement issued on May 22, 1973, that the purpose of the plumbers "was to plug leaks of vital security information. . . ." In such efforts, he was not without substantial precedent. From the Alien and Sedition Acts early in United States history, through the detention camps for Japanese-Americans during World War II, through the McCarthy era of the 1950s, even including the intelligence operations of the Kennedy and Johnson presidencies—Richard Nixon could find ample precedent to use repressive techniques in the name of national security.

But the unusually partisan quality of the Nixon techniques finally couldn't be covered with the national security blanket, even when stretched to its fullest. The unusual paranoia in the White House (which the tapes revealed when made public) confused the maintenance of the Nixon administration with the security of the political system. The inability to justify the actions as essential to the country's security made Watergate at the very least a national embarrassment. The resulting concealment, the steady duplicity, at last made the series of actions known as Watergate a national scandal causing a president to resign from office for the first time in American history.

The obvious threats to democratic arrangements that Watergate presented are of two sorts. First, the repressive measures themselves were contrary to democratic values. An administration that spies on its citizens and discredits its rivals clearly destroys basic conditions for democratic rule. One might argue that domestic conditions at the time required at least some of the measures the Nixon administration adopted. Although it is far from clear that this argument holds, even accepting it leaves the main point untouched: a repressive government is opposed to popular sovereignty. What the argument suggests is that domestic disorders can require undemocratic responses from the political system. Put another way, if citizens resort to extraordinary means, such as violence, to change policy, then the people are not acting on the pragmatic values central to democracies. With either a repressive government or citizen violence democratic procedures and norms are set aside.

Second, the chronic tendency of the Nixon administration to conceal information, to mislead even close supporters, even to attempt to rewrite history (basic documents on the assassination of South Vietnam's President

Diem during the Kennedy administration were altered by the plumbers)
undermined the access of citizens to information needed for the effective
exercise of power. Even members of Congress were unable to obtain accurate information and make valid decisions in the face of Nixon's duplicity:
several of his Congressional supporters were seriously compromised as
members of the House Impeachment Committee when they presented the
"facts" of the case from Nixon's point of view and these "facts" later turned
out to be utterly false. Like those of the people at large, representatives'
decisions are frequently no better or worse than the information on which
they are based.

EXECUTIVE PRIVILEGE

The issues of government repression and government duplicity are obviously important threats to democratic conditions. But perhaps the more
profound significance of Watergate for the American political system is its
role in the less dramatic and more subtle relationship between "executive
privilege" and democratic political arrangements, a relationship that
Watergate renewed and, in part, redefined.

The basis for executive privilege originates in the constitutional separation of legislative and executive power. Article I, Section I, of the U.S.
Constitution states that "all legislative Powers herein granted shall be vested
in a Congress of the United States. . . ." Since the power to legislate requires
information, the power to investigate (especially to get information) is also
part of the legislative authority. But the power of the executive to withhold
information may also be read into the Constitution. Article II states that
"The executive power shall be vested in a President of the United States of
America" and, in the last clause in Section 3, Article II, "He shall take care
that the laws be faithfully executed." Several presidents have interpreted
this last clause as giving them an "executive privilege" to deny Congress
access to information on and from the executive branch of government.

Claims of executive privilege go back to the origins of the U.S. political
system. In 1792, a committee of the House of Representatives investigated a
military disaster in the war against the British. The committee called for
"such persons, papers, and records, as may be necessary to assist their
inquiries." President Washington called a cabinet meeting and, though the
cabinet decided publicly that "neither the committee nor House had a right
to call upon the head of a Department who and whose papers were under the
President alone," Thomas Jefferson's notes of that meeting indicated that the
group judged "there was not a paper which might not be properly produced"
(Berger, 1974, Appendix A).

The Supreme Court very early in U.S. history (*Marbury* v. *Madison*,

1803) established that it was the final arbiter in what the Constitution meant and thus was the agency to resolve constitutional disputes between branches of government. In *United States* v. *Burr* (1807) Aaron Burr requested a letter written by a U.S. general to President Thomas Jefferson, maintaining that the letter was necessary for his defense. The president refused on grounds that certain portions of the letter should not be made public. Chief Justice John Marshall endorsed the idea that "the president of the United States may be subpoenaed, and examined as a witness, and required to produce any paper in his possession. . . ." (*U.S.* v. *Burr*). But, Marshall continued, the wishes of the President to withhold information might be considered conclusive unless the letter were absolutely necessary for defense. Jefferson produced an abridged version of the letter (Breckenridge, 1974).

Recent efforts by presidents to withhold information requested by other branches of government date to President Dwight Eisenhower's May 17, 1954, letter invoking executive privilege. Eisenhower directed Secretary of Defense Charles Wilson not to testify about certain advisory communications before a special subcommittee of the Senate Government Operations Committee. This letter was frequently cited over the next several years by members of the executive branch saying *no* to Congressional efforts to get information. The special counsel for the Army in the McCarthy hearings in 1954 used the letter to prevent testimony on a meeting involving White House aides. The use of executive privilege in these years was widely applauded by the press and the public.

Presidents Kennedy, Johnson, and Nixon continued to claim and use executive privilege. President Kennedy, however, in his letter of February 8, 1962, directing Secretary of Defense Robert MacNamara not to give certain information to a congressional subcommittee, restricted the doctrine of executive privilege to a case-by-case use and, in a later extension of the letter, to use by the president only. Lyndon Johnson affirmed that no other member of the executive branch could claim executive privilege without specific presidential approval. Richard Nixon codified the procedure for invoking executive privilege, firmly lodging it on approval by the president only. However, one study (Berger, 1974) suggests that subordinates in each of these three administrations still on occasion claimed executive privilege in congressional investigations without actual presidential approval.

WATERGATE AND EXECUTIVE PRIVILEGE

The Senate Hearings into the June 1972 burglary of the Democratic National Committee offices in the Watergate Apartments turned up an astonishing fact almost by accident: that the President of the United States was recording the conversations in his offices. These tape recordings of conversations between President Nixon and his chief advisors aroused the interests of many people, among them Special Prosecutor Archibald Cox. Cox had been appointed to investigate the Watergate break-in and cover-up. He requested that several of these tapes be surrendered to his office. The president refused. Judge John Sirica then issued a subpoena for the tapes, the first subpoena to a president since the *Burr* case in 1807.

In *Nixon* v. *Sirica* (1973), the Court of Appeals dismissed the president's appeal. The court ruled that the president "was not above the law's commands." While admitting the importance of the free and candid discussions that privacy affords, the court maintained that it is finally up to the courts rather than the president to decide whether executive privilege can be used in a particular case. The court conceded only a presumptive privilege for presidential communications, set aside in this case by the grand jury's need for the relevant material. The president did not appeal the decision any further.

The dispute over the tapes continued. In March 1974 a grand jury in Washington, D.C., indicted several top White House aides for conspiracy to obstruct justice in the Watergate cover-up. President Nixon was named as an unindicted coconspirator. The special prosecutor, now Leon Jaworski, requested more tapes to help prosecute those who were indicted. The president did not comply with the request. Instead, he publicly released edited versions of some of the requested tapes. The president also appealed the subpoena for the tapes, the appeal reaching the Supreme Court that same spring.

The main issue before the Supreme Court in *United States* v. *Nixon* was executive privilege. The president's appeal to quash the lower court subpoena was based on two claims: (1) that the separation of powers in the American political system simply precluded judicial review of his claim for privilege, and (2) even if the first claim is not accepted, the claim for executive privilege ought to override the special prosecutor's request in this case. The president based his second claim on the need to maintain confidentiality in conversations between the president and his advisors, a need he maintained must be met in order to carry out the executive function successfully.

The Supreme Court, not surprisingly, rejected any absolute privilege on the separation-of-powers doctrine, maintaining instead the ancient doctrine that it is the prerogative of the judiciary to interpret the law precisely because of the separation of powers. Absolute privilege against disclosure, the Court further determined, exists only where state or military secrets are involved. Otherwise, executive privilege must be weighed against other needs—in particular, the administration of criminal justice. In the absence of "military, diplomatic, or sensitive national security secrets," *in camera* inspection by the judiciary of even the most confidential executive communications is warranted. In Nixon's appeal, only the need to maintain the confidentiality of presidential communications was at issue, not the protection of state or military secrets. So, in this case, the Court judged the need for evidence in the criminal proceeding as stronger than the presidential need for privileged communication. In general, however, the Court was careful to affirm the need for confidentiality in government communications (*U.S.* v. *Nixon*, 1974).

It is symptomatic of the conflict between the Nixon presidency and the Court that, three years after leaving office, Nixon in the David Frost television interviews maintained an authority for the president to interpret the law roughly comparable to the authority traditionally reserved for judges. The following month Nixon wrote in a letter to the *Washington Star* defending the views he expressed on television, "Every day courts are required to interpret the written law in light of experience. Presidents have a comparable experience." In the television interview, Nixon had said that a president could, in certain emergencies, make an illegal action legal merely by ordering it to be done. On this assertion of inherent powers in the presidency, Nixon attempted to justify his authorization of wiretapping, burglaries, and other illegal actions against antiwar dissenters.

FREEDOM OF INFORMATION

Perhaps the most important outcome of *United States* v. *Nixon* was the Court's willingness to balance executive privilege against other needs except where state or military secrets are concerned. Though still recognizing the importance of privileged communication within the executive branch, the Court decided that this privilege is not absolute.

One general consequence of the "balancing" provision is the effect it is sure to have on the information available to ordinary citizens (Barton, 1975). In 1966, Congress passed the Freedom of Information Act (FIA). This act gives the public at large access to government information, with several exemptions. (Military secrets and inter- and intra-agency memoranda are protected, as well as some other types of information.) But the FIA, and the later amendments to the act in 1974, does require that general rules and statements of policy, plus internal dissents and interpretations, be made available to the public *upon request*. (No "need to know" has to be demonstrated to get the information.) The courts have held that all "final" determinations, especially of any material used as a basis for action by an agency of the government against a private party, cannot be protected (*American Mail Line, Ltd.* v. *Gulick*, 1969).

Since the traditional assertion of executive privilege has usually covered (1) secrets, and (2) internal memoranda or letters, the Supreme Court's decision in the *Nixon* case suggests how the types of information at issue will be handled. Secrets will likely go on being secrets. But, since the Nixon tapes are probably covered by one of the FIA exemptions—internal communications—the confidentiality of internal executive communications can be expected to be tested against competing interests. Certainly criminal trials now have at least a provisional priority for securing information and government claims for confidential communications can be expected to receive hard judicial scrutiny in the future. Since the public is being provided with such tools against government confidentiality, the doctrine of executive privilege is, for the moment, in a weaker position than it has been.

INFORMATION IN A DEMOCRACY

The obsessive secrecy of the later Nixon years as that administration attempted to cover up the Watergate break-in seems a classic lesson in civics. The litany goes like this: An "open" government is good; therefore, Nixon and his men were bad to hide things. The theme is not new to American society. Woodrow Wilson endorsed "open diplomacy" and even Dwight Eisenhower, no friend of public candor, urged an "open skies" foreign policy (unpoliced inspection from aircraft of each country's military installations—a harbinger of "spy satellites"). President Jimmy Carter was quick to capitalize on the mistakes of his predecessors, endorsing an "open administration" in general, and even—at first—opening cabinet meetings to the press.

The rationale for open politics is so wonderful as to be almost beyond challenge. A democracy, as suggested earlier, requires the dissemination of information to effectively realize popular sovereignty. The people need to know in order to have power, and knowing what the government is doing also helps prevent an oppressive government. One of the remarkable outcomes of the Freedom of Information Act was the release, upon their request, of dossiers on private people that U.S. intelligence agencies had developed for the most frivolous, or treacherous, of reasons. Also, keeping the politicians in the open seems a good way of keeping them honest: if you can see the moves in public, maybe the old shell game will be harder to play on the people.

Unfortunately, open politics has never worked out quite so well as its rationale suggests. Both the Wilson and Eisenhower proposals died natural deaths, lingering in the first case and stillborn in the second. Carter quietly closed the doors to his administration's deliberations soon after he took office. Nor could the closed doors be explained wholly by the tendencies of the world leaders toward intrigue. An open executive system, one where the public knows all the moves or at least all the words said, can discourage (a) candor, (b) compromise, and (c) speculative observation, all arguably necessary for effective government.

Let's start with the premise that representatives in a modern democracy have political power by consent of the people. It then follows that public statements of elected officials are sensitive to public opinion, on the reasonable grounds that the public is the broad source of the officials' power. Candor, on the other hand, is the quality of being outspoken, speaking honestly and directly without regard to the opinions of others. Though the candid politician may find himself blessed with public support, it is also easy to see how the need to appeal to one's constituents can work against candor.

The same conflict is suggested in compromise and speculative observation. Compromise can easily suggest weakness and vacillation: witness the press critiques of politicians (for example, Jimmy Carter in the 1976 Presidential campaign) who change their positions on issues in response to group pressure. Speculative observation can appear as dreadfully wrong advice when the speculation turns out to be mistaken. Yet honest appraisal, give-and-take adjustments of policy proposals, and even wild speculation on possible outcomes may all be helpful in government formation of policy. Thus, opening the doors wide to the public may lead to that carefully phrased and guarded government attitude that public access is supposed to dissipate.

Then there is the problem of acquiring information. It is conceivable that government agencies will find ways to circumvent any set of procedures designed to provide the public with information. Tape recorders are out by now. But perhaps all written records will be avoided on sensitive issues. It has been said by critics of the economic system that price-fixing among giant corporations went on at weekend golf games, where there were no secretaries, subordinates—and written records. Even the quality of available information may be suspect or, even worse, difficult to tell whether it ought to be suspected. A government intentionally obscuring its own documents, avoiding anything in writing or "on the record," may not produce any more successful a democracy than one shrouded in secrecy.

Quite obviously, the case for freedom of information is more complicated, and more difficult to implement, than first perceived. The people must have information if power to be dispersed democratically. But governments may also need privacy to conduct business effectively. Usually the press is seen in an adversary relationship with government. The healthy opposition of interests in such a relationship may accurately characterize the conflict between the people's quest for information and the government's privilege to withhold it.

DEMOCRATIC PLANNING: BIOMEDICAL TECHNOLOGY

Policies in a democracy are linked to popular demand. Policy planning, on the other hand, may require more than a *response* to demands or even current conditions in society. Projections involving substantial periods of time and comprehensive resources may be part of the logic in certain policy issues. We have suggested that popular sovereignty may require, in addition to information, both the capacity of the political system to respond effectively to citizen preferences and the absence of peremptory values. What happens, however, if a policy issue is, first, unavoidable, and, second, peremptory by definition? Does system capacity to treat the issue shift from citizen preferences to other values?

Biomedical technology, from many points of view, has reached a critical point in its development. Molecular genetics, in particular, offers a variety of hazards and benefits complicating traditional decision-models of public policy. One issue that has reached the stage of policy discussion is genetic research into micro-organisms. The city council in Cambridge, Massachusetts, voted in July of 1976 to ask Harvard University to halt construction of a new laboratory for genetic research until a full discussion of the issues could take place.

The "Cambridge decision" was plagued by a disagreement among scientists on the danger of experimenting with a new form of DNA (deoxyribonucleic acid), the basic substance that controls growth and reproduction in all living cells. The new DNA, "recombinant DNA," is an artificial substance easily made in the laboratory with DNA pieces taken from different cells. Recombinant DNA has the intriguing power to enter a host cell, becoming a permanent part of its genetic structure.

The potential benefits and hazards of recombinant DNA are provided by its chameleon-like capacity to assume the characteristics of each form of DNA pieced together to make it. Combining fragments of cancer and bacteria DNA, for example, produces a recombinant DNA that is, in effect, a bacterial cancer. Mixing this new DNA with other bacteria will then produce limitless numbers of bacterial cancer as the bacteria manufacture them. This frightening prospect holds great promise when more helpful fragments of DNA are combined. If, say, the fragments of genes that produce vitamins, antibodies, hormones, insulin, can be combined with bacteria, then the bacteria would produce these materials in the laboratory with little cost or effort. In June 1977, one of these breakthroughs occurred when University of California scientists successfully induced an insulin gene to reproduce itself in *E. coli* bacteria, a major step in the artificial production of insulin. Some scientists have even held out the possibility of developing new types of plants that would contain bacteria capable of converting atmospheric nitrogen directly into fertilizer. Food crops would then no longer be dependent on the availability of soil fertilizers, an obvious advantage for the world's food supply.

The dangers of research with recombinant DNA lie in the uncertainties of new genetic agents and the universal presence of the host bacteria to be used in research. In any experiment, fragments of DNA may combine in unknown ways, opening the door to the possibility of a lethal agent impossible to control. Some scientists, though only a small minority, feel that the whole earth could be contaminated, perhaps fatally, before anything could be done. The possibility of widespread contamination is suggested because of the bacteria used in experiments: *E. coli. E. coli* bacteria are present in harmless form all over the world. Moreover, they have a strong capacity to transfer genetic material from one cell to another.

A "worst-possible" outcome would be the transfer of a new and dangerous genetic agent to all forms of animal life, with possibly fatal and irreversible consequences. Even genes known to be harmful might be spread if combined with *E. coli* bacteria. DNA from cancer viruses has already been placed in a weakened type of *E. coli* bacteria. If *E. coli* bacteria with cancer were to escape from the laboratory, the recombinant DNA with cancer genes might be transferred to human cells. A cancer epidemic might occur as the *E. coli* bacteria spread to the world's population. Stopping the recombinant DNA carried by *E. coli* bacteria might be impossible.

The debate among scientists before the Cambridge city council focused on the reliability of safeguards to prevent such catastrophes. Two safety guidelines have been adopted. One is *physical* containment. Laboratories are designed to avoid the escape of specimens. The other is *biological* containment. Only weakened strains of bacteria (weakened *E. coli,* for example) are used in experiments, so that if they do somehow get out of the laboratory, they cannot live long enough to do damage. Critics, however, point out that physical containment has never worked successfully (Cavalieri, 1976). Army research on biological warfare, for example, was plagued by accidental escapes of lethal agents in spite of extraordinary precautions. Also, the enfeeblement of organisms is said to be risky. The genetic experiments themselves may give new strength to the organisms used, a possibility that can't be eliminated without doing the research in the first place and thus creating the dangers such enfeeblement is designed to avoid.

Scientists have lined up on both sides of the controversy. Most, mindful of benefits to mankind, inspired by research payoffs, and convinced of the effectiveness of the safeguards, have urged that the experiments continue with all deliberate speed under the accepted safety guidelines. A few, aware of the potential for extensive and irreversible damage to human existence, have argued for an immediate halt to all genetic research until more reliable specimens and procedures can be developed. The basic uncertainty of the controversy even extends to the firmness with which scientists take stands on the issue. Shortly after condemning genetic research, some scientists have dramatically reversed themselves. Most have quietly dismissed the earlier disaster projections. Others have openly admitted to having been alarmists. Dr. James D. Watson, a Nobel Prize cowinner for his work on DNA, was among the original signers of a 1974 call for a moratorium on DNA research.

In 1977, Dr. Watson admitted that "the vision of the hysterics has so peopled biological laboratories with monsters and superbugs that I often feel the discussion has descended to the realm of a surrealistic nightmare" (quoted in the *New York Times*, 7/31/77).

The city council of Cambridge faced a problem all policy authorities will encounter with more frequency in the future: what should be done when the stakes for good and bad are limitless and the experts disagree?

DEMOCRATIC DECISION-MAKING IN CONDITIONS OF RISK AND UNCERTAINTY

Any method of making decisions weighs gains against losses. If information on the outcomes of action is good, the probability of a gain or a loss can also be calculated (see Chapter 2). But with genetic research, neither the probabilities of gains nor losses can be securely counted. Risk (the probability of loss in this case) is what is in greatest dispute by the experts. The policy decision on whether to continue with genetic experiments must calculate on the possibility, not probability, of enormous risk (threats to the survival of the human race) against enormous potential benefits (gigantic increases in the world's food supply, cheap production of vital drugs, correction of genetic defects, and so on).

Even the acknowledged benefits may present a mixed bag of good and bad things. Alteration of plants may bring increased food supplies, but we now know enough about the balance of nature to suspect disturbances elsewhere from even beneficial changes. The increased use of fertilizer since the Second World War brought a "green" revolution that has since been re-evaluated with our fuller understanding of nitrogen pollution and increasing soil damage that follow from such practices. The rapid change of genetic engineering may disrupt nature on a broader scale, given the slow, evolutionary pace at which species of life evolve.

Human institutions may also be damaged by the beneficial results of genetic discoveries (Golding, 1968). If, for example, it were possible to create the "Six Million-Dollar Man" easily and inexpensively, the implications of a race of superheroes would still be unclear. Whether supremely intelligent and physically powerful people would be forces for good or evil is just not certain. What we do know is that a rapid increase in immensely gifted people could well upset the balance of current social practices. The institution of the family, for example, long nurtured on human dependence, might wither and die with undesirable consequences for other social norms. Moreover, the social mechanisms needed to implement genetic benefits might lead to undesirable results. If, for example, a lottery system were devised to distribute limited genetic benefits, a redistribution in social power paralleling the new mental and physical giants in the population might radically transform our society into one of oppressive elite rule.

Great uncertainty and the possibility of grave risks, then, coupled with the vision of unprecedented gains, are present in policy decisions about genetic research. That policy decisions must be made is the only certainty: not only are public resources frequently used to construct facilities and educate scientists, but even privately financed efforts pose the same risks and benefits to the general population. The question is: How do we make rational policy decisions?

In the absence of that authority vested in *expertise*, the natural reference in democratic systems is the people, especially those affected by a decision. We saw in Chapter 4 that the state of California turned to a referendum to decide the issue of safety in the future construction of nuclear plants. Again, the experts disagreed, with each side supported by prominent scientists. The people voted *no* on Proposition 15, setting aside the more stringent safety requirements Proposition 15 would have required for nuclear plants. Voters chose the freer development of nuclear energy over the warnings outlined by supporters of the proposition. In genetic research, a similar referendum could conceivably be held: *yes* or *no* on continuing the experiments.

The appeal of such a referendum is primarily *moral*, however, not rational. If the experts in a field cannot settle an issue on its merits, then neither can the people in a referendum. A referendum can determine whether those who might be subject to harm are willing to accept the risk. The vote on Proposition 15 in California did not establish the correct course of action. It determined the course of action acceptable to the people affected by the alternatives. The difficulties with the moral appeal are, unfortunately, rather profound. There is first the fact of a division in the electorate, and those who oppose going ahead with scientific research or energy development must face the risks equally with those who have accepted these risks. Then there is the matter of establishing the relevant population in genetic research. Since all mankind could be adversely affected, including all future generations, a fair constituency is impossible to locate.

To avoid these and other difficulties, some (Mazur, 1973) have suggested the establishment of a "science court," where divisive scientific issues can be argued out in an adversary hearing before a panel of neutral experts. The logic of a "science court" is exactly the logic of a court of law: advocates for opposing views can, under the guidance of strict rules of evidence and argument, fully develop a case for each alternative course of action. The cool and rational deliberation we have come to associate with well-conducted legal proceedings ought to facilitate an inspection of benefits and harms in scientific proposals.

Unfortunately, there is one problem: how to assemble a panel of truly neutral experts. In any important scientific controversy, most experts in the field will have strong opinions, as we witnessed with Proposition 15 in California. A bevy of neutral scientists on an issue probably means that the issue is not yet a concern for public policy. Of course, experts from a field of science outside the one at issue may be organized into a "science court" panel. But we have a right to suspect their expert status, given the current specialization in science. Would a panel of, say, physicists do that much better than a layman in weighing arguments over genetic research? Possibly. But they may not, especially if their neutrality is purchased at the price of ignorance in the field being debated.

When expert advice, referendums,· and adversary proceedings fail, there is still one easy answer: temporize, or do nothing until the picture is clearer. But this final option has its own sad consequences. For one thing, issues may never become clearer, no matter how long the delay. For another, delay may not be possible. The issue of genetic research must be faced now because of the simplicity of making and using E. coli bacteria with recombinant DNA. If any schoolboy can conduct his own genetic research, delaying a decision on regulatory laws covering the activity amounts to endorsing a no-control policy.

The melancholy conclusion is that a high-risk, high-return decision on basic uncertainty and forced-choice conditions (no delay) may be impossible to make on rational criteria; if the outcomes are peremptory—involving such irrevocable and total considerations as the future of the human race—then the moral strategy of a referendum is impossible also. Certainly the democratic reliance on citizen preference fares no better than authoritarian alternatives. "Blind intuition" may not be too strong a depiction of decision-criteria.

Finally, the concept of government regulation of science, no matter how rationally conceived, is an issue in itself. The spectre of Lysenko comes too easily to mind: the Soviet government in effect destroyed genetic research in Russia during the 1930s and 1940s by decreeing that one scientific approach, the one adopted by Trofim D. Lysenko, was right and all its rivals were wrong. Some of the world's leading geneticists, firmly located in the rival camp, were exiled or imprisoned. Lysenko's methods were applied to agriculture with disastrous results. Government intervention on the wrong side of a scientific dispute reduced Soviet genetic research to a travesty. Critics of United States regulatory policies toward science do not expect another Lysenko debacle. American officials are largely motivated by safety concerns, not ideological convictions, in their efforts to regulate genetic research. But they do cite the real dangers of political legislation in a field that thrives on open, unrestricted inquiry, as science does.

The National Institute of Health, in response to a plea for guidance by a group of scientists formed by the National Academy of Sciences, organized an advisory committee in 1975 to set up guidelines for scientific research into recombinant DNA. These guidelines describe in detail four sets of special practices, equipment, and laboratory conditions that define escalating levels of physical containment for DNA organisms. The N.I.H. guidelines also specify types of *E. coli* bacteria to use in DNA experiments. The medical microbiologists on the N.I.H. committee have asserted that *E. coli* bacteria cannot produce a pathological epidemic when inserted with recombinant DNA. Though without the force of law, the N.I.H. guidelines have been generally adopted by the scientific community.

The Cambridge city council, by the way, finally decided to allow the construction of the Harvard laboratory under the safety guidelines established by the N.I.H. Little was said to suggest that the council had grasped the full complexities of the scientific issues involved.

ENERGY PROBLEMS

If biomedical technology presents issues that escape solution in the form of rational public policies, energy problems in Western societies pull at least some rational solutions and democratic decision-rules in opposite directions. The stretch between the rational and the democratic has convinced some (Heilbroner, 1974) that democracy will not survive into the next century. Let's look at the problems.

The finite status of fossil fuels was given renewed dramatic emphasis in the bitter winter of 1977. Natural gas, long sold and promoted at artificially low prices, became a *publicly* scarce resource. The word *public* is important in this observation, because natural gas had been relatively scarce for years before the winter crisis of 1977. The persistently low temperatures of that winter, however, seriously disrupted the fragile balancing system that had supplied the nation with natural gas in the past. Factories closed across the Northeast. Schools took forced vacations. Only private homes were spared, and they just barely, as the abrupt rationing of natural gas applied to industry and schools. But John F. O'Leary, federal energy administrator in the new Carter administration, told the public that "the 65-degree home will become a feature of the future" (on the program "Issues and Answers," 2/13/77).

The natural gas shortage has a proximate and a long-term cause. The proximate cause is mandatory low prices that cause casual and unrealistic consumption. The 1938 Natural Gas Act has been administered and legally interpreted to keep the lid on the price of gas sold in interstate commerce. The U.S. Supreme Court ruled, in *Phillips Petroleum Co. v. State of Wisconsin*, 1954, that the Natural Gas Act applied to the prices set by producers who sold gas to the pipelines as well as to the interstate pipeline prices themselves. The low government-regulated prices for natural gas have not reflected market value, resulting in increased consumption of natural gas. Industrial consumers and electric utilities have promoted natural gas. It is clean, safe, and, until now, very cheap. California home owners even heated their swimming pools with natural gas. Consumption in the United States quadrupled between 1950 and 1970. This artificial bubble burst in 1977.

The long-range cause is a shortage of natural gas in the environment. Though critics contend that the gas companies hoard supplies to drive up prices, which may be true in limited cases, the evidence suggests that not enough natural gas is available to satisfy needs. In 1968, for the first time, discovery and extraction of new natural gas fell short of consumption. Reserves were used, and for almost every year since then, reserves have fallen (293 trillion feet in 1967 to 228 trillion feet in 1975). Natural gas supplies almost one-third of the U.S. energy market. Though new discoveries, such as the reserves found in Alaska, are possible, the finite supply of natural gas simply cannot, in the long run, continue to fuel the American economy. Alternative sources of energy must be found.

The proximate cause of gas shortages is relatively easy to remedy. Regulations keeping prices low can be relaxed or suspended. President Carter's proposal to deregulate natural gas newly committed to interstate sales (though not to gas already flowing) is one step in this direction. Deregulation would alleviate future imbalances in the distribution of natural gas across the

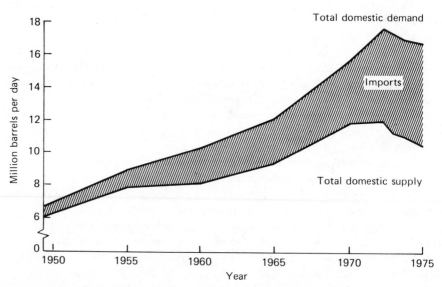

Source: U.S. Federal Energy Administration. Reprinted from Edward Teller, Hans Mark, and John S. Foster, Jr., *Power and Security* (Lexington, Mass.: D.C. Heath & Co., 1976), p. 102.

country. Eastern states in the winter of 1977, for example, were denied some natural gas because producers could get higher prices for the gas within their own states, where the price regulations did not apply.

If, however, deregulation allows natural gas to reach normal market prices, these prices may cause severe disruptions in the economy. The United States became dependent on natural gas because it was, for so long, a cheap source of energy. Household, school, and industrial budgets could be turned inside out if prices skyrocket, which they are likely to do. Although conversion to other sources of fuel is one answer, basic changes in energy use for existing buildings can be expensive. And the question, even with the absorption of conversion costs, is: What alternative energy source is available?

Oil, the most prominent alternative to gas, is currently consumed in the United States at a rate of about 15 million barrels per day. Approximately 43 percent of this total is imported. Domestic production of oil has gone down in recent years, from a high of 9.6 million barrels a day in 1970 to 8.2 million barrels in 1976. Alaska's North Slope oil increases domestic production, but experts believe that U.S. production of oil has already peaked and will not increase substantially in the future. The imported oil comes predominantly from the Middle East. The Arab oil embargo of 1973 and the newly found muscle of the oil cartel pose a continuing problem for the U.S. economy. The cartel can raise and lower prices, or institute another embargo. Greater U.S. reliance on oil will extend this dependence with the expected damage to American economic security. Also, oil will fare no better than natural gas in the long run. Most estimates place a thirty-year limit on the current oil abundance, calculating that world oil supplies will begin a permanent decline early in the next century.

Coal, once the staple energy source for Western societies, is in relatively plentiful supply. But the full use of this supply is difficult. The contraction of the domestic market for coal in the 1940s was abrupt and unsettling to the coal industry. The shift by railroads from coal-fired steam locomotives to diesel engines after World War II and the change from coal furnaces to oil, gas, or electricity in most private homes caused a 36 percent drop in coal production between 1947 and 1962. Periodic mine disasters and recognition of "black lung" disease added to the industry's problems throughout the 1960s. The Coal Mine Health and Safety Act of 1969, desperately needed to protect the health and safety of coal workers, cut severely into coal mine production. But the most important factor arresting coal use is that it is a dirty fuel. The Clean Air Act of 1970 set standards for oxides of sulfur, released by burning coal, that caused more shifts away from coal as a power source. To return to heavy coal use would mean, on existing technology, trading off even moderate clean-air standards for energy.

Nuclear energy, the only other major energy source in American soci-

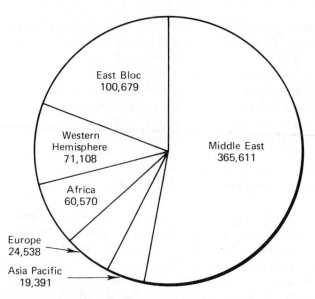

Worldwide Oil Reserves (In thousand million barrels, as of January 1, 1977)
Source: New York Times, 10/2/77, and *International Monetary Fund, Oil and Gas Journal.*

ety, was once viewed as the savior of our energy-dependent civilization. It is, so far, an energy form that is economical (if we exclude research and development costs) and practically inexhaustible. Nuclear power furnished about 5 percent of the nation's electricity in 1973, and the number of nuclear power plants are to increase 12 to 15 times by 1985 and an additional 3 to 4 times by the year 2000, according to the U.S. Atomic Energy Commission.

The chronic problem with nuclear energy has been safety. Like the prospect of recombinant DNA research, nuclear power is at once extremely promising and potentially very dangerous. Radioactive wastes from nuclear power plants are lethal materials that must be somehow removed from the environment for thousands of years. The length of time these wastes must be effectively isolated staggers the imagination. Safeguards must be maintained for a period of time longer than all civilizations and religions have existed from the beginnings of human history. Indeed, the responsibility for insuring safety from radioactive contamination may extend into the future beyond the length of time that man has already existed on the earth. If these safety procedures are not steadily maintained in the future, a serious accident could bring catastrophe to the entire human race.

In addition to waste dangers, the production of power in nuclear plants is hazardous. Release of radioactive material in use can kill or cause serious illness to hundreds, perhaps thousands, of people. Accidents are possible in many stages of the fuel cycle, including reprocessing of nuclear material, transportation, storage, and generation of power at the plants themselves. There is also the risk of losing, through theft or negligence, the radioactive material. Critics charge that present methods of safeguarding nuclear material are grossly inadequate (Willrich and Taylor, 1974).

Some recent events seem to support this charge. The federal government's Energy Research and Development Administration (ERDA) admitted in August of 1977, for example, that it had no idea what had happened to more than four tons of uranium and plutonium used in the last thirty years to make atomic bombs. Although ERDA saw no evidence of any theft, some commentators stressed the fact that enough material was missing to make almost 500 nuclear weapons. Since atomic bombs are easily made with the right material, such as plutonium, the threat of nuclear proliferation at virtually the household level is a possibility. One of the bittersweet news stories of early 1977 was that of the Princeton senior who drew up a design for a homemade atomic bomb costing less than $2,000 to make. He got an A on the paper and inquiries from several nonatomic countries (*New York Times*, 2/11/77).

Changes in technology, especially those brought about by important scientific discoveries, can alter the basic analysis of any social practice. But on the basis of what we know now, the energy crunch has not passed. Rather, it lies ahead. Policy decisions will be required on consumptive patterns of current energy sources, perhaps involving trade-offs of safety and a clean environment for additional fuel; and also on new energy sources once existing fossil fuels are depleted.

CHOICES

To someone responsible for policy in a democratic polity, the options open on energy range from the obvious to the almost unthinkable. The two standard efforts are increased production and reduced consumption.

1. *Increased Production.* Production of energy can be increased in the United States by using more of the available sources of fuel. Fields currently off limits to development could be opened, such as the Elk Hills Naval Petroleum Reserve in California earmarked for military emergencies. Marginally productive sources of acceptable fuel could be developed. Stripper wells, those that produce less than 10 barrels of oil per day, could produce more than 1 million barrels per day if all were put into production. Unacceptable fuel, such as coal, could be mined more effectively. Nuclear power plants could be developed at a greater pace. Such activity would produce more energy for the U.S. economy.

Unfortunately, the costs of production increases are high, socially and monetarily. Aside from security considerations in using fields reserved for the military, increasing production on any giant scale will require either price increases, the relaxation of safety standards, or a toleration of pollution, if not all three of these costs.

Assuming a market system, only increases in price will make the exploration of marginal energy sources worthwhile. Stripper wells, for example, will not be kept productive unless crude oil prices go up. Coal cannot be successfully used unless pollution standards are relaxed and labor grievances with the miners settled. The four and one-half day work-week is an unwelcome reality in the coal industry because of labor strikes. Strip mining, long opposed by environmentalists because of its devastating effects on the land, would also have to be accepted, at least in Appalachia and the Midwest where machinery for strip mining exists. Environmental impact studies and legal challenges by consumer groups have slowed the granting of licenses for construction of nuclear power plants. (Though speeding up recently, the Atomic Energy Commission granted only one license for plant construction

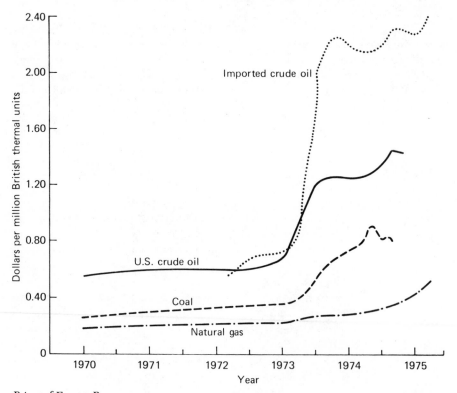

Prices of Energy Resources

Source: Reprinted from *Environmental Quality* (Washington, D.C.: U.S. Government Printing Office, 1976), p. 105

Table 8.1
1985 ESTIMATES OF DOMESTIC ENERGY SUPPLIES
(ALL FIGURES IN QUADS PER YEAR = 10^{15} BTU's PER YEAR)

	Oil	Natural Gas	Coal	Nuclear	Other*	Totals
FEA[1] Maximum production						
Levels						
Oil at $11 per barrel						
Business as Usual	31.8	23.4	24.8	7.0	4.6	
Accelerated Development	42.4	29.3	47.3	8.2	8.7	
Ford Foundation[2]						
Historical Growth						
High Domestic Oil and Gas	32	29	25	10	9	105
High Nuclear	32	29	23	12	9	105
Technical Fix						
Self-Sufficiency	30	27	16	8	4	85
Environmental Protection	29	26	14	5	4	78
CED[3]	28.5	26.5	21.5	10	8.5	95
NAE[4]	28.8	33.1	21.2	17.6	3.6	104.3
This Report	35	28	33	12	8	116

*Includes shale oil, synthetic oil and gas, hydroelectric, geothermal, solid waste, solar, etc.
Sources:
1. Federal Energy Administration, *Project Independence Report,* November 1974.
2. Ford Foundation Energy Policy Project, *A Time to Choose,* 1974.
3. Committee for Economic Development, *Achieving Energy Independence,* December 1974.
4. National Academy of Engineering, *U.S. Energy Prospects: An Engineering Viewpoint,* 1974.
Reprinted from Edward Teller, Hans Mark, and John S. Foster, Jr., *Power and Security.* Lexington, Mass.: D.C. Heath & Co., 1976, p. 27.

in 1971.) The concern over safety in nuclear generation, in many cases a reasonably based concern, would have to be suspended in a total commitment to use all energy sources.

The glum fact is that a full-scale development of energy sources would make our world more expensive, dirtier, uglier, and more dangerous. Not all these conditions would necessarily occur at once. But more aggressive production of dwindling fuel reserves would lead to some or all of these conditions in progressively greater amounts.

2. *Reduced Consumption.* The other choice is reduced consumption of energy. The United States, with only 6 percent of the world's population, consumes one-third of the world's energy. The rest of the world is increasing its consumption faster than the United States is, but American consumption is enormous by any standards. Residential energy use increased by 50 percent during the 1960s, reflecting a greater reliance by Americans on private households, often single-family dwellings, and easier life styles dependent on increased lighting, heat, television, and other high-energy-use appliances. Commercial energy use has increased 5.4 percent per year since 1960, primarily in space heating and cooling (office buildings without win-

Table 8.2
ENERGY DEMAND AND SUPPLY
(ROUNDED TO NEAREST 0.1 QUAD PER YEAR)

Demand		1973 Actual		1985 Target
Electricity[1]		19.8		33
Residential & Commercial[2]		15.4		18
Industry[2]		18.2		24
Non-Energy[3]		3.4		6
Transportation[2]		18.8		22
Subtotal–Domestic		75.6		103
Export		2.0		15
Liquids	0.5		6	
Gas	0.1		0	
Coal	1.4		9	
Totals		77.6		118
Supply				
Liquids		35.2		39
Conventional	22.2		35	
Shale	0.0		2	
Synthetic	0.0		1	
Imports	13.0		1	
Gas		23.6		29
Conventional	22.5		28	
Synthetic	0.0		2	
Imports	1.1		1	
Converted[4]	0.0		−2	
Coal		15.0		33
Nuclear		0.9		12
Hydroelectric		2.9		3
Other		0.0		2
Totals		77.6		118

1. Primary fuel demands–energy consumed by the electric utilities to produce electricity.
2. End-use sector totals exclude electricity consumed.
3. Includes 0.3 quads of liquids not accounted for in 1973. The item "non-energy" is the production of materials such as fertilizer and plastics which use coal or hydrocarbons for their substance rather than as a source of energy.
4. Gas which is converted to synthetic liquids (methanol).
Reprinted from Edward Teller, Hans Mark, and John S. Foster, Jr., *Power and Security*. Lexington, Mass.: D.C. Heath & Co., 1976, p. 14.

dows that open: heated in winter, air-conditioned in summer), lighting, and office equipment.

Transportation also absorbs great quantities of energy. Total vehicle miles driven in the United States has doubled every 15 years since 1940 while transportation efficiency has gone down. Public transportation has declined while the use of automobiles has risen (to 95 percent of all urban passenger traffic in 1970). The American car got more than 14 miles per gallon in 1958, less than 12 miles per gallon in 1973. Industrial use of energy accounts for more than 40 percent of domestic use and it too has grown in the last two decades. (Figures from *Exploring Energy Choices*, Ford Foundation Report, 1974)

Americans, in short, are gluttons for energy. Since the 1960s, serious efforts have been made to reduce or at least check this consumption. The Environmental Protection Agency reported that the average efficiency of 1976 American cars was 17.6 miles per gallon. Government officials have urged that thermostats be lowered in businesses and homes. Considerable slack also exists in how both commerical and private buildings use heat. Better insulation could reduce energy use. All of these conservation measures have a strong voluntary component: people must decide to buy smaller, more efficient cars, keep thermostats at low temperatures, purchase insulating equipment.

Voluntary action may not be enough, however. From 1973 through 1976, energy consumption in Germany fell 5.5 percent relative to national production. In the United States, consumption did not drop at all relative to production in the same time period. One important reason for the difference

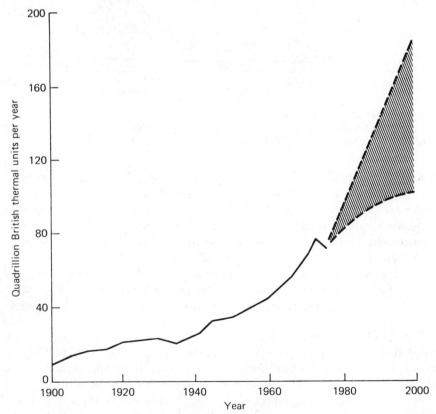

U.S. Gross Energy Consumption for 1900–1975 and Range of Projections to the Year 2000. *Source:* Reprinted from *Environmental Quality* (Washington, D.C.: U.S. Government Printing Office, 1976), p. 189.

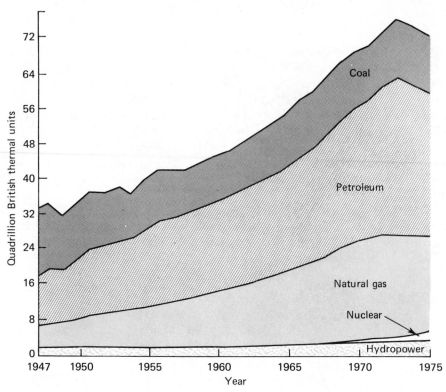

U.S. Gross Energy Consumption by Source: 1947–1975.
Source: U.S. Department of the Interior, Bureau of Mines. Reprinted from Environmental Quality (Washington, D.C.: U.S. Government Printing Office, 1976), p. 103.

is that Germany, like most other European countries, has a high and growing tax on gasoline. The United States has maintained a low tax of 12 cents a gallon on gasoline. The high tax in Europe forces gasoline prices up to what Americans would consider exhorbitant levels: in 1977, $1.85 per gallon in France and $1.38 in Germany, for example. It is not through voluntary action that European cars are smaller and more efficient than their American counterparts. They simply must be, given what it costs to run them. The American love affair with big gas-guzzling automobiles will likely be ended only by gasoline prices nearer the European level, not through voluntary choice.

Most effective conservation measures are also expensive to implement. Insulation costs money. Even more important, many of the wasteful features of American society are built into the very structure of American life. The absence of decent public transportation, buildings constructed on an assumption of cheap energy, high-energy appliances—all of these features of American life are expensive and difficult to change. To convert plants to the production of high-speed trains, to modify existing buildings and re-design appliances, to build cities with public transportation facilities, and so on will

294

in the short run cost more in energy than will be saved. Real conservation requires a heavy investment in conversion costs and quite possibly a funda-mental rearrangement of American life styles; these costs and changes will pay off only in the long run.

DEMOCRACY AND ENERGY PLANNING

Each of the two approaches to energy problems, increased production and reduced consumption, presents problems especially difficult to solve in democracies, where public demand plays so heavy a role in policies.

Production increases go less sharply against the grain of public demand since there is little evidence that the public will hold to environmental concerns, whether oriented toward pollution or hazards, when faced with sharp reductions in energy supplies. Both offshore oil drilling and the Alas-kan pipeline found easier acceptance after the 1973 Arab oil embargo. Even price increases may be somehow accommodated by income adjustments, though any substantial increase in energy costs to the consumer will severely harm those on fixed incomes (pensioners, for example). The real difficulty with the option of increased production is that it is a short-run solution. Eventually we will run out of fossil fuel, and we have no guarantee that atomic energy is a manageable long-range alternative.

The option of reduced consumption is more difficult to negotiate in democratic societies. If, as seems likely, voluntary conservation is not adequate, then some form of compulsory allocation and rationing becomes necessary. The mandatory rearrangement of basic life styles apt to be re-quired in such compulsory policies could produce major social disruptions. The disruptive possibility is especially strong if change comes more quickly than habit formed on years of excessive energy consumption can tolerate. Put bluntly, the American people may not readily accept the strong ad-justments that could be required to meet energy problems.

Compounding this reluctance may be the serious equity problems built into such social change. Explosive increases in profits to energy industries in the early years of the 1970s, coming exactly at the time of greatest price increases for fuel, created bitter public attitudes. Inequities of this sort, however, are intractable without strong control of the market, producers and consumers alike. Authoritative measures may therefore be required at all ends of the social spectrum, no problem for authoritarian systems but dif-ficult in democratic arrangements.

The long-range ability of democratic decision-rules to resolve energy problems may be even more severely tested if economies must operate on a zero-energy-growth model. A zero-energy-growth model (ZEG) anticipates a suspension of the production of energy sometime in the near future, say in the early 1980s, and then requires social arrangements to adust to the fixed supply (Ford Foundation, 1974). Though the timetable of ZEG is perhaps flexible, the earth is limited in its capacity to provide useful energy (even atomic energy must be balanced against the ecosphere's capacity to absorb radioactive waste). Thus, at some future point a ZEG model is likely. One important consequence of ZEG is that economic growth could no longer be assured. Service industries might grow, but the constant growth factor we have come to accept as a necessary part of the Gross National Product will be a thing of the past. Fixed points of reference, like stability and durability, will more closely fit the psychology of a ZEG society.

The issue is whether democratic arrangements can successfully moderate the forces for equality in a ZEG society. Increases in living standards have traditionally been provided in Western society by production growth. With a stationary, or near-stationary, economy, material life can improve only through redistributions of social resources, with direct losses to those in the upper and middle levels of society. Since the economic mobility that historically has eased the demand for equalization of income may itself be a casualty of the stationary economy, pressures for redistribution may become unbearable exactly as they are most painful to achieve. A greater concentration of coercive authority may be required to accommodate these fundamental changes, authority that democracy once more won't be able to supply (Heilbroner, 1974). In terms of the earlier observations made here, "system capacity" may have to be judged on efficiency and effectiveness (whether economic or political) in doing what is required rather than what the people prefer, on the basic grounds that survival itself is at issue.

It is at least as reasonable, however, to speculate on the decentralization of social power that energy problems may eventually bring. One of the more accommodating sights in recent history—at once nostalgic and hopeful—is the growing development of local energy sources: wind and sun, especially. The Sun-Belt states in America may come to rely on solar energy instead of fossil fuels or atomic power. General Electric is experimenting with windmills. In a test program sponsored by the Energy Research and Development Administration (ERDA) and the National Aeronautics and Space Administration (NASA), GE's Space Division built two structures twelve stories high with two-hundred-foot blades in Pennsylvania in 1977 to see if wind can produce cheap electricity. GE engineers have estimated that about 55,000 square miles in the United States have enough wind to make wind turbine generators feasible.

The ghost of Don Quixote, resurrected to sanity, may finally mark out the future of public policies in energy. Local sources of energy could fragment society into regional units, each autonomous and self-sufficient. Instead of an autocratic society with rational, centralized planning, the energy crisis may push us all back to those smaller and simpler social arrangements that traditional political philosophers have seen as the utopian end and logic of democratic decision-rules.

Anyway, as Jake says to Brett at the end of Hemingway's *The Sun Also Rises:* "Yes. Isn't it pretty to think so?"

ARE POLITICIANS AND POLITICS "SCURVY"?

At the beginning of our journey through the ideas and issues discussed in this book, it was suggested that various standards to judge "politicians" and "politics" would be identified as we traveled along. Certainly by now the reader is equipped to make such judgments, for we have surveyed not only rational but also moral principles in this study of public policy.

A few observations on ethics and politics are surely appropriate at this late stage. Let us describe these observations as reasons why politicians sometimes appear to be scurvy but really are not.

1. The nature of politics often works against the practical relevance of ethical principles. Some political transactions—for example, bargaining—require a compromise of principle; and while adjusting one's values to the wants and needs of others may appear reprehensible to the hidebound moralist, it is not only frequently good politics but essentially required in the use of decision-rules that *are* moral—like democratic ones.

2. Ethical norms sometimes conflict with one another in politics. It is morally good to consult with those affected by a decision (as Rousseau saw clearly). But conflicts of interest cover exactly those cases where interested parties are allowed to influence policy decisions. So we have a moral paradox: prior consultation is good, and prior consultation is bad. No wonder the poor politician seems scurvy. Another example: sunshine laws require open meetings of public officials, but private communications are highly valued as protection against hasty or unexamined judgments. The list could be extended. The point is mercifully brief, however: what is unethical in politics from one moral perspective is often, though *not* always, ethical from another.

3. The enforcement of moral values in politics sometimes (perhaps frequently) leads to results *contrary* to the values enforced. Thus, another paradox. The plight of President Carter's "human rights" appeals to the Soviet Union, where public support may have led to *less,* not more, respect for human rights in Russia, is a more general and dramatic example of a routine problem. Laws requiring crash helmets on motorcyclists may be enforcing an accepted moral value, protection of life. But the fact of enforcement robs the motorcyclists of that free choice even to do himself harm that John Stuart Mill developed as the effective basis for good government.

The problem that any society has in enforcing moral values is that social enforcement, whether through the law or through other more subtle instruments, is abrasive to the very nature of the stress in morality on voluntary choice of action by moral agents. A citizen compelled to be moral by his political system has lost the chance to be a moral agent freely choosing and carrying out moral ends (Hart, 1963). So moral enforcement may produce the paradox of nonmoral behavior. Of course, if the political system also lacks enforcement power, as is typically the case between sovereign states, then moral rhetoric might bring even the moral reverse of what is intended.

Purists longing for the fusion of ethics and politics of classical political philosophy will reject these closing comments. But at least a reasonable zone of pragmatism can be cut out between "scurvy" and "ethical," a zone we might *hope* that politicians choose to occupy if they find morality too strenuous an exercise.

SUMMARY

1.   *Democracy* is a term with many partisan meanings, but at its center is the idea of *popular sovereignty.*

2.   Several conditions are usually associated with popular sovereignty. The most important are (a) consensus on the "rules of the game" or a functional equivalent like "apathy"; (b) political equality, and its possible correlate of economic parity; (c) system capacity to respond effectively to citizen preferences; (d) the absence of peremptory values; and (e) dissemination of information.

3.   The events of Watergate presented challenges to democracy in controlling government repression and duplicity, but the court restrictions on "executive privilege" growing out of Watergate may have beneficial consequences for democracy. However, the "open government" sought by many may bring mixed blessings to its citizens.

4.   The issues in biomedical technology today, because of their high risk–high benefit status for the entire human race, may have to be decided on "blind" criteria equally acceptable with democratic and non-democratic decision-rules.

5.   Energy problems, however, may actually favor authoritarian decision-rules in the long run. The eventual change to a stationary economy may, in particular, require an authoritarian system unresponsive to popular demand.

6.   The other alternative in long-range energy policies is the possibility of local political units with decentralized power, oriented toward local power sources.

7.   Politicians don't have to choose between being "scurvy" *or* "ethical"; they can be pragmatic instead.

FOR FURTHER READING

DEMOCRACY

BACHRACH, PETER, *The Theory of Democratic Elitism: A Critique*. Boston: Little, Brown, 1967.

BARRY, BRIAN, "Review Article: *Size and Democracy*," *Government and Opposition*, Vol. 9, No. 4 (Fall 1974).

DAHL, ROBERT, *A Preface to Democratic Theory*. Chicago: University of Chicago Press, 1956.

———, *Who Governs*. New Haven, Conn.: Yale University Press, 1961.

———, *After the Revolution*. New Haven, Conn.: Yale University Press, 1970.

———, *Polyarchy*. New Haven, Conn.: Yale University Press, 1973.

———, *Size and Democracy*. Stanford, Calif.: Stanford University Press, 1974.

DAHL, ROBERT, AND EDWARD R. TUFTE, "Further Reflections on 'The Elitist Theory of Democracy,'" *American Political Science Review* 60 (June 1966).

DYE, THOMAS, AND HARMON ZIEGLER, *The Irony of Democracy*. Belmont, Calif.: Wadsworth, 1970.

GALBRAITH, JOHN KENNETH, *The New Industrial State*. Boston: Houghton Mifflin, 1967.

HACKER, ANDREW, *The End of the American Era*. New York: Atheneum, 1970.

HOLDEN, BARRY, *The Nature of Democracy*. New York: Harper & Row, 1974.

MACPHERSON, C. B., *Democratic Theory: Essays in Retrieval*. Oxford: Oxford University Press, 1973.

———, *The Real World of Democracy*. Oxford: Oxford University Press, 1972.

MAYO, HENRY, *An Introduction to Democratic Theory*. New York: Oxford University Press, 1960.

MCCLOSKY, HERBERT, PAUL J. HOFFMAN, AND ROSEMARY O'HARA, "Consensus and Ideology in American Politics," *American Political Science Review* 54 (June 1964).

MILLS, C. WRIGHT, *The Power Elite*. New York: Oxford University Press, 1956.

PARENTI, MICHAEL, *Democracy for the Few*. New York: St. Martin's, 1974.

POPPER, KARL, *The Logic of Scientific Discovery*. New York: Harper & Row, 1959.

PROTHRO, J. W., AND C. M. GRIGG, "Fundamental Principles of Democracy: Bases of Agreement and Disagreement," *Journal of Politics*, Vol. 22 (1960), pp. 276–294, reprinted in *Empirical Democratic Theory*, eds. C. F. Cnudde and D. E. Neubauer. Chicago: Markham, 1969.

SMITH, JAMES WARD, *Theme for Reason*. Princeton, N.J.: Princeton University Press, 1957.

STOUFFER, SAMUEL, *Communism, Conformity, and Civil Liberties*. New York: Doubleday, 1955.

THORSON, THOMAS, *The Logic of Democracy*. New York: Holt, Rinehart, & Winston, 1962.

WALKER, JACK, "A Critique of the Elitist Theory of Democracy," *American Political Science Review* 60 (June 1966).

———, "A Reply to 'Further Reflections on the Elitist Theory of Democracy,'" *American Political Science Review* 60 (June 1966).

WATERGATE AND "EXECUTIVE PRIVILEGE"

BARTON, ANSLEY B., "Comments: United States v. Nixon and the Freedom of Information Act: New Impetus for Agency Disclosure?" *Emory Law Journal* 24 (1975).

BRECKENRIDGE, ADAM CARLYE, *The Executive Privilege*. Lincoln, Neb.: University of Nebraska Press, 1974.
BERGER, RAOUL, *Executive Privilege: A Constitutional Myth*. Cambridge, Mass.: Harvard University Press, 1974.
THE WASHINGTON POST, *The Presidential Transcripts*. New York: Dell, 1974.
WESTIN, ALAN, AND LEON FRIEDMAN, EDS., *United States v. Nixon*. New York: Chelsea House Publishers, in association with R. R. Bowker, 1974.
WOODWARD, BOB, AND CARL BERNSTEIN, *All the President's Men*. New York: Simon & Schuster, 1974.
———, *The Final Days*. New York: Avon Books, 1977.

GENETIC RESEARCH

CAVALIERI, LIEBE F., "New Strains of Life—or Death," *New York Times Magazine*, Aug. 22, 1976.
GOLDING, MARTIN, "Ethical Issues in Biological Engineering, " *University of California Law Review* 15 (1968).
KASS, LEON, "The New Biology: What Price Relieving Man's Estate?" *Science*, November 1971.
MAZUR, ALLAN, "Disputes Between Experts," *Minerva*, April 1973.

ENERGY

BELL, DANIEL, *The Coming of the Post Industrial Society*. New York: Basic Books, 1973.
FORD FOUNDATION, *Exploring Energy Choices*. 1974.
HEILBRONER, ROBERT, *An Inquiry into the Human Prospect*. New York: Norton, 1974.
INSTITUTE FOR CONTEMPORARY STUDIES, *No Time to Confuse*. San Francisco, Calif., 1975. (A collection of essays critical of the Ford Foundation Report, *Exploring Energy Choices*.)
MEADOWS, D. L., WILLIAM W. BEHRENS, III, DONELLA H. MEADOWS, ROGER F. NAILL, JORGEN RANDERS, AND ERICH K. O. ZAHN, *The Limits to Growth*. New York: Universe Books, 1972.
TELLER, EDWARD, HANS MARK, AND JOHN S. FOSTER, JR., *Power and Security*. Lexington, Mass.: D. C. Heath, 1976.
WILLRICH, MASON, AND THEODORE TAYLOR, *Nuclear Theft: Risks and Safeguards*. Cambridge, Mass.: Ballinger, 1974.

LAW AND MORALITY

DEVLIN, PATRICK, *The Enforcement of Morals*. Oxford: Oxford University Press, 1965.
FINEBERG, JOEL, "Moral Enforcement and the Harm Principle," in *Social Philosophy*. Englewood Cliffs, N.J.: Prentice-Hall, 1973.
HART, H. L. A., *Law, Liberty, and Morality*. New York: Vintage Books, 1963.
NAGEL, ERNEST, "The Enforcement of Morals," *The Humanist* 28, No. 3 (May/June 1968).

fourteenth amendment to the constitution

appendix A

SECTION 1

All persons born or naturalized in the United States, and subject to the jurisdiction thereof, are citizens of the United States and of the State wherein they reside. No state shall make or enforce any law which shall abridge the privileges or immunities of citizens of the United States; nor shall any State deprive any person of life, liberty, or property, without due process of law; nor deny to any person within its jurisdiction the equal protection of the laws.

PLESSY v. *FERGUSON* 163 U.S. 537 (1896)

OPINION

We consider the underlying fallacy of the plaintiff's argument to consist in the assumption that the enforced separation of the two races stamps the colored race with a badge of inferiority. If this be so, it is not by anything found in the act, but solely because the colored race chooses to put that construction upon it. . . . If the civil and political rights of both races be equal one cannot be inferior to the other civilly or politically. If one race be inferior to the other socially, the Constitution of the United States cannot put them on the same plane.

OPENING COMMENT OF JUSTICE BROWN

The object of the [Fourteenth] amendment was undoubtedly to enforce the absolute equality of the two races before the law, but in the nature of things before the law, it could not have been intended to abolish distinctions based upon color, or to enforce social, as distinguished from political equality, or a commingling of the two races upon terms unsatisfactory to either. Laws permitting, even requiring, their separation in places where they are liable to be brought into contact do not necessarily imply the inferiority of either race to the other, and have generally, if not universally, recognized as within the competency of the state legislatures in the exercise of their police power.

HARLAN DISSENT

The white race deems itself to be the dominant race in this country. And so it is, in prestige, in achievements, in education, in wealth and in power. So, I doubt not it will continue to be for all time, if it remains true to its great heritage and holds fast to the principles of constitutional liberty. But in view of the Constitution, in the eye of the law, there is in this country, no superior, dominant, ruling class of citizens.

KOREMATSU v. UNITED STATES 323 U.S. 214 (1944) [Japanese Internment World War II Case]

It should be noted, to begin with, that all legal restrictions which curtail the civil rights of any single racial group are immediately suspect. That is not to say that all such restrictions are unconstitutional. It is to say that courts must subject them to the most rigid scrutiny. Pressing public necessity may sometimes justify the existence of such restrictions. Racial antagonism never can. But here the requisite "pressing public necessity" was found.

JUSTICE BLACK (CONCURRING)

Compulsory exclusion of large groups of citizens from their homes, except under circumstances of direct emergency and peril, is inconsistent with our basic governmental institutions. But when under conditions of modern warfare our shores are threatened by hostile forces, the power to protect must be commensurate with the threatened danger. [Korematsu's case is unique] because we are at war with the Japanese Empire, because the properly constituted military authorities feared an invasion of our West Coast and felt constrained to take proper security measures, because they decided that the military urgency of the situation demanded that all citizens of Japanese ancestry be segregated from the West Coast temporarily, and finally, because Congress, reposing its confidence in this time of war in our military leaders—as inevitably it must—determined that they should have the power to do just this. There was evidence of disloyalty on the part of some, the military authorities considered that the need for action was great and time was short. We cannot—by availing ourselves of the calm perspective of hindsight—now say that at that time these actions were unjustified.

BROWN v. BOARD OF EDUCATION 347 U.S. 483 (1954)

Does segregation of children in public schools solely on the basis of race, even though the physical facilities and other "tangible" factors may be equal, deprive the children of the minority group of educational opportunities? We believe it does.... We conclude that in the field of public education the doctrine of "separate but equal" has no place. Separate educational facilities are inherently unequal. Therefore, we hold that the plaintiffs and others similarly situated for whom the actions have been brought are, by reason of the segregation complained of, deprived of the equal protection of the laws guaranteed in the Fourteenth Amendment.

an overview of prominent black organizations

appendix B

An acquaintance with the principal black organizations in American politics may help provide substantive content to the points on interest group theory outlined in Chapter 3.

THE NATIONAL ASSOCIATION FOR THE ADVANCEMENT OF COLORED PEOPLE

The NAACP was founded in 1909. Since its origin it has attacked the legal aspects of segregation, primarily using the Fourteenth and Fifteenth Amendments to bring about integration in various parts of American society. The early history of the organization was influenced by W. E. B. DuBois, one of its founders. DuBois, in contrast to his rival, Booker T. Washington, was a militant of the times. Washington, operating from Tuskegee Institute, argued that blacks required a separate and special kind of education, "vocational" in type. DuBois, on the other hand, called for "color-blind" educational arrangements, where talent and not race determined entrance and outcomes. Washington was a realist, a moderate, a popular figure with the white establishment. DuBois, and the then incipient NAACP, were considered "radical" in their insistence on equal legal treatment for all races.

Beginning primarily in the 1940s, the NAACP scored an impressive series of court victories at the federal level against segregation. The case of *Smith* v. *Alwright* (1944), where the white primary election was declared unconstitutional, and *Brown* v. *Board of Education* (1954), which outlawed segregation in public schools, are two examples of these efforts. After 1944, the NAACP worked with voters leagues to register black voters, concentrating on the South. Some initial successes were achieved. In the southeastern states, for example, registration among blacks was increased from 223,000 in 1940 to about 1,100,000 in 1952. During this period, the NAACP also worked for fair employment and fair housing acts in the North and for integrated public recreational facilities in the upper South.

Another tactic successfully used by the NAACP has been political pressure on both the Chief Executive and Congress. President Truman's executive order to integrate military facilities was influenced by the NAACP. The denial of confirming votes in the Senate to individuals nominated by the president for the Supreme Court is a dramatic example of such pressure. For example, the NAACP was instrumental in securing a negative vote in the Senate against John Parker, nominated by President Hoover for the Supreme Court. The NAACP judged Parker racist in his views and successfully lobbied to keep him off the highest Court. More recently, the NAACP successfully fought against the confirmation of two judges nominated by President Nixon, Clement Haynsworth and G. Harold Carswell. In each of these cases, the NAACP operated as a pressure group on the U.S. Senate.

There is little question that the NAACP is the most tightly organized of black groups today. It has a well-developed bureaucracy and a complicated procedure for internal elections. As one might expect, one result of this tight organization is that new members are slow to attain positions of leadership. The NAACP has also always had a fixed constituency for integration (Rudwick/Meier, 1970). As a result, the NAACP resisted the strong pressures for change in black organizations that occurred in the 1960s, change that in some cases required the rejection of racial integration as a social goal. The NAACP is today generally considered to be among the more conservative of black organizations, in part because of its resistance to the mass movements of recent history. Valid or not, the judgment of conservative versus radical is obviously a matter of historical context. Legal challenges, tactics considered radical in the early part of this century, are now viewed as conservative, at least in part in contrast to recent mass demonstrations and riots. The NAACP has not *become* conservative; it has simply maintained the same tactics in the face of radical changes in the black movement.

THE URBAN LEAGUE

The most amiable and nonradical black organization historically has been the Urban League. It was founded in 1916 by a combination of philanthropists, social workers, and professional leaders. Its early and enduring concern has been twofold: to smooth over the abrasive points of race relations and to seek jobs for black workers. The overriding emphasis of the early

Urban League was "goodwill" between the races. It was an organization frequently used by whites to restore race relations during periods of racial unrest—for example, in the riots of 1919. More recently, the Urban League has become more militant, though it has consistently maintained the goal of racial harmony in American society through peaceful accommodation.

THE CONGRESS OF RACIAL EQUALITY

CORE was established in 1942. In its beginnings it was composed primarily of whites, a distribution maintained even to 1950. Since 1968 it has limited its membership to blacks. CORE was a product of the Depression, originating in a Quaker organization, the Fellowship of Reconciliation. From its inception, and even earlier in the Fellowship, CORE's tactics for social change emphasized the sit-in, a combination of Ghandi's *satyagraha* (nonviolent passive resistance) with the sit-*down* tactics employed in 1940 by the Detroit autoworkers. CORE was an informally organized group in its beginnings, subsisting on donations of both money and work. (It did not have a paid field worker until 1950.) Its early efforts were directed at integrating public accommodations, though since about 1963 its efforts have included attempts to alleviate black unemployment.

The history of CORE, perhaps more than that of any other black group, represents in microcosm the changes that the black movement has undergone in this century. In its first period, CORE engaged in numerous small-scale actions against segregation, including some early attempts (1946) to integrate public transportation. In the second period, from about 1961 to 1964, it engaged in the mass civil rights demonstrations. CORE was in the forefront of the Freedom Riders of 1961, aimed at breaking the racial barriers in public transportation in the South. The third period, from 1964 to the present, has been a time of black separatism for CORE. The organization adopted the slogan of "black power," by which they meant electioneering in, and organization of, the black community.

Unlike the NAACP, CORE has always been relatively decentralized. Any organization has oligarchic tendencies, but CORE has retained a simple organizational structure, a direct annual election of membership to its National Action Council, and an antibureaucratic ethos. Such decentralization naturally allows fluid changes in elites and ideology. Such change did occur in the 1960s, when both the membership and its leaders rapidly turned over in response to a change in CORE's constituency. From a pro-integration elite-formulated group, CORE became a uniformly black separatist organization. In many ways, CORE is the seismograph of social change, while the NAACP is not (Rudwick/Meier, 1970).

SOUTHERN CHRISTIAN LEADERSHIP CONFERENCE

The SCLC was a direct outgrowth of the Montgomery bus boycott of 1955–56. Like so many subsequent events to follow in the 1960s, the events leading to the Montgomery bus boycott began with a simple and spontaneous gesture: a black woman, Rosa Marie Parks, refused to move to the back of a Montgomery, Alabama, city bus. The incident triggered mass protest of segregated public transportation. The then-unknown Baptist minister, Martin Luther King, organized the boycott of Birmingham buses and founded the SCLC. The qualified success of the boycott and the charismatic personality of King launched the SCLC as a vital force in future civil rights activity.

The dominant tactic employed by SCLC has been "nonviolence." Martin Luther King's philosophy embraced the strategy that Ghandi adopted against the British in India: mass resistance to the law without employing overt violence. The tactic of nonviolence has not been without its critics, both in and out of the black movement. Floyd McKissick, while head of CORE in 1966, declared that "you can't have white people who practice violence and expect black people to remain passive." But King did expect that and continued to endorse nonviolence up to the time of his assassination by a sniper's bullet in 1968.

The tragic irony of King's death was of course paralleled by Ghandi's earlier and equally violent assassination. One might well feel compelled to ask, is "nonviolence" a prelude to fatal results? Any assessment of nonviolent tactics for social change must understand that certain conditions are required for its success. It is generally acknowledged now that nonviolence is more successfully used against direct tyranny than subtle oppression. It also helps if the oppressed people are the majority. Both these conditions were present in India, where Ghandi's movement was successful in liberating India from British rule. Only the first condition, direct oppression, was present in the South when the SCLC first began its movement. Even so, King was moderately successful.

The tactics of nonviolence seem to depend heavily on (a) the presence of a moral conscience among society's members, (b) the effectiveness of this moral conscience in restraining or bringing about action, and (c) the possibility of direct confrontation with the symbols of oppression. The importance of these general conditions is graphically illustrated in the success of black efforts in places like Selma, Alabama; Jackson, Mississippi; and Birmingham, Alabama. The first, abortive, march to Selma ended with state troopers attacking the marchers, the slaying of Medgar Evars, and the use of police dogs by Police Commissioner Eugene "Bull" Conner—these acts of violence and others, either initiated by the authorities or unchecked by them, were televised worldwide. The public outrage mobilized such outside authorities as the U.S. Attorney General's Office to intervene.

The tactics of nonviolence were not as successful where direct confron-
tation could not be arranged, or where outrage was not so readily available.
Such was the case, for example, with King's efforts in Chicago in 1966. The
SCLC Fair Housing Drive had unclear results, largely because racism in
Chicago was more tacit and therefore less tractable to mass action.

STUDENT NONVIOLENT COORDINATING COMMITTEE

The Student Nonviolent Coordinating Committee was organized at
Shaw University in 1960 under Martin Luther King's auspices. Like many
other black organizations of the 1960s, SNCC was a result of a spontaneous
action. Several college students decided to demand service at an all-white
cafeteria in a department store. When refused service, they continued to
"sit-in," thus effectively disrupting operations and immediately popularizing
what would later be one of the favorite tactics of civil rights groups in the
early 1960s. The visibility of SNCC in black politics was like a flare, brilliant
and brief. Stokeley Carmichael, its first leader, was by all accounts a charismatic figure. He coined the phrase "black power" and frequently opposed
Martin Luther King on the tactics and goals of the black movement. He was
succeeded as head of SNCC by N. "Rap" Brown, an even more militant
black leader who was soon forced underground to escape legal prosecution
by American authorities. SNCC lost prominence with the growing legal
difficulties of its leaders.

BLACK MUSLIMS

At the far extreme from traditional integrationist organizations like the
NAACP are the Black Muslims. The Muslims originated in a combination of
economic despair and hope: the high unemployment of blacks coupled with
the religious and revolutionary expectation of the Muslim movement. Unlike
most black organizations, the Muslims demand a total commitment from its
members for personal reform. Muslims are expected to forego eating pork,
use of alcohol and tobacco, and engaging in extramarital sex. A rigorous code
also regiments dress, cooking, and other details of one's personal life (Howard, 1966; Malcolm X, 1966). The difference in social goals between civil
rights groups and Muslims is also one of often stark contrast: while civil
rights groups pursue racial integration, the Muslims espouse black
separatism.

Some forms of black separatism have infused a wide segment of otherwise traditional civil rights organizations. CORE excludes whites from its

membership. SNCC has stressed power for blacks as a distinct group. More-over, the Black Muslims are like traditional civil rights organizations in other important respects today. All black organizations currently reject any impli-cation of black inferiority and white supremacy. All have been influenced by the emergence of the new African states, though they differ in their degree of identification with African units. Most black groups in America today also are more or less dissatisfied with *otherworldly* Christianity. (Even the SCLC doesn't counsel the rejection of social change in favor of rewards in the afterlife.) Finally, almost all black groups have rejected the older doctrines of *gradualism* in favor of immediate implementation of black goals. On all of these issues the black movement's stand is similar, from the traditional civil rights organizations to the Black Muslims.

The Muslims, however, are unlike many black organizations in impor-tant respects. It is helpful to distinguish between (1) black separatism as a concept and device to gain control over the black movement with the aim of increasing black autonomy and dignity, and (2) black separatism as an end in itself. Most of the black movement, with a legacy in both the older civil rights struggles and the black power strategies of the 1960s, embraces the first type of black separatism.

In the 1960s, for example, even black leaders who criticized the idea of black power could find some measure of the concept consistent with their own ends. Stokeley Carmichael inconsistently saw black power as (some-times) merely political and economic power for blacks and (at other times) war against whites. But, while Roy Wilkins of the NAACP viewed the idea as fanaticism, both Floyd McKissick and Adam Clayton Powell interpreted black power as simply standing for the self-determination of blacks in gen-eral. Even Martin Luther King, squarely in the tradition of civil rights, defined black power as the "development of a situation in which the gov-ernment finds it useful and prudent to collaborate with us" (Franklin, 1969). The point is this: the separatist ideas represented by such phrases as black power could be accepted by the main body of the black movement as in-strumental to the rearrangement of power relations in American society in a way more favorable to blacks.

The separatism of the Black Muslims, on the other hand, seems gener-ally indifferent to power relationships. It is a separatism that appears authen-tic *in itself,* with intrinsic merit to Muslims. The Nation of Islam clearly regards whites as devils, a regard buttressed by an elaborate philosophy of history and metaphysics. It would seem, then, that Muslim separatism is vital to the very identity of its black membership, and is not intended as an instrument for rendering change in American society. On this point, the Black Muslims are significantly different from other black organizations in the movement.

the voting paradoxes

appendix C

ARROW'S GENERAL POSSIBILITY THEOREM

In the most developed version of the voting paradoxes, Kenneth Arrow has advanced a general theory that attempts to prove that, under certain reasonable conditions, it is impossible to aggregate individual preferences into a state of collective preference that meets the transitivity requirement. The conditions are these:

UNIVERSAL DOMAIN

For any given set of orderings, the social choice function can be derived from an ordering. This condition means, generally, that individuals can and do order their preferences, and that the social outcome (or choice) is in some way produced from the choices of individuals. If we are trying to decide whether, for example, to have local or national systems of financial aid to education, the choice will be governed by some rule that maps from the preferences of individuals in the society. Stated more precisely, this first condition states that for each profile (a combination of preference orderings from each individual) over a set of alternatives, a social welfare rule gives a weak order, or map, into the set. Not all possible individual orderings are generated by the social welfare rule, but all possible profiles constitute the domain of the social welfare rule.

NONDICTATORSHIP

There is no individual whose preferences are automatically society's preferences independent of the preferences of all other individuals. This condition rules out the imposition of a single ordering of preferences on the entire society if only one individual supports the preferential ordering. If, for example, everyone supports federal aid to education except for one person, who supports local financing of education, it is impossible for the social outcome to be local financing of education. Ruled out with this condition are all forms of dictatorship as a means of arriving at social outcomes, including older ideas of monarchy.

THE PARETO PRINCIPLE

If alternative A is preferred to alternative B by every single individual according to his ordering, then the social ordering also ranks A above B. We not only expect the absence of both external imposition (first condition) and internal imposition (second condition), but we also expect the unanimous expression of individual preferences to be transformed directly into social outcomes. Not included in Arrow's conditions, it is worth noticing, are any inverse transformations and faulty social reflections of individual preferences. For example, a "hung jury," where the social, or group, outcome is inversely derived from the positive (though divided) preferences of jury members, is not a recognized social outcome in Arrow's theory.

THE INDEPENDENCE OF IRRELEVANT ALTERNATIVES

The social choice made for any environment depends only on the individuals' orderings of alternatives in that environment. This is quite possibly the most controversial of Arrow's conditions. It requires that rankings between pairs of alternatives not be affected by attitudes toward additional alternatives. If I prefer A to B, then my attitude toward C cannot (under this condition) alter the $A > B$ (read: A is preferred to B) relationship in any set of pair-wise comparisons. Put in simple, individual terms, I cannot prefer steak over chicken and then, when the waiter announces that fish is also available, say, "In that case, since I love fish, bring me the chicken." More precisely, and in terms of social choice, for any two profiles which agree on any pair of alternatives (A, B), and for any social welfare function, F, no matter how the profiles differ with respect to other pairs than (A, B), the social preference orderings will rank A and B in the same way relative to each other.

If, for example, state support of education is preferred to a system of private schools, then the presence of a third alternative, say a federal system of education, cannot, under Arrow's condition of the "independence of ir-relevant alternatives," alter the ranking of state-private schooling, though a federal system may be ranked above, in-between, or below, the original ranking. For example, a society may prefer A > B (state > private schools). A third alternative, C (federal schools), is also a possibility. The society cannot re-rank B > A just because of attitudes toward C without appearing as irrational as the man suddenly preferring chicken on his love (or hate) of fish.

In addition to the four conditions given above, certain definitions and axioms play a vital role in the development of the theorem. First, *connectivity* is assumed. This means that all alternatives are comparable. One does not have what used to be called incommensurate items (as choosing between two children whom one loves equally). Second, *transitivity* is accepted as an indicator of rationality, even intelligibility. We will recall from Chapter 2 that transitivity is a logical relationship: if a R b and b R c, then a R c. In Arrow's theorem, the absence of transitivity is equivalent to nonrationality. Third, comparisons are made between *pairs* of alternatives. This means that among alternatives A, B, and C, each alternative can be compared to any one of the others (A–B, A–C, etc.), but the three may not be compared in a general ranking (A–B–C, etc.).

The third axiom, pair-wise comparisons, rests on the acceptance of what has been called the Condorcet criterion for winning. This criterion requires that the winning alternative score a simple majority over every other alternative in a series of head-to-head contests. Thus, if we have alternatives A, B, and C, and $A > B$, $A > C$ by 10 people, $B > A$, $B > C$ by 8 people, and $C > A$ and $C > B$ by 3 people, then A wins on the Condorcet criterion. This criterion is generally recognized (Riker/Ordeshook, 1973; Fishburn, 1974) as distinct from the other major criterion for winning, the Borda criterion.

In a Borda system, points are assigned to alternatives in terms of their preferential standing, and the alternative with the most points is declared the winner. For example, a system of 3 points for first place, 2 for second, 1 for third, with the largest sum determining the winner, is a Borda-criterion system. One of the fundamental assumptions in Arrow's theorem is that only Condorcet winners are authentic winners. "The independence of irrelevant alternatives" condition, as described above, requires Condorcet winners. So the Borda system is ruled out, a ruling the axiom of pair-wise comparisons directly expresses.

Arrow's theorem proves that no constitution, or system of social choice, simultaneously satisfies the four conditions of (1) Universal Domain, (2) Nondictatorship, (3) the Pareto Principle, and (4) the Independence of Irrelevant Alternatives, while maintaining the three axioms (or definitions) of (1) connectivity, (2) transitivity, and (3) pair-wise comparisons. More specifically: every method of aggregating the preferences of individuals that satisfies the four conditions will violate one or more of the axioms. Even more specifically: any genuine expression of individual preferences that is consistent with the three axioms will violate the condition of nondictatorship. More generally: the acceptance of Arrow's four conditions and three axioms makes it impossible to move successfully from individual preferences to a social state that is not paradoxical (in terms of the transitivity requirement).

The theorem that Arrow has developed is obviously important for a variety of disciplines, including the study of public policy. In terms of the discussion here, it indicates the paradoxical nature of linking individuals to aggregates under certain conditions. To assess its more general importance, we will want to know (1) how frequently the paradoxes of voting can be expected to occur (discussed in Chapter 4), and (2) the reasonableness of the conditions and axioms required in the theorem.

THE CONDITIONS OF VOTING PARADOXES

The formal conditions required in order to develop a general theorem for the voting paradoxes, conditions outlined here as part of Arrow's general theorem, put into relief the significance of the problem for political theory. Obviously a number of political arrangements, primarily those imposing social outcomes on individual preferences, are immune from these particular types of paradoxes. Let us call such arrangements "imposition-systems," since they are characterized by the denial of preferences in social policy on one ground or another. Some imposition-systems, those which are authentic dictatorships or generally authoritarian, are (one would think) eminently undesirable on their own terms. It would take a rare character to prefer a dictatorship to a preferential system just because the latter encountered paradoxes from time to time. So we can dismiss certain imposition-systems on other grounds, and accept Arrow's theorem as setting out fair or equitable conditions when compared to at least some alternative social arrangements.

But it is not at all clear that Arrow's conditions *exhaust* desirable social arrangements. We might come up with arrangements that do not quite fit the theorem's conditions and yet are not so bad, in fact may even be preferable in their own right. Let's start with the simple distinction between a *want* and an *interest*. It is clear that a person can prefer that which is not in his interests, or—in more general terms—which is undesirable on any of a number of grounds (including his own reflections from a more knowledgeable point of view). If a distinction can be introduced between preferences and interests at the individual level, there is no reason to suppose that it cannot be also maintained at the aggregate level. We may say that the best, or most desirable, or even most preferable, social outcome is one that accords not with the aggregated preferences of individuals, but one that meets the requirements of some imposed standard.

We need not turn to the lofty principles of natural law to bring such standards into focus. Procedural norms qualify, including the very rules used to express preferences. Even the most democratic system will typically not allow its basic decision-rules to be overturned on preference alone. Either some "balancing" unit, such as the court system, is required to pass on such rules, or a limiting procedure is adopted, like a two-thirds vote of all of some class of units (for example, two-thirds of the states must ratify constitutional amendments in the United States), or some other system that restricts preferences is used. All such methods can be considered as at least procedural impositions.

Substantive impositions are also common in developed democracies. A measure can be supported not because it is preferred by a majority of the citizens, but because it increases social welfare. The military draft, any increase in taxes, special allocations for the poor (or the rich)—any social system is filled with policies that would have a hard time generating majority support but are justifiable nonetheless because they directly or indirectly increase the general welfare.

Policy outcomes, and the institutions that produce them, are rational or warranted not *merely* because they are products of aggregated preferences, but also because they are worthwhile impositions on individual preferences. Among these worthwhile impositions might be a wide range of policies accepted because they are the outcomes of a fair and previously endorsed decision-rule (see the discussion in Chapter 4 of the moral paradox in voting). That some types of imposition-systems on procedural or general-welfare criteria are acceptable means that the conditions of Arrow's theorem do not have a monopoly on all justifiable political arrangements for making policy.

The warrantability of some types of imposition-systems restricts Arrow's theorem to certain types of fairness, or equity, or legitimacy: it does not extend to all acceptable political forms. Internal limitations of the theorem's conditions cut even deeper into the significance of the paradoxes for politics in general. Let us focus on the fourth condition, "the independence of irrelevant alternatives." This condition, it will be recalled, requires that the alternatives of preference be confined to the environment of the individual ordering his preferences. Several criticisms can be made of this condition.

1. It is possible to interpret this condition in two ways. First, alternatives are irrelevant if they are unavailable. Second, the introduction or deletion of any alternative is not to have an effect on the orderings of the other alternatives. (Each of these interpretations stresses one of the two key words in the condition—the first *irrelevance*, the second *independence*.)

The first interpretation is designed to establish an environment (S) for preference orderings. Only those alternatives available, in the sense of physical possibility, are to count as S. Arrow offers the example of a list of candidates to be voted on in an election. One candidate dies after his name is placed on the list. Surely then, Arrow maintains, the dead candidate's name should be blotted out, for otherwise "would be to make the result of the election dependent on the obviously accidental circumstance of whether a candidate died before or after the date of polling" (Arrow, 1966, p. 26). In a later example (1969), Arrow rules out such considerations as instantaneous travel (of the Star Trek variety—reassembling molecules in different locations). Generally, this first interpretation of the fourth condition limits the expression of preferences to realistically feasible alternatives.

The second interpretation disallows the possibility that attitudes toward additional alternatives can affect pair-wise rankings. For example, if I prefer $A > B$ and $B > C$, then (on transitivity) $A > C$, my attitude toward any X is irrelevant to the $A > B > C$ ranking. I might rank X in any of the following ways: $X > A > B > X$, or $A > X > B > C$, or $A > B > X > C$, or $A > B > C > X$. What I cannot do on the "irrelevance" condition is allow change or stability in my preferences for X to produce a change in the rankings of $A > B > C$.

Difficulties can be found in both interpretations of the fourth condition. But the more interesting troubles lie in the second interpretation, in part because it plays a more vital role in the development of Arrow's theorem. Contrary to Arrow's assumption, it does seem possible that changes in attitudes toward additional alternatives can rationally justify changes in the rankings of other alternatives while maintaining the evaluative method of pair-wise comparisons.

Suppose the following. A voter ranks three candidates, $A > B > C$, on the moderation of their views. (Moderation, in this case, is translatable as non-aggressiveness on the use of government to express ideological doctrines.) All three candidates are conservative, but A is the most moderate, B and C not moderate at all. Our voter is politically "left" himself, and so understandably wants, among the alternatives available to him, the most moderate of the conservative candidates. Now a radical leftist, candidate D, unexpectedly enters the race. The voter of course now prefers D to all others, but he also prefers B and C to A. His preference ordering becomes $D > B > C > A$. Why? Because, he tells us, he does not want to risk the possibility of a D-A coalition government (if A does well in the election); and the possibility of a coalition is directly related to the moderation of the second-place candidate's views. No intensities produce the new ordering. The *reason* for the rankings has changed with the attitudes toward a new candidate, thus rationally justifying a rearrangement of preferences on pair-wise comparisons.

If the thought of a coalition government suggests a Borda method of ranking, then consider this example. Again, a voter ranks three candidates $A > B > C$, this time on the morality of their views (A is the most moral, then

B, then C). Standing on the sidelines is D, the moral *guru* of both our voter and candidate A. D's refusal to run for office is generally accepted as denoting his satisfaction with A. Suddenly D decides to enter the race. The message is clear to the followers: A must have done something terribly bad. *Because* D decides to run, and what his activation as a candidate communicates, our voter alters his preference ordering to $D > B > C > A$. Again, no intensities produce the alteration. The changed circumstances of the election, with new things to consider and new reasons for arranging the preferences, have justified a re-ordering of preferences.

Arrow's main use of "irrelevant alternatives" is designed to deny that rankings between pairs of alternatives can be affected by attitudes (fixed or changing) toward other alternatives while maintaining a Condorcet criterion of winning. These two examples suggest that such an alteration is rationally possible on pair-wise comparisons, without the introduction of intensities. One could of course go even further: alternatives not *in fact* open to a society (not part of its environment of preference) may be quite relevant to preferential ordering. Thoughts of what might have been, of utopias, dreams—an entire school of thought (as we have seen—Chapter 3)—maintains that hypothetical possibilities are vital to evaluating, and even listing, "true" preferences for social policies, thus presenting a challenge to the first interpretation of the fourth condition as a limitation of preferences to "realistic" alternatives. But the two rather commonplace examples used here indicate that the "independence of irrelevant alternatives" condition faces hard going even in realistic political settings.

2. The acceptance of the fourth condition also rules out a variety of political activities that are both warranted on their own and so commonly practiced that we distort the concept of politics if they are excluded. Consider a typical legislative maneuver variously labeled as "logrolling," or "bargaining" (Buchanan and Tullock, 1962). A group of Senators supports proposal A. Another group of Senators, smaller than the first, supports proposal B. If the group for B feels strongly enough about their proposal, and at least some members of the group supporting A are willing to compromise, then the group for B may offer a "deal": they will agree to vote for some other measure, C, which those supporting A feel more strongly about, *if* the A-supporters will abstain or change their votes on measure A. If successful, the senators have in effect traded votes on measures A and C. Such a move is disallowed by the independence of irrelevant alternatives condition for, on its most common interpretation, attitudes toward third, or additional, alternatives cannot alter the pair-wise rankings of proposals. But, of course, not only is vote-trading among the most common of political tactics, but it is also a device its users find eminently convenient.

The reason why logrolling is so convenient, even attractive, is that it reflects (however roughly) the varying *intensities* with which legislators view bills. It would make no sense to trade votes unless different groups supported different measures with uneven commitments. In the example the A-supporters feel more strongly about C than A, the B-supporters feel more strongly about B than C. But the introduction of intensities, while seen as reasonable and even basic by a number of political theorists (Dahl, 1956), is a rough form of Borda-criterion winning—one where alternatives are scaled as to high or low preference rating. Thus we have once more the possibility that winners on a Condorcet criterion (an axiomatic element in Arrow's theorem) will lose out on a scalar preference system. Logrolling, therefore, introduces the factor of intensities, which, while attractive and perhaps even necessary as a political ingredient, is contrary to the independence of irrelevant alternatives condition and its complement, the Condorcet criterion of winning.

This conflict between logrolling and the Condorcet criterion of winning reasonably turns our attention to the criterion itself. It is a criterion having to carry an enormous weight, for finally we can dismiss logrolling as a way to avoid the paradoxes of voting only by maintaining the Condorcet criterion of winning against all versions of the Borda criterion. The issue is simple and direct: (a) logrolling avoids the paradox by assuming intensity, but (b) intensity re-introduces the Borda criterion of winning, and (c) the Borda criterion provides for "irrelevant alternatives" in letting (under certain conditions) some preferences win in violation of the Condorcet criterion. The question is this: Why accept only the Condorcet criterion of winning? Here a basic issue in the general importance of Arrow's theorem is joined, but unlikely to be resolved. It is enough to suggest that the case for the Condorcet criterion is at the very least not conclusive.

Let's look at one final example of voting. This time let's shift the issue to environmental policy, a policy area discussed in the text. Again, let us consider three alternatives: first, nuclear plant construction unchecked by safety standards (A); second, no nuclear plant construction except with rigid safety standards (B); third, no nuclear plant construction except with moderate safety standards (C). The situation is this: in a series of pair-wise comparisons, A wins over B and C. But when an extraneous issue is introduced, let us say offshore oil exploration (Z), the supporters of A are willing to deal. (No issue for vote-trading can be completely extraneous, for at least—as in this case—the supporters of one of the primary three alternatives have an interest in the "extraneous" issue.) A-supporters happen to have a stronger preference for the bill permitting offshore drilling for oil. They trade support for A and Z so that C wins over A and B. The Condorcet winner, A, loses in the bargain.

Is such an outcome inequitable? It is easy to see why supporters of pair-wise voting think so: according to the Condorcet criterion a "loser" (C) ends up a "winner," and a "true" winner (A) eventually loses (Riker/ Ordeshook, 1973, p. 109). But we must realize that "winners" and "losers" are terms that make sense only with the adoption of one type of decision-rule or another. The acceptance of A as a "true" winner can only be bought by the purchase of the Condorcet criterion in the first place, which is precisely what is being placed at issue here. Let's look at other considerations. One way to judge the equitability of a decision-rule is in terms of its outcome, not simply because it might have led to a judicious result in a single example (though long-run results are important) or even necessarily because any kind of substantive outcomes occur. We might simply ask: Do the outcomes reflect the preferences of those who use the rule?

It is difficult to see why the Borda criterion is not as suitable in this regard as the Condorcet criterion. Intensity is surely as important in reflecting preferences as pair-wise comparisons; allowing a second-place alternative to win in order to insure the passage of a more important bill (as in logrolling) seems the very essence of maximizing preferences. Such action is at the heart of politics, leading (as we saw in Chapter 4 in the discussion of the moral paradox of voting) to that longitudinal maintenance of decision-rules even when outcomes are undesirable in the short-run.

The bottom-line opposition to "intensity" is that it leads to that ultimate quagmire, interpersonal comparisons of value. If I prefer wine to beer to water with dinner ($X > Y > Z$), and you prefer beer to wine to water ($Y > X > Z$), we may be able to resolve our impasse with an intensity scale: I may *love* wine and *hate* beer or water as distant prospects, while you may love *both* beer and wine as a close contest with water a distant third. In such case wine is the most palatable drink for us both. But the notorious problem with such resolutions is that we have no cardinal scale to compare loves and hates between people. Not only can we not get inside anyone's skin, but the measure of intensity may be unique for each person, not interpersonally comparable.

The answer to this objection is sweet reason itself: logrolling is the perfect *political* instrument to measure intensity because it involves each individual calculating what he is willing to trade for what. If we work with a strong preferential system, then interpersonal comparisons of value can work out to the actual values each person is willing to attach to alternatives as he trades preferences with others. In short: the problem of comparing values interpersonally may be solved pragmatically by the very method the problem seeks to dismiss—vote-trading.

These remarks, while not decisive for the Borda criterion against the Condorcet criterion, should indicate that the case is at least a bit mixed, and that the mixture makes the Arrow paradox less formidable as a barrier between individual preferences and social outcomes.

THE APPEAL OF ISOLATED ORDERINGS IN POLICY

Finally, transitivity itself may not be strictly required in public policy. Imagine for a moment that A, B, and C are groups, or units of people, who order their preferences in terms of different interests. Let us also say (in a variation on an earlier example) that x, y, and z are the following policy proposals: x is federal aid to secular education; y is local aid to secular education; and z is federal aid to parochial schools. Now if A is the National Council of Churches, the $x>y$, $y>z$ preference set may be rational; if B is a bloc of Southern Congressmen in the 1950s when integrated schools was still a volatile issue in the South, and racial integration is required in all social units subsidized by the federal goverment, the $y>z$ and $z>x$ may be rational from their perspective; and if C is the Catholic Church, then $z>x$ and $x>y$ may also be rational (if local aid permits racial segregation on a regional basis).

What do we have with these preference orderings? Obviously we have different considerations for a rational ordering ranged along a social structure of the society. The heterogeneous arrangement of the aggregate may nullify the condition of "connectivity": the preference sets may not be exactly comparable because in each case the supporting interests that make the separate orderings rational are, or can be, exclusive for each of the three groups. The social conditions in this example are roughly analogous to an individual who prefers water to wine, wine to cognac, thus water to cognac, on a hot summer day, but then cognac to wine, wine to water, thus cognac to water, on a cold winter day. In both cases, the individual is drinking to slake his thirst, but the context of his preferences—after playing tennis under a hot sun versus after walking in the snow—makes a different ordering rational in each of the two conditions.

If we "sum" or aggregate the separate preference orderings in these examples, then an intransitive ordering occurs. But the point to notice is that the separate conditions in which the preferences are expressed make an aggregation of the separate preference orderings to a single unified ordering unintelligible. To ask our vigorous and hence thirsty individual if he prefers water to cognac, or cognac to water, is to risk the obvious answer: *yes* and *no* on each comparison, depending on the situation. The voting paradoxes *are* paradoxical only by ignoring the differential arrangements of action that may provide the supporting reasons justifying each preference ordering. It is an important feature of voting that, in the language used in the text here, a numerical aggregate (each person voting as a discrete unit) is transformed into a mass aggregate (the electorate as a unitary agent expressing an outcome or "decision"). But it should not be surprising if transitivity cannot be maintained in a unitary preference set initially expressed as separate sets in

319

varying circumstances, anymore than we would be struck by the incoherence of trying to put together an individual's preferences expressed in widely differing circumstances.

A closer look at public policy, however, suggests that transitivity need not be a requirement in all types of aggregate rationality. The rationality of policy may be supervenient on reasons of interest as well as logic: the coherence of the proposals may be a variable of their acceptability for the affected parties as much as their logical consistency in a single ordering. The 1965 Elementary and Secondary Education Act comes close to representing such an outcome. Groups A and C were given enough of a trade-off between x and z to enlist lukewarm support for the bill, while group B was finessed by the earlier passage of the 1964 Civil Rights Act. The separate orderings were not amalgamated to provide a single, unitary ordering. Pieces of each of two alternatives (x, z) were spliced together, while the second (y) was cancelled out by shifting the rational considerations supporting its preferential status. A "bargained" outcome was the result, perfectly coherent though not amenable to a transitive ordering of component parts.

Is "coherence" itself rational in the absence of transitivity? An individual may maintain the rationality of preferences grouped without a transitive ordering so long as the circumstances of his preferences warrant different orderings when separately considered (for example, hot sun conditions versus snow conditions). Our drinking individual may even happily operate with a more general rule which says, "Drink cognac in winter, water in summer." Such general rules prescribe different actions in different conditions while resisting a single ordering of actions.

A social, or aggregate, directive is similarly rational so long as the heterogeneity of social arrangements provides local systems of ordering, even if these orderings cannot be combined into a single transitive ordering. Policies can respect such heterogeneity by reflecting it: loose arrangements of items in parcels satisfactory to the affected parties. A coherent policy, as we are constantly reminded by champions of piecemeal engineering and disjointed incrementalism, may be a joining of measures compatible only on the single feature of consensus itself. To consensus we can add the general rules that provide direction variable to local conditions. The absence of a single intelligible ordering, an absence occasioned by the separateness of social arrangements (the lack of "connectivity"), is thus filled with the less rigorous criterion of "coherence" provided by such rules as "Respect local differences."

It should not escape notice that both individuals and public authorities may reason on pluralistic circumstances. In a sense, the individual who constructs a directive for himself on drinking water and cognac is legislating for multiple selves in separate contexts, much as the public authority is legislating a policy for separate groups in different circumstances. In both cases, the transitivity of the items considered can be set aside as a condition of rationality by virtue of the heterogeneity of the circumstances under consideration. The notion of aggregate arrangements, in this case the *structure* of action, provides considerations that can defeat even the logical requirement of transitivity found in single-unit reasoning.

What we have in the absence of "connectivity" is a preference ordering separated by space or time. That the same policy can be coherent when drawn out, illogical when compressed, should be clear by now to anyone who has read this text. The paradoxes of voting come into prominence when conditions require that policy alternatives be judged by standards drawn from a single criterion indifferent to separate orderings. All policies do not currently face such hard requirements, though (as suggested in Chapters 5 and 8) the energy crisis forecast by many *may* force a replacement of the loose notion of "coherence" with some tighter version of central "rationality" containing all or most of the conditions in Arrow's theorem.

FOR FURTHER READING

(APPENDIXES A, B, AND C)

ARROW, KENNETH, *Social Choice and Individual Values*. New York: John Wiley, 1963.

————, "Values and Collective Decision-Making," in *Philosophy, Politics, and Society*, eds. Peter Laslett and W. G. Runciman, Third Series. Oxford: Basil Blackwell, 1969.

BLAU, JULIAN, "A Direct Proof of Arrow's Theorm," *Econometrica* 40 (January 1972), pp. 61–67. (One of many helpful, brief proofs of Arrow's Theorem.)

BUCHANAN, WILLIAM, AND GORDON TULLOCK, *The Calculus of Consent*. Ann Arbor, Michigan: The University of Michigan Press, 1962.

DAHL, ROBERT, *A Preface to Democratic Theory*. Chicago: University of Chicago Press, 1956.

FISHBURN, PETER, "Paradoxes of Voting," *American Political Science Review* 68 (June 1974), pp. 537–546.

FRANKLIN, RAYMOND S., "The Political Economy of Black Power," *Social Problems* 16 (Winter 1969), pp. 286–301.

HOWARD, JOHN, "The Making of a Black Muslim," in *The Black Revolt*, ed. James Geschwender, pp. 449–458.

LITTLE, MALCOLM, *The Autobiography of Malcolm X*. New York: Grove Press, 1966.

MEIER, AUGUST, AND ELLIOT RUDWICK, *Black Protest in the Sixties*. Chicago: Quadrangle, 1970.

PLOTT, CHARLES, "Axiomatic Social Choice Theory: An Overview and Interpretation," *American Journal of Political Science* 20 (August 1976), pp. 511–596.

RIKER, WILLIAM, AND PETER ORDESHOOK, *An Introduction to Positive Political Theory*. Englewood Cliffs, N.J.: Prentice-Hall, 1973.

index

Abortion issue, 14, 250-59
  legal reforms, 2, 252-55
  solutions for, 257-59
  theoretical issues, 255-57
Access control, pollution control by, 164,
    172
Aid for the Blind program, 197
Aid to Families with Dependent Chil-
    dren (AFDC), 13, 196, 197, 201
Air Pollution Control Act (1955), 166
Alien and Sedition Acts, 273
Allison, Graham, 105
Allocation in political systems, 5-6
Allocationist politics, 7
Allport, Gordon, 38
Almond, Gabriel, 9
Amendments, Constitutional
  Eighth, 129
  Ninth, 254
  Thirteenth, 84
  Fourteenth, 41, 84, 232, 233, 301-303
  Fifteenth, 84
  Seventeenth, 136
  Nineteenth, 85
American Medical Association, 20
American Women Suffrage Associa-
    tion, 84
Anderson, Jack, 223
Animal Farm (Orwell), 225
Apathy, political, 267

Aristotle, 203, 266, 255, 264, 267
Armour, David, 40-43
Arrow, Kenneth, 135, 310-21
Arrow's probability theorem, 310-21
Association, defined, 67
Authoritative, defined, 4-5
Authoritative allocative of values, 3-8
Authority, types, 147

Bakke, Allan, 232-33
Bardwick, Judith, 88-89
Bargaining as political activity, 10
Barton, Allen, 148
Beard, Charles, 268
Bentley, Arthur, 64
Berman, Edgar, 89
Biomedical technology, democratic
    planning and, 279-82
Black Muslims, 308-9
Black politics, 74-84, 304-9
  civil rights movement phase, 75-76,
    77
  early period in, 75
  elite concepts and, 82-84
  income and employment level of
    blacks, 78-79
  interest groups of blacks, 79-82
  rights sought by blacks, 80-81
  urban riots, 76-78
Blackmun, Harry, 254